THE UNIVERSAL POSTAL UNION

THE

UNIVERSAL

POSTAL

UNION

Coordinator of the

International Mails

GEORGE A. CODDING, JR.

New York University Press 1964

Publication of this work was aided by a partial subvention from THE FORD FOUNDATION, to whom the publishers make grateful acknowledgment.

To Lonnie

PREFACE

ONE of the more extraordinary phenomena of the twentieth century is the reliance of nations on international organizations to provide the conditions necessary to attack recognized common problems, the solution of which can be achieved only by cooperative action. There are over one hundred and fifty such agencies, including the United Nations, the specialized agencies, and many other lesser known ones. Almost every sphere of human activity is encompassed within their terms of reference, thousands of highly trained individuals are employed in their secretariats, and large sums of money are expended annually to support their work. Indeed, the budgets of more than one international organization exceed those of a large number of nation-states. International organizations have become an essential factor in the relations of states.

The Universal Postal Union is one of these organizations, with the title of specialized agency of the United Nations, and its domain is the international mails. As a result of the accomplishments of the UPU, an individual can post a letter and expect it to be delivered safely to any designated place in the world within a relatively short span of time. This includes the ordinary citizen as well as the commercial enterprise. Books, magazines, and newspapers, all essential to the free flow of information between nations, cross frontiers in a manner which would not be possible without the rules and regulations created by the UPU. There are many other related postal services that are provided for the user of the mails by the UPU. Last, but not least, national postal administrations are the beneficiaries in the reduced cost and increased efficiency which result from the labors of the UPU and its organs.

While the task that the UPU undertakes for mankind is an essential one, its uniqueness as an international organization lies elsewhere. In the first place, the UPU has attained an age equalled by few other international organizations. It was created in the nineteenth century when the concept of international organization was completely new, and as a result had to find its own way relatively unaided. Most other international organizations at least had the experience of the UPU to use as a guide. Secondly, the UPU was able to survive intact despite World War I, the great depression of the 1930's, World War II, and the demise of the League of Nations. The UPU's activities were slowed down or delayed, it is true, but the organization was never destroyed. There is only one other comparable international organization which shares these two attributes with the UPU, its sister organization, the International Telecommunication Union.

Oddly enough, despite the wealth of experience that the UPU can offer the student of international relations, no one has previously attempted a truly comprehensive study of its structure and organization. The UPU is often talked about, but little known. The purpose of this book, therefore, is to make up for this obvious lack in the literature of international organizations. A serious attempt will be made to determine the factors which dictated that the mails should be one of the first objects of international endeavor and, above all, the elements in its structure and authority which have contributed to its longevity and continued success despite the vicissitudes of international politics. In addition, an attempt will be made to discover whether its organization and structure have evolved sufficiently to permit it to continue to provide a focus for international cooperation to improve the international mails.

The organization of the book is as follows. The first chapter will deal with the forces — economic, political, and technical — which created the conditions necessary for its coming into existence. The second chapter will be devoted to the story of the first UPU congress and the slow but steady development of the UPU from a mere idea in the minds of men to the universal cooperative mechanism that it is today. Inasmuch as its history stretches over so long a period of time, and includes so many conferences and meetings, this chapter will have as its aim the tracing of the general outline of progress rather than an exhaustive historical study. Many of the details will be reserved for the following chapters, especially those concerning the changes that occurred after World War II. Chapter Three is an account of the constitution of the UPU, in the sense of its fundamental principles and basic legal structure. Included are sections on its aims and purposes, its membership, the nature of its basic acts, interpretation of these acts, and financing. The fourth chapter is a description and analysis of the structure and functions of the major representative organs of the UPU, while the fifth chapter does the same for the UPU's secretariat, known as the International Bureau. The sixth chapter deals with the relations between the UPU and other international organizations, including the regional postal unions. The seventh chapter will contain the author's conclusions.

THIS BOOK could never have been written without the help and support of a number of people. This includes colleagues, postal experts, and members of the staff of the international bureau of the UPU. The author is aware of his tremendous debt of gratitude to these many helpful people and hopes that they realize that it would be impossible to thank each and every one by name. The author also hopes that they will forgive him for acknowledging his special thanks to a few of their number. In particular, I would like to mention Dr. Fritz Hess, the former director of the UPU's international bureau, who so generously gave his assistance during the months the author was in Berne, and Mr. William A. Reid, second secretary at the international bureau, who has gone out of his way with consistent good will to guide me along the difficult path of achieving a true understanding of the UPU. I would also like to mention Mr. Greever Allan, director of the International Service of the United States Post Office Department, who read parts of the completed manuscript. No words can express the depth of my gratitude to my wife, to whom this book is dedicated. The author, of course, assumes responsibility for any inaccuracies and errors that remain.

FOREWORD

SINCE joining the International Bureau I have never ceased to contemplate with satisfaction and pride the momentous worth of the part the Universal Postal Union plays in international collaboration and appreciate the humanitarian overtones arising from its services to individuals and nations. In our age when distances have largely disappeared and the fate of mankind is more than ever a common problem, the Union stands as a happy example of fruitful achievement in the field of international human relations.

Mr. Codding is not a postal officer and his account, therefore, can be considered as essentially objective. We are grateful to him for the understanding shown in his description of our organization — a story that is well worth the telling. His book will undoubtedly become the authoritative standard work, of equal benefit to postal historians and students of international organizations.

The author has rightly emphasized the originality, universality and durability of the Union. His work comes at a time critical in the evolution of our institution. I commend this book as one of great interest and as an inspiration to men of goodwill throughout the world.

E. Weber

DIRECTOR,
INTERNATIONAL BUREAU OF THE
UNIVERSAL POSTAL UNION

Berne
March, 1964

CONTENTS

THE UNIVERSAL POSTAL UNION

ONE

Origins of the Universal Postal Union

O F ALL THE FACETS of the Universal Postal Union, one of the most interesting and least understood is the manner in which it was created. Although postal systems have been in existence since earliest recorded history and international postal treaties for the exchange of mail were drafted as early as 1601, the UPU did not come into being until 1874. Why did nations wait so long to bring order into international postal affairs? And, since few international organizations are as old as the UPU, why should the international post be one of the first subjects of international cooperation rather than commerce, health, or one of the many other subjects of worldwide importance?

To find an answer to these two questions it is necessary to trace the evolution of postal systems to the point where international cooperation was necessary for further development and to seek out the forces that were responsible for the creation of the UPU as the agency for such cooperation. Some attention will be paid to the primitive postal systems which existed in the Middle Ages and even to those of ancient times.

Although many of the ancient postal systems achieved a high degree of speed and efficiency, they cannot be compared to modern postal systems. The older postal organization consisted mainly of specially designated individuals whose task it was to carry official messages on foot or on horseback wherever there was governmental business to transact. Rarely if ever were these services made available to the public. It was not until the rise of the nation-state and the extension of education and commerce that postal systems began to take on their present form.

A special section of this chapter will deal exclusively with the revolutionary postal reforms achieved in England in the first half of the nineteenth century by Sir Rowland Hill. These reforms provided the impetus for the general lowering of domestic postal rates throughout the world which placed postal communication within the reach of the average citizen. The final sections will deal with the subsequent agitation for a similar reform of the international mails and the first international postal conference (Paris, 1863) that paved the way for the establishment of the Universal Postal Union.

A. Origins of the Post

EVIDENCE OF THE EXISTENCE of postal systems is found in the earliest available historical records. From Egypt, for example, comes the fragmentary record of a conversation, dating from the twelfth Pharaonic Dynasty (circa 2000 B.C.), in which a scribe warns his son that if he is determined to be a government letter carrier, he should draw up his will immediately. Letter carriers, according to the scribe, were in constant danger from wild animals and unfriendly tribes.[1]

Both the ancient Chinese and Persian governments had extensive messenger services. The first recorded postal system in China dates from the Chou Dynasty (1122 to 255 B.C.) and was composed of both foot and mounted couriers whose routes carried them throughout the empire and Manchuria. It was this system that Marco Polo was purported to have encountered.[2] The Persian postal system of Cyrus the Great (558 to 528 B.C.) has been described in detail and with great admiration by chroniclers of the times. Xenophon notes that in order to speed the service, Cyrus established relays or post houses along the major posting routes of his empire at exactly one day's ride from each other, where horses could be changed and the courier might seek food and rest. Mules and camels also were used where conditions warranted them. Herodotus too paid tribute to the speed and capabilities of this courier system which must have contributed much to Cyrus's successful control over his huge empire.[3]

One of the best known, and perhaps the best organized, of the ancient postal systems was the famous *cursus publicus* of the Roman Empire. As soon as the Romans began expanding beyond the borders of the city of Rome, and especially when the conquest went beyond the Italian peninsula, there arose the need for a competent, swift messenger system whereby orders and messages could be exchanged between offi-

1. Egypt, Ministry of Communication, *Les postes en Egypte* (Cairo, 1934), pp. 19–20.
2. China, Postal Administration, "Historical Survey of the Postal Services in China," *Union Postale*, L, No. 5 (May, 1925), 67. See also C. Ruger, "The Development of the Postal Service in China," *Union Postale*, LXV, No. 10 (October, 1940), 289.
3. See Eugene Gallois, *La Poste et les moyens de communication* (Paris, 1894), pp. 24–26. The words of Herodotus describing the Persian courier system, inscribed on the pediment of the New York Post Office, are still the best known tribute to the world's postmen: "Neither snow nor rain nor heat nor gloom of night stays these couriers from the swift completion of their appointed rounds."

cials and contact maintained with the military. The Roman postal system grew with the needs of the empire until it provided swift service to any part of the Roman world, first for messages, then baggage, and finally official passengers. According to one claim, a passenger could travel over 280 kilometers in a little less than 24 hours.[4]

The relay stations, the foundation of the *cursus publicus,* were composed of the official depots and stopping places along all the major Roman military roads where official couriers were provided with fresh horses and lodging as the need arose. Under Augustus the system was expanded to carry materials of war in addition to dispatches and officials on mission. An idea of the extent of the *cursus publicus* can be gained when one realizes that complete facilities were available along the five great Roman roads leading toward Carthage, Macedonia, Thracia, Spain, and Germany and Britain. Where there were stretches of water to be crossed, boats were held in readiness to accommodate the Roman postmen and their passengers. It should be noted that in Roman times as at present, the speed and dependability of the mail rested largely upon the status of the roads. During the height of the Roman Empire the roads were good and the service of the mail was swift.[5]

Just as it succeeded to the control of large areas of the Roman Empire, the Islamic Empire also took over part of the old Roman postal system. At its height, there were throughout the country some 930 postal stations situated along the six great roads fanning out from the capital at Bagdad. Although the califates also constructed their own excellent roads, wherever the Arabian postal routes crossed territory which had belonged to the Roman Empire they utilized the old Roman roads. Along those portions of the system which traversed the Arabian desert, the posting stations were often the only settlements within many miles. Not only was the speed of the post often equal to that achieved by the Romans, but at times whole military detachments, from 50 to 100 men, were transferred by the postal system to places where they were needed. One calif is reported to have stated: "My throne rests on four pillars, and my power on four men: a blameless Kadi [judge], an energetic chief of police, an honest minister of finances, and a faithful postmaster, who gives me reliable information on everything."[6] As had occurred in Rome, the decay of the Mohammedan Empire brought with it the decline and eventual end of the Arabian postal system.

Little is known of the extent of postal arrangements during the Dark Ages. Such letters as were written were conveyed from place to

4. Arthur de Rothschild, *Histoire de la Poste aux lettres et du timbre-poste* (Paris, 1876), p. 55.

5. For a more detailed discussion of the *cursus publicus,* see Rothschild, *op. cit.,* pp. 34–82. (See also, "The Cursus Publicus of the Romans," *Union Postale,* IV, No. 9, September, 1879, 175–82, and Dr. Werner Hürlimann, "The Cursus Publicus," *Union Postale,* LXXXVI, No. 1, January, 1961, 8A–13A.)

6. Thieme, "The Posts of the Califs," *Union Postale,* IV, No. 12 (December, 1879), 242.

place by means of itinerant traders, friars, or others whose business took them in the desired direction. Despite the payment of excessive fees, there was no guarantee that letters would arrive at their destination.

In the Middle Ages postal systems again assumed an important place in the affairs of mankind. However, the systems of this period differed greatly from those that had gone before. While the postal arrangements of antiquity were created by absolute governments for their official business, and were imposed upon the people, the postal services in the Middle Ages grew with the needs of various classes of society. Thus, instead of a centralized and uniform state post, there arose exceedingly diverse postal services made up of many hundreds of independent institutions. Princes, religious orders, and universities all created private messenger facilities. With the increase of trade and industry, independent cities, leagues, and commercial enterprises also found a need for the exchange of messages. Many of these services were placed at the disposal of the public, a development which was almost unheard of in earlier times.

The university messenger services were among the remarkable features of the Middle Ages, and reflect the period's spirit and character. There was a need for a communication system between the students (many of whom came from great distances) and their homes for the exchange of personal news and the forwarding of expense money. Most universities consequently created for their students, and also for professors, special messenger services which were soon recognized and granted certain privileges by the ruling authorities.

The messenger service of the University of Paris was particularly outstanding.[7] This service, already in existence when mentioned for the first time in a document of 1297, continued until it was merged with the royal messenger service in 1719. At first the organization consisted only of the *petit* (or flying) messengers, reliable individuals from the home towns of the students, appointed by the university. The petit messengers, who paid a nominal fee to the university for the job, were permitted to carry messages between the students' homes and Paris for a fixed sum per dispatch. These messengers probably made their rounds on foot at first. Later they employed horses and, later still, added carts and wagons to convey passengers and luggage as well. The messengers made the rounds from Paris to the various home cities of the students and returned on fixed days.

Because of the affinity of the University of Paris with the Roman Catholic Church and the desire on the part of French rulers to be in good standing with the church, the students and faculty were given many

7. Other universities for which there is evidence of a messenger service in the thirteenth and fourteenth centuries are those of Bologna, Naples, Toulouse, Vienna, and Heidelberg. Furthermore, it seems clear that most of the major European universities, including those in England and Spain, had private messenger systems. See Loeper, "Contribution to the History of the University Messenger Service," *Union Postale*, IX, No. 8 (August, 1884), 165–77; No. 9 (September, 1884), 189–97; and No. 10 (October, 1884), 210–22.

privileges. Since the messengers were important to the life of the universities, they too became recipients of many of these privileges. They did not have to pay certain taxes, they were exempt from some civic duties, and above all they were given royal protection.

This royal protection of the messengers in their travels, combined with the extent of their rounds — students came to Paris from all over France — resulted in their being entrusted with letters from individuals having no relationship to the university. Such carrying of public mail provided for a substantial increase in the earnings of the messengers and in turn became a service to the country as a whole.

Although the various private systems seem to have met the need for communication in the Middle Ages, new forces soon came into being that were to have a profound effect on the evolution of the post. The first and foremost was, of course, the rise of the nation-state. As monarchs slowly but surely succeeded in consolidating their power, a need arose for a more rapid and secure means of official communication. In answer to this need, ruling monarchs in Western Europe began to create royal posts, similar in many respects to those which had existed in ancient times, for the transportation of official messages. The first nation on record to take this step was France. In 1477 Louis XI of France decreed the establishment of a Royal Postal Service, and organized a body of 230 couriers for this purpose.[8] During his war with Scotland in 1481, Edward IV of England ordered a continuous system of posts, consisting of relays of horses and messengers every 20 miles, to facilitate the transmission of news from the battlefront to the English capital. When peace was restored, the system was allowed to fall into disuse but was revived during the reign of Henry VIII, who put it on a permanent basis.[9] Other European monarchs followed suit.

The second major force in the evolution of postal services resulted from the discovery of the printing press, the general extension of education, and the expansion of commerce. As a result of these innovations there arose a substantial nonofficial demand for rapid and secure postal communication. In many areas of Western Europe, the private postal systems were inadequate. In 1635, Thomas Witherings, postmaster of the English Royal Post, noted: "Private letters being now carried by carriers or persons travelling on foot, it is sometimes full two months before any answer can be received from Scotland or Ireland to London." [10] In France, private citizens took advantage of the greater speed,

8. While most historians prior to World War II placed the establishment of the French Royal Post at 1464, subsequent research, especially that undertaken by Professor Zeller of the University of Strasbourg and Eugène Vaillé, custodian of the French postal museum, has revealed that in all probability the correct date was closer to 1477. For an account of this research, and the proofs offered, see Eugène Vaillé, *Histoire générale des postes françaises*, II (Paris, 1947), pp. 5-23.

9. See William Lewins, *Her Majesty's Mails* (London, 1864), p. 5.

10. Quoted in Lewins, *op. cit.*, p. 19. When Witherings was given permission only a few months later to carry private mail, he established a postal service between "Edinburgh in Scotland and the City of London, to go thither and back again in 6 days" (*ibid.*, p. 20).

regularity, and security of the governmental system by bribing royal couriers to carry their letters on regular rounds.[11]

The next step was an authorization given to the official postal service to accept private letters and finally, the proclamation of a royal monopoly on all letter carrying. There were two major reasons for these actions. The first was revenue. The charges levied on private use of the royal mails proved an excellent means of subsidizing the official service. The second was security. In an official publication of the British post-master-general in 1911 it was stated bluntly that the decision to make letter carrying a royal monopoly was "primarily political and designed to prevent secret communication of the King's enemies at home and abroad." [12] The public service aspect of providing more rapid and secure postal communication was only secondary. By the early part of the nine-teenth century, the transition to governmental monopoly and the liquida-tion of private postal services was almost complete in every independent country.

Along with the transition from private mail systems to state monop-oly there occurred a slow but steady increase in the number of services offered to the public and in the efficiency of the mails.[13] Public post offices were established in major cities and roving mailmen made regular collections in the streets. City delivery and, in some cases, rural delivery of mail was begun.[14] Stagecoaches were substituted for slower means of conveyance of mail and passengers. Also, the procedure of routing all mail through the capital cities was abandoned and "cross posts" were established to provide direct mail services between major and minor cities.[15]

In the light of modern postal practice, there still remained one or two highly irritating elements. The more important was the high cost of mailing a letter. If the recipient lived more than a few miles from the sender, the rate was extremely high. Only the well-to-do were able to make more than casual use of the postal services for distances over a hundred miles. Furthermore, letters were generally taxed according to the number of pages they contained rather than by their overall weight. An additional difficulty was created by the method of collecting postage. With few exceptions, a letter was paid for on receipt. It was the often

11. See Vaillé, op. cit., passim.

12. Great Britain, Postmaster-General, The Post Office: An Historical Sum-mary (London, 1911), p. 121.

13. It should be noted that many of these services were originated by the operators of private mail services but all were eventually incorporated in the state systems.

14. City delivery was begun in London in 1680. After two false starts, one in 1653 and one in 1692, Paris initiated a city delivery in 1758. France was the first to start a rural delivery service, in 1829.

15. Stagecoaches were introduced in England for the conveyance of mail in 1784 following a large-scale road-building program. For a detailed and competent discussion of the development of British posts, see Howard Robinson, The British Post Office: A History (Princeton, N.J., 1948). For information on other mail services during the early days of the nineteenth century, see Alvin F. Harlow, Old Post Bags (New York, 1928), pp. 204–24.

exasperating and time-consuming duty of the postman to find the recipient of a letter and to collect from him what was owed. This practice naturally tended to delay the delivery of mail and to involve the postal administration in complicated accounting procedures.

It is at this point in the development of the post that we turn to the postal reforms of Sir Rowland Hill.

B. Postal Reform and Sir Rowland Hill

ONE OTHER INNOVATION was necessary to transform the post offce into a genuine public service institution. That was the lowering of postage rates to the point where they were within the reach of the average citizen. The Englishman Sir Rowland Hill [16] is given credit internationally for launching the movement to bring postal rates into some sort of relationship with the costs of the service, and, in general, for leadership in postal reform.

British domestic postal rates in Hill's time were as follows: [17]

Not exceeding 15 miles	4d	From 50 to 80 miles	8d
From 15 to 20 miles	5d	From 80 to 120 miles	9d
From 20 to 30 miles	6d	From 120 to 170 miles	10d
From 30 to 50 miles	7d	From 170 to 230 miles	11d
		From 230 to 300 miles	12d

For every additional 100 miles, or fraction thereof, there was an additional charge. These charges, it must be noted, were for single letters only, e.g., letters comprising a single sheet of paper. If the letter consisted of two pages, or an enclosure had been made, the rate doubled. Three times the above rates was the charge for a three-page letter, and so on. There was also a twopenny post for the London district, that is, for service within three miles from the General Post Office, and a three-penny post for service from three to twelve miles from the General Post Office. [18]

In addition to causing widespread dissatisfaction, the high postal rates in England resulted in extensive smuggling of letters by other means. Travelers almost invariably took with them as many letters for friends and acquaintances as they could carry. In fact almost anyone whose business took him regularly from one part of England to another could and did transport letters, sometimes at a personal profit. Even mail carriers and stagecoach drivers carried private mail on the side. During one raid by the police, a government mail carrier was found to have a bag containing no less than 1,000 private letters which he was going to deliver for a fee. One of Hill's informants, "a highly respectable

16. 1795–1879.
17. Robinson, *op. cit.,* p. 256.
18. *Ibid.,* pp. 252–56.

merchant and manufacturer" of Birmingham, was of the opinion that the number of letters distributed in the region of Birmingham without the consent of the post office "very greatly exceeded the number distributed in the same district by the Post Office." [19]

Another problem related to high postal rates that confronted the British postal system was the abuse of the franking privilege. Over the years members of Parliament and other officials of the government had been given the right to use the mails without charge. Not only did these individuals send enormous amounts of mail under this right to circumvent the high postage rates, but they also permitted friends and constituents to use their names to evade postage. In 1839 almost ten percent of all the British mail consisted of franked letters.[20] Others, even Hill and his family, found it expedient at times to sign the name of a member of Parliament to messages. As Hill pointed out, any feeling of compunction was lost "as we learnt the monstrous abuses which had grown up in connection with the franking system." [21]

The results of Hill's observations of the abuses in the postal service and his suggestions for their reform were summarized in a pamphlet under his authorship entitled *Post Office Reform: Its Importance and Practicability,* which was published in London in 1837.[22] Hill had two interrelated purposes in mind when he wrote his pamphlet. The first was the drastic lowering of postage rates. The second was to put the operation of the post office on a more efficient and economical basis. In both of these objectives he was successful.[23]

Hill first set out to prove that the British Post Office was not being operated on a sound basis. Upon analyzing the post office receipts for the preceding 20-year period he found that revenue had not only failed to increase, but on the contrary showed a steady decline. Hill considered that such a trend was difficult to accept in view of the increase, over

19. G. B. and Sir Rowland Hill, *The Life of Sir Rowland Hill and the History of Penny Postage* (London, 1880), I, p. 252.

20. Great Britain, Postmaster-General, *op. cit.,* p. 10.

21. G. B. Hill, *op. cit.,* p. 241. During an official investigation in 1763 it was revealed that "one man had, in the course of five months, counterfeited 1,000 dozen franks of different members of Parliament" (*The Post Office: An Historical Summary,* p. 125).

22. Three editions were published in the year 1837.

23. "While . . . confirmed in my belief that, even from a financial point of view, the postal rates were injuriously high, I also became more and more convinced . . . that the fiscal loss was not the most serious injury thus inflicted on the public; that yet more serious evil resulted from the obstruction thus raised to the moral and intellectual progress of the people; and that the Post Office, if put on a sound footing, would assume the new and important character of a powerful engine of civilisation; that though now rendered feeble and inefficient by erroneous financial arrangements, it was capable of performing a distinguished part in the great work of national education. I became also more alive to the consideration that the duty of rendering its operation as beneficial as possible, incumbent as this must be on any institution, became doubly so on the Post Office, from its being a monopoly; that, as it forbade all others to perform its functions, it was bound to render its own performance as complete as possible" (G. B. Hill, *op. cit.,* pp. 245–46).

the same period of time, in population, education, trade, and national prosperity. In support of his conclusion he analyzed the income from stagecoaches for the same period of time and found that the yield had doubled.[24]

Having concluded that the British Post Office was in effect being operated in an unsound fiscal manner, Hill attempted to prove that a lowering of rates was the primary remedy. Hill based his argument on the classic assumption that if the rates were lowered there would be a great increase in the use of the official post which would over a period of time bring in the same or more revenue. Lower rates would attract not only those who had never used the post before, but also those whose practice it was to smuggle letters by means other than the official post. Hill supported his argument with reference to instances where a decrease in duties, or in prices, produced a corresponding increase in consumption.[25] He also pointed to the French postal system — the rates were "less exorbitant than with us" — where both the use of the mails and the profits of the post office had tended to increase steadily.[26] There was, of course, a limit as to how far this rule could be applied. The problem was, therefore, to find a new low rate by which "the maximum of relief may be afforded to the public with the minimum of injury to the revenue." [27]

What better basis for finding a proper rate could be found than the actual expense involved in sending a letter from one place to another, or, in the words of Hill, "the natural cost of distribution?" For this purpose Hill divided the estimated number of letters and newspapers passing annually through the post office by the expense involved in their handling and conveying. He found that the apparent cost of the primary distribution, "viz., the receipt, conveyance and distribution," of a letter or newspaper within the United Kingdom was, on the average, only 84 hundredths of a penny.[28]

Investigation into the conveyance part of the postage bill led Hill to two additional discoveries. First, the cost of conveyance for a given distance was, under ordinary circumstances, in proportion to the weight carried. Secondly, using the mail from London to Edinburgh as a test, Hill found that the actual cost of conveying an ordinary paying letter was only about one thirty-sixth part of a penny. And, the four hundred miles between London and Edinburgh constituted a distance far above the average for a letter posted in the United Kingdom.[29]

24. Rowland Hill, *Post Office Reform: Its Importance and Practicability* (3d ed., London, 1837), pp. 3–4. Hill reasoned that "it seemed scarcely to be doubted that the demand for the conveyance of letters had increased in the same ratio as that for the conveyance of persons and parcels."

25. *Ibid.*, p. 7.

26. *Ibid.*, p. 4.

27. G. B. Hill, *op. cit.*, p. 243.

28. Rowland Hill, *op. cit.*, pp. 8–14.

29. It should be noted that Hill was basing his calculations on the expense of paying letters only and did not include newspapers and franked letters which were on an average much heavier.

Hill thus came to the conclusion that the existing practice of varying the amount of postage according to the distance over which an inland
letter was conveyed had no foundation in principle and that, consequently, there should be only a single low rate for the whole of the
United Kingdom. Weight alone should be the determining factor. Not
only would this innovation be much more equitable to the public, but
the simplicity of a single rate would have the additional advantage of
eliminating much of the post office's burden of calculating and accounting.[30]

Realizing that any further reforms which would lower operating
costs would help materially in the introduction of his plan for a single
low letter rate, Hill turned his attention to the handling of letters, then
as now the post office's most expensive operation. He found that there
were three major sources of expense in these procedures. The first was
in the "taxing" of letters, e.g., ascertaining the distance a letter was to
travel, or, under his new plan, the weight, and marking the postage to
be charged on each letter.[31] The second was the complicated accounting
procedure necessitated by the collect-on-delivery system: ". . . Postmasters having to be debited with unpaid postage on letters transmitted
to their offices, and credited with their payments made in return," the
accounts of the individual letters having to be received and verified at
each subsidiary post office, and finally the periodic collection and verification of all transactions at the central post office. The third was in
the delivery of letters. Although this expense was naturally very large,
he felt that it was almost doubled by requiring the postman to collect
the postage due at the time of delivery. Both the second and third
categories, he felt, could be drastically reduced by the simple expedient
of requiring wherever possible the payment of postage at the time the
letters were sent.[32]

Hill concluded his examination of post office procedures by advocating that for the internal service there should be one single rate,
irrespective of distance; the rate should depend upon the weight of the

30. Hill did point out that the cost of conveying a letter varied according
to the number of letters conveyed, the cost being much lower as the number of
letters increased. However, "as such increase would certainly follow reduction of
postage, it followed that, if a great reduction could be effected, the cost of conveyance, per letter, already so small, might be deemed absolutely insignificant"
(G. B. Hill, *op. cit.,* p. 250).

31. Letters also were often "candled" to ascertain if they were made up of
more than one page.

32. Rowland Hill, *op. cit.,* pp. 15–31. As Robinson points out, it was not
until the second edition of *Post Office Reform* that Hill suggested that prepayment
could be carried out by the purchase of "stamped covers and sheets of paper."
While as a result of this suggestion some thus consider Hill to have discovered
the idea of the postage stamp, Hill himself acknowledged that his proposal was
the outgrowth of a previous suggestion by Charles Knight, one of his collaborators
(Robinson, *op. cit.,* p. 268). For a discussion of even earlier suggestions for the use
of postage stamps, see, for example, Gallois, *op. cit.,* pp. 278–88 and Joseph K. F.
Nauman, "Letters in the Course of the Ages," *Union Postale,* LXX, No. 1 (January, 1945), 17.

letter and not the number of sheets of paper; the rate for the minimum weight should be one penny; and all postage should be prepaid.[33]

It would not be consistent with the purpose of this study to go into a detailed account of Hill's fight to have his proposals adopted by Parliament and his later fight in and outside the post office to have them actually introduced into practice. Suffice it to say that Hill's proposals found solid backing in Parliament, in educational circles, and in commercial organizations. Above all, the "penny post" became a popular slogan and Hill's reforms became a popular cause. All of his major reforms were eventually introduced in the United Kingdom.[34]

The British lead was soon followed in other countries. The impact of the British reforms was felt almost immediately in France and eventually led to the sweeping postal reforms that took place there in 1848. Immediate effects were also felt in Belgium and Switzerland and, not long after, in Russia and Spain. Prussia made partial reforms in 1844 and major reforms in 1850. In the United States reforms were started in 1845. By the time of the opening of the first international postal conference in 1863, scarcely a major postal system had escaped the effects of Hill's reforms.[35]

It would be an error to leave this important juncture in postal history without a word of clarification concerning the significance of Hill's contribution. He was not the first nor the only person in England interested in postal reform. However, he did build on the foundation laid by many individuals who preceded him and others who aided him throughout his fight. Nor was England the only country at that time to be giving serious consideration to ways and means of making the post office a truly public service organization. At the same time few would deny Hill a place of eminence in postal history. The scope of his ideas and their importance to efficient postal operation are without equal.

From the point of view of international postal organization, several of Hill's ideas were to have a profound effect. First there was the principle that letters should be charged according to their weight and not according to the number of enclosures. Second, was the principle that letters should, as far as possible, be prepaid — in other words, the financial transaction should take place at the moment of posting a letter. Third, was the discovery that the cost of transportation is an exceedingly small item in the overall postal bill.[36]

The importance of Hill's principles in the smooth working of the international mails and the impact that his ideas had on international conferences will become abundantly clear as this history progresses.

33. Rowland Hill, *ibid.,* pp. 43–45.
34. See Robinson, *op. cit.,* pp. 273–99, for an account of the political bargaining that took place before the penny post, i.e., one penny for each ½ ounce, was introduced in 1840.
35. For a general discussion of the effect of the British postal reforms on other countries, see *ibid.,* pp. 371–86.
36. True at least until the introduction of airmail.

c. Beginnings of the International Post

UP TO THIS POINT we have been concerned with the story of the development of the post from its inception as an official messenger service to its emergence as a public service institution. We have followed the mail from the time it was a political and even military weapon of ancient emperors, through the rise of independent messenger services to meet special needs, and the transition to royal monopolies with the idea of financial gain foremost, to its final form as a postal system available to the public. In addition, using Hill's reforms as the base, we have discussed the basic economic principles of the operation of the post office and its organization to serve the public. Emphasis has been primarily on the domestic features of postal systems.

It is now time to turn to the international aspects of the mail. Although, for this purpose, it will be necessary to turn back again to an earlier time, we will not have to go back as far as we did previously. The term "international" alone would set the starting date around the seventeenth century when the concept of the nation-state emerged in Europe. Only when there existed independent states did there occur international postal arrangements in the modern sense of the term. These arrangements consisted, fundamentally, of a treaty providing for the carrying of mails by a national organization to the border of another country, at which point the mails were to be transferred to a national postal organization for transshipment or delivery.[37]

There were three major stages in this development: first, the movement of couriers of the independent messenger systems through territories under the control of rulers other than those of their places of origin; second, the stationing of representatives of official posts in foreign countries for the purpose of sending and receiving mail; and third, the closing of frontiers to representatives of foreign official mail services, requiring the making of treaties between representatives of heads of states for the forwarding of mail to or across state frontiers.

There are many instances of private messengers crossing boundaries in the Middle Ages. Many of the early independent messenger services traversed Europe. The monastery of Benedictine de Cluny near Mâcon, in France, had mounted couriers who traveled as far as the heart of Spain and the frontiers of Hungary and Poland.[38] The University of Paris had students from all over Europe, including England and Scotland, whose messengers were constantly traveling from Paris to the students' homes. In the thirteenth century there was a very competent Italian messenger organization which maintained contact with several Italian

37. See, however, Hürlimann, *op. cit.*, p. 8A, for a partial account of a treaty, dated 562 A.D., relating to the exchange of mail between the East Roman Empire and the Persian Empire.
38. Vaillé, *op. cit.*, I, 328.

cities, including Florence and Genoa, and the periodic trade fairs held in Champagne, France. The postal service of the Hanseatic League tied together a great part of northern Europe and succeeded in establishing schedules of great precision. Mention should also be made of the messenger service of the Order of Teutonic Knights, the butcher post, the messenger service of the Fuggers, and the Stranger's Post between the continent and England.[39]

From one point of view, the task of messengers in the Middle Ages was fairly easy. There were few official restrictions on their movement. In general the roads and byways that existed were free to all users. On the other hand, the conditions of the roads and the problems of travel in general were such that journeys of any length were difficult in the extreme. If a messenger in the Middle Ages did not injure himself in fording a river or climbing a difficult mountain pass, he was still prey to lone robbers or bands of brigands. It should be noted also that the number of messages carried was relatively small. Few persons could write, commerce had not developed to any great extent, and in general the movement from one country to another of individuals who would be expected to remain in contact with their original home was limited.

The creation of royal messenger services brought about the second stage in the development of international mails. Little by little the official systems took over from the independent messenger services. There were few of the latter which had the organization and financial backing to compete successfully. And, as would be expected, the state placed more and more of its official mail, such as that for diplomatic establishments, in the hands of the official services.

The French royal messenger service, for instance, carried official mail to and from London, and sometimes Scotland, Holland, Spain, Flanders, and Germany in the sixteenth century.[40] In the case of some of the Swiss states, where the French had special privileges, there were French postmasters and post offices where all mail going to France had to be deposited, and through which mails came from France to the Swiss states.[41] In England, by 1607, there was a regular service by English postmen to and from Brussels to pick up the continental mail.[42] When

---

39. For a discussion of various private messenger services of this epoch, see, for instance, Loeper, "The Post in Universal Literature," *Union Postale*, IX, No. 1 (January, 1884), 28–30, and "The Most Ancient Town Post Arrangements." *Union Postale*, VI, No. 12 (December, 1881), 249–60, and VII, No. 1 (January, 1882), 1–13; and Harlow, *op. cit.*, pp. 24–57.

40. See Vaillé, *op. cit.*, II, pp. 335–65.

41. See Marc Henrioud, "The Franco-Swiss Postal Relations from the 13th Century to the Year 1815," *Union Postale*, LVIII, No. 6 (June, 1933), 196–212. The French mails were not always allowed to pass freely into Swiss cities, however. In March 1563, for instance, the Council of Lausanne decreed that the post rider of the king of France had to pay wine to the value of one gold crown to the keepers of the gates of St. Pierre and St. François for having the gates opened at night for the passage of mail (*ibid.*, p. 199).

42. Robinson, *op. cit.*, p. 24.

the regular Swedish postal system was inaugurated in 1620, official service was immediately begun to Denmark and south to Hamburg.[43] The first Russian postmaster, appointed in 1665, set up a postal route from Moscow to Riga to pick up and send official dispatches to Western Europe even before there was a domestic service in Russia itself.[44]

One of the most extensive official international services of this period was that maintained by the Taxis family for members of the Hapsburg Dynasty.[45] The Taxis post started out as a court post to maintain local postal routes which were established on payment of compensation and discontinued or transferred to other areas as circumstances required. At the beginning of the sixteenth century, however, this Austrian territorial post developed into an international system. On January 18, 1505, Francis von Taxis was commissioned to establish regular communication between the Netherlands, the court of Maximilian I in Germany, the court of the French king wherever it might be held, and the Spanish court. He undertook to carry letters from Brussels, the headquarters of the Dutch government, to Innsbruck in 5½ days (6¼ in winter), to Paris in 44 hours, to Lyons in 4 days, to Granada in 15 days, and to Toledo in 12 days. In 1512 a new agreement was concluded between the Taxis family and the king of Spain adding, among others, the cities of Verona, Rome, and Naples to the existing postal system. By the end of the sixteenth century almost all of Europe was crossed by the Taxis postal system.[46] Some time during the sixteenth century, because of the depleted state of the royal treasury, the Taxis post was permitted to carry private mail in order to augment its earnings.[47]

The decision to run the Taxis post across France, necessitating among other arrangements the establishment of relay stations, was taken unilaterally. There is no record of an agreement between the Hapsburgs and the French monarch, and no record of any protest or reluctance on the part of the French king to the arrangement. The concept of freedom of movement along the highways of Europe was still important,

43. Swedish Post Office, "The Swedish Posts Before 1636," *Union Postale* XXXIII, No. 8 (August, 1908), 113–18.

44. N. J. Sokolow, "Historical Facts Respecting the Origin and Growth of the Russian Post," *Union Postale,* XXI, No. 11 (December, 1896), 186.

45. At different times the name of Taxis was spelled: Tasso, Tassi, Tassus, Tassis, Tasis, Thassis, Tässis, Tarsis, Targis, Targes, Taxus, Taxius, Taxis, Täxis.

46. Joseph Rübsam, "Francis von Taxis, the Founder of the Modern Post, and Johann Baptista von Taxis, his Nephew," *Union Postale,* XVII, No. 8 (August, 1892), 127.

47. Joseph Rübsam, "History of the Oldest Postal Arrangements in Tirol and Adjacent Countries," *Union Postale,* XVI, No. 12 (December, 1891), 202. For a more complete history of the Taxis family and the Taxis post, see Eugène Vaillé, "The Postal, Feudal and Hereditary Rights of the Family of Taxis, as Discussed in 1775 by a French Diplomat," *Union Postale,* LXXIII, No. 3 (March, 1948), 70–92; No. 4 (April, 1948), 126–36; and No. 5 (May, 1948), 166–76. See also Dr. Guillaume Beck, "Postal Monopoly of the Tour-and-Taxis Family in the Papal States (1522–23)," *Union Postale,* LXXXV, No. 5 (May, 1960), 76A–80A.

and it can be assumed that the king of France found some advantage in such communication.[48] In the case of the Swedish official post that ran to Hamburg, mentioned earlier, there was no treaty concerning the use of Danish territory in transit, but only an acceptance of the fact under an agreement of 1580 whereby subjects of Sweden and Denmark were permitted to travel throughout the two countries unhindered.[49]

The final stage in the transformation of the international posts took place in the eighteenth and early nineteenth centuries. Just as political and financial considerations resulted in the elimination of independent domestic messenger services, leading finally to a state monopoly, they led also to increasing controls over foreign postmen crossing national territory. These controls began by obliging foreign postmen to carry special passports, restricting the routes over which they could travel, and limiting the types of correspondence that could be carried.[50]

From the restriction of movement of foreign postmen it was only a short step to the decision to take over the foreign postal routes and to use official domestic postmen for the carrying of transit mails. One of the first arrangements of this kind, and very likely one of the first postal conventions on record, was concluded in 1601 between D. Juan Taxis, Correo mayor of Spain, and G. Fouquet de la Varne, superintendent of French Posts. This agreement established the French posts as the primary carrier of transit mails between Spain and Rome and Spain and the Netherlands. All mails from Spain to Rome were to enter France by the town of Irun (between St. Sebastian and Bayonne), from which city they were transported to Lyon by way of Bordeaux, and there turned over to French couriers. The French couriers were obliged to transport the transit mail from Lyon to Rome in 11 days in summer and 12 days in winter. At the last relay but one, the French courier turned over the Spanish transit mails to a Spanish courier who took them into Rome. The French courier continued his journey in charge of any French mail to Rome that had been entrusted to him. For this service the Spanish post was to pay Fouquet 3 sols per letter ounce or 200 gold crowns per delivery. Letters from Spain for Flanders were carried by Spanish post to Bordeaux where they were turned over to the French authorities. The French couriers then carried the mail to Antwerp by way of Paris. This journey was also to be carried out in 11 days in summer and 12 days in winter. The quantity of mail exchanged between Spain and Italy at this time amounted to about 630 letters per month.[51]

This agreement not only affirmed the principle that the French government was responsible for the transit of foreign mails across its

48. Vaillé, *op. cit.*, II, 346.
49. "The Swedish Posts Before 1636," *op. cit.*
50. For a general discussion of the progressive imposition of restrictions on foreign messengers, see Vaillé, *op. cit.*, II, pp. 287–99.
51. "History of the Posts in Spain," *Union Postale*, VII, No. 4 (April, 1882), 73–75.

territory, but also declared that it should be entitled to a transit fee for this service. It was superseded by a new treaty signed in 1660, one year after the so-called Peace of the Pyrenees was concluded between France and Spain. This new treaty added some important provisions. Instead of permitting the Spanish post to carry the mails for the Netherlands as far as Bordeaux, or those for Rome as far as Lyon, all Spanish mail bags were to be turned over to the French at the border town of Irun. The French administration agreed to carry the mail between Irun and Paris at a minimum speed of 5 to 5½ days in spring and summer and 6 to 6½ days in autumn and winter. That section of the route between Paris and Brussels was to be covered in not more than 40 to 42 hours in the spring and summer and 48 to 50 in the autumn and winter. Further, the Spanish postal administration was permitted to use this service for mail destined for France and the French postal administration in turn could use the service for mail destined to Spain. Neither administration, however, was permitted to charge for this service. An additional article, which is interesting in relation to free postage for certain classes of mail, provided that the Spanish ambassadorial mail be forwarded free in both directions.[52]

Without going further into the history of the development of international postal relations, it will suffice for our purposes to point out that these early French treaties contained within their provisions the general outline of the form that international postal relations were eventually to achieve throughout the world. First, all mail, foreign or domestic, within a given country was handled by that country's official mail service. Foreign mails were deposited at the frontier where they were picked up and sent on to their destination within that country or to the border of another country where they were claimed for reshipment. Second, for the task of transmitting the mail, the domestic post office was to receive payment. The idea of a special charge for transit occurred as soon as the privileges for foreign postmen to cross domestic territory were ended. In short, although the handling of mails in any country became a monopoly of that country's official postal system, the system itself was placed at the service of other countries on the payment of charges fixed by agreement.

As postal relations were extended geographically with the increase in commercial relations, the development of new colonies, and the general widening of education, countries were forced to add new postal treaties. By the middle of the nineteenth century a European country's normal postal relations necessitated at least a dozen treaties. In 1873, Germany alone was the signatory of 17 different bilateral postal agreements. France was not far behind with 16, Belgium with 15, and England with 12.[53]

52. "An International Postal Treaty of the Year 1660," *Union Postale*, xx, No. 9 (September, 1895), 146–56.
53. Alexis Belloc, *Les postes français* (Paris, 1886), p. 616.

The rules governing international postal traffic increased in complexity in almost direct proportion to the number of treaties. No uniform formula for postal treaties existed, each country making the best possible bargain it could for itself. Depending upon the countries involved, there were different classifications of mail content, rates of postage, weight, and even letter size admitted. The United States and Great Britain used the ounce as the unit of weight for calculating rates; France, Belgium, and Italy, the gramme; and Germany and Austria, the zolloth. Transit rates often differed for the same distance, depending upon the route employed. A letter overland from Germany to Rome, for example, would be charged any one of three different transit rates: (1) by way of Switzerland, 68 pfennige; by way of Austria, 48 pfennige; and by way of France, 85 pfennige.[54] A letter from the United States to Australia would be charged 5, 33, 45, 55, 60 cents, or one dollar and 2 cents per ½ ounce, depending upon which one of the six available routes was used.[55]

The difficulties involved for the sender of a letter and for the various postal administrations were enormous. The sender did not know how much postage would be required for his letter until he went to a post office which had an up-to-date register of postal rates, where the path the letter was to take was determined, the weight of the letter was transposed into the weight units of the countries through which it would pass, and all of the charges were added up.[56] As stated by the United States postmaster general, "the complicated accounts necessary to be kept with the several foreign countries with whom we had postal treaty relations, and each of which had to be credited with its portion of the sum prepaid on each article (not on the aggregate weights of the mails), and the minute details required to be entered in the Letter Bill sent with each mail, are almost beyond belief; for these accounts were kept by the 'rate' and according to the standard weight of the creditor country, so that the credits were by the English ounce, the French gram, and the German 'loth,' and the unit of rate was with some countries one sheet of paper, with some a quarter of an ounce, with some a third of an ounce, with some a half ounce, and with some two-thirds of an ounce." [57]

In view of the expanding need for rapid and inexpensive postal services between countries, the international postal service was not living

54. A German Postal Officer, "Past and Present," *Union Postale*, xv, No. 6 (June, 1890), 86.
55. U. S., *Annual Report of the Postmaster General, 1895* (Washington, D.C., 1895), p. 449.
56. ". . . correspondents used to write their letters to countries beyond the seas on a special kind of thin paper, with blue ink, which is said to be lighter than ordinary black ink; no cover was used, but the letter was folded, and closed by means of a very light wafer. It is no exaggeration to say that the difficulty of expediting such letters combined with the expensive postage, deterred many people from writing at all" (from "A German Postal Officer," *op. cit.*, No. 8, August, 1890, p. 119).
57. *Annual Report of the Postmaster General, 1895, op. cit.*, p. 449.

up to its responsibilities. As we shall see, the forces that brought about worldwide domestic reform were soon to have their effect on the international mails.

D. International Postal Reform Movement

ALMOST IMMEDIATELY after the introduction of Hill's domestic postal reforms in Great Britain, agitation began for the reform of the international postal system. Proving that something could be done to make the posts cheaper and the procedures simpler, despite official inertia, was a tremendous stimulus to those who felt that the international service should be improved. And, as we have seen, the international posts in the nineteenth century were in definite need of improvement.

One of the first to take up the banner of reform was the German economist J. von Herrfeldt, of Frankfurt am Main. In two articles, appearing in 1841 and 1842, Herrfeldt advocated several specific reforms and the establishment of an international organization through which they could be achieved.[58] First, the international postal service should be speeded up. All important cities should be interconnected by the most rapid method of transporting mails; all mail transmitted by the shortest possible routes; and international mails exchanged at least once a day. Second, rates should be lowered and simplified. Herrfeldt advocated that there be a single uniform rate for international mails and no charge for transit. He defended his elimination of transit rates on the basis that the costs involved were in reality very small, and that transit administrations would be recompensed by the same service rendered to their mails by other countries. In these proposals, the influence of Hill's reforms are evident. Third, an international organization should be created in which all the states could get together to discuss international postal legislative and organizational problems. This should include periodic postal congresses, meeting once every three years, and a permanent office to serve as an intermediary between all postal administrations.[59] No official action followed on von Herrfeldt's proposals.

Ten years later a much more important effort at bringing about reforms in the international mails was initiated. In 1851 a private organization named the "International and Colonial Postage Association" was formed in London, the aim of which was to achieve for the world a simplified, uniform postal service with moderate postage rates.[60]

58. See C. J. Beelenkamp, *Les lois postales universelles* (The Hague, 1910), pp. 521–24.

59. *Ibid.*, pp. 522–24. For a definition of transit rates and a discussion of the transportation charges they give rise to, see below, p. 29.

60. The association did not attempt to go into detail as to the reforms it wanted, keeping in general to the concept of a simple and uniform international postal service with moderate rates. One of the exceptions, however, was the important suggestion that the sender country should keep all the postage collected, relying upon the idea that the mails between any two countries would in general

The International and Colonial Postage Association carried out an intensive propaganda campaign. Its first step was to inform the representatives of the countries accredited to the Court of St. James of its activities and to solicit their support. Favorable replies were soon received from the embassies, legations, or consulates of Austria, Belgium, Bremen, Brazil, Spain, France, Greece, Lubeck, Mecklenburg-Schwerin, New Granada, Oldenburg, Netherlands, Portugal, Prussia, Sardinia, Sweden and Norway, Switzerland, Turkey, and United States. The association also made a concentrated effort to publicize its aims in Great Britain. Among other accomplishments, the association obtained promises to consider the application of the penny post between the metropolis and its colonies; the support of Rowland Hill to the principle that it would be desirable to apply to letters in the international service the same rules as prevailed in the inland service; and a recommendation by representatives of the United Kingdom chambers of commerce that British commerce should support their movement.

Encouraged by its early successes the association decided in October 1852 to send a delegate to European governments to obtain more precise information concerning their attitude toward the proposed reforms. The mission was entrusted to its honorary secretary, Manuel de Ysasi, the honorary consul-general of Spain in London. Ysasi visited, and discussed his association's purposes, with officials in Austria, Belgium, Netherlands, Russia, Sardinia, Spain, Tunis, and Tuscany. Almost without exception, he was well received and in several cases obtained offers of cooperation.

The high point in the association's existence came when the International Statistical Congress, meeting in Brussels in 1853, adopted a recommendation to the effect that the congress wanted to see the postal reforms that had been carried out in various countries introduced into international postal relations.[61] To the honor of the association, the recommendation was passed in the manner framed by Ysasi himself. Twenty-seven countries were represented at the statistical congress.

Although by this time the association had branches, or correspondents, in some 52 countries, and plans for calling an international postal conference to meet in Paris during the Exhibition of 1855, it ceased to exist with the death of its prime mover, Ysasi. While the association could not point to any tangible results, it had planted the idea of international postal reforms in the minds of officials and the general public in countries all over the world.

Another event, the formation of the Austro-German Postal Union, did much to prepare the way for international postal reform and the creation of the Universal Postal Union. In 1850, after several years of intermittent negotiations, Austria and Prussia signed a treaty regulating their postal arrangements. Among other things, the treaty provided for

be equal (Marc Henrioud, "A Proposal for the Reform of the International Postal Service," *Union Postale,* LV, No. 10, October, 1930, 363).

61. *Ibid.,* p. 364.

the right of the sending administration to choose the most rapid route in the other country for the transit of the mail, guaranteed the right of transit on the payment of moderate fees, and set up a system of uniform rates. Perhaps the most important detail of the treaty was a provision inviting other administrations to adhere. Starting with Bavaria, all 15 of the other German postal administrations, including the postal administration of the Taxis family, subsequently adhered, thus creating what was known as the Austro-German Postal Union.[62]

"This Postal Union aimed at developing the postal service in a uniform way within its frontiers and at adopting uniform rules in the transactions with countries outside the union. It consequently obliged the contracting parties to modify the contracts they had concluded with other foreign administrations. Bavaria, which had concluded such conventions with Switzerland and France, was thus obliged to enter into negotiations with these two countries. In the years 1852 and 1858 new conventions were made with them on the basis of the Austro-German Postal Union." [63]

Although the union was later dissolved because of political complications, the dozen years of its existence did prove that sovereign states could adopt uniform rules for postal transactions and work together to make them effective.

E. Paris Postal Conference of 1863 and Its Results

"SIR: Many embarrassments to foreign correspondence exist in this and probably in other postal departments which can be remedied only by international concert of action. The difference in postal principles, as well as postal details of arrangement, in the several countries of both continents contributes to this result. Great diversity of rates prevails between the same points, in some instances as many as six different rates, according to the route of transit. Mistakes are perpetually recurring, arising from the complexity of present arrangements, and operate to the serious delay and expense of correspondents." [64] So reads the opening paragraph in a letter dated August 4, 1862, from U. S. Postmaster General Montgomery Blair to the United States Secretary of State, a letter that was to prepare the way for the last step but one in the creation of the Universal Postal Union.

Postmaster General Blair suggested that his government set the procedure in motion for the calling of an international conference to discuss common problems and to recommend measures to overcome

62. See "History of the German Post," *Union Postale*, III, No. 8 (August, 1878), 160–61, and, "Organization of the Administration of the Imperial German Posts," *Union Postale*, V, No. 1 (January, 1880), 1–4.

63. "The First 100 Years of the Bavarian Royal State Posts," *Union Postale*. XXXVI, No. 10 (October, 1911), 155.

64. U. S., *Annual Report of the Postmaster General, 1894* (Washington, D.C., 1894), p. 39.

them. It was not to be an ordinary diplomatic conference, however. "The practical knowledge of details necessary, and the special character of the interests involved, indicate the propriety of a conference between postal representatives to arrange the propositions of improvement, rather than to submit them to the usual dilatory course of diplomacy. . . ." [65] The government of the United States acted immediately on the suggestion of Blair and sounded out other countries on the idea of holding a postal conference. Sixteen countries agreed, and one, France, offered to be the host. The date set was May 1863, and the place chosen was Paris.[66]

The Paris Conference convened on May 11, 1863, with representatives of 15 countries in attendance: Austria, Belgium, Costa Rica, Denmark, France, Great Britain, the Hanseatic cities, Italy, Netherlands, Portugal, Prussia, the Sandwich Islands, Spain, Switzerland and United States.[67] A list of 36 questions had been drawn up by the French administration from suggestions received, as a basis for discussion.[68] In essence these questions had three general aims: uniformity of weights, uniformity of rates, and simplification of administrative procedure.

The organization of the meeting was simple. The director general of the French Post Office was chosen unanimously as chairman and a lesser official of the French administration was appointed secretary. Every representative was permitted to speak, and all decisions were taken by a majority of the countries represented. In the beginning it was agreed that each of the 36 questions would be submitted to the full assembly for discussion. This was soon changed, however. Although the first session lasted a whole day, agreement was reached on only two points; the major part of the time was devoted to a general discussion of the merits of the post office's being a state monopoly, rather than to the substantive issues. At the next session it was unanimously decided to turn over the questions to a committee of five members for preliminary consideration and to adopt opinions to be submitted to the plenary meeting. With the help of the committee, the conference was able to pronounce on the remaining 34 questions in only five sessions.[69]

There is no evidence that the United States in its instigation of the conference nor the other countries in accepting considered that the Paris

65. *Ibid.*, p. 40.

66. The documents of the conference were published by the French government under the title *Commission international des postes, Paris, 1863* (Paris, 1863). Documents relating to the calling of the conference are found therein on pp. 13–17.

67. Of the countries which had approved the idea of calling the conference, only Ecuador did not send a representative. Of those which were invited, only Ecuador and Russia did not attend (*ibid.*, pp. 10 and 27).

68. The United States had submitted 14 topics and Great Britain, 13. The French administration had redrafted these into a series of 34 questions to which two more were added during the conference at the suggestion of the United States (*ibid.*, pp. 18–23 and 28).

69. Nine plenary sessions were held in all. No substantive questions were discussed at the opening and closing meetings, and the third meeting was held only to set up the special committee. The committee was made up of representatives from France, Great Britain, Prussia, Switzerland, and United States (*ibid.*, p. 44).

meeting would create a binding international treaty. In Blair's letter suggesting the need for a conference on postal problems he stated: "The powers of the postal representatives, it is presumed, will be limited to discussion and recommendation of measures for the adoption of their respective administrations." [70] In the first meeting, Kasson, the American delegate, stated in response to a question that the feeling of his government was that the results of the deliberations would not engage those who were represented.[71]

Since the decisions of the delegates were in no way binding upon their respective governments, the final acts of the conference did not contain any new principles nor did they attempt to lay down any hard and fast rules for international postal behavior. The final document, entitled simply "Result of the Deliberations of the International Postal Commission at Paris," was, in essence, a list of 31 general principles representing what the majority considered to be a reflection of actual international usage. Its purpose was to point out the majority practice and to suggest to the minority a basis on which their systems could be brought into uniformity with the others.[72]

A few examples taken from the final acts give an indication of the point of view of postal administrations at that time. Article 1 lists six classes of articles which "must or may be forwarded by the Post from one country to another": ordinary letters; registered letters; registered letters with declared value (an early type of insured letter); commercial papers; samples of merchandise without intrinsic value; and printed matter. Articles 27 and 31 suggested that the international mails would not suffer if administrations also introduced money order and special delivery services. The possibility of adopting a low uniform rate for international letters was raised in Article 29 which stated: "In the adjustment of uniform postal rates, the greatest possible number of countries should be included in the same zone, and subject to the same rate."

The problem of high transit rates, undoubtedly one of the more important reasons for calling the conference, received more detailed treatment. After discussing, and turning down, an Italian proposal to eliminate all transit fees, the conference adopted two important principles:[73] Article 25 stated that "as the high transit charges upon correspondence present an insurmountable obstacle to the establishment of an international system of correspondence upon conditions advantageous to the public, the transit charge for each country shall never be higher than one half of the interior rate of the transit country; and for countries of small territorial extent this transit charge shall be even less." Article 26 added that "the cost of sea conveyance claimed by one country from

70. *Annual Report of the Postmaster General, 1894,* p. 40.
71. Docs., Paris Postal Conference (1863), p. 9.
72. Although the document is in French, an English translation of the final decisions is appended.
73. *Ibid.,* pp. 71–72 and 77–90.

another shall in no case be higher than the rate charged upon its own correspondence by the country by whose vessels the conveyance shall be effected."

On the point of uniform weights there was almost unanimous agreement. It was suggested that postage should be based on the weight of the article and that all countries should use the metric system.[74] The first unit for letter postage should be 15 grammes and for commercial papers and samples of merchandise it should be 40 grammes.

Other decisions of importance included the following items: "Wherever possible" postage should be prepaid; international accounts should be simplified by eliminating acknowledgments of the receipt of mail; post offices should draw up international accounts on the basis of the weight of closed mails;[75] official postal correspondence should be conveyed free of charge; and there should be no additional charge for forwarding a letter unless it had to be sent to a country other than the country of original destination.[76]

Despite the limited scope of the decisions taken at Paris, and despite the numerous escape clauses, the principles laid down were incorporated in many subsequently negotiated treaties and did bring advantages to postal administrations. In the two years following the Paris Conference, the United States alone renegotiated nine of its postal treaties along the lines suggested. So many other countries did the same that the American delegate was able at the next postal conference, eleven years later, to declare that "the principles recognized at the conference of Paris have been generally adopted."[77] In addition to the resulting simplification of methods in making up the mails and in transit accounting, the new treaties drastically reduced the cost of long-distance letters. For example, the three separate rates for letters from the United States to Austria which had existed before the Paris Conference were reduced to two, one of six cents and one of seven cents. The number of rates from the United States to Australia fell from six (the highest being $1.02) to two, of 16 cents and 22 cents, respectively.[78]

By the end of the 1860's, therefore, there existed several factors which invited the calling of an international conference to draft a binding postal treaty that would standardize international postal relations. First, there was the success of the Austro-Prussian Postal Union. Second, there were the benefits that had accrued from the Paris Postal Conference, and the confirmation that many nations were willing to meet together to discuss their postal problems. Third, the public had been

74. It is interesting to note that one of the strongest speeches in support of a universal adoption of the decimal system of weights was made by the delegate from the United States (*ibid.*, p. 55).

75. Some administrations opened all mailbags and examined the correspondence letter by letter to determine the amount due.

76. *Ibid.*, Articles 2, 20, 21, 22, 23, and 30.

77. Union générale des Postes, *Documents du Congrès postal international de Berne, 1874* (Berne, 1875), p. 36.

78. *Annual Report of the Postmaster General, 1895*, p. 451.

aroused to the need for postal reform through the efforts of Hill and the International and Colonial Postage Association.

An additional stimulus was provided in 1865 when representatives of twenty European states met in Paris to discuss common telegraph problems. Not only did this group prepare a treaty containing international telegraph regulations which would eliminate charges based on zones and reduce rates, but they also created an international organization, the International Telegraph Union, under whose auspices the countries of the world could meet regularly to discuss new problems as they arose.[79] If telegraphic communications could be organized successfully, why not postal communications?

Consequently, all that was needed was for someone to set the process in motion. The man who is given credit for this act was Heinrich von Stephan, director of posts for the North German Confederation. In 1868 he laid before the German government his plan for the calling of a general postal congress to conclude a universal postal treaty. In general, Stephan's scheme was to do for the international mails what Hill's reform had done for domestic mails. Stephan proposed the unification and lowering of postage rates and the simplification and unification of administrative procedures.[80]

After two false starts, von Stephan was successful. In 1869 the German postal administration, acting on his suggestion, proposed to the other nations of the world that they meet somewhere in Europe to negotiate a binding international postal treaty. Before any definite plans could be made, however, the Franco-Prussian War intervened. At the conclusion of the war, the German postal administration, again at the instigation of von Stephan, suggested the calling of a conference in a neutral country in the fall of 1873. This time it was the Russian and French governments which caused a delay. Russia hesitated in accepting the German offer because she was awaiting the results of several recently introduced postal reforms and because of general financial difficulties. France did not want to enter into an agreement that might lower her postal receipts at a time when the budget was under the financial strain imposed by the paying of a war indemnity to Prussia. Finally the two countries agreed to go ahead and the date for the conference was set for September 15, 1874. The Swiss government agreed to act as host.[81]

79. See G. A. Codding, Jr., *The International Telecommunication Union* (Leiden, 1952), pp. 20–23.
80. Beelenkamp, *op. cit.,* pp. 543–47.
81. *Ibid.,* p. 547.

Birth and Development of the UPU

THE POSTAL CONGRESS of 1874, meeting in Berne, Switzerland, translated the dreams of Heinrich von Stephan into reality. After only
three weeks of discussion, a treaty was drafted and signed that transformed the territories of 21 nations into a single unit for the exchange of
postal correspondence, standardized and simplified postal rates and procedures, and created the second oldest international organization.

Since the inaugural conference of 1874, the Universal Postal Union
has held a dozen regular conferences, one extraordinary conference,
several administrative conferences, and numerous meetings of committees
and study groups in an unremitting search for methods to improve the
flow of mail across frontiers.[1] A knowledge of the manner in which
the organization and its functions evolved over the years is essential
to an understanding of the raison d'être of the present-day structure
of the Universal Postal Union and the services which it performs.
Consequently, this chapter will present an historical summary of the
activities of the Universal Postal Union, concentrating mainly on three
major developments: *1*] the search for uniform postal rates; *2*] the
continual increase in the number of services offered to the users of the
international postal service and the search for acceptable regulations;
and *3*] the evolution of the organization itself.

A. The Congress of Berne, 1874

THE FIRST INTERNATIONAL postal congress met in Berne, Switzerland,
on September 15, 1874, at the invitation of the Swiss government.[2]

1. See Annex I for a list of the conferences and meetings held under the
auspices of the Universal Postal Union.
2. The meeting place was the building which formerly housed the Diet of
the old Swiss Confederation.

Twenty-one countries sent delegations: Austria-Hungary, Belgium, Denmark, Egypt, France, Germany, Great Britain, Greece, Italy, Luxembourg, Netherlands, Norway, Portugal, Rumania, Russia, Serbia, Spain, Sweden, Switzerland, Turkey, and United States. Forty individuals in all took part in the meeting, ten of whom were the directors of the postal services in their respective countries. The largest single delegation was that of the host country, Switzerland, with five representatives.[3]

1. Organization

The organization of the Berne Congress was similar to that of the 1863 Paris Conference. The delegates to the Berne Congress were also able to take advantage of the experience of the International Telegraph Union which had already had two conferences (Vienna in 1868 and Rome in 1871–72) since its founding in Paris in 1865. Not only was the subject matter similar but, in those days as at present, the posts and the telegraphs of most European countries were run by the government and in many cases grouped under the same department of government. Thus, delegates to the Berne Postal Congress had either personal experience in telegraph conferences or were able to draw on the advice of those within the same governmental department. The director of the postal administration of the host country, Mr. Eugene Borel, was designated chairman of the conference, and the Swiss postal administration provided the secretariat. According to the rules of procedure, drafted by the Swiss government and accepted without change by the congress, all delegates were given permission to participate in the discussions, but only one vote was allowed to each country represented. French was adopted as the official language for debates and for the drafting of the final documents, and it was agreed that decisions should be taken by majority vote. Voting by proxy was accepted, but no delegation was permitted to dispose of more than one other vote. Periodic reports were released to the press, who along with the public were excluded because of the limited space available in the meeting room.[4]

Two committees were created, a general committee to discuss specific questions submitted by the plenary assembly, and a special committee charged with drafting detailed regulations necessary for the implementation of the general provisions to be included in the anticipated postal convention. The General Committee was made up of Austria-Hungary, Belgium, Egypt, Germany, Italy, Netherlands, Portugal, Russia, Serbia, Spain, and Switzerland. The delegates of France and Great Britain refused to participate in the general committee on the grounds that the terms of their authority did not permit them to accept such a

3. Docs., Berne Postal Congress (1874), pp. 11–12, 35, and 69. The delegates of the United States did not arrive until the third meeting. The two principal French delegates did not arrive at all, having been injured in a train wreck on the way to the congress (*ibid.*, pp. 13 and 35).

4. *Ibid.*, pp. 15–16.

commission. Lack of authority did not deter the delegates of Egypt and Italy, however, whose credentials were no more complete than those of France and Great Britain. The Special Committee was made up of Austria-Hungary, Belgium, Netherlands, Rumania, Russia, Serbia, Spain, and Switzerland. In both cases delegations, rather than individuals, were named.[5] It was decided further to use a draft treaty prepared by the German postal administration as the basis for discussion.[6]

When the credentials of the assembled delegates were finally examined, it was found that only 13 had the authority to negotiate and to sign a treaty, five had the authority to represent their governments but no authority to sign a treaty, and three were without any authority whatsoever. To overcome the problem thus posed, it was decided to open the discussion to everyone while the delinquent delegates took the necessary steps to secure proper credentials from their respective governments. By the end of the conference, all but the French had secured the necessary powers.[7]

2. *The International Postal Service*

After the establishment of the organization of the first postal congress but before debate could begin on the two major issues — uniform rates and transit fees — the Universal Postal Union was confronted with its first political problem. The Turkish delegate pointed out that Turkey was not master of her own house in the exploitation of the postal service. Certain unnamed countries had post offices on Turkish territory which participated in the internal postal communication and which had a monopoly on all of Turkey's postal relations with the outside world. The Turkish delegate was of the opinion that a meeting attended by representatives of all the postal authorities involved would be the ideal forum to eliminate this "abnormal" situation in an equitable manner. The chairman, however, ruled that the question was outside the jurisdiction of the congress, and since it did not have the power to consider it, any decisions would be valueless. He suggested that the Turkish government take up the problem directly, on a diplomatic basis, with the countries involved. The chairman's decision and suggestion were supported by the delegates from Germany, Austria, Great Britain, and France.[8] Thus, at the first

5. *Ibid.*, pp. 16–17 and 43.
6. *Ibid.*, pp. 3–7, 16, and 25.
7. *Ibid.*, pp. 19–20, 54–55, 70, 73–74, 85, 100, 109, and 125. The manner in which it was arranged for France to become a charter member of the Universal Postal Union despite the inability of her delegate to sign the postal treaty will be discussed below, p. 34.
8. *Ibid.*, pp. 20–23. The Austro-Hungarian Empire sent a combined delegation of four men to the Berne Congress and the final acts listed "Austria-Hungary" as a single contracting party. Nevertheless, the congress usually treated Austria and Hungary as separate entities. One of the two principal delegates was permitted to speak as "the delegate of Austria" and the other as "the delegate of Hungary." Both countries were given a vote, and the final acts were signed separately. (The signatures of the delegates of Hungary, however, followed immediately on those

postal congress the principle was established that the Universal Postal Union should confine itself primarily to technical problems and avoid wherever possible questions of a primarily political nature.[9]

The main issue of the Berne Congress, as it had been for the Paris Conference and would be for most UPU meetings in the future, was the simplification of postal rates. Despite the gains that had been made since the Paris Conference, there were still a great number of different rates in use throughout the world "creating difficulties for commercial relations, industry and families." [10] All other improvements that might be made in the international postal service could be of only secondary importance.

While the achievements of the Berne Congress in simplifying postal rates were enormous, they were not complete. At first it was agreed unanimously that uniformity was desired and that the rates should be as low as possible. Low rates in the international service, it was expected, would lead to the same beneficial effects as the low rates almost universally adopted for internal mails. A basic letter rate of 25 centimes was therefore adopted for a basic weight unit of 15 grammes. The first compromise on the principle of uniformity occurred when it was agreed, as a transitory measure, to permit a variation in the basic letter charge, up to 32 centimes or down to 20 centimes. Although the reason given was that some countries did not have monetary units corresponding to the 25-centime rate, it was clear that some postal administrations simply wanted to charge more and others less.[11] The second compromise in principle was the decision to permit the charging of a surtax, not to exceed half of the ordinary rate, on all letters forwarded by sea for distances of over 300 miles.[12] The rates for postcards were fixed at half the rate for letters.

In addition to letter mail, the following categories of mail were recognized: books, newspapers and other printed matter, samples of merchandise, and commercial papers. The compromises for letter mail were extended to the other classes of mail. Wherever admitted to the international mail, these classes of mail paid a basic rate of 7 centimes for each 50 grammes of weight. Again as a transitory measure, each country was permitted to charge up to a maximum of 11 centimes or down to a minimum of 5 centimes. As with letter mail, countries were permitted to charge a surtax on these articles, not to exceed one half of

---

of the Austrians rather than being placed in the proper alphabetical order.) This same procedure was followed until the Congress of Rome in 1906 when, for the first time, Austria and Hungary were made completely separate entities for the purposes of the UPU. Nonetheless, the official documents of the UPU list both Austria and Hungary individually as having become members of the UPU on July 1, 1875, the date when the Berne treaty came into force.

9. The Turkish delegate did get his point across, however, and later, through direct diplomatic negotiations, the countries involved agreed to relinquish their extraterritorial postal rights in Turkey.

10. *Ibid.*, p. 23.

11. *Ibid.*, pp. 4, 23–24, 39–41, 45–46, 53, and 89.

12. *Ibid.*, p. 40.

the ordinary rate, when they were forwarded by sea for a distance of over 300 miles. A maximum weight of 250 grammes was fixed for samples of merchandise and a maximum of 1,000 grammes for other articles.[13]

The second issue of importance, and the one which resulted in the longest and most acrimonious discussion, concerned transit fees. As at the Paris Conference, a majority of the delegates at the Berne Congress had instructions to do all in their power to eliminate payments to postal administrations of intermediate countries whose sole task consisted of transshipping the mails. If transit fees could be eliminated, it was argued, everyone would benefit. Administrative expenses would be cut by the elimination of accounting between postal administrations, and the savings could be passed on to the user of the mails.[14] Hill's logic of the 1830's was used when it was pointed out that the actual cost of any form of surface transportation was very low in relation to that incurred at the two terminals, and that almost everywhere ordinary means of conveyance were used for the transit of mails. The proposal to eliminate transit fees, however, met with determined opposition from several countries whose geographical position placed them at what they considered to be a special disadvantage. France, for instance, categorically rejected the principle of free transit. The French government had already reduced its transit fees at a considerable sacrifice to the treasury and was not prepared to lose any more revenues. The Belgian delegate stated that his country was the major transit center of Europe, rendering twenty times the service to other administrations that was rendered to her. The expenses were too great to forego transit fees. The delegate from Turkey asked that, whatever the decision, his country be permitted to charge a special fee in view of the difficulty in transporting mails across her territory.[15]

In view of the amount and the intensity of opposition, the concept of free transit was finally abandoned and the attention of the conference was turned to the problem of fixing adequate and equitable transit fees. The solution found was in four parts. First, the general transit fee for each intermediate country was fixed at 2 francs per kilogram for letters

13. *Ibid.*, pp. 41–42, 46–47, and 65.
14. A clear understanding of the meaning of transit mails is important at this point since the problem of payment for this service has continued to be one of the thornier issues facing the international postal service throughout the history of the UPU. The issue does not arise when mail is exchanged only between two neighboring postal administrations. In this case, the sending administration pays the cost of the transport of the mail to its neighbor's border and the neighboring administration pays the cost of transport of the mails from its own border to the destination within the country. The problem of "transit" only arises when the mail must also cross the territory of one or more intermediate countries. It has been the general rule since the Congress of 1874, although often debated, that the cost of the transshipment of mails across the territory of intermediate countries is chargeable to the country of origin. (The country of destination, as in the case of exchanges between neighbors, pays for the final leg of the journey.)
15. *Ibid.*, pp. 23–24, 38–39, 47–48, and 50–52.

and postcards, and at 25 centimes per kilogram for other articles. Second, the rates were increased to 4 francs and 50 centimes, respectively, where the distance of transmission exceeded 750 kilometers over the territory of any one postal administration. Third, in cases where sea transit was involved exceeding 300 nautical miles, the country of expedition was required to pay the administration providing the service a fee not to exceed 6 francs 50 centimes per kilogram for letters and postcards, and 50 centimes per kilogram for other articles. Fourth, the transit fees for mail using the Indian Mail Service and the United States transcontinental lines were to be determined by special agreements between interested administrations.[16]

Once the two major issues had been resolved, the congress was able to come to an agreement on important related areas. It was agreed in principle that, wherever possible, mail should be prepaid by means of postage stamps and prestamped envelopes. The expediting country would retain all the proceeds from the sale of such stamps and stamped envelopes, thus eliminating any accounting between the country of expedition and the country of destination. The justification was that each letter would elicit a reply, thus equalizing in principle the receipts of the two administrations. However, since there were still postal administrations that did not require prepayment of postage, it was agreed to permit the sending of nonprepaid mail at double the ordinary prepaid mail rate. In these cases, the postal administration of the country of destination would retain the entire amount collected.[17]

If transit fees had been abolished, the decision to permit administrations to keep all charges collected would have eliminated almost all accounting from the international postal service. However, since it was not possible to abolish transit fees, as we have seen, the congress did do its best to ameliorate the consequences by simplifying the remaining accounting procedures. In order to determine the transit charges, it was agreed to weigh transit mail for a period of seven consecutive days twice a year, rather than to examine every piece or sack, with yearly accounts made up on the basis of these biannual inspections. Postal administrations were permitted to request a revision of the annual accounts in cases where an important change occurred in the flow of mails.[18]

The delegates at Berne made a number of other important decisions concerning the future of the international postal service. All international mail was to be reexpedited without charge in the case of a change in residence of the addressee. However, a fee equal to the local mail rate was to be charged by the postal administration of destination in cases where local mail was forwarded to another country. Only official postal administration mail was to be admitted without charge in the interna-

16. The United States refused to accept any fee less than 5 francs per kilogram for transit mail between New York and San Francisco. *Ibid.*, p. 49. (See also pp. 47–52 and 65.)
    17. *Ibid.*, pp. 24–25 and 30–31.
    18. *Ibid.*, pp. 51–52, 54, and 88.

tional mails. The registration of letters was to be permitted among the signatory states at a supplementary fee not to exceed that for local registered mail. An indemnity of 50 francs was to be paid for the loss of registered mail except when such loss was due to a circumstance beyond the control of the postal service. In addition, no charges were to be made on international mail other than that specifically permitted in the postal treaty. Of special importance was the decision that mail should be transmitted by the most rapid means available. The Paris Conference had recommended only that it be transmitted by the means that would "best serve the public interest." [19] Finally, administrations were permitted to refuse to transport and distribute anything, except letters, forbidden by local law.[20]

3. *The General Postal Union*

Of all the decisions of the Berne Congress, one of the most far-reaching was that establishing a continuing international postal organization. The congress had before it the example of the International Telegraph Union, which it followed in general outline.[21] The name chosen was the General Postal Union, and all of the signatories of the Berne treaty became charter members. Meetings were to be held every three years for the purpose of revising the basic treaty and discussing matters of common interest. In all such meetings, each country was to be given one vote and, while proxy voting was to be permitted, the maximum number of votes permitted to any country was to be two. Any conflicts which arose between members of the union were to be settled by arbitration. New members were permitted to join after consultation with members with which it had postal relations and following the approval of all members.[22]

19. Docs., Paris Postal Conference (1863), *Principes généraux* Art. 17.
20. Docs., Berne Postal Congress (1874), *Traité concernant la création d'une Union générale des postes*, Arts. 4, 5, 7, 8, 9, and 10.
21. See Codding, *op. cit.*, pp. 13–80.
22. Berne Postal Treaty (1874), Art. 17. The original text of this article was as follows:
L'entrée dans l'Union des pays d'outre-mer n'en faisant pas encore partie sera admise aux conditions suivantes:
1] *Ils déposeront leur déclaration entre les mains de l'Administration chargée de la gestion du Bureau international de l'Union.*
2] *Ils se soumettront aux stipulations du traité de l'Union, sauf entente ultérieure au sujet des frais de transport maritime.*
3] *Leur adhésion à l'Union doit être précédée d'une entente entre les Administrations ayant des conventions postales ou des relations directes avec eux.*
4] *Pour amener cette entente, l'Administration gérante convoquera, le cas échéant, une réunion des Administrations intéressées et de l'Administration qui demande l'accès.*
5] *L'entente établie, l'Administration gérante en avisera tous les membres de l'Union générale des postes.*
6] *Si dans un délai de six semaines, à partir de la date de cette communication, des objections ne sont pas présentées, l'adhésion sera considérée comme*

At the suggestion of the Belgian delegate, the congress also created a permanent bureau of the postal union. This bureau was given the general tasks of distributing information of interest to the international postal service; giving its advice, when requested by the parties involved, on legal questions; informing members of requests for changes in the postal regulations attached to the treaty and notifying them of changes adopted; helping to settle international postal accounts; and making studies and performing other tasks given it. The bureau was to be under the supervision of a postal administration designated by the congress, and its expenses were to be met by all of the members of the union.[23]

Except for a provision requesting members to keep all postage collected when mail was exchanged with nonmembers, the Berne Congress left members freedom of interchange with other countries and with one another on matters not covered by the treaty. Article 14, for instance, provided:

"The stipulations of the present treaty do not alter the internal postal legislation of any member country nor do they restrict the right of the contracting parties to maintain or to conclude treaties, or to maintain or establish limited unions for the progressive amelioration of postal relations." [24]

4. Detailed Regulations

It should be noted that the discussions and decisions reviewed up to this point have dealt with the content of the new postal treaty. As mentioned earlier, the Berne Congress also established a special committee to draw up a document containing detailed regulations of a more transitory nature necessary for the implementation of the general provisions included in the postal treaty. This document was appended to the general postal treaty and given the same authority and duration.[25] The major difference in form consisted in the provision that it could be revised in the period between the general diplomatic conferences "by common agreement between the administrations of the Union." [26] Although not spelled out in either the treaty or the regulations, it was assumed that such revision would take place at any time that a proposal to do so was made and accepted by all member administrations. The bureau was given the duty of circulating such proposals to all members and notifying them later as to whether or not all were in agreement.

---

accomplie et il en sera fait communication par l'Administration gérante à l'Administration adhérente. — L'adhésion définitive sera constatée par un acte diplomatique entre le Gouvernement de l'Administration gérante et le Gouvernement de l'Administration admise dans l'Union.

23. Docs., Berne Postal Congress (1874), pp. 32–33, 43, and 55; and Berne Postal Treaty (1874), Art. 15.

24. Ibid., Arts. 11, 12, 13, and 14.

25. Docs., Berne Postal Congress (1874), pp. 153–64, Règlement de détail et d'ordre pour l'exécution du traité concernant la création d'une Union générale des Postes.

26. Ibid., Art. 30; and Berne Postal Treaty (1874), Art. 13.

Of the 30 articles in the regulations, 26 dealt with details of the uniform operation of the international postal service, including such matters as directions for the proper cancellation of stamps and the wrapping and handling of mail; the tying and tagging of mailbags; making out of bills of lading (including model forms), and other such items. Common procedures were set forth for handling items with insufficient postage or mail for which it was impossible to find the intended recipient. The manner of accounting for transit mail was indicated in detail and the dates for compiling transit statistics were established.

The regulations also treated of the establishment and the functions of the bureau of the union. The Swiss government was designated as the organizer of the bureau and supervisor of its functions.[27] The budget was fixed at 75,000 Swiss francs a year, with costs to be divided among the members of the union according to a six-class scale. Members were permitted to choose the class they preferred, which determined the amount that they would contribute to the bureau's budget.[28]

The new bureau was given the following specific duties by the postal regulations: (1) to compile and distribute annual statistics on the international postal service; (2) to publish an official journal containing matters of interest to postal administrations in three languages: French, English, and German; (3) to circularize administrations on questions of common interest and to relay the results (administrations not replying within four months to be considered as consenting); (4) to furnish, in general, information requested by administrations; (5) to help in the preparation for union conferences; (6) and to prepare and distribute an annual report on its own activities. French was made the official language of the bureau, and the director of the bureau was given the right to participate in congresses without, however, the right to vote.[29]

5. *Implementation of the Treaty and Regulations*

It was decided that the treaty and regulations would come into force on July 1, 1875, and would remain in force for a period of three years. If it were not possible to hold a new congress before the end of that period, however, the treaty and regulations were to continue in force indefinitely, with each contracting party given the right to withdraw from

27. See Docs., Berne Postal Congress (1874), pp. 82, 85–86, and 99–100. (See also below, p. 187.)

28. The classes established and the units of payment were as follows: 1st class, 25 units; 2d class, 20 units; 3d class, 15 units; 4th class, 10 units; 5th class, 5 units; and 6th class, one unit. The amount that each unit represented was obtained by dividing the total expenses of the bureau by the total number of units subscribed to by member countries. The countries represented at the Berne Congress chose the following classes: 1st class, Austria-Hungary, France, Germany, Great Britain, Italy, Russia, Turkey, and United States; 2d class, Spain; 3d class, Belgium, Egypt, Netherlands, Rumania, and Sweden; 4th class, Denmark, Norway, Portugal, and Switzerland; 5th class, Greece and Serbia; and 6th class, Luxembourg. (Berne Postal Regulations (1874), Art. 27.)

29. *Ibid.*

the union on a year's notice. As soon as the treaty came into force, all other treaties between the member countries inconsistent with its provisions were to be considered abrogated. The next postal congress was scheduled for Paris in 1877 and it was agreed to meet in Berne at least three months before the treaty was to come into effect to exchange ratifications.[30]

The Berne Postal Treaty was signed in Berne on October 9, 1874, by representatives of all the countries which participated in the congress, with the exception of France. The French delegate stated that the economic consequences of the treaty were such that his government would not even permit him to sign until approval had been obtained from the French Parliament. The importance of France to the success of the treaty, and to the postal union, was such that a special protocol was added to the treaty permitting France to sign at a later date on equal terms with the other signatories.[31]

On May 3, 1875, the participants of the Berne Congress met again in Berne to exchange ratifications. The French representative announced at the meeting that his country was prepared to accept the postal treaty on the condition that she could bring its provisions into force on January 1, 1876, rather than July 1, 1875; that the rates would not be changed before the next congress except by unanimous consent of all members; and that she would be permitted to charge transit rates on the basis of the actual distance the mail was carried. These reservations were agreed to, and France made the necessary decisions to become a member of the General Postal Union.[32] Montenegro, which had been invited to the Berne Postal Congress but was unable to send a representative, was permitted to become a member of the union upon a simple declaration of adherence to the treaty. The declaration was made in time for the treaty to become operative for Montenegro on July 1, 1875, with the others.[33]

B. Toward Universality:
The UPU from 1875 to 1919

THE PERIOD from the coming into force of the Berne Postal Treaty (July 1, 1875) to World War I was one of experimentation for the new international postal organization. Together with the International Tele-

---

30. Berne Postal Treaty (1874), Arts, 18, 19, and 20.

31. Docs., Berne Postal Congress (1874), pp. 69–70, 129–30, and 151. For further information on the reasons for the refusal of the French delegate to sign, see Georges Lacroix, *Exposé du Système Général de l'Union postale universelle* (Toulouse, 1910), pp. 82–84.

32. Docs., Berne Postal Congress (1874), pp. 165–67. See also, UPU, *L'Union postale universelle, sa fondation et son développement, 1874–1949, Mémoire,* p. 34. (This document will be referred to hereafter as *Mémoire.*)

33. *Ibid.*

graph Union, the new postal union was pioneering a new field of human endeavor, the bringing together of representatives of nations to attack, on a continuing basis, problems that could be dealt with effectively only by international cooperation. The task was not an easy one. Almost every problem that arose demanded a new and unique answer, whether it concerned membership, organization of conferences, functions of the international bureau, or postal rates and services to be offered to the public. That the postal union was able to find satisfactory answers to the problems of organization and of regulation of postal communications was reflected in the increasing numbers of countries which participated in the union's meetings. Twenty-one countries sent representatives to the Berne Postal Congress of 1874. The number had grown to 54 by the Lisbon Congress of 1885 and to 71 in Rome in 1906, the last congress held before World War I.

This section will concentrate on the major changes and innovations that occurred during the period from 1875 to World War I concerning organization, especially the increase in membership, new services offered to the user of the international postal service, and postal rates. Most of these developments took place at the five regular congresses: Paris, 1878; Lisbon, 1885; Vienna, 1891; Washington, D.C., 1897; and Rome, 1906. Four other special conferences and meetings were held in this same period under the auspices of the union: one in Berne in 1876 to decide on the admission of new members; one in Paris in 1880 to draw up a new agreement on parcel post; one in Brussels in 1890 to draw up a draft agreement on a newspaper subscription service; and one in Berne in 1900 to celebrate the 25th anniversary of the union.

1. Membership and Organization

Almost immediately after the Berne Postal Treaty came into force the new international organization was faced with a problem concerning admission of new members, specifically, whether colonies or territories should participate in the union's conferences and meetings on a basis of equality with the states which had created the postal union. The Berne treaty did not contain a general admission article. The pertinent article, described earlier, provided that an "overseas country," not a member of the union, would be admitted only after agreement between it and the countries with which it had postal treaties or direct postal relations on the matter of sea transit rates, and its acceptance, at least tacitly, by all other union members.[34] The problem was raised when Great Britain applied on November 15, 1875, for the admission of British India to the union.[35] Accordingly, the Swiss government called a special conference of all interested administrations to decide on the sea transit rates to be

34. Berne Treaty (1874), Art. 17.
35. The British had requested and obtained membership in a like manner for British India in the International Telegraph Union four years previously. (See Codding, *op. cit.,* pp. 39–40.)

permitted between British India and the members of the union. Before
the conference had convened on January 18, 1876, there were also
requests of a similar nature from France and the Netherlands, and during the conference the Spanish delegate announced the intention of his
government to request admission for the Spanish colonies.[36] The question
of membership of dependent territories was answered, in principle, in
the affirmative when the conference agreed on sea transport rates for
British India and the French colonies and set July 1, 1876, as the date
for their admission to the union. After the refusal of the British to discuss the admission of the Dutch and Spanish colonies, the conference
agreed that the problem of their admission would have to be taken up
by the union at a later date.[37]

The ramifications of the decisions of the Berne Conference of 1876,
which established the acceptance of nonindependent territories as members of the union, were not lost on the governments of countries with
such territories. In 1877 the Swiss government received word that nine
British colonies were entering the union (the Bermudas, Ceylon, British
Guinea, Hong Kong, Jamaica, Labuan, Mauritius, the Straits-Settlements
and Trinidad), as well as the colonies of Denmark, Spain, Netherlands,
and Portugal.[38] The Congress of Paris in 1878 accepted the precedent
established by the Berne conference and in a special article recognized
that seven colonies or groups of colonies were to be considered as "a
single country or a single administration, as the case may be" for the
purposes of the postal treaty. The seven included the two admitted by
the 1876 Berne Congress, British India and the French colonies, the
Danish, Dutch, Portuguese and Spanish colonies, and the Dominion of
Canada.[39] The latter became a voting member of the union when Great
Britain requested and received approval during the congress to turn
over to Canada the vote granted to it for the British colonies.[40]

The number of nonindependent members of the union continued
to increase up to World War I. Only a few voices were raised against
this attempt to obtain "supplemental" votes, but none was successful in
putting an end to it. Even some of the opponents to such membership
finally capitulated and requested extra memberships. By the end of the
Congress of Rome (1906) there were 17 such memberships as follows:

1] German protectorates in Africa;
2] German protectorates in Asia and Australasia;
3] The Empire of British India;

36. UPU, *Actes de la Conférence postale de Berne, Janvier 1876* (Berne, 1876; réimpression 1944), pp. 15, 23, 24, and 27, and Annexes, I–III.

37. *Ibid.*, pp. 47–50. The conference, in fact, adopted a recommendation that a special conference be held in London on June 1, 1876, for the purpose of con-sidering the admission of the Dutch and Spanish colonies. No action was taken on the recommendation, however (*ibid.*, p. 34).

38. *Mémoire*, p. 43.

39. UPU, *Documents du Congrès postal de Paris, 1878* (Berne, 1879), *Convention postale universelle*, Art. 21.

40. Docs., Paris Postal Congress (1878), pp. 397–398.

4] The Dominion of Canada;
5] The Commonwealth of Australia, with British Guinea;
6] British colonies and protectorates in South Africa;
7] All other British colonies;
8] Insular possessions of the United States, comprising the Hawaiian Islands, the Philippine Islands, and the islands of Puerto Rico and Guam;
9] Danish colonies;
10] Spanish colonies;
11] Algeria;
12] French colonies and protectorates in Indochina;
13] All other French colonies;
14] Italian colonies;
15] Dutch colonies;
16] Portuguese African colonies; and
17] All other Portuguese colonies.[41]

The Paris Congress also filled the gap in the Berne treaty concerning the admission of "sovereign" countries. The old provision of calling a special conference for "overseas countries" was discarded entirely, and any country, overseas or otherwise, was permitted to become a member by a simple declaration of adherence. The pertinent article of the Paris Convention read as follows:

1] Countries which are not bound by the present Convention are permitted to adhere to it by request;
2] This adherence is notified, by diplomatic procedure, to the government of the Swiss confederation and, by that government, to all the countries of the union.[42]

The number of countries which took advantage of this simplified procedure, or which participated in succeeding conferences and signed and ratified the final acts, soon included almost all of the independent countries of the world. The Far East was represented with the joining of Japan in 1877 and China in 1914; Latin America, when 19 independent republics became members between 1877 and 1888; and Africa, when Egypt was joined by Liberia in 1879 and Ethiopia in 1908.[43]

With the exception of the question of membership, very few essential changes were made in the organization of the union from 1874 to World War I. Of a minor but important nature, however, was the change in the name of the union from the General Postal Union to the Universal Postal Union, made at the Paris Congress of 1878, and the change in the

41. UPU, *Documents du Congrès postal de Rome, 1906* (Berne, 1906), II, *Convention postale universelle*, Art. 27.
42. *Ibid.*, Art. 18.
43. The three independent countries of Brazil, Japan, and Persia notified their adherence to the Berne Postal Treaty of 1874 in 1877. Although the treaty did not at that time provide for countries joining the union by means of a simple act of adherence, these three were permitted to attend the Paris Postal Congress of 1878 as regular members, and their date of membership was inscribed in all subsequent union documents as 1877.

name of the basic document from a "treaty" to a "convention." The name of the union was changed in order to make it better reflect its geographical scope, and the change in nomenclature of the basic document was made both to reflect what was considered to be its unique nature and to differentiate it from ordinary bilateral and multilateral treaties.[44] The Paris Congress also decided that a three-year interval between congresses was too short and that therefore future congresses would be held at five-year intervals from the date of the coming into force of the revised conventions.[45] Another decision provided that if a problem should arise which required a more immediate decision, an extraordinary congress could be held between regular congresses, if a request for such a conference were approved by two thirds of the member governments. Further, if an administrative problem should arise which created a need for a consultation of experts rather than delegates with plenipotentiary powers, an administrative conference could be held upon request and approval of two thirds of the "member administrations." [46]

Also of importance was the decision of the Paris Congress to tighten up the article of the convention which permitted postal administrations to make agreements on postal matters outside the aegis of the UPU, by the addition of the provision: ". . . provided that these agreements do not derogate from the present Convention." [47]

The international bureau also received some attention from the postal congresses preceding World War I. The Vienna Postal Congress of 1891, for example, gave the bureau the task of operating a clearing house for the liquidation of any international postal accounts arising between members of the union.[48] To enable the bureau to carry out the increased burden resulting from the addition of new members, larger conferences, and additional functions, the bureau's budget was increased to 100,000 Swiss francs a year by the Congress of Paris in 1878 and to 125,000 francs a year by the Congress of Vienna in 1891.[49]

Just as important as the formal changes in the structure of the bureau, perhaps, were the informal ones. The Berne Postal Congress, it will be recalled, gave the director of the bureau the right to attend union meetings and to participate in the discussions, although withholding his

44. Docs., Paris Postal Congress (1878), pp. 21, 243, 378, 486–87, and 627.

45. *Ibid.*, pp. 48, 250, 396, and 635.

46. Paris Postal Convention (1878), Arts. 4, 5, 6, and 71, and *Règlement,* Art. 4.

47. Docs., Paris Postal Congress (1878), pp. 45–46, 248, and 633–34. The permissive limits of such outside agreements were clarified even further at Stockholm in 1924 when the following phrase was substituted for the one adopted in 1878: ". . . on the condition that they do not introduce provisions less favorable to the public than those provided in the Acts of the Union." (See UPU, *Documents du Congrès postal de Stockholm, 1924* (Berne, 1924), II, 168, 387, 658, and 845. Each succeeding postal convention has contained a similar provision.

48. UPU, *Documents du Congrès postal universel de Vienne, 1891* (Berne, 1892), pp. 331–56, 454–60, 495–96, 498, 726, 754, 789, and 790.

49. Paris Postal Convention (1878), Regulations, Art. 28, and Vienna Postal Convention (1891), *Règlement,* Art. 26, or 32, or 35, or 36.

right to vote. A temporary addition to the powers of the director made him the proxy for a member country in the Conference of Berne in 1876, and the congresses of Lisbon in 1885, Vienna in 1891, and Rome in 1906.[50] The position of the director of the bureau was further enhanced when he was made the vice chairman of congresses, starting at Vienna in 1891.[51]

2. Services Offered to the Public

Another important characteristic of the period from 1875 to World War I was the increase of services instigated by the UPU for those using the international post. Some of these new services, such as the introduction of "special delivery," dealt primarily with the exchange of the mails; and others, such as the parcel post or postal money orders, dealt with nonmail services. Provisions for new mail services, with the possible exception of insured letters and boxes, were added directly to the basic postal convention and its regulations for execution. The introduction of many of these new mail services became obligatory upon members of the union on the date when the revised convention itself came into effect. Others were introduced on an optional basis.

The major new non-letter services were, almost without exception, set forth in an additional document called an agreement, having the same standing as the postal convention, with appended regulations for execution. The major exception was the parcel post instrument which was given the title "Convention." These agreements, and the parcel post convention, were made binding only on those countries which signed and ratified them, or those which subsequently deposited an act of adherence.

Among the new mail services offered to the users of the international post were: special delivery, with an additional 30-centime charge (1885); the admission of packages containing samples of liquids between those countries which consented to such admission (1891); the addition of natural-history specimens in the samples of merchandise class (1897); and the introduction of a new postage reply coupon, issued by the international bureau, which could be used by the recipient in exchange for one of his own country's stamps (1906).[52]

Postcards provide a good example of the stages through which some of the mail services passed in the early years of the postal union.

50. Docs., Berne Postal Conference (1876), p. 19; UPU, *Documents du Congrès postal de Lisbonne, 1885* (Berne, 1886), II, 3; Docs., Vienna Postal Congress (1891), p. 361; and UPU, *Documents du Congrès postal de Rome, 1906* (Berne, 1906), II, 7.

51. Docs., Vienna Postal Congress (1891), pp. 365–67; UPU, *Documents du Congrès postal de Washington, 1897* (Berne, 1898), pp. 369 and 371; and Docs., Rome Postal Congress (1906), II, 17.

52. Docs., Lisbon Postal Congress (1885), pp. 45–46, 74, 248–49, 504, and 634; Docs., Vienna Postal Congress (1891), pp. 74–75, 438–40, 722–23, and 777–78; Docs., Washington D.C. Postal Congress (1897), pp. 122, 459–60, 500, 710–11, and 760–61; and Docs., Rome Postal Congress (1906), II, 26–28, 61, 66–67, 71, 126–29, 207, 240–41, 252, 313–14, 328–29, 353, and 585–86.

The Berne Postal Congress of 1874 admitted ordinary postcards to the international postal service. The Lisbon Postal Congress of 1885 admitted reply-paid postcards to the international postal service, but on a voluntary basis. Those countries which wished to issue such cards were permitted to do so, but all the members of the union were obliged to return the reply half. The Congress of Vienna in 1891 made the issuance of reply cards obligatory on all postal administrations. Privately manufactured postcards, and reply-paid postcards were not admitted until the 1897 Washington Postal Congress.[53] The Lisbon Congress of 1885 added Braille materials to the printed matter category, and the Congress of Rome in 1906, at the request of The Hague Peace Conference of 1899, provided that mail for prisoners of war should pass through the international mails free of charge.[54]

By the time of the Rome Postal Congress of 1906, the Universal Postal Convention had six annexes to it, each of which was optional and each of which provided for a different postal service. The first to appear were the Agreement concerning Insured Letters and the Agreement concerning Postal Money Orders, both created by the Congress of Paris in 1878. The agreements laid down the major principles involved and the two attached regulations contained the common administrative rules necessary to put the insured letters service and the postal money order service into operation. Delegates of 16 countries signed the money order agreement and 20 signed the insured letter agreement.[55] These were followed by the Parcel Post Agreement, a Collection of Bills Agreement and a Postal Identity Card Agreement in 1885, and an Agreement on Subscriptions to Newspapers and Periodicals in 1891. Only the Agreement on Postal Identity Cards was considered simple and short enough to eliminate the need for an attached regulation for execution.[56]

In the case of the Agreement for Subscriptions to Newspapers and Periodicals, the original proposals made at the Congress of Lisbon in 1885 received so little support that it was not considered worthwhile to hold a full-scale discussion; the international bureau was directed to give it further study and, if necessary, call a special conference of interested parties.[57] The international bureau called a special study committee of delegates from Austria, Belgium, Germany, and Portugal, which met in

53. Docs., Lisbon Postal Congress (1885), I, 4, 96, and 566, II, 61, 110–11. 402, and 422–23; Docs., Vienna Postal Congress (1891), pp. 3 and 380; and Docs., Washington D.C. Postal Congress (1897), pp. 110, 455–56, and 497.

54. Docs., Lisbon Postal Congress (1885), pp. 115–17 and 423–24, and Docs., Rome Postal Congress (1906), II, 136–37 and 313.

55. See *Mémoire*, pp. 51–52, and Docs., Paris Postal Congress (1878), pp. 689–748.

56. Docs., Lisbon Postal Congress (1885), II, *Arrangement concernant le service des recouvrements,* and *Arrangement concernant l'introduction de livrets d'identité dans le trafic postal international.* Docs., Vienna Postal Congress (1891), pp. 945–49, *Arrangement concernant l'intervention de la poste dans les abonnements aux journaux et publication périodiques.*

57. *Mémoire*, p. 68.

Brussels from June 26 to July 1, 1890, and drew up a draft agreement for the next regularly scheduled congress.[58] The draft was submitted to the Congress of Vienna in 1891, accepted, and attached to the international postal convention.[59]

The procedure for the drafting of the agreement on parcel post was slightly different. The possibility of drafting such an agreement was first raised by the delegate from Germany at the Paris Congress in 1878, but in view of its importance and the fact that the delegates had not come prepared to discuss it, the project was referred to the international bureau for consideration and the possible calling of a conference to deal with it.[60] After study, the international bureau circulated a draft agreement to the members of the union. As a result of the tremendous number of revisions suggested by administrations, the international bureau notified the French government that the calling of a special conference was in order. The latter agreed, and the members of the UPU were invited to meet in the French capital on October 9, 1880.[61]

The bureau gave an interesting reason for suggesting that Paris be the meeting site. In the first place, the size and geographical position of France made it a key country in any such scheme. Secondly, it was felt that the main obstacle to an agreement on the international exchange of small parcels lay in the fact that in many countries the conveyance of parcels was a function not of the post office, but of railway administrations or other transportation enterprises. Since France was one of these countries, it would be of value to the conference to have the benefit of its experience and the counsel of the enterprises which carried its small parcels. As a matter of fact, all the major French railway lines and the three French maritime enterprises which carried small parcels were allowed to send representatives to the conference as observers.[62]

The Paris Postal Conference met from October 9 to November 3, 1880. It was attended by delegates from 23 countries who succeeded in drafting a parcel post convention and regulations for its execution. Briefly, the convention provided for the exchange of small parcels between the contracting postal administrations, set rates and transit fees, established methods of handling, and fixed the maximum size of packages. Of significance for the postal service in general was the decision of the participants that there would be a single transit fee of 50 centimes for each territorial transit, and five rates for maritime transit: 25 centimes up to 500 maritime miles; 50 centimes between 500 and 1,000 miles;

58. UPU, *Documents de la Conférence tenue à Bruxelles pour l'élaboration d'un projet d'arrangement concernant le service international des abonnements aux journaux et aux publications périodiques, 1890* (Berne, 1890), pp. 1–51.

59. Docs., Vienna Postal Congress (1891), *ibid.*

60. Docs., Paris Postal Congress (1878), pp. 592–93.

61. UPU, *Documents de la Conférence postale de Paris, 1880* (Berne, 1880), pp. 37–40.

62. See "The Postal Conference of Paris in the Year 1880," *Union Postale,* v, No. 12 (December, 1880), 248.

1 franc between 1,000 and 3,000 miles; 2 francs between 3,000 and 6,000 miles; and 3 francs for any maritime route that extended more than 6,000 miles.[63]

The parcel post convention was signed on November 3, 1880, by 19 of the participating delegations, and came into effect on October 1, 1881. A special provision permitted the four nonsigners — British India, Great Britain, Netherlands, and Persia — to delay signing until July 1, 1881, and to postpone the execution of the convention and regulations until April 1, 1882.[64]

3. Rates for Letter Mail

The principle of uniform postal rates, agreed to in the Berne Congress of 1874, became a reality following the decisions of the Paris Congress of 1878. The formula adopted, it will be recalled, was to set a common rate but to allow countries to deviate from that rate within a certain maximum and minimum. In the case of the letter post, the rate was fixed at 25 centimes for each 15 grammes, with a maximum deviation up to 32 centimes and a minimum down to 20 centimes. Countries were thus permitted fairly wide leeway for experiment until the time came for making a new decision.

By the Paris Congress of 1878, sufficient countries had found the letter rate of 25 centimes for 15 grammes to their liking so that they were willing to forego the permissible deviations. The formula arrived at, in view of the still-existing differences in monetary units between many members of the union, was to fix 25 centimes as the rate in the basic convention and to add to the regulations a table in which each member country set forth the equivalent of 25 centimes in its own currency.[65] The same formula was used for the other classes of letter mail, postcards and printed matter, commercial papers and samples of merchandise.[66] Further, the Paris Congress of 1878 reduced the basic rate of postcards to 10 centimes per article, and other articles from 7 centimes per 50 grammes to 5 centimes per 50 grammes. Countries were permitted to renegotiate their equivalents between conferences, in the event of a change in the monetary system or "an important modification of the value of its money," with the Swiss postal administration.[67]

Concerning low postal rates, as contrasted to uniform postal rates, the basic rate for letter post fixed in 1874 and those for postcards and other items of the letter post set in 1878 remained unchanged until the last conference before World War I, held in Rome in 1906. Isolated

63. Docs., Paris Postal Conference (1880), pp. 187–93.
64. Ibid., pp. 192–93.
65. Docs., Paris Postal Congress (1878), pp. 27–35, 60–66, 88–89, 244–45, 382–83, 410–11, 418–19, 492–93, 495–96, and 530. It is interesting to note that "equivalent" was used to replace "the closest equivalent" used in the draft presented by France and the international bureau (ibid., pp. 88–89 and 530).
66. Ibid., p. 530.
67. Paris Postal Convention (1878), Art. 4 and Regulations, Art. 4.

attempts to lower the basic rate for letters were made by France and Serbia in 1878, Netherlands in 1885, and Serbia in 1897, but in each case were decisively defeated.[68] The justification for not lowering the letter rate included arguments that it might make it difficult for new countries to join the union, it would result in serious financial sacrifices for postal administrations, and in general it was not being asked for by the public.[69]

However, by 1906 there was increased pressure for a lowering of the 25-centime letter rate. The most extreme proposal at the Rome Congress came from the delegate of the British colonies of Australasia who wanted the international letter rate lowered from 25 to 10 centimes. Many countries, argued the Australasian delegate, had lowered their internal letter rates to 10 centimes. Although, as in the case of Australia and New Zealand, the new low rate would result in immediate losses to the postal administration, it was expected that the tremendous increase in use of the mails would eventually result in a profit. In any case, the benefits to the mail users were considered to far outweigh any losses. The advantage of cheaper postage in the international field, in increased communication between peoples, was important enough to encourage the congress to lower its international letter rate to 10 centimes.[70]

Another group of nations, led by Japan, also felt that the time had come for a lowering of the basic letter rate. This group presented a more modest proposal, a reduction from 25 centimes to 20 centimes. Ten centimes was considered to be too low a rate for the international service, since there was no guarantee that there would be sufficient increase in the use of the international mail to make up for the immediate losses entailed. However, since there was popular pressure for lower rates, it was felt that the congress should at least set the basic rate at 20 centimes.[71]

A third group, mostly European, were adamant in their refusal to consider any reduction. The Belgian delegate, for example, argued that there was no guarantee that a reduction would result in an increased use of the international mails; and even if there were such an increase, there was no guarantee that the additional cost of processing such an increase would be covered by additional revenue. After all, he continued, the international mails were used mainly for commercial purposes, and those in commerce could not be expected to use the mails more often simply because the letter rate was lowered.[72]

The Australasian proposal was defeated in committee by a vote of 18 to 3. Only the British Australasian colonies, Egypt, and the United States voted in favor; Canada, Great Britain, India, and Japan abstained;

68. Docs., Paris Postal Congress (1878), pp. 27–35, 60–66, 244–45, and 492–93. Docs., Lisbon Postal Congress (1885), I, pp. 21, 22, 561 and 594. Docs., Washington, D.C., Postal Congress (1897), pp. 27 and 422.
69. See, for example, Docs., Paris Postal Congress (1878), pp. 60–66.
70. Docs., Rome Postal Congress (1906), II, 165–73.
71. *Ibid.*, 174–75.
72. *Ibid.*, 177–78.

and all the rest voted no.[73] It is interesting to note that a subsidiary Australasian proposal to require other countries to accept and deliver any such 10-centime mail that they wished to send was attacked because it would raise public pressure on the receiving countries to lower their rate accordingly. The Japanese proposal was defeated in committee by a vote of 13 to 10, with 2 abstentions.[74] The Australasian proposal was not raised in plenary session. However, the proposal to reduce the rate from 25 to 20 was presented, but it was defeated by 34 votes to 17, with 8 abstentions.[75]

The user of the international mails was not completely ignored. A group of six European countries — Germany, Austria, Denmark, Hungary, Luxembourg, and Switzerland — proposed and gained widespread acceptance for the raising of the basic weight limit for letter mail from 15 to 20 grammes. The proposal was defended on the grounds that it was difficult to keep letters below the 15-gramme limit, requiring constant testing by postal employees. This was an inconvenience to the public and the postal administrations. In addition, it was argued, the public was anticipating some concessions, and this would be as good a way as any to meet that desire. The opposition argued that a change in the weight unit would necessitate an expense to administrations in changing post office scales, and many persons would use the post in preference to parcel post, to the detriment of the latter. Nevertheless, accepted in committee by 13 to 12, the proposal to raise the basic limit to 20 grammes was approved in plenary session by 30 to 26, with 3 abstentions.[76] It was also agreed that the charge would be 15 centimes for every 20 grammes over the basic weight limit.[77]

The question of transit rates — rates charged by intermediate countries for the transportation of mail from one border to another — was raised at every conference. These rates bore a close tie to ordinary mail rates, inasmuch as the support of some countries for proposals to lower basic mail rates was made dependent upon transit rates. At each congress proposals were introduced to eliminate transit rates completely. In the discussions that followed there was always a group of countries that successfully defended the charging of transit fees, from the point of view of their geographical position, which made them the natural transit countries; of their extreme size or the difficulty of transportation; or from the point of view of the special expensive sea transportation involved.[78]

73. *Ibid.*, p. 181.
74. *Ibid.*, pp. 177 and 181. The countries voting in favor were: Australasia, British India, Canada, Egypt, Great Britain, Japan, Netherlands, Spain, Sweden, and United States. Those voting against were: Argentina, Austria, Belgium, Denmark, France, Germany, Italy, Mexico, Norway, Portugal, Russia, Turkey, and Uruguay. Switzerland and Hungary abstained.
75. *Ibid.*, pp. 572–75.
76. *Ibid.*, pp. 78, 163–65, 174–85, and 575–79.
77. Rome Postal Convention (1906), Art. 5.
78. See, for example, Docs., Vienna Postal Congress (1891), pp. 383–90.

On the other hand, at almost every congress in the period in question, transit fees became progressively lower. By the Congress of Rome in 1906, the transit fees applicable for closed mail between members of the union were as follows:

1. Land Transit:

A]   Up to 3,000 kilometers — 1 franc 50 centimes for letters and postcards and 20 centimes per kilogram for other mailable matter.

B]   3,000 to 6,000 kilometers — 3 francs per kilogram for letters and postcards and 40 centimes per kilogram for other mailable matter.

C]   6,000 to 9,000 kilometers — 4 francs 50 centimes for letters and postcards and 60 centimes per kilogram for other mailable matter.

D]   Over 9,000 kilometers — 6 francs per kilogram of letters and postcards and 80 centimes per kilogram for other mailable matter.

2. Sea Transit:

A]   Up to 300 maritime miles — 1 franc 50 centimes per kilogram for letters and postcards and 20 centimes per kilogram for other mailable matter (free if the administration providing such transport already received remuneration for land transit).

B]   Over 300 maritime miles between countries in Europe, between Europe and ports in Africa and Asia in the Mediterranean and the North Sea, between Europe and North America, between two ports of the same state and between the ports of two states served by the same maritime company up to 1,500 maritime miles — 4 francs per kilogram for letters and postcards and 50 centimes for other mailable objects.

C]   Other than A] and B] — 8 francs per kilogram for letters and postcards and 1 franc per kilogram for other objects.[79]

In no case were the transit fees to exceed 8 francs per kilogram of letters and postcards and 1 franc per kilogram for other objects. For open mail (*à découvert* mail), there would be a standard charge of 6 centimes for letters, 2½ centimes for postcards, and 2½ centimes for other mailable objects.[80]

4. Effects of World War I

One of the first effects of World War I on the work of the Universal Postal Union was the indefinite postponement of its seventh postal congress. The Congress of Rome in 1906 had decided that the seventh

79. Rome Postal Convention (1906), Art. 4.
80. *Ibid.*

congress would be held in Madrid five years from October 1, 1907, the effective date of the final acts of the congress. Discussions were held between Spain, the international bureau, and interested countries during the latter part of 1912 and 1913, on the exact date for the opening of the Madrid congress, but because of prevailing conditions the opening was postponed until September 1914. War broke out in August of that year, however, and it was decided to postpone the seventh congress until such time as nations would be prepared once again to discuss international postal matters.[81]

The international postal service suffered seriously from the effects of World War I. The rule of "freedom of transit" of the mails between members of the UPU broke down completely. In some cases countries refused to permit the sending of mail to certain belligerents; in others, the progress of the war itself eliminated postal communication. As announced by its delegate at the Madrid Postal Congress of 1920, for example, Hungary was cut off completely from any foreign mail for a period of 52 days during the war.[82] Censorship of mails was a common practice, and many types of services, such as money orders, were suspended for the duration.[83] The routing of international mail in many cases did not depend upon the expense involved, but only upon the probability of its being delivered.

About the only portions of the postal convention remaining in force during World War I were the articles concerning the international bureau and those providing for free transportation of mail to and from prisoners of war. The two countries most responsible for the exchange of prisoner of war mail were Sweden and Switzerland. Switzerland alone handled 529,161,367 such letters and 92,946,096 packages.[84]

Since it was in Switzerland, the international bureau was able to carry out much of its normal work. Its publications reached the members of the union with more or less regularity, including its multilanguage periodical, the *Union Postale*. The bureau even had the time in 1916 to carry out a survey on the subject of whether war could be considered a *force majeure* affecting the responsibility of administrations for the loss of registered letters and insured letters and boxes. Of the 24 replies to the bureau's questionnaire, 22 were in the affirmative — some with slight reservations; Luxembourg declared that it did not consider war a *force*

81. *Mémoire*, p. 119.
82. UPU, *Documents du Congrès postal de Madrid, 1920* (Berne, 1920–21), II, p. 30. In justification for refusing to support a Swiss proposal at the Madrid Congress to add a provision to the postal convention guaranteeing the "liberty of transit" of mails even in wartime, the delegates of Britain and France pointed out that in times of war postal administrations do not have the liberty of choice, but are entirely under the orders of the military (*ibid.*, p. 196).
83. For a discussion of French censorship during World War I, see Raoul Blayac, *Origine, évolution et organisation de l'Union postale universelle* (Montpellier, 1932), pp. 98–101.
84. "The War Prisoners' Post in Switzerland," *Union Postale*, LXIV, No. 4 (April, 1919), 56–58.

majeure and Russia declared that it would be necessary to examine each case separately on its merits.[85]

At the end of hostilities the nations of the world quickly turned their efforts toward the restoration of normal postal relations. Wartime laws dealing with such matters as censorship were eliminated, restrictions on postal relations were lifted, and in general the regulation of international postal matters was returned to individual postal administrations. With reference to the Universal Postal Union, the peace treaties recognized the 1906 Postal Convention of Rome as part of the body of continuing international law, and the international bureau and the Spanish administration began preparing for the long-delayed Madrid Postal Congress.[86] Administrations were requested to review the proposals prepared for the abortive 1914 congress and bring them up to date. Finally, in consultation with the international bureau, the Spanish government invited the members of the union, including the former enemy states, to meet in Madrid on October 1, 1920, for the UPU's seventh regular postal congress.[87] It should also be noted that a special conference, outside the auspices of the UPU, was held in Paris, July 7 to 13, 1920, to plan for the reestablishment of communications in wartorn Europe. One of the areas which was considered was postal communications.[88]

c. Toward Maturity:
The UPU from 1919 to 1946

THE UNIVERSAL POSTAL UNION held five congresses in the period between World War I and World War II: Madrid in 1920, Stockholm in 1924, London in 1929, Cairo in 1934, and Buenos Aires in 1939. The first two congresses were dominated by economic problems arising out of World War I, and the work of the last two was already overshadowed by the coming of the second worldwide conflict; only the Congress of London in 1929 could be called an "ordinary" postal congress. Much constructive work was accomplished during this period, however. A new

85. "Responsibility for Cases Beyond Control," *Union Postale*, XLI, No. 6 (June, 1916), 83–85. For further information on the activities of the international bureau during wartime see its *Rapport de Gestion* for the years 1914 to 1919, and issues of *Union Postale* for the same period. The UPU's *Rapport de Gestion*, the title of which was changed to *Rapport sur les activités de l'Union* in 1953, will be designated hereafter as *Annual Report*.

86. Treaty of Versailles, Art. 283; Treaty of St. Germain, Art. 232; Treaty of Trianon, Art. 218; Treaty of Neuilly, Art. 163; Treaty of Sèvres, Art. 170; and Treaty of Lausanne, Art. 99.

87. *Mémoire*, p. 119.

88. See, France, Ministère des Travaux Publiques, sous-secrétariat d'État des Postes et des Télégraphes, *Conférence internationale pour l'amélioration des Communications postales et ferroviaires, télégraphiques et téléphoniques et radiotélégraphiqes (7–13 juillet 1920)*, Paris, 1920.

method of determining rates was established to accommodate the fluctuations in national currencies; transit rates were lowered, with further simplification of international accounting; and several new services were inaugurated for the users of the international mails.

The period between the wars was also marked by the development of a new method for the transport of mail. Experiences of the military with heavier-than-air craft during World War I were quickly adapted to the internal transport of mail in several countries, and later between neighboring countries. Although the range and capacity of aircraft were expanded during this period, they were never extended far enough to permit airmail to become universal. Nevertheless, experience with this new means of mail delivery was sufficient to merit the calling of several conferences at which the countries of Europe outlined the basic rules for its use. The expertise developed in these conferences was invaluable for the whole of the union when airmail became universal after World War II.

1. Organization of the Union

The most important change that occurred in the union's organization in the interwar years was the continued increase in membership. Much of that increase was because of the rearrangement of frontiers by the peace treaties following World War I and other political activities outside of the union which resulted in the independence or self-administration of areas previously under the control of, or belonging to, member governments. More important perhaps was the joining of independent countries which had not heretofore held membership and the acceptance of the UPU's rules and regulations by colonial governments for colonies and territories not previously bound by them.

After the Congress of Madrid in 1920, for example, there were 59 regular members and 19 dependent areas considered, for the purposes of the convention, to be members of the union.[89] By the London Postal Congress in 1929, the number of regular members had increased to 73 and the number of dependent area members stood at 14.[90] Further, in

89. Docs., Madrid Postal Congress (1920), II, *Convention postale universelle,* Préambule and Art. 27.

90. Regular members included: Afghanistan, Albania, Argentina, Australia, Austria, Belgium, Bolivia, Brazil, Bulgaria, Canada, Chile, China, Colombia, Costa Rica, Cuba, Czechoslovakia, Danzig, Denmark, Dominican Republic, Ecuador, Egypt, Estonia, Ethiopia, Finland, France, Great Britain, Germany, Greece, Guatemala, Haiti, Hedjaz, Nejd, and dependencies (after 1934, Saudi Arabia), Honduras, Hungary, Iceland, India, Iraq, Ireland, Italy, Japan, Latvia, Liberia, Lithuania, Luxembourg, Morocco (excluding the Spanish Zone), Morocco (Spanish), Mexico, Netherlands, New Zealand, Nicaragua, Norway, Panama, Paraguay, Persia, Peru, Poland, Portugal, Rumania, Saar, Salvador (El), San Marino, Serbs, Croats, and Slovenes, Kingdom of (after Oct. 3, 1929, Yugoslavia), Siam, South Africa, Spain, Sweden, Switzerland, Tunisia, Turkey, United States, USSR, Uruguay, Vatican City, and Venezuela. The 14 dependent areas were: Algeria, Belgian Congo, Chosen (Korea), Dutch colonies in America, Dutch East Indies, French colonies, French colonies and protectorates in Indochina, Italian colonies,

1929, there was a group of eight territories for which regular members were responsible for postal relations and for enforcing the UPU's rules and regulations.[91]

So all-encompassing was the influence of the UPU, in fact, that the London congress decided that there was no longer any reason to retain the provisions of the convention concerning relations between members and nonmembers.[92]

The period between the two wars was also notable for the search by the union for methods to expedite the work of the postal congresses. The increasing range of topics under the jurisdiction of the union and its steadily expanding membership tended to place an ever-enlarging burden on succeeding congresses. While before the war proposals to amend the various conventions, agreements, and regulations numbered in the hundreds, after the war they increased to thousands. The time necessary to examine, discuss, and decide on changes to the union's documents grew from one month to two months. Expenses became increasingly heavy for the host country of the congress and for the postal administrations which paid the expenses of their delegations. Further, member administrations became increasingly disturbed at the prospect of having their high administrative officials absent from their duties over long periods of time.[93]

Two different methods were used in an attempt to expedite the work of the postal congresses: experimentation with the internal organization of congresses, including the use of the different numbers and types of committees, and the creation of committees to meet between the regular congresses to do preparatory work. Concerning internal organization, the first two congresses were able to manage with only two committees. In 1885 the number was raised to three, the first committee dealing with the convention and the other two dividing up the various agreements and their regulations. From 1920 to the Congress of Buenos Aires in 1939, the union used, in principle, four major and one or two minor committees, as the bulk of the work demanded. The Congress of Buenos Aires, for example, had a committee devoted to the convention and airmail, two committees dealing with the various agreements and their regulations, and a drafting committee. In addition to the various sub-

---

Japanese dependencies, Philippine Islands, Portuguese colonies in Africa, Portuguese colonies in Asia and Oceania, Spanish colonies, and United States insular possessions. See UPU, *Documents du Congrès postal de Londres 1929* (Berne, 1929), *Convention postale universelle*, Préambule and Art. 8.

91. The Principality of Liechtenstein, by the Swiss postal administration; The Faroes Islands and Greenland, by Denmark; Spanish possessions on the northern coast of Africa; The Valley of Andorra, by the Spanish and French postal administrations; The Principality of Monaco, by the French postal administration; and Walvis Bay, by the Union of South Africa, and Basutoland, by the postal administration of the Union of South Africa. *Ibid.*, Art. 9.

92. Docs., London Postal Congress (1929), I, 2, 19, 21, 117, 221, 292–95, 593, 1421, 1441, 1467, and 1529; and II, 136 and 651.

93. See, for example, the discussions in Docs., Stockholm Postal Congress (1924), II, 719 and 794–97.

committees of the four major committees, there was a credentials committee and one to verify the accounts of the union.[94]

Three attempts were made in the interwar years to use committees, meeting between regular congresses, to prepare the way for succeeding congresses: with the study committee of 1921 and 1922 which met in Zermatt and Nice to prepare for the Stockholm Congress of 1924, the London preparatory committee which met in Paris in 1928, and the Cairo preparatory committee which met in Ottawa in 1933. Each had a restricted membership of wide geographical distribution and included delegates from countries in which the postal services had achieved a high state of efficiency. The committee of 1921–22 had delegates from seven countries, the London preparatory committee had 14, and the Cairo preparatory committee had 14, with two observers. All three committees had the task of gathering the proposals for changes in the union documents, arranging and evaluating them, and presenting a draft for the succeeding congress. The committee of 1921–22 had the additional task of redrafting the basic documents of the union along more logical and simplified lines, to eliminate discrepancies, repetitions, and the like.[95]

The use of preparatory committees, however, was abolished by the Cairo Postal Congress of 1934. Some difficulties were encountered in seeking proper geographical distribution among the countries to be represented and in the costs of the committees (both in money and in the time lost from the work of their own administrations by the expert delegates). Further, it was difficult for a group representing only a dozen or more countries to make decisions having any lasting utility, inasmuch as the delegates to the congresses wanted to make their own decisions. In general, the time gained was too little to warrant further such experiments. It was decided that the functions of preparatory committees could be better attained by changes in the internal organization of congresses and that, therefore, they should be dropped.[96]

2. Postal Rates

The principle of low uniform postal rates received a setback in World War I from which it did not recover until a few years before the outbreak of World War II. The nature of the debates on rates at the Madrid Congress of 1920 took an almost 180° turn. While before the war there had always been an active minority pushing for a lowering of rates, and a majority wavering between lowering rates and maintain-

94. UPU, *Documents du Congrès de Buenos Aires, 1939* (Berne, 1939), II, 18–19, 22–25, and 518–19.

95. See *Union Postale*, XLVIII, No. 2 (February, 1923), 17 and 18; Docs., London Postal Congress (1929), I, 1359–1658; and UPU, *Documents du Congrès postal du Caire*, 1934 (Berne, 1933–34), I, 1–2; and UPU, Commission d'Etudes Zermatt-Nice, 1921–1922, *Projets de Convention et d'Arrangements* (Berne, 1923).

96. See the proposals and discussions in the Cairo Preparatory Committee, Docs., Cairo Postal Congress (1934), I, 224, 226, 1309–10, 1366–71, 1413–14, and in the congress itself in *ibid.*, II, 59, 152, and 179–84.

ing the status quo, at Madrid there was an active vocal minority pushing for a raise in rates and a majority divided between raising rates and keeping the status quo. The arguments of the minority at Madrid centered around the necessity for covering the losses sustained as a result of currency depreciation in many countries and the necessity for making a profit in order to help in the payment of reconstruction costs and reparations.[97] A compromise was finally reached which satisfied both those who wanted an increase and those who wished to maintain the status quo, a compromise similar to the one used at the first postal congress in 1874: the establishing of a common rate with minimum and maximum limits, within which countries were permitted to fix their actual charge. First, the regular postal rate was raised to 50 centimes for each 20 grammes plus 25 centimes for every additional 20 grammes or fraction thereof. Postcards were raised to 30 centimes per card. Other categories of mail received similar treatment.[98] Second, a clause was added to a final protocol permitting each member country to fix its equivalents to the rates in its own currency in consultation with the Swiss postal administration. Such rates could not be higher than those set forth in the Madrid convention but could be as low as those in force for the country in question on October 1, 1920, the date of the beginning of the Madrid Congress. Further, each member country could modify its equivalent to cover monetary fluctuations, but in no case should such equivalents be lower than the rates fixed at the Congress of Rome in 1906.[99]

By 1924 the economies of most countries had overcome most of the major immediate effects of World War I, and pressures existed for a return to low uniform rates. Nevertheless, many countries were having difficulties with currency stability and did not want to see rates fixed so low that they would not be able to maneuver them to provide what they considered to be a fair return from the postal administrations. This second group, combined with a small group of countries that had always felt that rates should be high enough to permit a substantial profit from the operations of postal administrations, was able to keep the low-rate countries from achieving all of their objectives.[100] First, at the insistence of the low-rate group, the prewar rate structure was reintroduced almost in its entirety. Rates for letters were fixed at 25 centimes for the first 20 grammes and 15 centimes for each additional 20 grammes. The rate for postcards was fixed at 15 centimes. Other classes of mailable items were given similar treatment. To pacify the nations which still wanted higher rates, and the very few which wanted even lower rates, the Madrid compromise was utilized, whereby upper and lower limits were fixed between which countries could establish their rates. In the final protocol

97. See the proposals in Docs., Madrid Postal Congress (1920), I, 566, 582–83, and 584–85, and II, 33, 43, and 99–100, and the discussions in II, 272–97.

98. See *ibid.*, pp. 801 and 860–61.

99. *Ibid.*, II, 875–79, and *Protocole final*, Art. 3.

100. See the proposals and discussions in Docs., Stockholm Postal Congress (1924), I, 18, 409, 459–60, and 467; and II, 42–43 and 174–79.

attached to the postal convention, each country was permitted to raise
the established rates by 60 percent, or to lower them by 20 percent.
After the Stockholm Congress the postage on an ordinary letter, for
example, could be as high as 40 centimes for the first 20 grammes, and
24 centimes for an additional 20 grammes, or as low as 20 centimes for
20 grammes and 12 centimes for an additional 20 grammes.[101]

In the two congresses which followed (London in 1929, and Cairo
in 1934) the general lineup of countries on the question of rates remained more or less the same. A vocal minority of delegates pressed for
higher rates and for the largest possible permissible maximum of deviation from those rates. A smaller minority held out for a lowering of
rates and for a decrease or elimination of the permissible deviations.
The majority gave lip service to the aim of reestablishing the low uniform rates that existed before World War I, but tended toward the
status quo. The result was the maintenance of the rate scale, but with
a slight reduction in the permissible maximums. In London the maximum
deviation was lowered from 60 to 50 percent, and in Cairo, from 50 to
40 percent.[102] In both cases it was agreed that the changes would not
have any appreciable effect in lowering rates, but at the same time
would be a concession to public opinion.[103]

By the Congress of Buenos Aires in 1939, the economic situation
of enough countries was sufficiently stable to put a majority of the group
in favor of a reduction of rates. After a long discussion, in which all
of the arguments for and against lower rates were aired, the first committee of the Buenos Aires Congress agreed to the lowering of rates
from 25 centimes for 20 grammes of weight to 20 centimes; and for
each additional 20 grammes up to a maximum of 2 kilograms, the rate
was lowered from 15 centimes to 12 centimes. The postcard rate was
lowered from 15 to 12 centimes and most other mailable articles were
similarly reduced.[104] The committee's vote of 29 to 23, with 6 abstentions, was reaffirmed by the congress as a whole (41 to 11).[105]

101. *Ibid.*, I, 460, and II, 54–55, 152–53, 176–77, 268–69, 272, 395, 661–63,
670, 720–24, 742–43, 779–80, 783, 852–53, and 870. See also II, *Protocole final*,
Art. 2.

102. See Docs., London Postal Congress (1929), II, 656–58; and Docs., Cairo
Postal Congress (1934), II, 702.

103. See, for example, the discussion in Docs., London Postal Congress
(1929), II, p. 246.

104. Docs., Buenos Aires Postal Congress (1939), II, 61–65.

105. *Ibid.*, pp. 65, 521–23, and 528. While the congress vote was made by a
show of hands, the lineup in the first committee vote was as follows: AFFIRMATIVE:
Argentina, Belgium, Belgian Congo, Bolivia, Brazil, Colombia, Cuba, Dominican
Republic, Ecuador, Finland, France, Great Britain, Ireland, Italy, Italian colonies,
the Levantine states (Syria and Lebanon), Luxembourg, Mexico, Nicaragua,
Panama, Netherlands, Curaçao and Surinam, Dutch East Indies, Siam, Sweden,
Switzerland, United States, United States insular possessions, and Venezuela.
AGAINST: Australia, Bulgaria, Chile, China, Danzig, Egypt, Germany, Hungary,
British India, Iran, Japan, Chosen, Liberia, New Zealand, Peru, Philippines,
Poland, Portugal, Portuguese colonies in West Africa, Portuguese colonies in East
Africa, Asia and Oceania, Rumania, South Africa, and Yugoslavia. Abstaining
from the vote were Canada, Denmark, Greece, Lithuania, Norway, and Uruguay.

The permissible variations from the fixed rates established at Cairo in 1934 were retained, despite heavy pressure to narrow them, so that after the documents of the conference came into effect, letters could cost anywhere from a minimum of 16 centimes to a maximum of 28 centimes. Additional weights of 20 grammes each would range from 9.6 centimes to 16.8 centimes, as would postcards. Other types of mailable articles were also subject to the 40 and 20 percent variation.[106]

The question of transit rates was also a continuing problem in the interwar years. At each congress there were proposals to abolish transit rates completely, and at each session the proposals were voted down by a fairly large number. At each congress there was a large group of delegates who accepted the necessity of transit rates, but who at the same time pressed for a lowering of the rates. When their proposals for the abolishing of transit rates were defeated, the first group joined the second to make a powerful voting force. These groups were opposed at each session by those who preferred the status quo, or who wished to raise transit rates.[107] In the interwar years, the attack on the principle of transit rates was led by Latin American countries, supported at various times by Spain and the Spanish colonies and the United States and its possessions. The proposal to abolish transit rates at the Madrid Congress in 1920, for example, was supported by United States, U.S. insular possessions, Argentina, Bolivia, Brazil, Chile, Colombia, Cuba, Dominican Republic, Ecuador, Guatemala, Honduras, Hungary, Mexico, Nicaragua, Panama, Paraguay, Peru, Salvador, Spain, Spanish colonies, Uruguay, and Venezuela.[108] In the London Congress of 1929, the following supported the proposal: Brazil, Chile, Colombia, Cuba, Guatemala, Honduras, Peru, Philippines, Salvador, Spain, Spanish colonies, Uruguay, and Venezuela.[109] Among the abstainers to these two votes one finds Germany (which was one of the strongest advocates of the elimination of transit rates before World War I), China, and Siam. Other countries moved in and out of the abstention column without any observable pattern. Among the traditional opponents to the elimination of transit rates were the United Kingdom, her colonies and territories, France and her territories, Portugal and her territories, Belgium and her territories, and other European countries. Of the non-European proponents of transit rates, one of the more persistent was Japan and her territories.

The abolitionists, however, never had any success either in committee or in the congresses of the union. The partisans of lower transit rates, on the other hand, were slightly more successful. Although transit

---

106. *Ibid.*, I, 152–56; II, 61–65, 113, and 258–59; and III, 34.

107. See, for example, the discussion in Docs., Madrid Postal Congress (1920), II, 758–65; Docs., Stockholm Postal Congress (1924), II, 230–65; Docs., London Postal Congress (1929), II, 221–41 and 589–94; Docs., Cairo Postal Congress (1934), I, 168–92 and II, 131–44; and Docs., Buenos Aires Postal Congress (1939), II, 100–13.

108. Docs., Madrid Postal Congress (1920), II, 763.

109. Docs., London Postal Congress (1929), II, 227.

rates were not raised at the Congress of Madrid in 1920, as were basic letter rates, at least the status quo was maintained. Transit rates were lowered at the Congress of Stockholm in 1924, and the status quo was maintained at the Congress of London in 1929. In Cairo in 1934 transit rates were lowered, but the Cairo rates were maintained by the Congress of Buenos Aires in 1939. The Cairo transit rates, which remained unchanged until 1947, were as follows:

Distance	Letters and Postcards	Other Objects (by kilogram)
LAND TRANSIT		
Up to 1,000 kilometers	0.60	0.08
From 1,000 to 2,000	0.80	0.12
From 2,000 to 3,000	1.20	0.16
From 3,000 to 6,000	2.00	0.24
From 6,000 to 9,000	2.80	0.32
Over 9,000	3.60	0.40
SEA TRANSIT		
Up to 300 maritime miles	0.60	0.08
From 300 to 1,500 maritime miles	1.60	0.20
Between Europe and North America	2.40	0.32
From 1,500 to 6,000 maritime miles	3.20	0.40
Over 6,000 maritime miles	4.80	0.60[110]

Before leaving this section, one other action of the Universal Postal Union should be noted, one that had an important impact on the whole question of rates. Prior to World War I, the monetary unit on which all international postal charges were based, was the franc of the countries belonging to the Latin Monetary Union. The breakdown of the international gold standard after World War I and the resulting fluctuations in national currencies destroyed the value of the Latin Monetary Union franc as a means of international postal accounting. The Madrid Congress of 1920, therefore, had to find a replacement. While the gold franc was finally chosen, it is interesting to note that the French delegation argued that only the U.S. dollar fulfilled all of the necessary conditions for a stable monetary unit.[111] The Congress of Stockholm in 1924 went one step further and described the gold franc, for purposes of international accounting, as a gold franc of 100 centimes with a weight of 10/31 of a gramme and a fineness of 0.900. Each member of the union was obliged to fix its postal charges on the basis of the closest possible equivalent to the value of this franc in its own currency.[112] This provision has never been changed.

110. Docs., Cairo Postal Congress (1934), II, *Convention postale universelle*, Art. 75.
111. Docs., Madrid Postal Congress (1920), I, 601, and II, 191, 196, 261–65, and 343–80.
112. Docs., Stockholm Postal Congress (1924), I, 14; and II, 171, 659, and 851.

3. New Services

Several new services for the users of the international post were inaugurated in the interwar period. The manner in which they were established, whether as part of the convention or the subject of an optional agreement varied radically. Although none was as fundamental as those created before World War I, most were beneficial to individuals in those countries which accepted their introduction.

The first of the new services was the international postal checking account transfer service (*virements postaux*). This service was inaugurated as an agreement annexed to the 1920 postal convention, with separate regulations for execution.[113] In essence, it permitted any person in a country which agreed to introduce the new service to transfer a sum from his own postal checking account into the account of a person in any other country also accepting the agreement, for a fee equal to one percent of the amount to be transferred. Among the details set forth in the agreement was the provision that the money would be paid in the currency of the recipient and that the conversion would be made according to the official exchange rate in force on the date of receipt. Postal administrations were given wide discretion in fixing the amounts that could be transferred as well as other details of the transaction.[114] Twenty-seven members of the union signed the agreement.[115] The Madrid Postal Congress also eliminated the Agreement concerning Postal Identity Cards and incorporated its provisions in the convention, while still leaving member countries the option of accepting it.[116]

The second of the new services inaugurated by the 1929 Congress of London was the "small packet." The small packet is a category of mail in general less expensive and rapid than the letter post but more expensive and more rapid than the parcel post, and containing materials subject to customs control. Small packets have a minimum charge, to rule out the possibility that regular letter mail would be sent by this method, and a maximum weight and size to eliminate competition with the parcel post. In addition, any mailable article of this category must be subject to inspection and must have a label describing its contents for customs purposes. In addition to the convenience to the user, the proposers of this new category pointed out that it would tend to eliminate bulky articles from the letter mail and at the same time do away with the necessity of customs control for letter mail, which could deteriorate into a censorship.[117] After long and heated discussions it was decided to add the small packet to the mailable articles in the postal convention,

113. See Docs., Madrid Postal Congress (1920), I, 692–731; and II, 689–735 and 793–94.
114. See *ibid.*, II, *Arrangement concernant le service des virements postaux,* and *Règlement d'exécution de l'arrangement concernant le service des virements postaux.*
115. *Ibid.*, II, pp. 1147–48.
116. *Ibid.*, I, 61; and II, 222, 435, 858, and 869.
117. See, for example, Docs., London Postal Congress (1929), I, 3–5.

rather than to establish a special agreement, as some delegates had suggested, but to permit countries to refuse to accept it if they wished.[118] The charge established was 15 centimes per 50 grammes, with a minimum charge of 50 centimes and a maximum weight of 1 kilogram.[119]

The two other services introduced in the interwar years were the international postal travelers checks and the "phonopost." The provisions for international postal travelers checks was created by the Congress of Cairo in 1934 and added to the Agreement concerning Postal Money Orders.[120] The phonopost, proposed by the host government at the Buenos Aires Congress of 1939, consisted of a special category of mailable articles composed of gramophone records at a reduced rate (15 centimes for the first weight unit of 20 grammes and 10 centimes for every additional 20 grammes). According to the host government, this new service would be of value to those who could not write and who could not afford to use the long-distance telephone service; for example, illiterates, children, and certain categories of sick persons. Probably in view of the fact that this was the first congress in Latin America, the host government's proposal was adopted unanimously.

As a result of the decisions of the five interwar congresses, the following classes of material were incorporated in the postal convention as mailable material: 1] letters;   2] postcards;   3] commercial papers; 4] printed material;   5] literature for the blind;   6] merchandise samples;   7] small packets; and   8] phonopost items. The two latter categories were exchanged only between those postal administrations which agreed to permit them. As for the "non-letter" services offered in the form of agreements annexed to the convention, and valid only between those countries which adhered to them, the following services were available at the beginning of World War II: 1] insured boxes and letters;   2] parcel post;   3] postal money orders and postal travelers checks;   4] transfers to and from postal checking accounts;   5] collection of bills; and   6] subscriptions to newspapers and periodicals. To each of these agreements was annexed a set of regulations containing details for the execution of the provisions of the agreements.[121]

4. The Beginnings of Airmail

A discussion of the UPU in the interwar years would not be complete without some mention of airmail. In this period the carrying of mails by aircraft developed from a promotional device to an important adjunct of the international mail transport system especially in Europe and in North America.

118. See *ibid.*, I, 1396–99; and II, 157–72, and 657.
119. *Ibid.*, II, *Convention postale universelle*, Art. 33.
120. See Docs., Cairo Postal Congress (1934), II, *Arrangement concernant les mandates de poste, Supplément concernant le service des bons postaux de voyage.*
121. See Docs., Buenos Aires Postal Congress (1939), III, 149–414.

International air transport, upon which airmail naturally depended, developed rapidly. Blériot flew across the English Channel in 1909, and by 1918 the British Royal Air Force was operating airmail services between London and Paris. Lindbergh flew nonstop across the Atlantic in 1927, and by the middle and late thirties there were limited, but regular, transatlantic services in operation. As international air transport expanded, the international airmail service also expanded. Although the quantity of airmail carried grew tremendously in this period, it was extremely small in comparison to the present amount. "The development of regular services was severely handicapped by the small capacity of aircraft, the low and irregular frequencies, the many hazards of flight, the slow development of night flying in most parts of the world, the extremely high costs of operation and, in general, insufficient technical development." [122] The extremely high airmail rates, especially in the long-distance international service, was also an important factor. In addition to the considerations mentioned above, the high rates were due also to the fact that airmail was being used as one of the major subsidies of air transport development. "Probably in no form of transport, especially international transport, has the postal service played so vital a part as in the development of aviation." [123]

This new means of transporting mail was quick to come to the attention of the Universal Postal Union, although the provisions adopted in the early 1920's were rudimentary. The Postal Convention of Madrid (1920) was the first to deal with airmail service. Article 5 of the Madrid convention assimilates the airmail service to "extraordinary" ground services, services whose high cost justified their exemption from the normal rate scale. Rates were left to agreement between interested administrations with the sole proviso that the charges for a given air service were to be uniform for all administrations using such a service.[124] The Congress of Stockholm in 1924 did not make any fundamental changes to these provisions but did lay down the principle that transit rates should not apply to air services.[125]

By the second half of the 1920's, however, the air transport industry overcame many obstacles and evolved, especially in North America and Europe, into a regular network on which international airmail could travel with reasonable speed and dependability. Consequently, at a meeting of the air transport committee of the International Chamber of Commerce, in Paris in 1926, a resolution was proposed and adopted calling the attention of postal administrations "to the advantages which might accrue to the mail services if a restricted official Conference could meet in the near future according to the provisions of . . . the Uni-

---

122. ICAO, *Air Mail Study*, Doc., 5348–AT/654 (Montreal, 1948), p. 3.
123. *Ibid.*, p. 2. The postal service also played a vital role in the development of land and sea transport.
124. See Docs., Madrid Postal Congress (1920), II, 190, 197, and 766–67.
125. Docs., Stockholm Postal Congress (1924), II, *Convention postale universelle*, Art. 74.

versal Postal Convention." [126] At the instigation of the postal administration of the USSR, the bureau of the UPU polled the members of the
union as to the advisability of such a conference. Upon receiving an
affirmative reply from 25 postal administrations, a special airmail conference was called to meet at The Hague on September 1, 1927.[127]

The Hague Airmail Conference was held in the Dutch capital from
September 1 to 10, 1927. Represented were 38 postal administrations,
mostly from Europe and North America, 14 air transport companies,
the International Air Transport Association, and the air transport committee of the International Chamber of Commerce. The air transport
companies and the international organizations were permitted to participate in the discussions but not to vote.[128] As stated in the inaugural
address, the purpose of the conference was to establish: cheap and uniform rates; just compensation for the air navigation companies; regular
transshipment of airmail; and a simplified system of international
accounting.[129]

The 1927 conference established regulations that went far to achieve
these purposes. The "low and uniform rate" for airmail was set at the
rate of an ordinary surface letter plus a surcharge not exceeding 25
centimes per 20 grammes for each 1,000 kilometers of air distance.
Postcards were given a surcharge of 25 gold centimes per 1,000 kilometers traveled. However, a provision was added that permitted the
raising of the rates for long-distance services whose upkeep entailed
"extraordinary expenses." [130] Just compensation for air navigation companies was provided for in the provisions establishing payments to them
of 6½ centimes per 100 grammes for each 100 kilometers flown, except
for especially difficult long-distance services where the payments could
be higher.[131] All signatory powers agreed to accept airmail and to deliver
it as rapidly as possible and to include it wherever possible in the first
delivery after its arrival. Administrations without air services were
obliged to expedite airmail by the most rapid means available.[132] Finally,
it was agreed that international airmail accounting between postal ad-

126. *Union Postale*, LII, No. 2 (February, 1927), 53–54.

127. *Union Postale*, LII, No. 6 (June, 1927), 157.

128. The postal administrations participating were from Algeria, Austria,
Belgian Congo, Belgium, British India, Canada, Chosen, Czechoslovakia, Danzig
(Free City of), Denmark, Dutch colonies in America, Dutch East Indies, Egypt,
Finland, France, Germany, Great Britain, Greece, Hungary, Italian colonies, Italy,
Japan, Japanese dependencies, Latvia, Luxembourg, Morocco, Netherlands, Nor-
way, Persia, Portugal, Saar, Spain, Sweden, Switzerland, Tunisia, Turkey, United
States, and USSR (UPU, *Documents de la Conférence sur la poste aérienne de La
Haye, Septembre, 1927* (Berne, 1927), pp. 99–100). The air transport companies
were from the following countries: Austria, Belgium, Czechoslovakia, France,
Germany, Great Britain, Italy, Netherlands, Poland, Sweden, Switzerland, and
USSR (*ibid.*, pp. 102, 104–105, and 121).

129. *Ibid.*, p. 95.

130. *Ibid.*, pp. 231–43, Annex No. 1, *Dispositions concernant le transport de
la poste aux lettres par voie aérienne*, Arts. 3 and 11.

131. Art. 11, paras. 10 and 11.

132. Arts. 5 and 7.

ministrations should be carried out on the basis of statistics taken in the second week of November and June, respectively, each year.[133] The Hague conference also created a separate agreement for air parcel post which was to be binding on those agreeing to it.[134]

It was agreed further by the representatives at The Hague conference that the new regulations should come into effect as of January 1, 1928, so that there would be at least one year of actual experience for the guidance of the next universal postal congress, due to meet in 1929.[135]

The Postal Congress of London, 1929, adopted the regulations established by The Hague conference with only minor alterations and annexed them to the regular universal postal convention.[136] The general pattern of regulation established by The Hague conference underwent no essential changes at the UPU congresses of Cairo in 1934 and Buenos Aires in 1939 with the exception that an upper limit of six francs per metric ton-kilometer was established as payment to air lines for airmail in the "ordinary" air transport services.[137]

Although the actions of the regular UPU congresses in the field of international airmail should not be discounted, the real progress in the interwar years was made in a series of conferences restricted to European countries but under the auspices of the Universal Postal Union. The first of these conferences was the Restricted European Airmail Conference of Brussels (1930), convened by the Belgian postal administration and attended by representatives from Belgium, Czechoslovakia, Denmark, Finland, France, Germany, Great Britain, Italy, Netherlands, Sweden, and Switzerland.[138] The purpose of the Brussels conference was not to promote the use of airmail nor even to establish stricter regulations over airmail, but rather to define the attitude of the major air transport countries toward the practice already introduced by some postal administrations of "sending mails by air without charging a special air fee or requiring the sender to indicate on his correspondence that he wished it sent by air." [139] Although there was opposition from some administrations which felt that such practices would result in too great an expense for postal administrations or would interfere with the handling of regular surtaxed airmail, the Brussels conference finally agreed that regular mail could be sent between countries without any additional charges and without prior authorization from the country of destination

133. Art. 15.

134. See *ibid.*, pp. 244–52, Annex No. 2, *Dispositions concernant le transport des colis postaux par voie aérienne.*

135. *Ibid.*, p. 54.

136. Docs., London Postal Congress (1929), II, *Dispositions concernant le transport de la poste aux lettres par voie aérienne*, and *Dispositions concernant le transport des colis postaux par voie aérienne.*

137. Docs., Buenos Aires Postal Congress (1939), II, *Convention postale universelle, Dispositions concernant le transport de la poste aux lettres par voie aérienne*, Art. 14, para. 8.

138. UPU, Conférence aéropostale européenne, 1930–31, *Documents de la Conférence*, 1ʳᵉ partie (Berne, 1933), p. v.

139. Air Mail Study (1948), p. 6.

providing: (1) the country of destination was informed in advance of any such arrangement; (2) previous agreement was reached with transit countries concerning the conveyance of such mail; and (3) the country of destination was not obliged to deliver such mail, if sent by night, in the morning delivery as was the rule with regular airmail.[140]

The 1930 European Airmail Conference also undertook a general discussion of the problems of airmail, including the possibility of establishing an airmail network which would provide for the swift and regular delivery of such mail throughout Europe. It was finally decided to circulate a questionnaire among all European postal administrations in order to gather the necessary information; to have this information examined by a preparatory committee called together by the international bureau; and to have the preparatory committee draft a plan for the establishment of a European airmail network that would be submitted to a special all-European postal conference.[141]

The European Airmail Conference preparatory committee met in Prague from June 8 to 18, 1931, and drew up a plan for a European airmail network to be submitted to administrations for study and for discussion at a regular European airmail conference to be held in Brussels in the autumn of the same year.[142] The conference was not held in the autumn, however. It was found that the delay was too short to obtain all of the information and comments needed, and it was therefore agreed to postpone the opening of the conference to the spring of 1932. In 1932 it was agreed that the economic consequences of the depression were such that it would not be advisable to attempt any scheme that would result in a further increase of the costs of postal administrations, and the opening of the European Airmail Conference was postponed sine die.[143]

By the time the long-delayed European Airmail Conference was convened in Brussels on June 16, 1938, the situation had changed entirely.[144] The problem was no longer one of making arrangements for a European airmail network; that had been accomplished in the interim without a conference. What was needed was an answer to the problem posed by the 1930 conference; what was to be done about nonsurcharged airmail? The answer found by the 1938 conference was that the time had come to regard air transport as the normal means of conveying all first class mail in Europe without any extra charge whatsoever to the general public.[145]

140. Docs., European Airmail Conference (1930–31), pp. V–XII.
141. Ibid., pp. XIII–XXXIV.
142. Ibid., pp. 153–200.
143. Mémoire, pp. 185 and 205.
144. In 1937 the idea of a conference was again taken up by the Belgian government. It was thought that the conference would be held in the first part of 1938, but it was postponed until June after a suggestion by Netherlands and France to hold two preparatory meetings of restricted membership. The preparatory meetings were held in The Hague from April 13 to 16, 1937, and in Paris from June 15 to 19, 1937. (See ibid., pp. 255–95.)
145. Ibid., p. 427.

Inasmuch as the implementation of such a policy required a substantial reduction in the cost to the postal administrations of transporting airmail, it was particularly necessary to obtain a reduction in the rates of payment to the operating airline agencies. This was accomplished with the cooperation of a private international agency of the airlines, the International Air Traffic Association (IATA). IATA presented the Brussels Conference of 1938 with a decision taken early in 1938 (after learning of the general consensus for lower rates expressed in the 1937 preliminary European airmail meetings), to lower the airline charges for first class mail to 2.50 francs per metric ton-kilometer in the event of a generalization of the transport of first class mail by air. IATA also promised to investigate the possibility of lowering charges even further at the end of a three-year trial period.[146] The Brussels conference accepted the offer from IATA and suggested that it consider the introduction of a two-franc charge as soon as possible.[147]

By the end of May 1940, 12 European nations had notified the international bureau that they were applying the Brussels decisions in their mutual postal relations: Belgium, Denmark, Finland, France, Germany, Great Britain, Luxembourg, Netherlands, Norway, Poland, Sweden, and Switzerland.[148]

The attempt to obtain recognition of the principles adopted by the Brussels European Airmail Conference of 1938 in the basic documents of the UPU at the Buenos Aires Postal Congress of 1939 was a failure, however. Although the Buenos Aires Congress made some changes in the provisions of the universal postal convention dealing with the transport of airmail, it rejected without much discussion all of the proposals from European postal administrations that would have done for the world what the Brussels conference had done for Europe.[149] As stated in the general observations submitted to the 1947 Paris Postal Congress by five Scandinavian countries, the refusal of the Buenos Aires Congress "was without doubt due more to the threatening international situation than to any reasons of a strictly postal nature." [150]

The Brussels European Airmail Conference and the Buenos Aires Postal Congress were the last two conferences held under the auspices of the UPU before such international cooperation was terminated by the "threatening international situation."

5. Effects of World War II

As would be expected, World War II had a distastrous effect on the development of international postal communication and a paralyzing

146. *Ibid.,* pp. 354 and 428. The UPU convention permitted a maximum charge of 6 gold francs for the transport of surcharged airmail.
147. *Ibid.,* p. 428.
148. Air Mail Study (1948), p. 7.
149. See the proposals in Docs., Buenos Aires Postal Congress (1939), I, 280–386, and the discussions in II, 121–23, 126, and 135.
150. UPU, *Documents du Congrès de Paris 1947* (Berne, 1948), I, 232.

influence on the work of the Universal Postal Union. During a conflict of the size and intensity of World War II, little time and energy can be expended on the matter of a smooth flow of mails between countries — even friendly countries.

Both belligerents and neutrals placed restrictions on the international mails. Some countries limited the weight of letters and packages that could be sent; registered mail was permitted for destination to some countries but not to others; and the money order service was suspended. Almost all countries instituted censorship of outgoing mail and, in many cases, of incoming mail. The exchange of mails between belligerents ceased both as a matter of policy and as a matter of expediency. Military action, especially on the high seas, often resulted in the destruction of the little mail that was permitted in ships alongside priority war materials.[151]

Although no conferences or meetings of the Universal Postal Union were held from 1939 to 1947, the international bureau of the UPU continued to function throughout the period. While it demanded a considerable effort and a high degree of improvisation, the bureau managed to act as a clearing house for postal information, publish and circulate the multilingual periodical *Union Postale,* serve as a clearinghouse for some international transit accounts, and in general do its best to carry on normally in an extremely difficult time.[152] By maintaining its activities throughout the war, even though they were seriously curtailed at times, the continuity of the Universal Postal Union was not eclipsed and there was a basis for the renewal of its activities after the cessation of hostilities.

One of the major factors that saved the international bureau, and thus the Universal Postal Union, from oblivion was its location on neutral Swiss soil. Switzerland, one of the very few countries in the world which remained truly neutral during World War II, was ideally situated between the two major blocs of warring powers. By the use of the good offices of the Swiss government the bureau was able to keep in continuous contact with almost all of the members of the UPU which, in effect, meant all of the countries of the world. As stated in an extract from the bureau's report for the year 1943: "Thanks . . . to the assistance given by the supervisory authority [the Swiss Government], the International Bureau has been able to remain in contact with almost all the Union Administrations." [153]

The international bureau was also able to make a significant con-

151. See, for example, the account of the effect of World War II on United States international mails in Helen G. Kelly, "International Mails During Wartime," *Union Postale,* LXX, No. 8 (August, 1945), 113–23.

152. See "Extract from the Report of the International Bureau of the Universal Postal Union for the Year 1941," *Union Postale,* LXVII, No. 4 (April, 1942), 85.

153. "Extract from the Report of the International Bureau of the Universal Postal Union for the Year 1943," *Union Postale,* LXIX, No. 3/4 (March/April, 1944), 43–61.

tribution to one of the brighter pages of World War II — the aid given to prisoners of war and civilian internees. The international bureau reminded the members of the UPU of the decision to extend to interned civilians the free postage privilege granted to prisoners of war, inquired for the International Red Cross of routes through neutral countries which could be used for the transit of mail for prisoners of war and interned civilians, and in general aided the International Red Cross in this humanitarian effort.[154] It should be noted too that in this effort the bureau's activities also were helped — one could almost say made possible — by the fact that it and the International Red Cross were both established on "neutral" Swiss territory and could avail themselves of the good offices of the Swiss government.

Although it was not an activity of the Universal Postal Union, one should not ignore the attempt made in the 1940's to create a European postal and telegraph union. During 1941–1942, Germany concluded with neighboring countries a number of bilateral agreements designed to reduce postage rates and to reduce or eliminate transit charges. In 1942, at the time when the Axis control over Europe was almost complete, the German Postal and Telegraph Administration in its own name and in the name of the Italian administration invited all the postal and telegraph administrations of Europe, both "friend and neutral," to attend a conference in Vienna in October to study measures for ameliorating and perfecting the European postal and telecommunication services. Thirteen administrations accepted the invitation and sent delegations, three sent official observers, one sent an "unofficial observer," and two declined.[155]

The European Postal and Telecommunication Conference, held in Vienna in October 1942, drew up a treaty which provided for the regulation of inter-European postal communication, including the introduction in Europe of lower and more simplified postal rates "based on German internal rates" and the abolition of land transit charges for letters.[156] The treaty also established a European Postal and Telecommunication Union with provision for conferences, a bureau to be located in Vienna, and a permanent study committee. It is interesting to note that the final agreement contained a clause to the effect that the bureau of the European union should be confined to the role of disseminator of information and center of consultation, and it was not to be substi-

154. See *ibid.* and Vincente Tuason, "Free Postage for Prisoners of War and Victims of War," *Union Postale,* xxx, No. 9 (September, 1945), 134–54.

155. The following countries sent delegates: Albania, Bulgaria, Croatia, Denmark, Finland, Germany, Hungary, Italy, Netherlands, Norway, Rumania, Slovakia, and San Marino. Regular observers came from Spain, Turkey, and Vatican City, and the Swiss sent an "unofficial observer." Both Portugal and Sweden declined the German invitation.

156. See *Europäischer Postkongress, Wien 1942, Berichte und Vereinbarungen* (Vienna, 1942). The official languages of the conference were German and Italian. Speeches in other languages were permitted, but translation was made only in German or Italian.

tuted for the two international bureaus already in existence (the bureaus of the Universal Postal Union and the International Telecommunication Union), and that the conventions, agreements, and regulations of the Universal Postal Union and the International Telecommunication Union should remain in effect for all of the signatories except where specifically regulated by the European Union's own agreement and regulations.[157]

The European Postal and Telecommunication Union came into being on April 1, 1943, for the 13 postal administrations which had sent regular delegations to the conference and had signed the final acts. None of the administrations which sent observers authorized its representatives to sign the final acts, and no country took advantage of the clause in the agreement permitting adherence at a later date. In view of the nature and obvious purpose of this organization, it ceased to exist with the defeat of Germany in World War II. As stated by Dr. Otfried Brauns-Packenius, Counsellor of Posts, Higher Postal Directorate, Frankfort on Main: "The European Postal Union of the Second World War period was a special case. It was based on enforced association and that is also why it disappeared when the motivating force collapsed at the end of the war." [158]

D. The UPU Since World War II

THE ACTIVITIES of the UPU returned to a normal basis with the convening of the twelfth Universal Postal Congress in Paris on May 8, 1947. Although only a relatively short time had elapsed since the end of World War II, the delegates at Paris were able to take up the threads of their work dropped eight years before without too great difficulty. Advances in technology, as applicable to the international mails, were topics of considerable importance, as was the future of airmail, which could take advantage of the great strides in air transportation made during the war years. The United Nations system had been created, and it was necessary to define the proper role of the UPU in that body. The organization of the UPU for the future also came under close scrutiny.

Two other congresses have been held to date, the Congress of

157. *Übereinkommen über den Europäischen Post- und Fernmeldeverein,* Preamble and Arts. 5 and 9. For further information on the 1942 conference in Vienna and the other activities of the European Postal and Telecommunication Union — one meeting of the permanent committee was held in Copenhagen in June 1943 — see *Europäischer Postkongress,* pp. 1–98; Dr. Risch, "The Tasks and Aims of a European Postal Union," *Union Postale,* LXVII, No. 9 (September 1942), 247–53; "European Congress of Vienna," *Union Postale,* LXVII, No. 10/11 (October/November, 1942), 291–99; and "Permanent Committee of the European Postal Union," *Union Postale,* LXIX, No. 2 (February, 1944), 24–26.

158. See "The Nature of Restricted Postal Unions," *Union Postale,* LXXXVII, No. 4 (April, 1962), 55A, and "Permanent Committee of the European Postal Union," *op. cit.* For further information on the nature and activities of this organization see *Union Postale,* LXVII, No. 9 (Sept., 1942), 247A–53A; No. 10/11 (October/November, 1942), 291A–99A; and LXIX, No. 2 (February, 1944), 25A–27A.

Brussels in 1952 and the Congress of Ottawa in 1957. Technology and its application to the postal services, domestic as well as international, were the dominant themes of these congresses. This final section of Chapter Two will present only an overall view of the work of the union from the end of World War II to the present. We will go into greater detail especially concerning the constitution and organization of the UPU, in following chapters.

1. The Congress of Paris (1947)

If it were not for the importance of its subject matter, the twelfth postal congress could have been postponed until the effects of the war had eased. By their nature, however, postal communications had an essential role to play in the difficult process of reconstruction and recovery. Consequently, the French government started almost immediately after the cessation of hostilities to prepare for the congress which had originally been scheduled for 1939 in France. After consulting the director of the bureau on the required procedures and details, the French government issued an invitation to the members of the UPU in October 1946, to meet in Paris on May 7, 1947, to take up the work which had been interrupted by the war.[159]

The 12th Universal Postal Congress which met in Paris from May 7 to July 5, 1947, was one of the largest ever held in the history of the UPU. Two hundred and seventy-one delegates took part in the deliberations, representing all the members of the union with the exception of Costa Rica, Morocco (Spanish Zone), Nicaragua, Spain, Spanish colonies, Transjordan, and Yemen. Included among the representatives were observers from the Allied Commission on Telecommunications and Posts in Berlin (to look after the interests of occupied Germany) and the Allied Control Authority of Japan (to do the same for occupied Japan). One regular member, Liberia, sent an observer rather than a delegate.[160] The number of proposals was small in comparison with the record submitted at the busy Congress of Madrid in 1920, 821 compared with 2,248.[161] In duration, however, the Paris Congress was only one day shorter than the Madrid Congress.

Concerning composition, the Paris Congress made two important innovations. First, a new committee (1 bis) was created to deal exclusively with questions concerning airmail. Long-range aircraft, developed during World War II, had been converted almost immediately to commercial purposes, permitting for the first time a truly international airmail system. The need to establish regulations for this new system, which was bound to grow in the future, made the creation of a new committee concerned only with airmail a necessity.[162] Second, for the first time in

159. See Circulaire No. 150 of October 18, 1946.
160. Docs., Paris Postal Congress (1947), II, 7–14, 59, 60, 180, 201, 265, 276, 377, 885, 1094, 1906, and 1907.
161. See ibid., Vol. 1.
162. Ibid., II, 43, 83, and 569–646.

the history of the UPU outside observers were permitted to participate in the work of a congress. Only two were admitted, however, and they were from the United Nations and the International Civil Aviation Organization.[163]

The Paris Postal Congress concentrated primarily on bringing the final acts of the Buenos Aires Congress of 1939 up to date. All in all nothing truly revolutionary was accomplished, changes being limited mostly to details. The new Agreement on Cash on Delivery Items, created by the congress, was no exception. The major provisions of this agreement and its regulations had been contained previously in the Agreement on Parcel Post and its Regulations.[164]

The major exception, as could be expected, occurred with regard to airmail. Committee 1 *bis* did an extensive job of overhauling the airmail regulations to bring them into line with the many developments since 1939. The most important decision, perhaps, was in regard to rates and transportation charges. In the first place, it was decided that airmail traffic should be divided into two classes, A and B. Class A was defined as intra-European air services and other air services in which operating expenses were similar, and Class B as all other services in which operating expenses were considered to be higher. It was then decided that, as a general rule, several types of mail (including letters and postcards) in Class A relations would be sent at ordinary mail rates for distances under 2,000 kilometers. Other types of mail would be charged an airmail surtax of 7½ centimes per 20 grammes for the same distances. Class A mail of all types which traveled distances of over 2,000 kilometers was liable to a surcharge of 7½ centimes per 20 grammes for each additional 1,000 kilometers. For all category B mail, the surcharge was fixed at 15 centimes per 20 grammes per 1,000 kilometers.[165] As regards the transportation charges due air lines for transporting the mail, the designations of Class A and B were also adopted and the maximum charge was set at 3 and 6 gold francs per ton-kilometer respectively. These charges were, in a real sense, an important achievement. Previously, all airmail traffic was classed as either ordinary or extraordinary. Rates for the ordinary services were 15 centimes per 20 grammes per 1,000 kilometers and the transportation charges were 6 gold francs per ton-kilometer. Rates and charges for extraordinary services were left to the discretion of postal administrations and air lines. Further, not only were the rates and charges for extraordinary services oftentimes extremely high, but as was pointed out by ICAO, almost all air services

163. The whole subject of relations between the UPU and international agencies, both intergovernmental and private, will be taken up in Chapter Five.

164. See Docs., Paris Postal Congress (1947), III, *Arrangement concernant les envois contre remboursement* (Paris, 1947).

165. *Ibid., Convention postale universelle, Dispositions concernant la poste aérienne*, Arts. 5 and 14. For the exceptions to the rule that certain types of Class A mail would be sent at ordinary mail rates for distances under 2,000 kilometers, see the Final Protocol to the Airmail Provisions, Art. 3.

were "classified as 'extraordinary', including all the domestic United States services, whose operating costs are among the lowest in the world." [166]

Permission was granted to send first class mail by air at the same rates as ordinary mail, although an attempt to make it a universal rule was defeated. Concerning these decisions, the chairman of the congress stated:

> There is no doubt that this bold reform, proposed since before the war and which aims at treating henceforth the airplane as a normal means of transport, like the railway and the ship, is the solution of the future. Unfortunately, air transport is still too expensive as compared with other means of transport. Also, in view of the financial condition of several countries, who have suffered severely from the war, I think we have acted wisely in merely initiating this reform and in following above all a policy of lowering transport rates. No doubt our successors, who will benefit from our efforts towards clarification and financial soundness, will be able to make progress along the road which we have traced and reach a more complete solution.[167]

Without doubt the most fundamental innovation of the Paris Congress was the creation of a new permanent organ for the UPU: the Executive and Liaison Committee. Prior to Paris, the UPU had carried out its work mainly through congresses and, in the interval between congresses, through the international bureau at Berne. Several factors pointed up the need of a more elaborate organizational structure for the UPU, two of which can be mentioned at this point.[168] Before World War II the postal services of individual nations, both domestic and international, were organized and run along lines that, though adequate, were somewhat antiquated. By 1947, however, it was clear that the world's postal services were in need of overhauling and modernization to keep up with more rapid international communication that was foreseen in the postwar period. This job could not be carried out adequately on an individual basis; it demanded cooperative action. The second reason was that by the time of the Paris Congress the UPU was well on its way to becoming an active element in the new United Nations system. As a specialized agency it would have need of a representative body which would permit the UPU to maintain closer contact with the UN and the other specialized agencies which had been created or were in the process of creation.[169]

166. See Air Mail Study (1948), p. 22. For the rates in effect prior to the Paris Postal Congress, see Buenos Aires Postal Convention (1939), Dispositions Concerning the Transportation of Letter Mail by Air, Arts. 5 and 14.

167. Docs., Paris Postal Congress (1947), II, 1101.

168. For a more detailed discussion of the creation of the ELC, see below, pp. 156–59.

169. See Paris Postal Convention (1947), Art. 18.

Finally, with regard to innovations, the Paris Postal Congress of 1947 drafted an agreement which made the UPU a specialized agency of the United Nations in November 1947.[170]

The delegates who departed from Paris on Saturday, July 5, 1947, left secure in the knowledge that the UPU had weathered successfully the storm of World War II and was prepared to meet the demands of the future.

2. The Brussels Postal Congress, 1952

The second post-World War II postal congress met in Brussels from May 14 to July 11, 1952. Ninety-one members out of 93 sent representatives, 297 in all; and six international organizations were permitted to send observers: United Nations, UN Educational, Social and Cultural Organization, World Health Organization, Postal Union of the Americas and Spain, Council of Europe, and International Air Transport Association.[171]

While the Paris Congress had been an innovator, the Brussels Congress was a revisor. The latter spent the major part of its time bringing provisions of the final acts of the Paris Congress up to date, as dictated by the experience of the past five years, and revising those areas of postal regulations which the Paris Congress had been forced to overlook in the press of time. Among the more obvious examples of this work was the complete revision of the agreement on insured letters and boxes and on newspaper and periodical subscriptions.[172] In other areas, the Brussels Congress revised the provisions dealing with the exemption from postal charges on mails for prisoners of war and interned civilians, to bring them into harmony with the 1949 Geneva convention for the protection of war victims.[173] It also liberalized the exemption from postal charges for postal matter for the blind, and added phonograph records and tapes to the class of mailable postal material known as "phonopost" articles.[174] No radical changes were made in the duties of the international bureau or the ELC, although the number of member countries serving on the latter was raised from 19 to 20.[175]

Postal rates and charges received mixed treatment. On the one hand, administrations were given permission to reduce the tariffs on printed papers by 50 percent, and on the other, they were permitted to charge a tariff 60 percent superior to the rates established for ordinary mail rather than the 40 percent permitted by the final acts of the Paris

170. The relations of the UPU with other international organizations, including the UN, will be discussed more fully in Chapter Six.
171. UPU, *Documents du Congrès de Bruxelles, 1952* (Berne, 1952–53), II, 182–92.
172. *Ibid.*, III, 149–79 and 427–52.
173. *Ibid., Convention postale universelle*, Art. 37.
174. *Ibid.*, Art. 38 and *Règlement*, Art. 140.
175. *Ibid.*, Art. 15.

Congress. A rule was also introduced that printed matter for the blind should be exempt from postal charges.[176]

Airmail rates received extensive treatment at Brussels. In the first place, an attempt was made to abolish the two different categories on which airmail surtaxes and air transportation charges were based, Class A (European and other services with comparable costs) and Class B (more expensive services). According to an ICAO report to the congress, the operating expenses for all services had become approximately equal. Therefore, the ICAO report continued, "we are of the opinion that at present the classification of services into two categories is no longer logically justified and, consequently, it should be abandoned as soon as possible." [177] The congress agreed in principle and eliminated the old A and B categories from the airmail regulations. In their place the congress substituted two classes of mail based on the type of material to be sent: LC, letter mail, and AO, other articles. Further, maximum air mail surcharges were dropped and each administration was given permission to fix its own. It was specified, however, that there must be a strict relation to the cost of transport and, as a general rule, the yield from rates must not exceed the whole of the transportation charges.[178]

As regards transportation charges, on which the new rates would depend, it was decided to fix the maximum that air lines could impose at 3 gold francs per ton-kilometer for LC articles and 1.25 for AO articles. Up to this point the objective of simplification of transportation charges had been advanced an important step. Some administrations operating lines of the old B classification were not convinced, however, that the new transportation charges were adequate to compensate their air lines, and asked for the right to charge more. Since this group was fairly large and obdurate, it was then decided to permit air services which had been charging more than 3 gold francs per ton-kilometer as of July 1, 1952, to charge an extra 1 gold franc per ton-kilometer for LC articles if they so desired. Another step backward was made when the UPU's members later agreed, via a poll, that any air line which was not in Class A prior to July 1, 1952, in other words any old Class B air line, would be permitted to charge 4 gold francs per ton-kilometer on any new air service that it should introduce.[179]

As a result of these actions, the Brussels congress first abolished the old A and B classifications and then turned around and re-introduced them in fact if not in form. As it has worked out in practice, the 3 franc LC transportation charge is valid only in Europe and the Mediterranean basin, which is now designated by IATA as Zone A, and the 4 franc LC transportation charge is used in all other areas of the world, now desig-

176. *Ibid.*, Arts. 38 and 48 and *Protocole final*, Art. III.
177. Docs., Brussels Postal Congress (1952), II, 656–57.
178. Brussels Postal Convention (1952), *Dispositions concernant la poste aérienne*, Art. 5.
179. *Ibid.*, Art. 15, and UPU, *Les Actes de l'Union postale universelle revisés à Ottawa, 1957* (Berne, 1959), *I*ᵉʳ *fascicule, Convention postale universelle*, p. 295, ftn. 5. (Hereafter this publication will be referred to as *Annotated Acts*.)

nated by IATA as Zone B.[180] The Ottawa congress, as we shall see, did nothing to change the situation.[181]

Perhaps the most dramatic action taken by the Brussels congress was the approval of the decision taken by the ELC and the Swiss government to erect a new building in Berne to house the international bureau.[182]

3. The Ottawa Postal Congress, 1957

The Ottawa Postal Congress, despite its distance from Europe, was the largest held in the history of the UPU. Ninety-five members were represented by almost 350 individuals, and six international organizations sent observers.[183] The congress lasted only 44 days, however, from August 14 to September 27, 1957, in comparison with the 60 of Paris; and the delegates had to consider only 1,288 proposals as compared with the 1,712 of Brussels.[184]

The accomplishments of the Ottawa Congress had two outstanding characteristics. In the first place it was an innovator equal at least to the Paris Congress. The biggest achievement in this area was the creation of a new permanent body of the union, the Consultative Committee on Postal Studies (CCPS). As mentioned earlier, the members of the UPU had become aware after World War II of the fact that the world's postal services were backward in comparison with other branches of communication. The first step in meeting this problem was the creation of the ELC. The second was the formation of the CCPS. In the words of the chairman of the committee which drafted the section of the postal convention dealing with the CCPS: "Well before the Congress and also at the Congress itself it was noted that the postal communications in the Member-Countries of the UPU were very backward in the technical and operational field in comparison with the other branches and were far behind the present-day requirements and further, that the work carried out by the different countries would be more useful if a special permanent body were set up within the framework of the UPU, in order to study and generalize the best achievements and the progress made by the Member-Countries of the UPU in the technical, economic and operational spheres of the postal service." [185] That the delegates at the Ottawa Postal Congress were of the same view is evidenced by the ease with which the congress accepted the proposal to create the CCPS and by the number of proposals submitted to the congress on questions which

180. It should be noted that if both Zone A and Zone B air services are used in transporting mail, a combined rate applies.

181. See below, p. 71.

182. *Union Postale*, LXXVII, No. 12 (December, 1952), 155A.

183. UPU, *Documents du Congrès d'Ottawa*, 1957 (Berne, 1958), II, 44–54.

184. *Ibid.*, Vol. I.

185. From a statement of the work done by the Committee for the Program of Technical Studies by its chairman, Mr. K. Sergueitchuk, in *Union Postale*, LXXXIII, No. 4 (April, 1958), 49A.

member countries felt should be included in the new committee's program of studies.[186]

The Ottawa Congress also drafted a new Agreement Concerning the International Savings Bank Service. Suggested by the Brussels Congress, and by a draft prepared by the ELC, the agreement provided a method whereby an individual with funds in his country's postal savings bank could transfer them by mail to a postal savings bank account in another country. The representatives of 15 countries signed the agreement.[187] The Ottawa Congress also admitted "perishable biological material" to the international mails and provided that letters in Braille for the blind should be sent without postage charges.[188]

The other characteristic of the Ottawa Congress was its tendency to raise postage rates. Basic postage rates for ordinary postal correspondence, for example, were increased by a flat 25 percent. The minimum charge for international postal reply coupons was raised from 32 centimes to 40; the maximum rate for money orders was raised from 20 to 25 centimes. The maximum fixed rates for C.O.D. items was raised from 40 and 20 centimes to 50 and 25 centimes. The maximum fee that administrations could charge for an inquiry or request for information by a sender of a mailed article was raised from 40 to 60 centimes, and the fee for advice of delivery was raised from 30 to 40 centimes.[189]

As regards airmail rates and charges, the Ottawa congress did little but reduce the transportation charges for AO articles to 1 gold franc per ton-kilometer.[190] All proposals to change the LC transportation charges, including several to eliminate the Zones A and B differential, fell when Committee 1 *bis* voted 52 to 39 to maintain the status quo, a decision maintained in plenary session by 61 to 32.[191]

By this decision, the Ottawa congress shifted the problem of possible unification of transportation charges to the next postal congress. Whether the next congress will be able to do any better, of course, remains to be seen. That it will have a busy time, however, is evident. Not only will it have to attack the problem of transportation rates again, but it will be forced to confront another problem which has since come to light. According to the most recent ICAO *Air Mail Study,* the provision adopted by the Brussels congress to the effect that the rate which the public pays for airmail letters must have a strict relation to the cost of transport is not being obeyed: ". . . postal administrations allow them-

186. *Ibid.* The creation of the CCPS will be discussed further in Chapter Four.

187. See Docs., Ottawa Postal Congress (1957), III, 471–95. The countries which accepted the agreement at Ottawa were: Belgium, Chile, Egypt, France, Germany, Italy, Japan, Netherlands, Norway, Paraguay, Spain, Spanish territories in Africa, Sweden, Turkey, and Viet Nam.

188. Ottawa Postal Convention (1957), Art. 40 and *Règlement,* Art. 139.

189. Ottawa Postal Convention (1957), Arts. 49, 56, 67, and 69; *Arrangement concernant les mandats de poste et les bons postaux de voyage,* Art. 6; and *Arrangement concernant les envois contre remboursement,* Art. 5.

190. *Ibid., Dispositions concernant la poste aérienne,* Art. 11, 1, b).

191. Docs., Ottawa Postal Congress (1957), II, 572 & 1136. See also the discussions on pp. 548–572 & 1135–1136.

selves considerable latitude in computing the costs in question, so that it is hard to determine just what the proper postage in relation to a given conveyance charge should be. Indeed, the evidence is overwhelming that many administrations simply disregard the Convention provision in question and charge postage at rates that cover conveyance charges several times over. Moreover, a comparison of the airmail surcharges in effect under the Paris Convention and under the Brussels Convention, which made a 33 percent reduction in most transportation charges, shows for many countries no corresponding reduction in surcharge." [192]

After reconvening to sign the final acts on October 3, 1957, the delegates to the fourteenth universal postal congress left for their homes to prepare for the opening of the fifteenth universal postal congress scheduled for Rio de Janeiro in 1962.[193] In 1960, however, after two years of negotiation between the international bureau and the Brazilian government, lack of facilities and, perhaps, political events in Brazil, resulted in a decision by the Brazilian government to renounce being host to the fifteenth congress. The Indian government, whose invitation had been turned down by the Ottawa Congress in favor of the one from Brazil, proceeded to renew its invitation which, in a consultation carried out by the bureau at the request of the ELC, was accepted "by a very strong majority" of the members of the union. The date for the convening of the fifteenth postal congress was then set by the Indian government for March 1, 1963, and New Delhi was chosen for the place of meeting.

Preparations to transfer the meeting place to New Delhi were well under way in December 1962, when the Indian posts and telegraphs administration telegraphed the bureau: "Owing Chinese invasion of Indian territory and consequent national emergency greatly regret unable to make conferences and accommodation arrangements for our guests Stop Most reluctantly compelled therefore to withdraw invitation for holding the postal congress in New Delhi Stop." [194] Subsequently, the Austrian postal administration renewed its invitation and, at the last report, the members of the UPU had accepted.[195] Thus, unless another like incident should occur, the fifteenth congress will be held in Vienna in the summer of 1964.

Leaving the history of the UPU at this point, we will now turn to a more detailed analysis of the nature and organization of the UPU.

192. ICAO, *Air Mail Study, 1962 Edition,* Doc. 8240–AT/716 (Montreal, 1962), p. 7.
193. *Union Postale,* LXXXIII, No. 4 (April, 1958), 67A.
194. *Union Postale,* LXXXVIII, No. 1 (January, 1963), 17A. (See also *Annual Report, 1961,* p. 17.)
195. "News from the International Bureau," *Union Postale,* LXXXVIII, No. 6 (June, 1963), 89A.

THREE

Constitution of the UPU

F OR AN INTERNATIONAL ORGANIZATION, or any social organization for that matter, to endure, it must perform a task that men and nations consider to be essential and it must be able to adapt itself to changing world conditions. Its more than eight decades of service to the world is ample proof that the UPU has these essential qualities in a large measure.

The purpose of this chapter is to explore the nature of the UPU, what the organization itself considers to be its contribution to the world community, and the methods which permit it to adapt to changing needs and circumstances.

A. Aims and Purposes

THE OFFICIAL AIMS and purposes of the UPU are two: to form "a single postal territory for the reciprocal exchange of correspondence"; and "to secure the organization and improvement of the postal services and to promote in this sphere the development of international collaboration." [1]

The aim of transforming the entire world into a single postal territory for the reciprocal exchange of the mails is a formula of long standing, introduced originally at the Congress of Berne in 1874 without discussion.[2] It was retained in Article 1 of succeeding postal conventions, and no attempt was made to spell out its implications until the Congress of Cairo in 1934 when the delegate of a relatively new member country, Lithuania, proposed that it be eliminated from the convention because it was an abstraction with no real meaning. In the discussions which followed the Lithuanian proposal (which was defeated), it was defined for the first time. First it was agreed that the term was primarily figura-

---

1. Ottawa Postal Convention (1957), Art. 1.
2. Docs., Berne Postal Congress (1874), pp. 3, 24, 86, and 139.

tive and could not, therefore, be taken in a literal sense. Literally it would mean the existence of a single worldwide postal administration, one common postal fund, and stamps issued by a central authority. This did not exist and there were no plans to make it a reality. On the other hand, the term symbolized the aim of the union to: (1) create regulations for the international mails that would permit them to be handled throughout the world in a uniform manner; (2) establish more or less equivalent charges for the use of the international mails; and (3) obtain agreement of all countries to handle incoming foreign mail in a manner at least equal to that of domestic mail. This was the great work of the UPU, it was explained, which was reflected in the universal postal conventions and other final documents of congresses.[3] This interpretation of the major aim of the UPU remains as true today as it was in 1934.

A corollary to the principle of a single postal territory, although not included in the aims and purposes section of the universal postal convention, is the principle of freedom of transit. This means the obligation on the part of all members of the union to provide efficient and rapid transportation across their territory for mails originating in one country and destined for a third country, an essential factor in making the mails truly international. In the words of Dr. E. Weber, director of the UPU's international bureau; ". . . the organization of the circulation of the international mail is based on the freedom of transit, which allows the utilization of the enormous world net of communications with all the means which science and modern technique offer for its use. As a result, therefore, only by insuring absolute freedom of transit can the effectual universality of the postal territory be attained." [4]

The principle of freedom of transit is expressed primarily in Article 34, para. 1, of the Ottawa Postal Convention (1957) which reads in part: "Freedom of transit is guaranteed throughout the entire territory of the Union." Article 169 of the detailed regulations elaborates this principle further: "Administrations may exchange, through the intermediary of one or more of their number, both closed mails and open mail according to the needs of the traffic and the requirements of the service." It is even more explicit in the first paragraph of Article 170 of the same detailed regulations: "Each Administration is obliged to forward by the most rapid routes that it uses for its own items . . . correspondence which is forwarded to it by another Administration."

While the concept of a single postal territory and its corollary freedom of transit are fundamental principles of the UPU, they cannot be considered absolutes, as an exception to each of these concepts will show. Others will become obvious as we proceed. First, the idea of uniformity of regulations inherent in the phrase "a single postal territory" does not preclude the creation of "restricted" international postal unions of member countries or "special agreements" between two or more member

3. See Docs., Cairo Postal Congress (1934), II, 597–98, 607–608, and 621.
4. "Freedom of Transit, a Fundamental Basis of the Universal Postal Union," *Union Postale,* LXXXVII, No. 4 (April, 1962), 49A.

countries to do such things as reduce postal charges below those set forth in the acts of the UPU or make other special arrangements for the handling of mail. There is a limitation on what can be done in restricted postal unions and special agreements, however, and that is that they must not introduce provisions "less favorable to the public" than those contained in the acts of the UPU.[5] In this sense, therefore, the idea of uniformity in international postal regulations should be considered primarily as a minimum standard of conduct below which member countries are not permitted to fall.

Secondly, as we have seen, the idea of freedom of transit does not preclude the imposition of a fee by the intermediate state for the service of transporting mails across its territory. There is a basic difference between free transit and transit without a fee. As stated by Dr. Weber: ". . . freedom of transit does not mean gratuity of transit and, consequently, in this question there are two distinct aspects, one legal and the other economic." [6] On the other hand, the UPU has made a consistent effort throughout the years to see that transit fees are at least more or less uniform over equivalent distances.[7]

The second section of Article 1 of the universal postal convention dealing with the aims and purposes of the UPU has two parts: (a) "to secure the organization and improvement of the postal services," and (b) "to promote in this sphere the development of international collaboration." The first part was added to the convention in 1924 and the second in 1947.[8] Despite its relatively late arrival in postal conventions, the securing of the organization and improvement of the postal services cannot be considered anything more than a restatement of a function that the UPU has had since it became operative in 1875. Almost everything that the union has done since 1875 has tended to organize and improve the postal services, including standardization of the methods of handling international mail, making rates uniform, and establishing responsibility for lost or damaged articles.

Improvement also reflects the results of the studies undertaken by congresses and conferences on certain aspects of the international mail service, as well as those completed on a cooperative basis through the intermediary of the international bureau, and the studies of the bureau itself. From the beginning, for instance, the bureau has been charged with "coordinating, publishing and distributing information of interest to the international postal services." [9] The official journal, *Union Postale,* has always carried articles dealing with special advances or special techniques introduced into the international mail service by member countries. Further, as will be discussed later, from the turn of the century

5. Ottawa Postal Convention (1957), Art. 8.
6. Weber, *op. cit.,* p. 50A.
7. See Ottawa Postal Convention (1957), Art. 79. For two exceptions to this rule, see *Protocole final,* Arts. 10 and 11.
8. See Docs., Stockholm Postal Congress (1924), II, p. 845 and Docs., Paris Postal Congress (1947), II, 907.
9. See Berne Postal Treaty (1874), Art. 15.

the bureau has used its good offices, at the request of a postal administration, to open inquiries among member countries on questions of common interest for the improvement of services.[10]

One point that may not be too clear from the history of the UPU is that it has not confined itself to questions relating only to the international postal service. Just as the implementation of the idea of a single postal territory has an impact on the international services of the various member countries, so does it also influence the various domestic services. In most postal administrations there is no clear differentiation between international and domestic services. Employees and facilities are used for both. Consequently, innovations in UPU regulations must have a definite impact on the domestic service. Further, the UPU has made a conscious effort to aid countries in improving their domestic mail. After all, it is clear that the speed and efficiency of the international mail depends upon the speed and efficiency of each postal administration that handles it. The bureau has always passed on information about improvements in one postal administration to all of the others. The *Union Postale* has always carried articles dealing with new techniques of domestic postal services. The Congress of London in 1929, in effect, legitimized this function of the bureau by adding a new paragraph to the detailed regulations by which the bureau was obliged to "be ready at all times to furnish the members of the union with any information on questions relating to the services of which they may have need." [11] If the bureau has the information it will supply it to administrations, whether it deals with the international service or directly with the domestic services. The bureau is always willing to open inquiries among members on any problems confronting administrations, either international or domestic.[12] And, as will be discussed later, the UPU has for a long time provided its own type of technical assistance to postal administrations which have needed such help, with no real distinction between domestic and international.[13]

The second part of the second section of Article 1, "to promote in this sphere the development of international collaboration," seems at first glance to be redundant. After all, the UPU has been promoting international collaboration in the field of postal affairs since 1874. The addition of this phrase by the Paris Postal Congress of 1947 was justified, however, by the *additional* postwar emphasis on international collaboration resulting from the desire of postal administrations to reap the benefits of new advances in automation and mechanization, the desire of the many new postwar nations to share the advantages of older civilizations, and the general welfare orientation of the United Nations system.

10. See below, pp. 197–98.
11. Docs., London Postal Congress (1929), II, 654.
12. See, for instance, the inquiry concerning the utility of using mobile post offices in *Annual Reports,* 1905, p. 5; 1906, p. 7; and 1907, p. 6.
13. See below, pp. 223 and 226.

The periodic congresses and the bureau's clearinghouse activities for information were excellent, but more was demanded. The first response to this demand was the creation of the permanent Executive and Liaison Committee by the Paris Congress, with the order to "study technical questions and problems of every kind connected with the international postal service and to communicate the results of such studies to the postal administrations." [14] At its first real working session in 1949 (the executive and liaison committee meets once a year), it began exploring a wide range of postal problems, some international and others that can be described only as domestic.[15]

The number of questions that needed study, both domestic and international, forced the 1957 Ottawa Congress to carry one step further the new emphasis on more frequent international collaboration. The executive and liaison committee was restricted to the study of "administrative, legislative and judicial problems connected with the international postal service," and a new permanent organ was created, the Consultative Committee for Postal Studies, charged with carrying out "studies and issuing opinions on technical, operational and economic questions concerning the postal service." [16] No attempt was made to confine the work of the consultative committee to purely international postal affairs and, as is evident in the first report of the consultative committee's sections, studies concerning the domestic postal services will take up a great deal of its time and energy.[17]

In order to obtain a complete picture of the aims and purposes of the UPU, a definition is due at this point. The international mails, as the term has been used thus far, include much more than just letter mail. Letter mail, as defined by article 48 of the Ottawa Postal Convention, includes "letters, single and reply-paid postcards, commercial papers, printed matter, literature for the blind, samples of merchandise, small packets, and phonopost items." As we have seen, throughout the years the UPU has established the rules and regulations of many other international services available to the public through the post office, including insured letters and boxes, parcel post, postal money orders and postal traveler's checks, transfers to and from postal checking accounts, cash on delivery, collection of bills, postal savings bank services, and subscriptions to newspapers and periodicals. As a general rule these services were first developed in domestic practice, then they became the subject of bilateral agreement between neighboring postal administrations, and finally, when they became extensive enough, they came under the auspices of the UPU. Although none of the rules and regulations for

14. Paris Postal Convention (1947), Art. 18, para. 11 b.
15. UPU, *Documents de la Commission exécutive et de liaison, Session de mai 1949, Compte rendu analytique* (Berne, 1949), p. 14.
16. Ottawa Postal Convention (1957), Art. 16, para. 6 (b), and Art. 17, para. 1.
17. UPU, *Documents de la Commission consultative des études postales (CCEP) et de son Conseil de gestion, Session d'Ottawa 1957 et de Bruxelles 1958* (Berne, 1958), *Compte rendu analytique*, pp. 10–12 and 13–15.

these services has been accepted by all of the members of the union, acceptance has been wide enough to make these "non-letter" services an important part of the work of the UPU.

Put together, the creation of a single postal territory with its corollary freedom of transit, the task of aiding the organization and improvement of the postal services both domestic and international, and the promotion of international collaboration for both letter mail and non-letter services, add up to a very comprehensive coverage of a subject matter the scope of which is important but very narrow. The international mails, with which the UPU is primarily concerned, do have an extremely important place in the relations of nations and in the concept of freedom of information. This cannot be denied, although perhaps one would not go so far as one writer who stated ". . . that the Union embodies the ideal of a bond of co-operation and harmony between all the peoples of the world, like a bridge which crosses the depth of incomprehension and antagonism which separate men, a bridge which leads to the ideal of peace and friendship, the supreme aim of humanity." [18]

On the other hand it would be amiss to compare the aims and purposes of the UPU, in terms of its scope or even in terms of its contribution to humanity, with those of the League of Nations, whose demise the UPU survived, or the United Nations, or even its sister specialized agencies such as UNESCO, WHO, or FAO. Nevertheless, none of these agencies has had such a long and fruitful history as the UPU. Perhaps the narrow scope of its terms of reference, and the highly technical nature of the subject matter with which it deals, may account in some manner for its longevity.

Before proceeding to the question of membership in the UPU, a word is in order about an obvious lacuna in the aims and purposes of the UPU. Nowhere in the postal convention, its attached detailed regulations, or the various agreements on non-letter services, is there a provision setting forth the rights of the individual to use the international mail or a declaration stating that the savings inherent in a rapid and efficient international postal service should be passed on to the individual user. The final acts of the UPU are oriented almost exclusively toward the rights and duties of postal administrations, and the improvements that are periodically made to these acts are justified on the basis of savings to postal administrations in time and personnel.

It could be argued that it is not the place of the UPU to worry about the user of the international mails. That perhaps should be left to the good intentions of the domestic postal authorities and to pressure group activity within each member country. However, all of the other specialized agencies of the UN, including the ITU, which is the most similar to the UPU and even older, make some reference to the individual in their basic treaties. One of the major purposes of the ITU, for instance, is to "promote the development of technical facilities and their most

18. Weber, *op. cit.,* p. 52A.

efficient operation with a view to improving the efficiency of telecommunication services, increasing their usefulness and making them, so far as possible, generally available to the public." Another purpose of the ITU is to "foster collaboration among its Members and Associate Members with a view to the establishment of rates at levels as low as possible consistent with an efficient service and taking into account the necessity for maintaining independent financial administration of telecommunication on a sound basis." [19]

The reason for this difference in attitude between the UPU and other international organizations is not readily apparent. It might be due to a lack of pressure from within member countries which would give credence to the argument that postal administrations do pass on the benefits of the UPU's rules and regulations to the domestic user. It is more likely that it is because "freedom of information" has definite political overtones, and thus the members of the UPU feel that it should be left to other international bodies such as UNESCO or the United Nations itself to encourage. The constant emphasis in the UPU on the technical nature of its work would give support to this theory. One might even draw the conclusion, more evidence of which will be given as we proceed, that the avoidance of political questions might have to be included as one of the basic aims of the UPU, or at least one of its basic tenets.

A slight change in this respect is foreseeable, however. In 1960 the executive and liaison committee drafted a new arrangement of the articles of the postal convention and detailed regulations, the "constitutional" section of which states that the document is being adopted in order "to promote the higher aims of cultural, social, and economic cooperation between peoples through the efficient functioning of the postal services." This statement is not a part of the operative provisions of the document in question, however, but merely the preamble to that document.

B. Membership

THE UPU has always deserved the title "universal." In contrast to what occurred in most other international organizations which came into being in the latter half of the nineteenth century, the UPU started out as an international organ rather than a regional one. The congress of 1874 had representation not only from Western Europe, but also from Scandinavia, the Near East, and North America. Within a few years Asia was represented in its congresses as was Latin America. Before the turn of the century, the membership of the UPU included practically all of the sovereign states then in existence.

19. See ITU, *International Telecommunication Convention, Buenos Aires, 1952* (Geneva, 1953), Art. 3, paras. 1 and 2. (See also Codding, *op. cit.*, pp. 272–75.)

There were two primary reasons for this phenomenon. The first was the nature of its terms of reference: to improve the international mails. The international mails have always been a primary means of communication. Membership in the UPU quickly became mandatory for any nation that wished to take advantage of this means of communication so necessary to trade and commerce. The second reason was the flexibility of the UPU's admission procedure. No independent nation that applied for membership was ever turned down, and many were accepted that under other circumstances might never have been considered for membership in an international agency. As a result, the entire world did, in reality, become a single postal territory.

Since World War II, as we shall see, strained international relations of a type never before seen have resulted in the dimming of the UPU's universality. Nevertheless, with a membership of over 120 at the end of 1963, the UPU still remains one of the most universal international organizations in existence.

1. Conditions of Membership

In its search for universality, the UPU had, until World War II, a very simple basic procedure for membership. From the coming into effect of the convention of 1878 to that of 1947, all that a country had to do to belong was to declare its adherence to the postal convention, through diplomatic channels, to the Swiss government. The Swiss government, in its turn, simply notified all the existing members.[20] No votes were taken, no consultation held; simply notification was given by the country of its adherence to the basic document.[21] In this manner the UPU built up its membership from the original 21 which participated in the Congress of Berne in 1874 to 64 in 1906, and 88 in 1939.[22]

As was also discussed in Chapter Two, not all of the countries which were considered full members of the union before World War II, with voting rights, were in fact independent. Starting in 1878 the union created a category for territories which were recognized as nonindependent but which were given all the rights of union membership afforded to clearly independent countries.[23] The justification for creating this additional category for membership in the union was, in general, that these territories covered such large geographical areas and had such large populations, with attendant individual problems, that their presence in the union was mutually desirable, besides the fact that they also had independent postal administrations.[24] While it might be difficult to deny that some benefits have accrued to the union from this additional

20. See, for example, Paris Postal Convention (1878), Art. 18.
21. For membership provisions from 1875 to 1878 see Chapter Two above, pp. 35–37.
22. See preamble of the Postal Treaty of Berne (1874), Rome Postal Convention (1906), and Buenos Aires Postal Convention (1939).
23. See above, pp. 36–37.
24. See, for instance, Docs., Congress of Paris (1878), p. 397.

kind of membership, it also seems clear that the primary purpose of the sponsoring great powers was to obtain additional votes in the congresses.[25] By 1939, for example, the Dutch delegation controlled four additional votes. Even the United States had an extra membership (and vote) for "the Whole of the Possessions of the United States of America, comprising Hawaii, Puerto Rico, Guam and the Virgin Islands of the United States of America." [26]

Inasmuch as these territories were listed in a separate article in the convention, the procedure for admission to membership was different from that for independent countries. First, a regular member, usually the colonial power, suggested to a congress that the name of its colony be added to the list of territories considered to be members of the union, and followed its suggestion with a statement of the importance of the colony in question and what it and the union would gain mutually from its membership. If the sponsoring country could then obtain at least a majority of votes the article was amended to add the name of the new colony, which then had membership from the time the new convention came into effect. While the number of colonial memberships increased regularly, there are instances where applications were turned down by congresses. At the Congress of Vienna in 1891, for example, the British delegate requested two memberships, and two votes, for its Australasian colonies — one vote for Western Australia, meridional Australia, Victoria, and Tasmania; and one vote for two other parts of Australia, New Zealand, New Guinea, and the Fijis. After a storm of opposition, the British settled for one membership, and one extra vote, for "the Whole of the British Colonies in Australasia." [27]

The "open" membership of the UPU came to an end, finally, at the Congress of Paris in 1947. Proposals for tightening the union's admission procedures were tabled at Paris by the United States, Great Britain, France, the USSR, Canada, Bulgaria, and Mexico, among other nations. The range of proposals spread from the simple to the complicated. For example, Bulgaria's provided that if one fifth of the membership of the United Nations were to declare that the country demanding admission did not fulfill the requirements of a "sovereign state," then two thirds of the members of the UPU could veto that state's admission; Mexico's would have simply eliminated the article of the convention which permitted nonindependent territories to exercise all the rights of union membership. There was a great variety of reasons offered for making the admission procedure more difficult. The one by the Russians, for

25. See the discussion of colonial voting in the ITU during this same period, in Codding, *op. cit.*, pp. 38–41 and 98–100.

26. See Buenos Aires Postal Convention (1939), Art. 8.

27. See Docs., Vienna Postal Congress (1891), pp. 381–83, and 643–49. It should be noted that in the next congress the British obtained an additional vote for "the Whole of the Other British Colonies" (Docs., Washington D.C. Postal Congress, 1897, pp. 715 and 720). Further discussions on the entire colonial voting question can be found in the proceedings of all the UPU congresses, from that of Paris (1878), to the most recent.

example, stressed the need for "equality of states in voting in Congresses and Conferences," or in other words attacked colonial or weighted voting.[28] The Mexican proposal also directly attacked those nations which in the past had obtained admission for their colonies in order to use the extra votes in meetings. The Bulgarian proposal had a similar ring. Other advocates agreed to a tightening of the rules, but not to the same extent. These argued along less clear lines, preferring to emphasize the necessity for having some sort of criterion for membership (a UPU criterion) and for making the admission standards conform to a greater extent to that of the UN, with which the UPU was negotiating an agreement to become a specialized agency. One interesting argument was that under the existing statutes the real decision as to membership qualifications was left to the Swiss government in its role as the accepting agency for applications.[29]

The admission article of the convention was initially sent to the first committee where a lengthy debate took place. Starting with admission procedures, the committee soon turned to a discussion of a proposal that a new associate membership be created for nonindependent countries with all the ordinary rights of membership except that of voting, and of the general question as to whether colonial voting should be abolished. The problem of admission procedures faded more and more into the background as the opponents of colonial voting emphasized the principle of "equality of states." Why, it was argued, should any state have at its disposal more than a single vote in an international organization of this type? The proponents, on the other hand, emphasized the contributions that colonies had made to the work of the UPU and the importance of tradition, and pointed out that colonies often had interests differing from those of the home country which had to be defended. The proponents of colonial voting also stressed the argument that the UPU was an organization of technicians and not of politicians, and therefore the concept of one vote for one independent country had less validity than it did in more politically oriented international organizations.[30]

The work of the first committee on the problem of admission to the union came to an anticlimactic end when a proposal to maintain the status quo was adopted by a vote of 40 to 28 (with 5 abstentions and 3 absences). Those who voted against the proposal were: Albania, Byelorussia, Brazil, British colonies, Chile, China, Colombia, Cuba, Czechoslovakia, Great Britain, Guatemala, Haiti, Hungary, India, Ireland, Italy, Mexico, New Zealand, Poland, Rumania, San Marino, Ukraine, United States, the whole of the United States possessions, Uruguay, USSR,

28. Docs., Paris Postal Congress (1947), I, 21. Later in the congress, Russia demanded and received membership for Byelorussia and the Ukraine.

29. *Ibid.*, pp. 20–21 and 29–35.

30. See *ibid.*, II, 234–64 and 276–94. Without citing concrete instances, the Mexican delegation argued that the colonial members had never voted against the home country, while the delegate of Indochina argued that it had occurred "many times" (*ibid.*, p. 291).

Venezuela and Yugoslavia. Abstainers were Australia, Bulgaria, Finland, Philippines, and Vatican City. The absent delegates were those from El Salvador, Honduras, and Panama.[31]

This decision did not end the matter, however. About two weeks later, the United States delegate raised the matter in a plenary session. According to this delegate, although the congress had decided that all present members of the union should continue to exercise full membership in the union's activities, it had not decided the fundamental question of future applications for membership. The United States proposed that in the future only "sovereign countries" should be members and that a procedure for assuring this rule should be clearly set forth in the postal convention. A two-thirds affirmative vote on future admissions was proposed. It was also pointed out — and this may have been the decisive argument — that the UN team which was negotiating the agreement to make the UPU a specialized agency had made it clear to the UPU negotiators that the status quo, agreed upon by the first committee, did not provide the union with the clear standard for admission which the UN group considered desirable.[32]

For some reason, perhaps because of something else which had occurred at the congress or perhaps because of new directives from governments, an almost completely new alignment of forces took place. Most of the delegates who had voted for the status quo in committee rallied to the United States proposal. It was agreed that the nature of the UPU demanded that only sovereign countries be admitted in the future and that a two-thirds affirmative vote for admission was quite proper. The communist bloc delegates, almost without exception, argued that any country should be granted membership upon its request.[33]

After a further heated discussion in which the communist bloc delegates presented various other arguments (including the legality of raising the question again in plenary meeting after the committee had made its decision, and the propriety of the UN negotiation team's making demands upon the UPU), the United States proposal was decisively approved. The key paragraph of the proposal, providing for a two-thirds majority for admission, was opposed by only seven delegations, i.e., Byelorussia, Bulgaria, Hungary, Rumania, Ukraine, USSR, and Yugoslavia. The following nine delegations abstained: Algeria, Austria, Belgian Congo, Czechoslovakia, Dutch Indies, French overseas territories, Indochina, Lebanon, and Poland. Delegations of Albania, Bolivia, Cuba, Dominican Republic, El Salvador, Ecuador, Ethiopia, Honduras, Peru, and Syria were absent.[34]

During the voting on the proposal, the United States delegate ac-

31. *Ibid.*, p. 294.
32. *Ibid.*, pp. 68–69.
33. The delegate of the USSR argued that the two-thirds vote was too restrictive despite the fact that the original Russian proposal had provided for just such a vote on admission (*ibid.*, pp. 68–80 and 907–21).
34. *Ibid.*, p. 920.

cepted an amendment from the Czechoslovakian delegate to the effect that those countries which failed to act on a request for admission within a four-month delay should be considered as having abstained and not as voting against the country seeking admission. This amendment made the American proposal potentially much less strict than it would have been in its original form.[35]

The present admissions procedure for the UPU, amended slightly since 1947 and only in wording and not intent, is as follows:

ARTICLE III

New admissions. Procedure.

1] Any sovereign country may apply for admission as a member of the Universal Postal Union.

2] The application is addressed through the diplomatic channel to the Government of the Swiss Confederation, and by the latter to the member-countries of the Union.

3] The country concerned is considered to be admitted as a member if its application is approved by at least two thirds of the member countries of the Union.

4] Member countries of the Union which have not answered within a period of four months are considered to have abstained.

5] Admission as a member is announced by the Government of the Swiss Confederation to the Governments of all the member countries of the Union.[36]

As far as can be determined, few if any requests have been turned down by the members of the union since the convention of 1947 came into effect.[37]

No substantive changes were made by the Paris Congress, or by succeeding congresses, to the provision of the convention providing for full voting membership for certain nonindependent territories. The idea of creating an "associate membership" was dropped when the first committee of the Paris Congress decided to retain the status quo, and was not raised in a plenary session. Consequently it is still possible for a member of the union to obtain an extra vote by obtaining the approval of a congress to add a dependent territory to the appropriate article of the convention. This did occur, in fact, at the Congress of Ottawa in 1957 when it was agreed, on the proposal of the executive and liaison committee, to give voting membership to "The Territory of Somaliland Under Italian Administration." [38] It is doubtful that there remain many dependent territories with independence in postal matters that could qualify for such membership, especially in view of the growing anti-

35. *Ibid.*, p. 919.
36. Ottawa Postal Convention (1957), Art. 3.
37. For a complete list of all of the members of the UPU and the dates of membership, see Annex IV.
38. See Docs., Ottawa Postal Congress (1957), I, 126; and II, 319.

colonial sentiment in certain parts of the world. The new excolonial members of the union, who share this feeling, would make it difficult to obtain the majority needed according to the rules of procedure of congresses.

On the other hand, territorial membership will become less of an issue as more former colonies become independent members of the community of nations. The Congress of Brussels (1952) dropped from this article the names of the Dutch Indies and Indochina for this reason.[39] Others will be dropped at the next congress.

2. Representation

The problem of admission is not the only problem of membership that confronts international organizations. States change their boundaries, and thus their size, and in some cases are absorbed into other political units. Some states aggress against others, and others are aggressed against. Almost all international organizations, the UPU no exception, at times have had to face the problem of deciding whether the changes that have occurred in the status of member states, or certain of their actions, warrant the deprivation of the right to participate in the activities of a particular international organization.

Prior to World War II, the problem of representation was much less acute. States came and went, territorial changes took place, and states engaged in wars. Although there were discussions in UPU congresses over these occurrences, sometimes with the exchange of heated words, wars and alterations of territorial boundaries through force or any other means were ultimately recognized as facts of international life and accepted as such without seriously disrupting the work of the union. The Congress of Rome (1906), for example, in reference to the disappearance of the independent states of Hawaii, Orange Free State, and Transvaal, came to the conclusion that a sovereign state which was subsequently deprived of its sovereignty was retired "automatically" from the list of contracting parties and therefore could no longer be represented at UPU sponsored meetings. The Rome Congress also agreed that "important territorial innovations" in member countries should be reported to the Swiss government, which in turn would notify the countries of the union, "mentioning expressly at the same time that the notification should in no way prejudice observations or protestations to which it might give rise on the part of interested states." [40] According to Reinhold Furrer, director of the bureau from 1938 to 1944, the interpretation of the Rome Congress was the correct one; a congress should accept automatically autonomous confirmation of important territorial alterations. "It would indeed ill suit the Universal Postal Congress," he wrote, "to have to vote and decide on the question as to whether a change of territorial sovereignty shall be recognized or not, for it is not

39. Docs., Brussels Postal Congress (1952), I, 150 and 151; and II, 327.
40. Docs., Rome Postal Congress (1906), II, p. 197. (See also pp. 561–63).

a political forum, and, if it wants to attain the aims of its founders, cannot become one." [41] The Congress of London (1929) in a like vein came to the conclusion that "diplomatic difficulties" should not influence or present any obstacle to the invitation of any member or to its representation in congresses and conferences.[42]

There were no problems of representation after World War I. By the time the first postwar congress was held, the former enemy states were already being accepted as fullfledged members of the international community and were permitted to attend the Congress of Madrid without opposition or even serious discussion.

By 1947 circumstances were different, and they have remained so to the present. It is not necessary, nor would it be appropriate, to review the international political climate of the post-World War II years at this point. Suffice it to say that the scope and intensity of World War II, and the periods of occupation of certain countries, were unlike anything the world had ever known, and induced a strong mood of moral indignation. The new United Nations was a reflection of this change in the international climate, and it had its impact on the UPU. To these two factors must be added the continued strain in the relations between the East and the West, popularly known as the "cold war." All three factors added up to a series of problems of representation for the UPU. These problems can be considered under three categories: (1) the ex-enemy states and Spain; (2) the Balkan states, whose political status underwent a substantial change during the course of World War II; and (3) the "divided states," Germany, China, Korea, and Viet Nam.

The problem of representation of the former states of Germany and Japan, and of Korea arose at the Paris Congress of 1947, at which time all three countries were still under Allied occupation. France, the host country, invited the Allied Control Councils of both Germany and Japan to send observers, which they did. These observers participated actively in the work of the congress, but the general feeling was that they should not be allowed to sign in the name of the countries which they represented. The observers from the Allied Control Council of Japan actually made a request to be permitted to act as the regular representatives of Japan and to vote, both for Japan and for Korea, and to sign the final acts. The request was not discussed or voted on; it was simply reproduced *in extenso* in the minutes of the meeting.[43]

On the other hand, there was no desire to terminate their membership, because all three had been members of the union for many years and were important elements in the concept of a "single postal territory." The solution, proposed by the chairman of the conference, Mr. Joseph-Jean Le Mouël, was to keep names of these countries in the preamble to the postal convention and to add a provision in the final protocol per-

41. See "Repeal and Ratification as Understood in the Universal Postal Convention," *Union Postale,* LXIV, No. 12 (December, 1939), 555–89.
42. Docs., London Postal Congress (1929), I, 1383; and II, 155.
43. Docs., Paris Postal Congress (1947), II, 233–34.

mitting them to adhere at a later date, without prejudice to their membership.[44] This provision read as follows:

> Germany, Japan, and Korea, temporarily precluded from acceding to the Convention and the Arrangements, may accede to these Acts without submitting to the formalities prescribed in Article 3 [membership provisions], at the time considered opportune by the responsible authority.[45]

The representation of Spain was a slightly different problem. While not an active belligerent in World War II, Spain's activities during that conflict and the nature of its leadership caused the United Nations, in December 1946, to pass a resolution recommending among other things, the exclusion of the Franco government from membership in the specialized agencies. Preceding the congress, the French government received a communication from the Secretary-General of the United Nations drawing its attention to the resolution and pointing out that the question of the relationship between the UN and the UPU would be discussed at the Paris Congress.[46] The French government did not invite Spain to participate in the Paris Postal Congress, which engendered a discussion on the legality of the French decision, as well as upon the disposition that should be made of Spanish representation until the UN resolution should become invalid.

While there was no basic opposition to the treatment of Japan, Germany, and Korea, there was considerable opposition to the decision of France not to invite Spain and to all suggestions that Spain be refused the right to maintain its active membership in the UPU. In taking up this problem (which lasted several days and produced heated debate), the delegates at the Paris Congress discussed not only the actions of Spain during World War II, but also the nature of the relationship between the United Nations and the UPU, as well as the basic nature of the UPU itself. In general, the opponents of the exclusion of Spain, led by the delegation from Argentina, based their arguments on: (1) the fact that the postal convention did not have an article which permitted the expulsion of a member and that an expulsion had never taken place in the UPU's history; (2) the fact that the convention required that "all" bona fide members of the union had to be invited to all congresses; and (3) the "non-political" nature of the UPU which, in their opinion, demanded that the type of government of a member country should have no influence on its relations to the union.

The supporters of the French government's action, including those who wished to see a decision excluding Spain from future participation in the activities of the union until there had been a change of government, based their arguments on: (1) the obligation imposed by the

44. *Ibid.*, pp. 88, 233–34, 462, 570, 745, and 903–907.
45. Paris Postal Convention (1947), *Protocole final*, Art. XVII, para. 2.
46. See UN, *General Assembly Resolution 39* (1), December 12, 1946, and Docs., Paris Postal Congress (1947), II, 251.

decision of the UN, of which most of the states represented at Paris were members; (2) the impact which a decision to permit the participation of Spain would have on future relations between the UN and the UPU; and (3) the opinion that, despite any provisions of the postal convention, the Paris Postal Congress was the supreme organ of the UPU, and thus could take any decision it chose. Others, such as the delegates of the USSR and Byelorussia, placed heavy emphasis on the behavior of Spain during World War II.[47]

The question of invitation to the Paris congress was decided in the first committee when the following proposal was approved, 47 to 12, with 12 abstentions (5 delegations were absent): "The Committee approves the statements of France concerning the non-invitation to the XII Congress of the UPU. . . ." Voting against the proposal were: Argentina, Brazil, Canada, Colombia, Cuba, Ireland, Paraguay, Portugal, Portuguese colonies of West Africa, Portuguese colonies of East Africa, Uruguay, and Vatican City. Abstentions were recorded for: Bolivia, Chile, Denmark, Egypt, Ecuador, Iceland, Lebanon, Norway, Peru, South Africa, Sweden, and Switzerland.[48] As to the future exclusion of Spain the congress decided to keep Spain's name in the preamble of the convention, as a member, and to place the exclusion in the final protocol, as was done in the case of Japan, Germany, and Korea.[49]

In both cases, for Spain and the Spanish colonies and for Germany, Japan, and Korea, the congress provided that accession to membership was to be made "by diplomatic channels to the Government of the French Republic." [50]

The General Assembly resolution on Spain was revoked in 1950, and Spain notified the French government of its accession to the final acts of the Paris Congress in January 1951.[51] The governments of Japan and the Republic of Korea notified the French government of their accession to the final acts of the Paris Congress in 1949, and the Federal Republic of Germany, in 1955.[52] The accession of Japan and Spain and her colonies did not give rise to any controversy, and these two countries participated as full members in the congress of 1952 as well as succeeding congresses. The problems that arose over the accession of the Federal Republic of Germany and the Republic of Korea will be discussed after a quick survey of the controversy over the three Baltic states.

The question at the Paris Congress of the representation of the three Baltic states of Latvia, Lithuania, and Estonia and their membership in the UPU, raised one of the most acrimonious disputes of this or any UPU congress. The question was first raised on the second day of the congress and prevailed until the last day but one. It involved

47. Docs., Paris Postal Congress (1947), II, 105–106, 147, 210, and 238–64.
48. *Ibid.,* p. 261.
49. Paris Postal Convention (1947), Final Protocol, Art. XVII, para. 1. See also Docs., Paris Postal Congress (1947), II, 266–68, 872, and 1013.
50. Paris Postal Convention (1947), Final Protocol, Art. XVII, para. 3.
51. *Annual Report, 1951,* p. 24.
52. See *Annual Reports, 1949,* p. 22; *1952,* p. 28; and *1955,* p. 26.

almost a dozen votes, one informal walkout of a delegation in a plenary session, and numerous statements and declarations including, at one point, a protest by the chairman of the congress against the statements of one of the delegations.[53]

The problem arose in the following manner. Latvia, Lithuania, and Estonia had been members in good standing of the UPU since just after World War I. In late 1940 the USSR had notified the members of the union through the bureau that these three states had been incorporated in the USSR and therefore ceased to be separate members of the UPU. On January 31, 1947, less than five months before the opening of the Paris Congress, the USSR notified the members that in conformity with the law promulgated by the Supreme Council of the Union of Soviet Socialist Republics of February 1, 1944, concerning the power of the Union Republics to carry out foreign relations, the government of the USSR was annulling the notification of 1940, and asked the bureau to notify the members of the union and change the bureau's documents accordingly. Telegrams were received from the postal administrations of the three countries in question stating that they had recommenced being members of the union, and notifying the bureau of the contributory class to which they wished to belong.[54]

The question posed to the Paris Congress, therefore, was whether the three Baltic states had the right to membership in the union and representation in the congress. The USSR, which was the prime supporter of their membership and representation, argued that it was not a case of new admissions, but one of "prolonging the status of membership" of existing members. In the first place, it was argued, the notification by the USSR in 1940 was not legally binding because it did not conform to the requirements of the convention which stipulated that all withdrawals must be accompanied by a "notification through diplomatic channels to the government of Switzerland." Secondly, since their withdrawal was invalid, the three states had the right to representation at the congress as full and equal members. Thirdly, the three states had undertaken all of the normal obligations of members vis-a-vis the final acts of the union, which they could do as "sovereign and independent" states in the Soviet Union.[55]

According to the delegation of Great Britain, which was among the many in opposition to the representation of the three states, regular membership in the union was confined to "sovereign countries." ". . . Lithuania, Latvia and Estonia were incorporated *de facto* into the Soviet Union in 1940 and ceased *de facto* to be sovereign states." As such they ceased to be members of the union and it was "impossible" to revive their membership except by a new act of accession to the con-

53. For a full account, see Docs., Paris Postal Congress (1947), II, 23, 49–53, 105–106, 147, 166–84, 893–98, 921–48, 1022–27, 1028, 1029–38, 1041–55, 1058–59, and 1063–77.
54. *Ibid.*, pp. 23 and 49–53.
55. *Ibid.*, I, 16–19.

vention.[56] As pointed out by the Canadian delegation, the acceptance of
the membership of these three states would constitute a gift to the USSR
of five additional votes (Byelorussia and the Ukraine had already been
admitted), and eventually 16.[57]

The problem of representation of the Baltic states was initially discussed in the first committee to which it had been sent by the plenary
assembly. At the eighth meeting of the first committee it was decided
by 28 votes to 11 that the Baltic states had ceased to be members of
the UPU in 1940 and therefore could not be represented at the congress.
Unfortunately for the committee, however, there were 36 abstentions on
the vote, and 6 delegations were absent.[58] The delegate of the USSR
immediately raised the point that fewer than half of the delegations to
the congress had voted; therefore, if it was not illegal it was at least
inconclusive. After another lengthy discussion, the committee voted 56
to 4 with 11 abstentions (6 delegations were absent) that the committee
had taken a valid vote. The four were Albania, Byelorussia, USSR, and
Yugoslavia. The 11 abstainers were Afghanistan, Austria, Bolivia, Bulgaria, Czechoslovakia, Ecuador, Finland, Hungary, Iran, Poland, and
Rumania.[59]

The Russian delegation was not content with the action of the first
committee, however, and raised the question again at the next plenary
meeting. A new complication was introduced when the French delegation, after being attacked by the Russian delegate for not inviting representatives of the Baltic countries to the congress, got its government to
issue invitations on the basis that the French government had not been
aware of the January 1947, message from the USSR.[60] For a while then
the representatives of the Baltic countries (which had been included
originally in the Russian delegation) participated in the discussions of
the congress, including the discussion on whether they were actually
members of the union with the right of representation! After a long and
bitter debate, the plenary assembly finally decided, by a vote of
27 to 13 (with 28 abstentions and 8 absentees) that the decision of the
first committee that the Baltic states were not members, despite the fact
that France had issued invitations, precluded the Baltic states from
participating in the congress.[61]

56. *Ibid.*, pp. 15–16.
57. *Ibid.*, II, 176.
58. *Ibid.*, pp. 179–80. The abstentions came from Afghanistan, Austria, Bel-
gium, Belgian Congo, Bolivia, Denmark, Ethiopia, France, Algeria, Indochina,
French overseas territories, Greece, Guatemala, Iraq, Iceland, Italy, Lebanon,
Luxembourg, French Morocco, Norway, Netherlands, Curaçao and Surinam,
Philippines, Portugal, Portuguese colonies of East Africa, Asia and Oceania,
Portuguese colonies of West Africa, San Marino, Siam, Sweden, Switzerland,
Tunisia, and Turkey. Those voting for representation were Albania, Byelorussia,
Bulgaria, Czechoslovakia, Ecuador, Finland, Hungary, Poland, Rumania, USSR,
and Yugoslavia.
59. *Ibid.*, pp. 180–84.
60. *Ibid.*, pp. 921–22.
61. *Ibid.*, pp. 893–98 and 921–48.

The representatives of the Baltic countries, in their turn, called into question the legality of this vote in a subsequent plenary session. After another acrimonious debate in which these individuals insisted on speaking in the name of their own countries and in which the chairman of the congress insisted that they speak only as part of the USSR delegation (the minutes of the meeting designate them as "the representative of" rather than the "delegate of" as was used for other speakers), another discussion took place on the legality of the assembly's vote and the legality of the chairman's enforcement of that vote. After further heated debate the assembly proceeded to a series of five votes, the legality of most of which was disputed by the delegates in the minority. The first vote was taken on a Bulgarian motion to the effect: "Must the Chairman apply votes which violate the Convention or which were secured in violation of the Rules of Procedure?" The question was answered in the negative by 51 votes. Three delegations abstained, 15 were absent at the time of the vote, and 7 delegations "refused to vote." Those which refused to vote were Argentina, Belgian Congo, Belgium, Mexico, Paraguay, USSR, and Vatican City. The refusals were based on the claim that the question was the wrong one to place before the assembly or that it was badly phrased.[62] Next the meeting agreed, by 50 votes to 5, with 8 abstentions and 1 "refusal to vote" (1 delegation was absent), that the chairman had made a correct application of the convention and the rules of procedure. The five delegations which voted in the negative were Albania, Byelorussia, Bulgaria, Ukraine, and USSR. The Yugoslavian delegation "refused to vote," and the abstentions came from Austria, Bolivia, Czechoslovakia, Finland, France, Hungary, Italy, and Rumania.[63] Next it was decided to vote on the question of whether France had acted correctly in inviting the Baltic states to send representatives to the Paris Congress. First, however, by 52 votes to 9 (with 7 abstentions), it was agreed to use a secret ballot. The secret ballot resulted in 24 votes in the affirmative, 37 votes in the negative, 5 blank ballots, 2 ballots carrying the notation "abstention," and 1 irregular ballot. The doyen of the congress, who was in charge of the committee to count the ballots, made the following statement immediately after the votes had been counted and it was decided that France's actions were irregular: ". . . I hope, from the bottom of my heart, that the vote does not imply any blame with regard to the French government towards which we have contracted an imperishable debt of gratitude." [64]

The question was not resolved, however. In the succeeding plenary assembly the chairman confessed that he was still in the dark as to whether the Baltic states would be permitted to sign the final acts. This led to another full-scale debate (which, in effect, covered most of the ground already covered in previous meetings) and two more votes. The first vote, carried out by means of raised hands, was on the point

62. *Ibid.*, pp. 1049–51.
63. *Ibid.*, pp. 1050–51.
64. *Ibid.*, pp. 1052–53, 1054–55, and 1058–59.

of order of whether the meeting should close the discussions and proceed to a vote on the status of the Balkan countries. Although it was agreed by 42 to 5 that discussion should be closed, another long and lively debate followed. Finally, again by secret ballot, it was agreed 51 to 15 (with 6 blank ballots) that the Baltic states were not members of the union. With the exception of a formal statement by the Russian delegation criticizing the actions of the congress, received two days after the congress had adjourned, the "affair of the Baltic countries" ended for the Paris Congress.[65] An attempt to put the names of the Baltic countries back in the preamble of the postal convention at the Congress of Brussels was defeated by a vote of 48 to 9 (all nine being communist countries), but the problem was not raised at the Congress of Ottawa in 1957.[66]

The UPU did not solve all its problems of representation with the action of the Congress of Paris, however. In the congresses of Brussels and of Ottawa, the delegates were confronted with an argument over the status vis-à-vis the UPU of those countries which were divided as a result of World War II, and succeeding international political events: China, Germany, Korea, and Viet Nam. And, as long as the international political complications known as the "cold war" continue, it is very likely that each succeeding congress will also be faced with this problem.

The first issue of this sort arose in the May 1950 session of the executive and liaison committee. By that time, it will be recalled, the nationalistic government of China had taken refuge on the island of Formosa and the Communist government had taken control of the mainland. China was one of the countries that had been elected to send a delegate to the ELC meeting, and arrangements had been made for receiving a delegate from the Chinese postal administration at Taipeh. Just ten days before the meeting opened in Montreux, Switzerland, on May 5, 1950, the director of the bureau received a telegram from the minister of Foreign Affairs of the central government of the People's Republic of China in Peking, stating that its government was "the only government representing the Chinese people" and that it had named a delegate to the ELC. The director replied that the ELC itself would have to decide on the question of the representation of China, which it did. After a rather long discussion, in which both legal and political arguments were raised, it was decided by a secret vote of 6 to 5 (with 4 abstentions) to seat the delegate of the People's Republic of China as the only qualified representative of China. It was also decided, in view of the fact that the United Nations had not yet made a decision on the same point, to wait until that decision was taken and then poll the members of the UPU for their advice regarding future meetings of the ELC. At this point the Nationalist Chinese delegate walked out of the meeting

65. *Ibid.*, pp. 1063–77.
66. See Docs., Brussels Postal Congress (1952), II, 321–22.

followed by the delegations of the USSR and Czechoslovakia. The latter two delegations explained that their action was due to the temporary nature of the ELC decision. The USSR returned to participate in the work of the ELC at its seventh meeting, and the Czechoslovaks at the eighth. The delegate of the People's Republic of China arrived in Montreux on May 24 and participated in the work of the ELC until the closing meeting on the 26th.[67]

By the next session of the ELC, in May–June, 1951, three pertinent events had taken place. The UN had decided that the Nationalist Chinese government had the right to representation in UN conferences and meetings; the Korean conflict had started and Communist Chinese forces had intervened; and the bureau had taken a poll of the members of the union, which showed a clear majority of the UPU members against granting representation to the People's Republic of China. The ELC, after much discussion, decided, by means of a secret ballot, to accept the poll and confine China's representation in the ELC to the Nationalist government.[68]

Since 1951 the question of the representation of China has been raised in each of the union's congresses and would probably have been raised each year in the ELC had not China been replaced on that body by another country in 1952. To that problem has been added that of Germany, Korea, and Viet Nam. In December 1949, the government of the Republic of Korea took advantage of Article XVIII of the final protocol of the Paris Postal Convention, discussed above, and notified the French government through diplomatic channels that she acceded to the Paris convention. The French government accepted the communication and notified the members of the UPU that Korea was thus a member in good standing. In 1951, Viet Nam (the southern part) made formal application for membership in the UPU, according to the procedure set forth in the new admissions article of the Paris convention. The Swiss government accepted the communication, canvassed the members of the UPU, and received a two-thirds majority vote in favor of Viet Nam's admission. Finally, the authorities of the Federal Republic of Germany had notified the Belgian government in 1955 that she also acceded to the Brussels Postal Convention. (The procedure laid down in the final protocol of the Paris convention had been renewed for Germany at the Brussels Congress in 1952 and the new host country had

67. UPU, *Documents de la Commission exécutive et de liaison, Session de mai 1950* (Berne, 1950), pp. 13–17 and 139–46, and *Compte rendu analytique,* pp. 6–7. The following countries were represented at the meeting in which the vote on China's representation took place: Australia, Colombia, Czechoslovakia, Egypt, France, Great Britain, India, Mexico, Netherlands, Portugal, Sweden, Switzerland, Turkey, United States, USSR, and Yugoslavia. A Nationalist Chinese delegate was present, but was not permitted to vote.

68. UPU, *Documents de la Commission exécutive et de liaison, Session de mai–juin 1951, Compte rendu analytique* (Berne, 1951), pp. 6–7. The results of the secret ballot were 10 (to accept the implications of the poll) to 6, with 3 abstentions.

been designated to receive Germany's accession.) The Belgian government had accepted the communication and notified the member countries.[69]

In the case of China, the delegation of the USSR, supported by one or more East European Communist delegations, argued at both the Brussels and Ottawa congresses that the People's Republic of China and not Nationalist China was the "true representative of the Chinese people" and that the work of the UPU would be seriously hampered by the absence of Communist China. On both occasions, the delegate of the USSR or one of the East European Communist delegates proposed to the congress that "the delegation from the reactionary Kuomintang clique" be expelled and an invitation be extended to the People's Republic of China. By 1952 the opponents of the admission of Communist China were much better organized than the opposition to the representation of the Baltic states had been at the Paris Congress. The discussions were kept to a minimum, consisting of statements from the nine Communist nations and one or two answers from countries opposed to Communist China's representation, and the subject was never brought to a vote directly but was resolved on points of procedure. In Brussels, it was decided (53 to 9) simply to end discussion on the matter, and at Ottawa it was done by defeating an Egyptian proposal to set up a special study group on the problem.[70] Both times the opponents relied heavily upon the previous decisions of the UN on the same matter.

Regarding Korea, Viet Nam, and Germany, the proponents of the representation of the Communist halves of these three countries used a different technique. Rather than demanding the expulsion of one set of delegates in order to substitute another, emphasis was placed on the argument that the actual representatives — those of the Federal Republic of Germany, the Republic of Korea, and Viet Nam (South) — could not be considered as representing the whole of the countries whose name they bore. Consequently, it was argued, to make the situation fit the facts it was necessary to send out *additional* invitations to the governments of the other halves: the German Democratic Republic, the Korean Popular Democratic Republic, and Viet Nam (North). Despite the difference in logic, the proponents were no more successful than they had been with regard to Communist China; one by one the congresses, by strong majorities, rejected their claims.[71]

In the overall problem of representation, it is worthwhile to note the importance of the host country. The host country is responsible for sending out invitations. The presence or absence of a delegation can have an important impact on the course of the deliberations. The host

69. See Docs., Brussels Postal Congress (1952), II, 226 and 228–29; and Docs., Ottawa Postal Congress (1957), II, 183–84.

70. Docs., Brussels Postal Congress (1952), II, 104, 216–26, and 323–24.

71. *Ibid.*, pp. 226–30 and 232–34; and Docs., Ottawa Postal Congress (1957), II, 179–93, 1166–67, and 1171.

country also receives notifications of ratifications and, in the case of Japan, Germany, Spain, and Korea, was made the recipient of acts of accession. For example, the French government received a communication from the German Democratic Republic through the intermediary of the Czechoslovakian government in 1952, stating that it was assuming membership in the union in accordance with Article XVII of the final protocol of the Paris convention. The French did not, however, follow up on the communication, thus leaving the field clear for a notification from the German Federal Republic. When the Federal Republic's communication arrived at Brussels, the Belgian government accepted it without question.[72]

Concerning new membership, on the other hand, it is the responsibility of the Swiss government to accept diplomatic notifications of accession to the postal convention. The Swiss government is more or less freed of responsibility for making unpopular decisions, however, because it is now protected by the clause which provides for a vote on each new admission and a two-thirds majority agreement before an applicant can become a member.

As long as major changes do not occur in the international political climate, there is a great deal of doubt whether the People's Republic of China, the German Democratic Republic, the Korean Popular Democratic Republic, and North Viet Nam will be permitted representation in the union. Just as clearly, the congresses of the union will be faced with requests for their representation for a long time to come. This lack of universality of membership, however, will not necessarily do damage to the universality of application of the rules of the UPU. According to the director of the UPU: "Even those (countries) which are not formally members — and they are very few — actually carry out the Acts." [73]

c. The Basic Acts of the UPU

THE ORGANIZATION of the UPU, its functions, and the principal record of its accomplishments are contained in the Universal Postal Convention and its various annexes and appended documents. The most recent postal convention, that dated 1957, is the direct successor of the Treaty Concerning the Creation of a General Postal Union of 1874. That the creators of the UPU found a valid formula for international cooperation is evidenced by the fact that the UPU has made some 14 major revisions to its basic treaty while maintaining the continuity of its search to improve the international mails. The finding of this formula is perhaps one of the most important achievements of the UPU.

72. See Docs., Brussels Postal Congress (1952), II, 230–32.
73. Dr. Edouard Weber, "The UPU Today and Tomorrow," *Union Postale,* LXXXVIII, No. 8 (August, 1963), 115A.

1. Nature of the Universal Postal Convention

The legal basis of the UPU is provided by the Universal Postal Convention, the union's basic document. The convention is an agreement between states, a treaty drafted by representatives of states with plenipotentiary powers and ratified or acceded to according to the constitutional process of each state. Once ratified, or acceded to, the provisions become obligatory upon the governments which have taken this action under the general rules of international law which govern all contractual relations between states, especially the principle of *pacta sunt servanda*.

This is true despite the preference of the drafters of the various postal conventions for the word "country" or the words "member countries" over the more conventional "states" and "member states," and the constant admonition that "administrations shall" and other numerous references to "administrations" and "member administrations." Article 1 of the Ottawa Postal Convention (1957), for instance, starts out: "The countries between which the present convention is concluded form . . ." and paragraph 1 of Article 3, dealing with membership, states: "Any sovereign country may apply for admission as a member of the Universal Postal Union." The use of the word "country" in preference to "state" is justified somewhat by the fact that, as discussed earlier, certain non-independent entities have been given the designation of member of the union with the same voting rights in congresses as truly independent states. One country took these variations from normal practice so seriously that it proposed, at the Congress of Vienna in 1891, that the appellation of representatives to congresses in the convention be changed from "plenipotentiaries" to simple "delegates" and "ratification" to "approval." For obvious reasons the proposal was decisively defeated and no similar proposals have since been made.[74] Consequently, nomenclature notwithstanding, the UPU follows the normal practice of most other international organizations with delegates to congresses armed with plenipotentiary powers conferred by the highest organ of the state, or the administering state as the case may be, and the postal conventions are ratified in the normal manner.

The use of the term "postal administration," or simply "administration," can be viewed in the same manner. It is justified to a certain extent in view of the fact that it is, in the final analysis, the postal administration which actually carries out most of the obligations regarding the international mail set forth in the postal convention, and that delegations to congresses are usually made up primarily of officials from postal administrations. Also it is true that some of the obligations in the convention can, in some states, be introduced into domestic practice without involving a nation's legislative process or without even reaching the desk of the chief executive. In this case, as in the previous one, the use of terms other than the normal ones should be

74. Docs., Vienna Postal Congress (1891), pp. 417–19, 691, and 713–15.

viewed only as a harmless fiction. It is abundantly clear that the universal postal conventions are the creation of the governments of states and that it is the state which has the ultimate responsibility for carrying out the obligations which are set forth.

The universal postal convention is in reality four documents. The Ottawa convention, for example, is made up of the convention proper, a Final Protocol, a Detailed Regulations for Implementing the Universal Postal Convention, and an annex entitled Provisions Concerning Airmail. To be considered a member of the UPU, states must accept the obligations set forth in all four documents.

The convention proper is divided into two parts, one dealing with the constitution of the union and the general rules of the international postal service, and the other dealing with provisions concerning the letter post. The first part is further subdivided into chapters covering the constitution of the union (the material that will be discussed in this chapter); the organization of the union, which includes the establishment of congresses and conferences, the two permanent committees and the international bureau; the final acts of the union; proposals to amend or interpret the acts of the union between congresses; and arbitration procedures. The first part of the convention also includes 14 articles setting forth the general rules of the international postal service including obligations upon all parties to: 1] provide freedom of transit of the mails of other contracting parties; 2] make no charges for postal services other than those set forth in the final acts; 3] exempt official mail, mail to or from prisoners of war and civil internees, and mail for the blind from all postal charges; 4] use the official forms for postal transactions described in the convention; 5] issue postage stamps; and 6] adopt, or "propose to the legislature of their countries," the adoption of penal measures for the punishment and prevention of certain undesirable acts such as the counterfeiting of stamps. Other articles in this category permit countries to suspend the transit of mails of those countries which refuse to reciprocate; suspend temporarily the international mail service under certain exceptional circumstances; and issue postal identity cards. Finally, a common monetary unit is established, equivalents of the monetary unit are described, and a general procedure is set forth for the settlement of accounts.[75]

The second part of the postal convention sets forth the general rules for the operation of the international letter post, including a definition of the items permitted in the letter post; types of charges and the method of payment; procedures for withdrawing letters from the mail and for the disposition of undeliverable items; rules concerning mail and the customs; provisions concerning international reply coupons; express items; and the procedure to be followed in handling inquiries and requests for information from the public. Also included is a section dealing with registered items and the allocation of charges among postal administrations, especially those stemming from the transit of mails. The pro-

75. See Ottawa Postal Convention (1957), Arts. 1–47.

visions in this section of the convention are mostly general in nature and, as is the case with the first part of the convention, are a mixture of obligations, procedures, and permissible activities.[76]

The universal postal convention ends with an article dealing with its entry into force and its duration, and is followed by the signatures of the plenipotentiary delegates who attended the congress which revised it. The pertinent article of the Ottawa Postal Convention (1957), Art. 84, reads as follows:

> *Entry into force and duration of the Convention.*
>
> The present Convention shall come into force on the 1st of April 1959, and shall remain in operation for an indefinite period.
>
> In faith whereof, the Plenipotentiaries of the Governments of the above named Countries have signed the present Convention in a single copy which shall lie in the Archives of the Government of Canada and of which a copy shall be delivered to each Party.
>
> Done at Ottawa, the 3rd of October 1957.

The final protocol is a separate document, attached to the convention proper and given the same force and effect, which sets forth reservations and derogations to the provisions of the universal postal convention. The use of this device is as old as the UPU itself, and no convention has been without one. The final protocol to the Treaty of 1874 left the treaty open to accession by the government of France, which had been forced to withhold its ratification, and provided that if France failed to accede, the convention would still be binding on the other ratifiers.[77]

Over the years as the provisions of the convention have become more numerous and complicated, the items in the final protocols have increased accordingly. The final protocol of the Ottawa convention, for example, has 18 articles, including seven general reservations to provisions of the convention, five specific reservations, and six of an operational nature. An example of the general reservations is the article, with which we became familiar in the historical section, which permits postal administrations to raise charges for various items in the letter post, fixed in the convention, by 60 percent or reduce them by 20 percent. Another example is Article 1 dealing with literature for the blind. Article 40 of the convention states that such literature is exempt from all charges. However, Article 1 of the final protocol states: "Notwithstanding the provision of Article 40 . . . those countries which do not concede free postage to literature for the blind, including letters in writing used by the blind posted unsealed, in their internal service have the option of making a charge which must not in any event exceed the one in their internal service." Exceptions to conventional provisions are also made

76. See *ibid.*, Arts. 48–83.
77. See Docs., Berne Postal Congress (1874), pp. 165–68.

for the low rates on commercial and printed matter and samples of merchandise, international reply coupons, registration and advice of delivery fees, and the use of the metric decimal system in calculating weights. Another general reservation permits administrations to refuse to accept items brought from some other country by other means to take advantage of lower postal rates.[78] Among the specific reservations in the final protocol is one which permits nine named countries to refuse to change the address on correspondence or to withdraw an item from the mails at the request of the sender; one which permits four countries to refuse registered letters with articles of value enclosed; two concerning exceptions to the conventional provisions dealing with transit; and one permitting special storage charges.[79] The six operational provisions in the final protocol permit states which have signed and ratified the convention to accede later to the agreements; permit members which were not present at the Ottawa Congress to accede at a later date; set the time limit for these accessions; make the provisions concerning airmail an integral part of the convention; and permit the executive and liaison committee and the consultative committee for postal studies to assume their functions as revised by the congress in advance of the entry into force of the convention.[80] The final protocol is concluded with a formula giving it the same force and effect as the convention and is followed by the same signatures as those which follow the convention.

The third basic document is the Detailed Regulations for Implementing the Universal Postal Convention. The legal basis for this document is found in Article 24 of the Ottawa Postal Convention which reads: "The Administrations of member countries draw up by common consent, in the Detailed Regulations, the detailed rules and procedures necessary for the implementation of the Convention . . ." The regulations contain a formula for its entry into force and duration.[81] This document, as its name indicates, contains more specific rules and regulations for the guidance of administrations in carrying out the general principles set forth in the convention. Its provisions are patterned, more or less, on the convention. There is a general constitutional section dealing with the details of the operation of the bodies of the union, especially the bureau; general provisions concerning postal services; provisions concerning the letter mail and all of its subcategories; and a long section

78. Ottawa Postal Convention (1957), Final Protocol, Arts. 1–4, 6, 7, and 9. The rules regarding the international reply coupon are an interesting variation. Article 56 of the Ottawa Postal Convention makes the issue of reply coupons obligatory. The final protocol, however, states that while all administrations must accept coupons from a foreign country and must issue a stamp in return, a country may refuse to sell a coupon to its own citizens. *Ibid.*, Art. VII.

79. *Ibid.*, Arts. 5, 7, and 10–12.

80. *Ibid.*, Arts. 13–17.

81. Article 191 of the Detailed Regulations of the Ottawa Postal Convention reads: "1. The present Detailed Regulations shall come into force on the day on which the Universal Postal Convention comes into operation. 2. They shall have the same duration as the Convention unless renewed by common consent between the parties concerned."

dealing with transit charges, including the method of statistical operations and the settlement of accounts. To give an idea of the relationship between the convention and the regulations, Article 48 of the convention sets forth the categories of articles that are admitted in the letter mail, while Article 124 of the regulations goes into detail on the matter of how items of the letter mail should be made up and addressed. Article 45 of the convention states that certain forms should be used between postal administrations, while the regulations contain over forty pages of models of the forms to be used, with indications of size and color.[82]

The concept of using two separate documents, one with the provisions dealing with the constitution and organization of the union and the basic principles of the international postal service, was introduced in Berne in 1874, and its purpose was to provide a means of organizing the work of the UPU meetings. If all the basic provisions were separate from the transitory ones of a primarily administrative nature, they could be discussed and revised at relatively longer intervals of time. The regulations, on the other hand, would have to be discussed and revised more frequently, and this task could be left to representatives of postal administrations without the necessity of having a regular diplomatic conference. Thus Article 18 of the Berne Postal Treaty of 1874 states: "At least every three years, a plenipotentiary Congress of the countries participating in the treaty will meet to perfect the system of the Union, to introduce the changes judged necessary and to discuss common affairs." On the other hand, Article 13, the predecessor of Article 24 of the present convention mentioned above, stated: "The postal administrations of the various countries which make up the Union are competent to fix, by common agreement, all the regulations and details necessary for the execution of the present treaty. It is understood that the provisions of this regulation can always be modified by common agreement among the Administrations of the Union." [83]

The concept did not work out as expected, however. Each succeeding congress has undertaken the revision of both the convention and the regulations and usually the same delegates sign both documents. One reason may have been that the drafters of the early conventions and regulations did not have the experience necessary to know what was fundamental and what was transitory. Later, tradition played an important role. Whatever the reason, the concept did not work for the UPU as it did for the International Telegraph Union.[84]

82. See *Annotated Acts* (1957), 1ᵉʳ fascicule, pp. 242–82.

83. See also Docs., Paris Postal Congress (1878), p. 8.

84. The Telegraph Union divided the subject matter of its final acts into a convention and regulations in 1865. For the first ten years the Telegraph Union found that it was revising both parts of its final documents at the regularly scheduled plenipotentiary conference, as was the case with the UPU. After it undertook a major redrafting of its fundamental documents in 1874, however, it was able to get along on administrative conferences only until its merger with the Radiotelegraph Union in 1932. Although the International Telecommunication Union (the name it took after the merger) has not been able since that time to go so

Many unsuccessful attempts were made, however, to realize this principle in the period before World War II. Proposals to rid the convention of all administrative and transitory details were introduced at the congresses of Vienna (1891), Washington, D.C. (1897), Rome (1906), Madrid (1920), and Buenos Aires (1939). All such proposals were turned down, usually on the basis that they would fly in the face of "history and tradition." [85] More to the point, however, was the fact that over the years more and more provisions of a permanent nature found their way into the regulations and more transitory details found their way into the postal conventions, to the point that the time involved for a revision was more than the delegates wanted to take.

There is hope now, however, that the union may be able to realize its long-sought principle. The Paris Congress of 1947 ordered the newly created Executive and Liaison Committee to undertake a study of the problem and to come up with proposals. The first proposals, presented to the Brussels Congress of 1952, which included very drastic revisions, were turned down, but a new modified proposal ordered by the Congress of Ottawa in 1957 is before the members of the union and has a good chance of providing the next congress with a satisfactory framework in which to make the long-desired changeover.[86]

The basic rules and regulations of the international airmail service are not in the postal convention itself, or in its regulations, but in a separate document entitled "Provisions concerning Airmail." However, the special article of the final protocol of the convention mentioned earlier, gives it the same force and effect as the convention, thus making it mandatory for all members of the UPU to subscribe to it. This article reads as follows: "The Provisions concerning airmail are annexed to the Universal Postal Convention and are regarded as forming an integral part of it and of its Detailed Regulations." [87] Despite the fact that it is an "integral part" of the convention and regulations, it too is signed separately by the delegations to the postal congresses.

The Provisions concerning Airmail have two operative sections. The first, general provisions, are broken down into: 1] Admission and Charges;   2] Routing, Delivery, Redirection and Return to Origin; and

long a period without a plenipotentiary conference, such conferences to revise the telecommunication convention have been more infrequent than administrative conferences. (See Codding, op. cit., pp. 27–30.)

85. See Docs., Buenos Aires Postal Congress (1939), II, 37–39. See also, Docs., Vienna Postal Congress (1891), pp. 1, 371–76, and 632–39; Docs., Washington D.C. Postal Congress (1897), pp. 16 and 407–409; and Docs., Rome Postal Congress (1906), pp. 302–306.

86. An account of the work of the ELC since Ottawa can be found in UPU, Documents de la Commission exécutive et de liaison (session de mai 1960) et de la Sous-Commission de la revision générale de la convention (réunions de septembre 1959 et de mars 1960) (Berne, 1960). See also Docs., Paris Postal Congress (1947), I, 52, and II, Docs., Brussels Postal Congress (1952), I, 56–57 and 109–608, and II, 282–93; and Docs., Ottawa Postal Congress (1957), I, 117–19, and II, 299–303, 325, and 329–30.

87. Ottawa Postal Convention (1957), Final Protocol, Art. 13.

3] Air Conveyance Charges. The second, operational provisions, is sub-divided into: *1*] Rules for Dispatch and Routing;   2] Accounting, Settlement of Accounts; and   *3*] Information to be Supplied by Postal Administrations and by the International Bureau. There are no separate regulations as in the case of the convention.[88]

Airmail regulations were placed in a separate document by the Congress of London in 1929 on the basis of work done by The Hague Airmail Conference of 1927, it will be recalled, because at that time international airmail did not concern all the members of the UPU, and it was felt that their revision could best be left to the countries directly concerned. Consequently, from 1929 to 1957, a provision was inserted in the final protocol to each convention providing that a special airmail conference could be called upon the demand of any three members of the union to revise these provisions.[89] Although several restricted airmail conferences were held in the 1930's, none made proposals directly concerning the annex to the convention. Contrary to what had been foreseen, it was the regular congresses that undertook the task of the revision of airmail regulations in the same manner as for the other provisions of the convention and regulations. This rather abnormal situation was discussed fully for the first time at the Congress of Ottawa (1957) and it was decided to direct the executive and liaison committee to study the possibility of eliminating the separate airmail provisions and to incorporate them into the body of the postal convention and its regulations.[90]

There are four basic documents then to which each member of the UPU must subscribe: The Universal Postal Convention; the Final Protocol to the Convention; the Detailed Regulations for Implementing the Universal Postal Convention; and the Provisions Concerning Airmail.

2. *Nature of the Agreements*

Over the years the UPU has extended its sphere of influence over other activities of international concern to postal administrations that are not directly connected to the letter post. The practice of the UPU has been to place the rules and regulations of these other services in separate documents known as Agreements. As stated in paragraph 3 of Article 22 of the Ottawa postal convention:

The other services are regulated by the following Agreements:
1)   Agreement concerning Insured Letters and Boxes;
2)   Agreement concerning Parcel Post;
3)   Agreement concerning Postal Money Orders and Postal Traveler's Checks;

88. See *ibid.*, Provisions Concerning Airmail.
89. See, for example, Docs., London Postal Congress (1929), II, 675.
90. Docs., Ottawa Postal Congress (1957), II, 59, 342–43, 372, 375, 1143, and 1157. The Congress of Ottawa also deleted the paragraphs in the final protocol which permitted the calling of restricted airmail conferences.

4) Agreement concerning Postal Checking Accounts;
5) Agreement concerning Cash on Delivery Items;
6) Agreement concerning Collection of Bills;
7) Agreement concerning the International Savings Bank Service; and
8) Agreement concerning Subscriptions to Newspapers and Periodicals.

While these documents take the form of a treaty similar to the postal convention itself, contrary to what is true concerning the convention the adherence of members of the UPU is entirely optional. Members may undertake the obligations set forth in one or more of these documents in the conventional manner (signature and ratification or accession), but only those delegations whose countries have undertaken that obligation may present proposals concerning these acts, and only those delegations whose countries have undertaken that obligation or who declare that they have been ordered by their government to sign at the end of the congress can vote in the deliberations.[91]

As a general rule, these eight additional treaties are similar in form and content to the universal postal convention with the exception that they do not make reference to the constitution and organization of the union. The Agreement concerning Insured Letters and Boxes, for example, is divided into five chapters, with a total of 18 separate articles. Chapter I, "General Provisions," is made up of two articles, one dealing with the nature of the agreement and one defining "insured value." Chapter II, "Conditions of Admission," has four articles dealing with conditions under which insured articles will be admitted into the international postal service, including weight and size, authorized enclosures, prohibited enclosures, and treatment of articles wrongly admitted. Chapter III, "Charges and Fees," sets forth the charges that will be collected from the sender, and exempts from charges all official insured letters between postal administrations and between postal administrations and the international bureau. Chapter IV, "Responsibility," sets forth the principle that postal administrations are responsible for loss of, theft from, or damage to, insured items; and then goes into detail about exceptions to the principle of responsibility, cessation of responsibility, how the sender is indemnified, and the manner in which responsibility is apportioned between postal administrations. Chapter V, "Miscellaneous and Final Provisions," includes articles dealing with the provisions of the universal postal convention that apply to the insured letter and box service, the manner in which revisions to the agreement can be made between congresses, and the date of entry into force and the duration of the agreement.[92]

Each of these eight agreements has its own Detailed Regulations for Implementing the Agreement, which contain the more transitory details of execution. The regulations have the same force and effect as

91. See Ottawa Postal Convention (1957), Art. 13, and Docs., Ottawa Postal Congress (1957), II, 35–43, *Règlement du Congrès,* Art. 2, para. 6, in Docs., Ottawa Postal Congress (1957), II, 35.
92. *Ibid.,* pp. 183–90.

the agreement to which they refer and are signed in the same manner by the delegations of the countries which participated in their drafting. Both the regulations and the agreements to which they refer are discussed and revised at the regular periodic congresses of the union. The agreements on Insured Letters and Boxes and Parcel Post also have a final protocol similar to that appended to the postal convention.

The agreements vary greatly in length. The longest is the Agreement concerning Parcel Post, with its 47 articles. The Regulations of the parcel post have an additional 45 articles. The smallest is the Agreement concerning the Subscriptions to Newspapers and Periodicals (16 articles) and its regulations of 15 articles. Because of the fact that each of the agreements deals with an object of intrinsic value or with the transfer of funds, the subject of responsibility is covered in detail. Also important are the details of handling and the rates to be charged for the various services.[93]

There is also a great variance in the number of countries which have become parties to the various agreements. The most popular agreement is that concerning parcel post and the least, that concerning the international savings bank service. According to the *Annual Report* of 1962, 88 countries had signed and ratified, or adhered to the parcel post agreement of 1957 by December 31, 1962 (18 additional countries had signed, but failed to ratify). The figures for the other agreements were as follows: Agreement on Insured Letters and Boxes, 81 (15); Agreement concerning Postal Money Orders and Postal Traveler's Checks, 66 (17); Agreement concerning Postal Checking Account Transfers, 46 (16); Agreement concerning Cash on Delivery Items, 57 (15); Agreement concerning the Collection of Bills, 51 (16); and the Agreement concerning Subscriptions to Newspapers and Periodicals, 41 (15). The international savings bank service agreement had only 14 countries which had signed and ratified or adhered (three other countries had signed but failed to ratify).[94]

There has never been a genuine attempt to make adherence to all of the agreements obligatory for members of the union. Each agreement was drafted originally by those countries which had already inaugurated the service in question in its own domestic relations. The members of the union seem content to leave the agreements to those countries which are interested, and are not willing to force any country to take up a new service.[95] There have been recent attempts, however, to encourage members to become parties to certain of the agreements. The Paris Congress in 1947, at the suggestion of the delegate from Uruguay, exhorted the union administrations to become parties at least to the agreements concerning Cash on Delivery Items and Subscriptions to Newspapers and

93. *Ibid.*, III, 181–526.
94. *Annual Report, 1962*, pp. 49–52.
95. For the approach of the ITU to a similar situation, see Codding, *op. cit.*, pp. 324–26.

Periodicals in order to promote "the cultural, economic and spiritual rapprochement of people." [96] The Brussels Congress of 1952 agreed unanimously to a similar recommendation, also proposed by the delegation of Uruguay, but which added the Agreement concerning Transfers to and from Postal Checking Accounts.[97] There is no positive evidence, however, that these exhortations have resulted in any increase in the number of contracting parties to the agreements in question.

3. Revision and Modification

The postal convention provides two principal methods for its revision and modification as well as that of the agreements and their respective regulations. The more important is the plenipotentiary congress which meets approximately every five years, and in which all members of the union may participate. Although it will be discussed in detail at a later point, in general the system is as follows: All provisions of the final acts are subject to amendment, and every member country has the right to make proposals concerning the convention and its regulations and every agreement and its regulations to which they adhere.[98]

Each congress draws up its own rules of procedure and thus establishes the method by which changes can be made. Prior to the 1947 Paris Congress, a simple majority in favor was all that was required to change any part of the final acts. Since 1947, the voting requirements have been stiffened. The rules of procedure of the Ottawa Congress in 1957, which are typical, require that proposals to modify Part I, Section 1, of the postal convention (that part dealing with the constitution and organization of the union) must receive more than half of the votes of all the countries represented at the congress and at least two thirds of all the members of the union represented at the congress and entitled to vote must be present at the moment of the vote. Changes in the remainder of the convention and all other official documents are decided by a majority of the members present and voting, provided that at least half of the countries represented at the congress are present at the time of voting. Abstentions, or blank or spoiled ballots, are not taken into consideration when determining the required majority.[99]

There is no need at this point to go into further detail on the method of revising and modifying the final acts of the UPU. Suffice it to say that member countries are not hesitant to make proposals for the modification of the postal treaties — over 1,000 were made at Ottawa alone — and the congresses have no hesitation in making changes when they are

96. Docs., Paris Postal Congress (1947), II, 1058.
97. Docs., Ottawa Postal Congress (1952), I, 92; and II, 319.
98. Ottawa Postal Convention (1957), Arts. 11 and 13 and Regulations, Art. 101.
99. See Docs., Ottawa Postal Congress (1957), II, 38. See also below, pp. 141–44.

considered necessary or even helpful to the union and the international postal system.[100]

The UPU is not content to make revisions at five-year intervals, and has provided a convenient method for revision of the convention and its regulations in the intervals between congresses. The procedure which follows, contained in the Ottawa Postal Convention, has had its equivalent in all the postal conventions, starting with that of Berne in 1874: (1) In the interval between congresses, any administration of a member country has the right to submit to the international bureau proposals for the modification of the convention and its regulations and to any agreement and its regulations to which it is a party. To be eligible for consideration, all such proposals must be supported by at least two other administrations. (2) The proposal is circulated by the bureau to all contracting parties for their observations. Amendments are not permitted. (3) The proposal and the observations are then submitted to all contracting parties with an invitation to pronounce for or against the proposal. A period of two months is provided for replies; all parties not replying within the two-month period are considered to have abstained. (4) The proposed modification becomes effective if it obtains:

A]   the unanimity of the votes if it involves amendments to the provisions of Articles 1 to 47 (Part I), 48, 49, 52, 55, 68, 69, 71 to 74, 76 to 83 (Part II), 84 (Part III) of the Convention, of any of the Articles of its Final Protocol, and of Articles 101, 102, 103, 106 (paras. 2–5), 112 (para. 1), 116, 117, 119, 134, 169, 173, 180, 184 and 191 of its Detailed Regulations;

B]   two thirds of the votes if it involves amendments of principle to provisions other than those mentioned under A];

C]   the majority of the votes if it is a question of:

> *1*) editorial amendments to the provisions of the Convention and its Detailed Regulations other than those mentioned under A];
>
> *2*) an interpretation of the provisions of the Convention, its Final Protocol and its Detailed Regulations, except in the case of a disagreement to be submitted to arbitration as provided in Article 33.[101]

The procedure for changes in the agreements and their detailed regulations is similar except for the fact that only those members which are parties may participate. Further, each of the agreements sets forth the conditions to be fulfilled for the approval of proposals, especially the voting majority needed for various provisions.[102]

---

100. For the proposals made at the Ottawa Congress, see Docs., Ottawa Postal Congress (1957), Vol. I. Volume III contains the final acts of the Ottawa Congress. All changes made by the congress in the final acts of the previous congress are italicized for easy reference.

101. Ottawa Postal Convention (1957), Art. 29, para. 1. (See also Arts. 27 and 28.)

102. See for example, Agreement concerning Postal Money Orders and Postal Traveler's Checks (1957), Art. 44; and Agreement concerning Cash on Delivery Items (1957), Art. 17.

As a general rule, unanimity of agreement is required for any change of substance in the convention and the agreements. Only lesser changes can get by with a two-thirds affirmative vote. In the case of the convention, for example, unanimity is necessary for all of the constitutional and organizational provisions, all of the articles dealing with the general rules concerning the international postal service, all of the articles dealing with transit charges and their allocation, and a majority of the articles dealing with registered items. Only in the general provisions concerning the letter post would a majority of the articles fall within the two-thirds rule. Even there, the more important articles dealing with postage fees would fall within the unanimity rule.

Successful proposals for changes in the final acts "do not take effect until at least three months" after their promulgation.[103] Promulgation of amendments to the convention, the agreements, the final protocols, and the annexes to those acts consist of a "diplomatic declaration" to that effect by the Swiss government to the governments of the member countries. Amendments to the various detailed regulations and their final protocols "are recorded and notified to Administrations by the International Bureau." [104]

Despite the strong majorities needed to modify the final acts between congresses, the UPU has made frequent use of this procedure. The following table gives the number of times proposals have been submitted and voted upon, the number of times the proposals have con-

MODIFICATION OF FINAL ACTS BETWEEN CONGRESSES

Period	Votes Held	Documents to which they referred					Approved	Disapproved
		C	ILB	PP	PMO	CB		
1878–1885	20	13	3	4	0	0	19	1
1885–1891	29	14	1	8	4	2	25	4
1891–1897	28	21	0	3	4	0	10	18
1897–1906	5	5	0	0	0	0	5	0
1906–1920	6	4	1	1	0	0	3	3
1920–1924	11	8	0	3	0	0	8	3
1924–1929	7	7	0	0	0	0	6	1
1929–1934	2	2	0	0	0	0	2	0
1934–1939	7	6	0	1	0	0	4	3
1939–1947	3	0	0	3	0	0	3	0
1947–1952	1	0	0	1	0	0	1	0
1952–1957	3	2	0	1	0	0	3	0
1957–1962*	0	0	0	0	0	0	0	0
Totals	122	82	5	25	8	2	89	33[105]

* Date of last available information. This period will not end until the convening of the 15th congress. (See Annual Reports, 1957–1962.)

103. Ottawa Postal Convention (1957), Art. 31.
104. *Ibid.*, Art. 30.
105. *Annotated Acts* (*1957*), 1ᵉʳ fascicule, p. 60.

cerned the Convention (C), and the Agreements concerning Insured Letters and Boxes (ILB), Parcel Post (PP), Postal Money Orders and Traveler's Checks (PMO), and Collection of Bills (CB) as well as their adoption and rejection.

4. Ratification and Its Problems

The procedure for ratification of the final acts of the UPU congresses is fairly simple. The Ottawa Postal Convention provides, for example:

> The Acts adopted by a Congress are ratified as soon as possible by the signatory Countries; the ratifications are communicated to the government of the country where the Congress was held and by that government to the governments of the signatory countries.

The Convention also provides that:

> As from the date fixed for the entry into force of the acts adopted by a Congress, the acts of the previous Congress are rescinded.[106]

Usually a relatively long period is provided between the conclusion of a congress and the date when the final acts come into force, to allow countries plenty of time to ratify before the previous final acts are rescinded, the average time being a little over a year.

Nevertheless, there are usually a large number of countries which fail to ratify the final acts before the new ones come into force, and even some which never ratify. The final acts of the Congress of Ottawa, for example, were signed on October 3, 1957, and did not come into force until April 1, 1959, almost 18 months later. By April 1, 1959, however, only 18 of the 96 signatories to the Ottawa convention had completed their ratification.[107] The countries which had ratified within the time limit were: Belgian Congo, Belgium, Canada, Denmark, Egypt, Finland, Japan, Jordan, Lebanon, Mexico, Norway, San Marino, Sweden, Switzerland, Syria, Tunisia, United States, and United States territories. By the end of 1962 the number had increased to only 78 out of 96.[108] Another example is in the ratifications of the final acts of the Congress of Brussels in 1952. A period of approximately twelve months was provided between the closing of the Congress of Brussels and the date on which the final acts came into force. Not only had a majority of members failed to ratify before the effective date of the final acts, but of the 90 signatories, 11 had failed to ratify by December 31, 1957, the year of the Congress of Ottawa. These countries were Afghanistan, Bolivia, Brazil, Colombia, Costa Rica, Ecuador, Iran, Iraq, Liberia, Panama, and

106. Ottawa Postal Convention (1957), Art. 25, paras. 1 and 3.
107. *Annual Report, 1959,* pp. 36–38.
108. *Annual Report, 1962,* p. 11.

Uruguay.[109] Further, by the date of the coming into effect of the final acts of the Congress of Ottawa, ten had still failed to ratify the final acts of the Congress of Brussels.[110]

The failure to ratify has plagued the UPU for many years. Only the Treaty of 1874 was almost exempt. Representatives of the signatories to the 1874 treaty held a special meeting on October 9, 1874, seven months after the postal conference, and exchanged ratifications in person. By a special protocol, it will be remembered, France was permitted to ratify late. The increased and widening membership of the UPU was given as the reason for discarding this method by succeeding congresses and for adopting a process of independent ratification.[111] From that time on, there have always been countries which have failed to ratify in time, and the question has arisen as to the status of those countries after the new final acts come into effect and the older ones are rescinded.

The question was raised at the Congress of Cairo (1934) and at the Congress of Brussels (1952). On the first occasion, Germany had presented a proposal to the effect that there be a temporary application of all new acts to all states which had been delinquent in ratifying. The German proposal was dropped by the sponsor after the Japanese delegation protested that it could not be done legally.[112] On the second occasion, the USSR introduced a proposal which would have prohibited those countries which had failed to ratify the new acts from voting in any union conferences and meetings and on the admission of new members between congresses. The Russian proposal was narrowly defeated in a secret ballot. The congress did recommend, however, that all members ratify as soon as possible.[113]

In general, those who supported the tightening of ratification requirements argued along legal grounds. The convention, it was stated, is a treaty. Legal obligations to carry out the treaty, and the other acts dependent upon it, arose only upon ratification. Those countries which failed to ratify, therefore, were under no obligation to carry out the rules and regulations of the international mails. Or, as stated by the Polish delegate, those which failed to ratify were benefiting from the rights of membership in the union without the responsibilities.

The proponents of the status quo, on the other hand, followed more practical lines. They argued that those countries which had deferred or entirely neglected ratification of the new convention had (although no facts were presented to support the contention) nevertheless *always* conformed to the rules laid down by the new convention and had put them into force without reserve or restriction. In a like manner, the

109. See *Annual Report, 1957*, p. 30.
110. See *Annual Report, 1959*, p. 33.
111. See *Annotated Acts (1957)*, 1ᵉʳ fascicule, pp. 58–59.
112. Docs., Cairo Postal Congress (1934), I, 23; and II, 97, 508, and 624.
113. Docs., Brussels Postal Congress (1952), I, 188; and II, 383. The vote was 33 for, 34 against, with 14 abstentions and 2 blank ballots.

countries which had ratified always applied the new provisions in their relations with all countries, including those which had failed to ratify. The purposes of the union demand universal application of the rules laid down in the convention. It was preferable, therefore, to maintain the status quo rather than risk the possibility of losing universal application on legal grounds.[114]

To the present, although the vote at the Brussels Congress might indicate the possibility of a change in the future, the position of the UPU on the problem of ratification and the rights of membership seems to be based on the following propositions: (1) Once a country ratifies a convention it remains a member without further formal action; and (2) the rights and duties of both those countries which have ratified and those which have not, are determined by the new convention from the date on which it comes into force. The justification for this variance from a strict interpretation of international law was well expressed by the German writer Scheuffler: "The interest which the union has in the maintenance of every membership is certainly greater and more vital than the need for improvement or for completing and revising the clauses of its statutes and its internal organization." [115]

5. Implementation and Enforcement

The basic documents of the UPU contain no provisions which would permit the UPU to bring formal sanctions to bear on governments which fail to carry out their treaty obligations. The UPU cannot order its members to cut off postal relations with recalcitrant states, and the postal convention does not contain any provision for their exclusion from membership. Congresses, permanent committees, and the international bureau can exhort, cajole, and beg but, in the final analysis, can take no real action. As we have seen, a state which fails to ratify the revised basic documents, even after the former ones have been "rescinded," still retains its membership.

Some of the reasons for the success of the UPU in obtaining and maintaining almost complete universal membership without an enforcement procedure are obvious. Above all, the subject matter with which it is concerned is important and unimportant in proper combination. The international mails are important in that they are an essential element in communication between peoples and nations, a service which nations cannot do without. Note the anguished cry of the Hungarian delegate at the Congress of Madrid in 1920 that Hungary had been

114. See Docs., Cairo Postal Congress (1934), I, 20–23, 97–98, 508, 1267–68, and 1409, and II, 69, 95–98, 151–52, and 624–26; Docs., Brussels Postal Congress (1952), I, 188, and II, 381–84.

115. "The Ratifications in the Universal Postal Union," *Union Postale,* LXVII, No. 10/11 (October/November, 1942), 261–91 (from an article in *Zeitschrift für Völkerrecht,* XXIV (1940), 50–59).

isolated from postal communication for 52 days during the height of World War I.[116] Recognizing the essential nature of the mails, although they do not have the monopoly in the field of communication they once did, nations are scrupulous in carrying out their obligations for fear of losing the benefits that accrue to them from this form of international cooperation.

The international mails are unimportant in the sense that there are no real political implications that would cause nations to hesitate in carrying out their obligations, and little in their nature that could enable nations to use them as an instrument in political conflict. There was a time when an increase in postal rates could be used to finance a large portion of a war effort, but that time is long past.

Another factor that is less apparent perhaps, but no less important, is to be found in the manner in which the UPU has treated the creation of legal obligations in the past. In international postal matters, in contrast to nonpostal matters such as representation or membership, the UPU has laid great stress on obtaining unanimous agreement on all important changes or innovations.[117] When unanimity, or near-unanimity, is not obtained, the UPU has tended to make important changes or innovations optional rather than obligatory. An example would be the language for forms employed by administrations for the transfer of mail. The Treaty of Berne stipulated that, "as a general rule," all forms should be made out in French. It was not until the Congress of Rome in 1906 that unanimous agreement was reached that all forms should be in French, at which time it was made obligatory.[118] Some of the rules of postal conventions always remain optional because of a strong minority opinion against them. The postal identity card, for instance, was created by the Congress of Lisbon in 1885. The provision dealing with postal identity cards in the most recent postal convention, however, still begins: "Each administration *may* issue to persons who apply for them, postal identity cards. . . ."[119] In other cases, especially those dealing with charges, optional clauses are surrounded by permissible limits. For instance, each member country "has the option of conceding a reduction of 50 percent of the ordinary tariff for printed papers to newspapers and periodicals . . ." [120] In extremis, exceptions to the rules can be set forth in the final protocol. These can be blanket exceptions, such as Article VII, which reads: "Administrations are permitted not to undertake the sale of international reply coupons or to limit their sale." Or,

116. Docs., Madrid Postal Congress (1920), II, 30.

117. See the statements reflecting the desire for unanimity in *Annotated Acts (1957)*, 1er fascicule, p. 26, fn. 1.

118. See Berne Postal Treaty (1874), Art. 28, and Docs., Rome Postal Congress (1906), I, 215–16, and II, 241, 261, and 747. A proposal to make the French language obligatory was dropped at the Congress of Lisbon in 1885 because of the opposition of only two member countries. (See Docs., Lisbon Postal Congress (1885), I, 127, and II, 128.)

119. Ottawa Postal Convention (1957), Art. 46, para. 1. Italics supplied.

120. *Ibid.*, Art. 49, para. 5.

more specific exceptions, such as Article XII which states: "Exceptionally, the Administration of Aden is authorized to collect a charge of 40 centimes per bag for all mails stored at Aden, provided that that Administration does not receive any fee in respect of land or sea transit for those mails." [121] In the Brussels Postal Convention and its regulations, combined with the final protocol, there were some 30 optional clauses providing almost 50 specific exceptions to the general rules which administrations could use as they liked.[122]

The agreements are no exception to the rule. First, whether or not to be bound to these treaties is in itself optional. Second, each of the agreements has numerous optional clauses, as is the case with the convention and regulations. Finally, the Agreement on Insured Letters and Boxes and the Agreement on Parcel Post both have appended final protocols containing additional exceptions to the rules and regulations of these two services.[123]

There is one exception to the nonenforcement rule. Article 35 of the Ottawa Postal Convention — a similar article has been included in postal conventions since 1920 — provides: "When a country fails to observe the provisions of Article 34 concerning freedom of transit the administrations of the other member countries are at liberty to discontinue their postal service with that country. They shall give prior notice of this step to the administrations concerned by telegram." It is important to note that this is an individual sanction, not a collective one. The other members have no obligation whatsoever to aid a country so isolated. Nevertheless it could be an important club to hold in the courts over a member who refused transit, or in arbitration, except for the following article, Article 36, which states: "When, owing to exceptional circumstances, a postal administration finds itself obliged to suspend its services temporarily, either wholly or in part, it is bound immediately to advise, if need be by telegram, the administration or administrations concerned." [124] In effect, then, an administration could avoid all legal responsibility for failure to give transit simply by invoking this article. This interpretation is supported by a decision of the Congress of Madrid

121. *Ibid.,* Final Protocol, Arts. VII and XII.

122. See UPU, *Recueil officiel des renseignements d'intérêt général concernant l'exécution de la Convention et de son Règlement* (revisés à Bruxelles en *1952*) (Berne, 1953). This document also contains information on the use countries make of these options.

123. For a compilation of the optional clauses contained in the various agreements appended to the Brussels Postal Convention of 1952 and the use made of them by postal administrations, see: UPU, *Recueil de renseignements concernant l'exécution de l'Arrangement des lettres et des boîtes avec valeur déclarée* (Berne, 1953); UPU, *Recueil de renseignements concernant l'exécution de l'Arrangement des colis postaux* (Berne, 1953); UPU, *Recueil des Articles d'argent. Mandats de poste et bons postaux de voyage. Virements et valeurs domiciliées dans les bureaux de chèques postaux. Remboursements et Recouvrements* (Berne, 1953); and UPU, *Recueil de renseignements concernant l'exécution de l'Arrangement des abonnements aux journaux et écrits périodiques* (Berne, 1954).

124. Ottawa Postal Convention (1957), Art. 36.

in 1920 that the administration which invokes the article is the sole judge of what constitutes "exceptional circumstances." [125]

This is the case at present vis-à-vis Israel. In 1960 and 1961 several Arab states informed the bureau, for the information of the other members of the UPU, that they were stopping all postal relations with Israel. One, Tunisia, specifically mentioned the invocation of Article 36 in its communication to the bureau.[126] Israel can invoke Article 35 if she wishes, which, under the circumstances, could not have a great deal of effect. The only other alternative, in view of the fact that the basic acts of the UPU do not have any provisions for sanctions, is appeal to one of the bodies of the UPU for a condemnation of the actions of the Arab states involved. It is likely that she will do so at the next congress. The action against Israel may account for the "special study" on freedom of transit and its importance to the success of the UPU, which appeared in the international bureau's annual report for 1961.[127]

D. Interpretation of Final Acts

OF ALL of the specialized agencies, the UPU has probably the most comprehensive set of procedures for the interpretation of its fundamental documents. The first method involves obtaining the opinion of members of the union, the second utilizes the international bureau, and the third is the more familiar procedure of arbitration.

The first method secures the "interpretation" of a congress, in the following manner. During committee meetings, a delegate may state his interpretation of a provision of the convention, an agreement or the attached regulations, and ask whether the committee agrees. The procedure is completed if the interpretation is accepted by a majority of the committee and if the report of the committee in which it is contained is approved by a plenary meeting. Records of such actions are not contained in the final acts of the congresses, but only in their minutes.

The use of the congress interpretation has a long history in the UPU, dating at least from the Congress of Rome in 1906. Application of this method increased tremendously in the interwar period, however, and has remained frequent since. The size of the final acts is one contributing factor, as well as the limitations that have been introduced since 1924 on the submission of substantive proposals during congresses. The Congress of Buenos Aires in 1939, dubbed by some as the "interpretation Congress" used this method some 70 times; so often, in fact, that it was accused of finding the "easy way out." [128] Suffice it to say that

125. Docs., Madrid Postal Congress (1920), II, 839–40.
126. See *Circulaire*, 1961, No. 137. See also, *Circulaire*, 1960, Nos. 128, 147, 179, 183, and 189; and 1961, Nos. 30, 104, 137, and 182.
127. *Annual Report, 1961*, pp. 33–34.
128. See C. J. Beelenkamp, *Réformes postales internationales* (Bloemendaal, 1947), pp. 24–25. See also Docs., Buenos Aires Postal Congress (1939), II, 549–57.

the minutes of UPU congresses have been spiced liberally with interpretations of the final documents.

For a time, interpretations of congresses were considered to have
the same force as provisions contained in the final documents signed
and ratified by the member countries. Starting in 1939, however, doubts
were raised as to the legality of the interpretations. How could they, it
was asked, have the same force as provisions in a treaty which is signed
and ratified? The director of the bureau, for example, asked the plenary
meeting of the Buenos Aires Congress what would be the fate of any
such decisions if they were not actually promulgated in the member
countries by internal legislation.[129] No answer was made to the director's
question, not even an observation. Professor Beelenkamp, an expert in
international postal legislation, in 1949 answered the director's question
in the negative. In his opinion such acts by the committees and the
plenary sessions of congresses could never have any true legal validity.[130]

A full-scale debate on the subject at the Brussels Congress of 1952
was sparked by an Indonesian suggestion that certain important interpretations of the past be introduced into the convention and the other
congress documents because, since it was assumed they had legal validity,
they should be readily available to administrations and not lost in the
minutes of meetings.[131] In the debate which took place at the third
meeting of the general committee, the delegates upheld the idea of
providing a means whereby the members of the union could request an
interpretation of the final acts from their colleagues in congresses, but
reluctantly agreed that the previous congresses had been in error; interpretations could not have the same legal validity as provisions of documents that had been ratified by the governments of member countries.
The resolution that ended the debate read in part: ". . . The interpretations and recommendations concerning the acts of the Union, adopted
by different congresses and set forth in the minutes of meetings, do not
have the same legal value as the acts to which they refer. These opinions,
interpretations, etc., have as their objective the eventual facilitation of
the interpretation of the Convention and the Agreements." [132] Interestingly enough, the procedure used in making this resolution was exactly
the same as that used in interpretations. The committee agreed to the
text, which was included in the minutes of the meeting. It was not
adopted formally by a plenary session except as a part of the approval of
the minutes of the general committee.

Notwithstanding the legal arguments, the "interpretation" does
provide a convenient method for a member country to determine the
attitude of representatives of other countries concerning provisions of
the final acts of congresses. Although there is no information on the use

129. See for instance Docs., Stockholm Postal Congress (1924), II, 288; and
Docs., Buenos Aires Postal Congress (1939), II, 532 and 541.

130. C. J. Beelenkamp, *La Cooperation Entre l'Organisation des Nations
Unies et l'Union postale universelle* (Overeen, 1949), p. 16.

131. Docs., Brussels Postal Congress (1952), I, 69–91.

132. *Ibid.*, II, 313–17.

of interpretations in legal disputes, it is evident that they would have a great deal of weight in the making of a decision. Perhaps the more important aspect of the interpretation is not in its use in legal disputes, but in its preventing of them. If a disagreement is in the making over a provision of the final acts, the interpretation of a congress cannot help but have the effect of supporting the case of one side or another and thus keeping the disagreement from erupting into a genuine dispute.

The same is true of investigations carried out by the bureau on the request of an administration as provided for in the detailed regulations of the convention. Article 106, para. 3, states that the international bureau "also conducts inquiries requested by administrations in order to learn the opinion of other administrations on a particular question." In order to eliminate any legal discussion, however, the following is added: "The result of an inquiry does not have the status of a vote and is not formally binding." This method of obtaining an interpretation of the final acts is available at any time to the members of the union, not just during congresses, as is the interpretation. Although this provision was not placed in the convention or regulations until 1952, the bureau has provided this service for member countries since 1877. From 1877 to the end of 1962, the bureau had opened over four hundred inquiries for members of the union. Although many deal with internal postal matters, a very large percentage deals with interpretations of the final acts of the union.[133]

The second method for obtaining an interpretation of the acts of the union involves an opinion from the international bureau. There are two procedures provided for in the basic documents. First, on the request of any member country, the bureau is authorized to give its interpretation of any of the union's acts. Secondly, in the case of a legal dispute, the bureau is authorized to give its interpretation of any of the acts of the union if requested by all parties to the dispute. In neither case, as was the rule concerning interpretations by congresses, are the opinions expressed by the bureau binding upon administrations. The actions of the bureau are more akin to conciliation and mediation than they are to arbitration. But again, the fact that the opinions of the respected bureau become known to the parties involved cannot help but have the effect of supporting one or the other disagreeing factions in the case and thus preventing the eruption of a genuine dispute.

The bureau has given its interpretation of acts of the union, on the request of a member administration, 317 times in the period from 1878, when the first request was made, to the end of 1962. In five cases the bureau refused to give an interpretation on the grounds that it did not have jurisdiction. The largest number of inquiries concerned the types and content of objects that are admitted in the various categories of letter mail, as for example, whether designs for tapestries drawn and colored by hand should be included under the category "commercial

133. See UPU, *Catalogue de l'UPU,* Tome II, Section Ga, and *Annual Reports* from 1955 to 1962.

papers," the maximum length of dedications permitted in "printed matter," and the like. Questions concerning the parcel post service and the proper handling of transit mail ran a close second, followed by problems concerning postage.[134]

While the number of inquiries handled by the bureau averages approximately 3.75 a year, there is a great deal of fluctuation from year to year. As a general rule, requests have a tendency to build up between congresses, tapering off as the date of the next congress approaches. The reason is fairly obvious. It takes a while for the weaknesses in new final acts of congresses to show up. As they become evident, the requests for interpretations by the bureau increase. As the time of the congress approaches, administrations have a tendency to postpone any requests for opinions, preferring to obtain a change in the final acts that will eliminate the problems or weaknesses, or at least to seek the opinion of the congress itself. The most requests for opinions in a congress year occurred in 1934, with four. There were three in 1952. All other congress years had two, one, or none. As would be expected, the number of requests for opinions also dropped sharply during World War I and World War II. In the period from 1914 to 1918, there were 10 requests for interpretations; and from 1939 to 1946 there were 20, six of which occurred in 1946 alone. Since World War II, the number of requests has risen to a respectable average of about 6 per year.

The international bureau has given its opinion in legal disputes between members of the union some 68 times since it was first asked in 1877. On four additional occasions the bureau has refused to give an opinion for want of jurisdiction. The most active period for the bureau was in the economically difficult interwar years, from 1920 to 1935, in which the bureau gave 31 legal opinions. The bureau gave only five opinions in a legal dispute in the years from 1875 to 1898. There was a steady trickle of opinions given during World War I, but from 1936 to 1945 there were only two. Two opinions were given in 1946, and one in 1947, 1949, 1951, and 1952. There have been no requests for opinions in legal disputes since 1952.

Concerning the nature of the legal disputes in which the bureau was called upon to give its opinion, the largest number involved the parcel post, including such problems as accounts between administrations and the responsibility for damage to packages. Insured boxes and letters were second with nine, and the admission of various types of mail into the international postal service was third, with eight cases. There were seven cases concerning the maritime transit of the mails, six of a general nature concerning transit, and six dealing with negotiable instruments. As an example of a recent case, in 1952 the bureau was called upon to decide whether a postal administration had the right to charge another administration a fee for the transit of mails between two islands

134. These figures and those that immediately follow are, unless otherwise noted, taken from *Catalogue de l'UPU,* Tome II, Sec. Go, and *Annual Reports, 1955* to *1962.*

both under the first administration's jurisdiction. The bureau concluded that it is a general rule in the international postal service that the country of origin is obliged to pay the costs of transport of its correspondence only to the frontier of the country of destination, and that all further transportation in the country of destination must be carried out by the latter country, no matter by what means. Consequently the bureau's opinion was that the maritime route between the two islands should be considered as interior transportation of the country of destination (despite the fact that both commercial and governmental transportation facilities were involved) and that, consequently, no transit fees were due from the country of origin.[135]

If countries cannot find satisfaction in interpretations by other members of the union, or by the international bureau, they always have the right to make use of the arbitration procedure provided in the postal convention. This procedure is as follows:

1] In the event of disagreement between two or more postal Administrations of member countries as to the interpretation of the Convention, the Agreements and their Final Protocols as well as their Detailed Regulations and their Final Protocols, or as to the responsibility imposed on a postal Administration by the application of these Acts, the question at issue is settled by arbitration.

2] To this end, each of the Administrations in the case selects an Administration of the Union not directly interested in the dispute. When several Administrations make common cause, they count as a single Administration for the purposes of this provision.

3] If one of the Administrations in disagreement does not act on a proposal for arbitration within a period of six months, the International Bureau, if requested, calls on the defaulting Administration to appoint an arbitrator or itself appoints one *ex officio.*

4] The parties in the case may agree to appoint a single arbitrator which may be the International Bureau.

5] The decision of the arbitrators is taken on a majority of votes.

6] If the voting is equal the arbitrators select another postal Administration also disinterested in the question at issue to settle the difference. Should they fail to agree on the choice, the Administration is appointed by the International Bureau from among members of the Union not proposed by the arbitrators.

7] If the dispute concerns one of the Agreements, the arbitrators may be appointed only from among the Administrations bound by that Agreement.[136]

Noticeable in these provisions is the position of the international bureau. If one of the parties to the dispute fails to act on a request for arbitration, the bureau has the power to appoint an *ex officio* arbitrator

---

135. See *Annual Report, 1952,* pp. 20–26. The international bureau regularly receives requests from private parties for legal interpretation which the Bureau just as regularly turns down. (See, for example, *Annual Report, 1947,* pp. 12–13.)

136. Ottawa Postal Convention (1957), Art. 33.

for that country. Further, if the two arbitrators fail to agree, and the parties to the dispute cannot compromise on a third arbitrator, the bureau again steps in to name the third arbitrator. Finally, if the parties agree, the bureau may be the sole arbitrator in a legal dispute. In none of the other specialized agencies of the United Nations is the secretariat placed in such a position in matters of legal dispute. Also of note is the failure to provide for any other means of settling a dispute, including especially the International Court. No mention is made of the use of the International Court in any of the UPU's final acts or in the UPU-UN agreement signed in 1947.

There are 26 known cases of arbitration on postal matters. In 19 cases the dispute was settled by the two arbitrators chosen by the parties to the dispute. In five cases it was necessary, as a result of disagreement, to choose a third arbitrator. In one case one of the parties to the dispute failed to name an arbitrator and it was done by the international bureau, and in one other case the international bureau acted as the sole arbitrator. In the one case where the bureau named the second arbitrator, it was a question of the correctness of an account between Portugal and Yugoslavia. It was Portugal which claimed that the accounts were in error in her favor and it was for Yugoslavia that the bureau named the second arbitrator. The case arose over postal relations in 1941 and 1943 and the decision was rendered in 1956. The case when the bureau was the sole arbitrator actually occurred before the relevant provision was inserted in the convention, and was accomplished by means of a special *compromis*.[137]

The largest number of arbitration cases (15) concerned problems of responsibility of administrations for loss or theft of all or part of the contents of articles of mail and related subjects. Seven concerned accounts between administrations. Three cases involved problems caused by the fluctuations of currencies or problems of conversion of currencies, and one involved inviolability of correspondence.[138] The case where the bureau acted as the sole arbitrator provides an interesting example of the UPU's arbitration procedure. In 1943 a parcel post package, insured for 980 gold francs, was deposited in a post office in Switzerland, addressed to a commercial firm in Turkey. The Turkish firm received the package and reexpedited it to a bank in Egyptian-administered territory. The package went first to Syria for transshipment to Egypt. By mistake it was then sent to Iraq. In Iraq the error was discovered and the package was sent back to Syria, where it was redirected to its correct destination in Egypt. On its arrival in Egypt, the Egyptian postal authorities found that the package had been pilfered and so notified the Turkish authorities. The Turkish postal authorities claimed that the loss must have occurred in Syria or Iraq. Syria was responsible for the full amount of the insurance, according to Turkey, since it was her fault that it had been misdirected to Iraq. The Syrian administration placed some of the blame

137. *Annual Reports, 1948,* pp. 14–22; and *1956,* p. 24.
138. See *Annotated Acts (1957),* 1ᵉʳ fascicule. pp. 64-71.

on Turkey and suggested that they divide the amount between them. Iraq, whom the Turkish authorities suggested might be responsible with Syria, declined responsibility for the insured value since the package had not been insured for its misdirected voyage to Iraq, but suggested that it would be willing to contribute a sum equal to the indemnity fixed by the UPU regulations for a noninsured parcel.

At the suggestion of the Iraq postal administration, the three countries drew up a special *compromis* making the bureau the sole arbitrator. The bureau's decision was handed down in 1948. The operative article of the Buenos Aires Parcel Post Agreement of 1939, which was in force at the time, provided that if loss occurred during transport and if it is not possible to establish on whose territory the loss occurred, all administrations concerned were equally responsible. The bureau was not able to determine where the loss occurred from the facts presented by the three countries, so it ordered the postal administrations of Turkey, Syria, and Iraq to pay equal parts of the 980-franc loss to the shipper of the package. The bureau, on the other hand, exonerated the Egyptian administration from any responsibility because it had discovered the loss at the moment of reception and had notified the expeditor in the proper manner laid down by the UPU's rules and regulations.[139]

In assessing the degree with which postal administrations carry out the decisions of postal arbitration boards, one can accept the statement of J. J. Le Mouël made in 1950:

> It may be asked, what action the UPU can take, in case of difficulty, in order to enforce an adjudication made either by an arbitrator or referee. I can answer by saying that, in our Organization, the question does not arise. All the arbitral decisions rendered over a period of 75 years in the UPU were simply carried out without any ill-will. There is no example, in our Union, of any country evading the adjudication of the arbitrators.[140]

While the UPU has probably gone further than most public international organizations in providing for peaceful methods of settling disputes that might arise from varied interpretations of the final acts, and perhaps has also made more use of those provided, there is also a greater need. In international postal relations there is a physical "object" that passes from one country to another. In an operation as vast as the international postal service there is always the possibility that items of mail may be damaged or lost in transit from one place to another. Consequently there are usually many occasions when questions of responsibility arise that must be settled easily and amicably if the concept of "one single postal territory" is to remain a reality.

In general it must be admitted that the services of conciliation,

139. See *Annual Report, 1948,* pp. 14–20.
140. "The Universal Postal Union," *Union Postale,* LXXV, No. 12 (December, 1950), 182–83.

mediation, and arbitration provided by the final acts of the UPU have been of value to the members of the union throughout the many years of existence of the UPU. The decline of the use of the bureau's good offices in legal disputes, and a similar decline in the use of the arbitration procedure, can be a cause for concern, however. It is hard to believe that conflicts are not occurring, because the use of the international mails continues to increase. If this tendency means that conflicts are not being resolved, it is to be deplored. If, on the other hand, countries are using traditional diplomatic methods of resolving their conflicts on the basis of "interpretations" of the bureau and congresses, which have not decreased, the situation is not so bad as it looks. In this respect it should be noted that countries have shown a general reluctance since World War II to make use of international courts and arbitration devices in all matters. Suffice it to say that the provisions of the final acts of the UPU provide a wide range of procedures that can, if the will is there, take care of almost any foreseeable problem of interpretation.

E. Financing the UPU

ASIDE FROM a relatively insignificant sum obtained from activities such as the sale of documents, the UPU is dependent for its finances on the contributions of member countries. The manner in which these contributions are made is laid down in the UPU's basic documents, and when a country becomes a member of the union it is legally obligated to make its share available. As with any international organization, the ability of the UPU to carry out its responsibilities is contingent upon the attitude of its members toward their financial obligations. Refusal to pay certain expenses, or consistent tardiness in making contributions available, can result in financial crises which endanger the very existence of the organization. Such has been the case of the UN in the late 1950's and early 1960's. A steady, adequate income, on the other hand, can provide a strong foundation that will enable the international organization to function on a well-organized basis. The UPU, in this respect, has always been fortunate. The amount of money available has been sufficient for its purposes, and its members usually make their contributions on time. The most obvious explanation would be that the cost of running the UPU has always remained relatively low and hence the burden on member countries has been light. However, one should not overlook the nonpolitical character of the UPU and especially the important service that it renders to all of its members.

1. Expenses and Income

The UPU is not an expensive organization to maintain. In 1962 its total expenditures amounted to 3,160,502.07 Swiss francs. After deduction of its few sources of independent income, only 3,059,529.00 Swiss francs remained to be paid by contributions from member countries.[141]

Nevertheless, the expenses of the UPU have risen since World War II. Prior to 1946, the gross expenses never exceeded 500,000 Swiss francs, except for 1939, the year of the Buenos Aires Postal Congress. Since that time they have increased considerably as evidenced in the following table:

GROSS ANNUAL EXPENDITURES OF THE UPU, 1946–1961
(SWISS FRANCS)

1946	565,367.76	1954	1,852,003.63
1947	721,646.04	1955	1,837,524.68
1948	888,679.23	1956	1,888,153.84
1949	1,272,823.12	1957	2,237,599.01
1950	1,291,860.74	1958	1,944,861.63
1951	1,515,543.54	1959	2,687,127.89
1952	1,805,514.65	1960	2,780,174.17
1953	1,863,568.49	1961	3,061,395.05
		1962	3,160,502.07[142]

Some of the increase has been because of the constantly rising cost of personnel and materials, and some because of the expansion in the membership of the union. More, however, results from the creation of the executive and liaison committee and the consultative committee for postal studies, and the expansion of functions that the existence of these two organs exemplify.

The expenses of the UPU are divided into two main categories, ordinary and extraordinary. Ordinary expenses include all the normal recurring costs of the operation of the international bureau, the ELC, and the CCPS. Of these three, the bureau's portion is by far the largest. Of the total expenses of the union in 1962, the sum of 2,137,587.58 Swiss francs was attributed to the expenses of the bureau and only 242,244.75 to the CCPS and 193,132.26 to the ELC. The wide discrepancy between the costs of the three organs is explained by the fact that the work of the bureau is a continuing operation while the committees meet only periodically, and that the secretariats of both the ELC and the CCPS are provided in the main by the bureau. It is not surprising, therefore, that the largest amount in the expenses of the bureau (1,516,953.85 Swiss francs) was attributed to personnel. The next largest item in the bureau's ordinary budget was a sum of 278,061.95 for printing and binding.[143]

141. *Annual Report, 1962*, p. 35. (One American dollar is equal to approximately 4.3 Swiss francs.)

142. See Docs., Buenos Aires Postal Congress (1939), II, 538; Docs., Paris Postal Congress (1947), II, 901; and *Annual Reports, 1947*, p. 22; *1948*, p. 37; *1949*, p. 35; *1950*, p. 30; *1951*, p. 31; *1952*, p. 35; *1953*, p. 28; *1954*, p. 31; *1955*, p. 29; *1956*, p. 39; *1957*, p. 31; *1958*, p. 40; *1959*, p. 40; *1960*, p. 37; *1961*, p. 37; and *1962*, p. 35.

143. *Annual Report, 1962*, p. 42.

The nonrecurring expenses of the UPU "occasioned by meetings of a Congress, conference or special committee and the expenses which may result from special tasks entrusted to the International Bureau" are classified as "extraordinary expenses." [144] In general, extraordinary expenses are small in comparison with ordinary expenses. In 1961, for example, extraordinary expenses amounted to only 587,537.48 Swiss francs.[145] The additional work occasioned by congresses, however, tends to make this category of expenses fluctuate. As a general rule, such expenses start building up a year or two before the congress is to take place, reaching a peak during the year it is in session, and then falling off gradually, as is demonstrated in the following table:

EXTRAORDINARY EXPENSES, 1955–1962
(SWISS FRANCS)

1955	63,444.10	1959	219,120.40
1956	129,155.98	1960	129,626.25
1957	778,792.90*	1961	260,914.40
1958	427,180.20	1962	587,537.48[146]

* Congress year.

The uses to which the extraordinary expenses are put also fluctuate, depending upon the proximity to a congress year. In 1957, the year of the Ottawa Congress, 701,700.70 Swiss francs of the union's extraordinary expenses were attributable to "congresses and conferences" and only 77,092.20 to the international bureau. The largest single item of the former part was 301,946.30 for simultaneous interpretation, followed by 230,422.30 for travel expenses of members of the secretariat to and from Ottawa, and 154,547.65 for printing and binding. The largest additional single item was 36,289.95 Swiss francs for temporary personnel. On the bureau's part, the largest single item was 60,003.60 for printing and binding, followed by 16,100.00 for temporary personnel.[147] In 1960, a between-congress year, only a single item of 33,204.70 Swiss francs for travel was attributed to congresses and conferences, while 96,421.55 were attributable to the international bureau. Of the latter, 45,336.45 francs were for printing and binding, 23,130.40 for temporary personnel, and 21,311.00 for the acquisition of furniture and technical equipment.[148]

Extraordinary expenses would undoubtedly account for a much larger part of the overall expenses of the union were it not for the fact that much of the cost of holding congresses is undertaken by other

144. Ottawa Postal Convention (1957), Art. 10, para. 1.
145. *Annual Report, 1962,* p. 42.
146. *Annual Reports, 1955,* p. 36; *1956,* p. 44; *1957,* p. 38; *1958,* p. 46; *1959,* p. 46; *1960,* p. 44; *1961,* p. 42; and *1962,* p. 42.
147. *Annual Report, 1957,* p. 38.
148. *Annual Report, 1960,* p. 44. It should be noted that in 1957 the CCPS had not come into existence and in 1960 there were no extraordinary expenses attributable to it.

agencies. In the first place, tradition dictates that the host country support the costs of housing the congress and the meetings of its committees, and supply a large part of the temporary secretariat from its own postal administration. Secondly, each country represented at a congress is responsible for all the expenses of its delegates. There are certain duties which fall to the bureau, however, which accounts for the existence of items in the extraordinary category such as the preparation of proposals, helping the host country make arrangements for congresses, providing expert members of the secretariat, and publishing the final acts.

The expenses of the UPU are met from two sources: payment for certain services and contributions from member countries. The first is comparatively small, amounting in 1962 to only 100,973.07 Swiss francs. The largest single item was from the sale of publications, including subscriptions to and advertisements in the union's journal, which amounted to 47,976.23. The next largest amount was 37,087.00 francs entitled "reimbursements" which included a sum returned by the Swiss government for a turnover tax which had been paid by the union and payments for the cost of simultaneous interpretation in meetings of the executive and liaison committee and the consultative committee for postal studies by member countries whose delegates elected to use a language other than French.[149] This was followed by 6,661.10 Swiss francs obtained from the rental to the Swiss government of part of the UPU's headquarters building for a post office and its share of the cost of heating. An additional "miscellaneous" item brought the income of the UPU in this category up to 100,973.07.[150] Although there has been an increase in income, as seen from the following table, the amount of money that the UPU can earn in addition to the contributions of its members is strictly limited by the nature of its functions.

GROSS ANNUAL INCOME OF THE UPU FROM SOURCES OTHER
THAN ANNUAL CONTRIBUTIONS OF MEMBERS
(IN SWISS FRANCS)

1946	15,135.76	1954	99,616.63
1947	18,926.04	1955	83,226.68
1948	21,799.23	1956	126,211.84
1949	58,945.12	1957	469,924.01
1950	71,670.74	1958	171,453.63
1951	108,695.54	1959	175,387.89
1952	56,949.65	1960	156,594.17
1953	115,003.49	1961	309,106.05
		1962	100,973.07[151]

149. The question of union languages is discussed below, pp. 144–46, 207–208.

150. *Annual Report, 1962*, p. 43. Of this total, 3,432.44 francs were placed on the "extraordinary" side of the accounts and the remainder was "ordinary" income.

151. *Annual Reports 1947*, p. 21; *1948*, p. 36; *1949*, p. 34; *1950*, p. 29; *1951*, p. 30; *1952*, p. 34; *1953*, p. 28; *1954*, p. 31; *1955*, p. 29; *1956*, p. 39; *1957*, p. 31; *1958*, p. 40; *1959*, p. 40; *1960*, p. 37; *1961*, p. 43; and *1962*, p. 43.

The remainder of the expenses, after the deduction of the income mentioned above, is met by contributions of member states. The manner in which the amount of contribution of each state is determined is the subject matter of the following section.

2. The Class-unit System

The UPU uses a class-unit system for fixing the contributions by member countries to its expenses. At present there are seven classes with unit values as follows:

1st class	25 units	4th class	10 units
2d class	20 units	5th class	5 units
3d class	15 units	6th class	3 units
	7th class	1 unit[152]	

Each year the total net expenses of the UPU are divided by the total number of units subscribed in order to determine the value of each unit. Members then pay the amount determined, by multiplying the number of units in their chosen class by the value of the single unit. In 1962, for example, the total net expenses were 3,059,529 Swiss francs and the total number of units subscribed by members was 957. By dividing the total net expenses by 957 units, the value of a single unit was determined to be 3,197 Swiss francs. Countries in the first class then paid 79,925 Swiss francs (957 × 25) and the lowest class paid 3,197 Swiss francs.[153]

The following table indicates the amount of a single unit from 1947 to 1961, in Swiss francs:

1947	768.00	1952	1,911.00	1957	1,911.00
1948	960.00	1953	1,911.00	1958	1,911.00
1949	1,318.00	1954	1,911.00	1959	2,695.00
1950	1,335.00	1955	1,911.00	1960	2,815.00
1951	1,516.00	1956	1,911.00	1961	2,885.00
				1962	3,197.00[154]

Since 1874 each postal convention or its regulations carried an article in which the name of the member country is listed along with its class of contribution. In the case of new admissions, "the Government of the Swiss Confederation fixes by common consent with the Government of the Country concerned the class in which the latter shall be placed for the apportionment of the expenditure." [155] The name of the new

152. Ottawa Postal Convention (1957), Art. 20, para. 1.

153. *Annual Report, 1962*, p. 37.

154. See *Annual Reports, 1947*, p. 22; *1948*, p. 37; *1949*, p. 35; *1950*, p. 28; *1951*, p. 29; *1952*, p. 33; *1953*, p. 28; *1954*, p. 32; *1955*, p. 30; *1956*, p. 40; *1957*, p. 32; *1958*, p. 41; *1959*, p. 41; *1960*, p. 38; *1961*, p. 38; and *1962*, p. 37.

155. See Ottawa Postal Convention (1957), Art. 20, para. 3. The provision concerning new admissions was introduced by the Paris Postal Congress (1878). (See Paris Postal Convention, 1878, Art. 18.)

member and its class of contribution are added to the pertinent article of the convention or its regulations by the next congress.

Inasmuch as the member's contribution class thus becomes registered in the UPU's basic documents, there are only two methods of changing it. The usual method is to submit a proposal to change the pertinent article at the next congress. If a majority of the delegates agree, as is always the case, the new classification will come into effect at the same time as the final acts of that congress. The most recent case of this kind occurred in 1947 when Poland requested and received permission to drop from Class 1 to Class 3.[156] Between congresses, under the provisions of Article 29 of the Ottawa Postal Convention, any requests for changes must receive the approbation of two thirds of the members of the UPU. The only occasion since 1947 when a member changed its classification between congresses occurred in 1954, when it was unanimously agreed to let the Belgian Congo move from Class 7 up to Class 6.[157]

The final acts of congresses are silent as to the qualifications for admission to the various contributive classes, but tradition dictates that account should be taken of the size of the population of the member country; the extent of its lines of postal communication; and the number of its post offices.[158] In practice, however, countries are permitted to move from one class to another without serious objection. At the end of 1962, the member countries and their classes were as follows:

1st class (25 units) — Argentina, Australia, Brazil, Canada, China, France, Germany, India, Italy, Japan, New Zealand, Pakistan, South Africa, Spain, United Kingdom, United States, and USSR (17).

2d class (20 units) — (none)

3d class (15 units) — Algeria, Belgium, British territories, Czechoslovakia, Egypt, French territories, Indonesia, Mexico, Netherlands, Poland, Rumania, Sweden, Switzerland, Turkey, Ukraine, United States territories, and Yugoslavia (17).

4th class (10 units) — Denmark, Finland, Hungary, Ireland, Korea, Morocco, Norway, Portuguese provinces in West Africa, Portuguese provinces in East Africa, Asia and Oceania, and Portugal (10).

5th class (5 units) — Austria, Byelorussia, Bulgaria, Ceylon, Chile, Colombia, Greece, Iran, Nigeria, Peru, and Tunisia (11).

6th class (3 units) — Afghanistan, Albania, Bolivia, Burma, Congo (Leopoldville), Costa Rica, Cuba, Dominican Republic, Ecuador, El Salvador, Ethiopia, Ghana, Guatemala, Guinea, Haiti, Honduras, Israel, Luxembourg, Malay Federation, Malagache Republic, Nepal, Nicaragua, Panama, Paraguay, Netherlands Antilles and Surinam, Senegal, Thailand, Uruguay, Venezuela, and Viet Nam (30).

156. See Docs., Paris Postal Congress (1947), I, 206; and II, 376, 567–68, and 876.

157. *Annual Report, 1954,* p. 27.

158. See Docs., Berne Postal Congress (1874), p. 57, and *Annotated Acts (1957),* 1ᵉʳ fascicule, p. 162, fn. 1.

7th class (1 unit) — Cambodia, Cameroons, Central African Republic, Congo (Brazzaville), Cyprus, Dahomey, Gabon, Iceland, Iraq, Ivory Coast, Jordan, Kuwait, Laos, Lebanon, Liberia, Libya, Liechtenstein, Mali, Monaco, Niger, Philippines, San Marino, Saudi Arabia, Sierra Leone, Somaliland, Spanish territories in Africa, Sudan, Syria, Tchad, Togoland, Vatican City, and Yemen (32).[159]

As is evident, the UPU is not one of the specialized agencies in which the United States maintains the major financial burden. In 1962 the United States, Great Britain, and France all shared first place with a total of 40 units for themselves and their territories. If one wished to add Byelorussia and the Ukraine to the Russian contribution, the 45 units paid by the USSR would put it at the top of the contributors to the UPU expenses. Prior to giving independence to various dependent territories, both France and Great Britain were by far the largest contributors.

As a general rule, members pay their contributions on time. In 1957, the last time this information was made public, only six countries had debts outstanding for a period of over a year and a half. One of the delinquent countries was from the Middle East, owing a very small amount, and the remainder were from Latin America. The total of such outstanding debts in June 1957 amounted to only 107,158.48 Swiss francs.[160] One reason for prompt payments by member countries is undoubtedly the provision of the convention regulations which states that any amount owed at the end of the year in which the bills are sent to debtor countries is liable to an interest rate of 5 percent a year in favor of the Swiss government, which is charged with advancing the bureau's operating funds.[161]

ARREARS IN PAYMENTS, 1948–1957

Year	Amount	Year	Amount
1948	359,200.00	1953	210,407.00
1949	219,347.00	1954	219,120.00
1950	248,832.00	1955	143,957.00
1951	157,495.00	1956	270,445.00
1952	147,486.00	1957 (to end of May)	107,158.00[162]

On several occasions suggestions have been made to change the UPU's system of contributions. Outside of the addition in 1878 of the seventh class (paying one unit), however, all such suggestions have been turned down.[163] Until World War I there seemed to be general

159. See *Annual Report, 1962*, pp. 53–62.
160. See UPU, *Rapport du Directeur du bureau international sur les finances de l'union*, June 30, 1957, Annex 6.
161. Ottawa Postal Convention (1957), Regulations, Art. 113, para. 3. The only additional benefit received by those in the higher contributory classes, it should be noted, is extra copies of documents (Art. 110, para. 7).
162. See Docs., Ottawa Postal Congress (1957), II, 73.
163. Docs., Paris Postal Congress (1878), pp. 121–22 and 430.

satisfaction with the class-unit system. In any event the cost of running the union was not a great burden even on the larger unit classes. Some members, as pointed out by the bureau, were able to make Class 1 contributions solely for "prestige purposes." [164] After World War I, however, monetary problems culminating in the great depression of the 1930's brought a tendency on the part of the union's members to move to a lower class of contribution, which led to an augmentation of the value of each unit and consequent complaints about the inequalities of the system. The preparatory committee of the 1934 Cairo Congress was confronted with four proposals, all of which attempted to set forth criteria for classification. The Greek proposal, for example, suggested the use of the figures for the total exterior postal traffic of each nation. All were turned down. In the congress proper, the same fate befell an Argentine-Colombia-Mexico proposal to reduce the classes of contributions to three, with 30, 15, and 5 units, respectively.[165]

The matter was raised again at the Paris Congress in 1947 when a record six proposals to change the class-unit system were introduced. All but one proposal either demanded a reduction in number of classes or suggested criteria for assignment to each class. The one exception was a proposal by Ecuador that the UPU adopt the United Nations system for the payment of expenses. This suggestion was the only one which got to the floor of the plenary meeting, where it was defeated, 47 to 16, with six abstentions.[166] Only one proposal to change the class-unit system was introduced at the Congress of Brussels in 1952 and none at Ottawa in 1957.[167] One would not be far wrong in suggesting that the UPU's class-unit system is in no great danger of being drastically modified unless the world is threatened by another great economic crisis, at least equal to that of the 1930's, and unless the expenses of the UPU rise to a much higher level than they are now.

3. Financial Controls

The UPU has a unique system of control over its finances, because of the position of the Swiss government as the direct supervisor of the international bureau.[168] This system has three major elements, the estab-

164. See the study made by the bureau contained in Docs., Paris Postal Congress (1947), II, 122–23. The League of Nations, in Article 6 of the Convenant, adopted the UPU's system but, in view of the inequalities that resulted from the relatively much higher expenses, soon abandoned it (*ibid.,* p. 122).

165. Docs., Cairo Postal Congress (1934), I, 28–30, 1269, and 1411.

166. See Docs., Paris Postal Congress (1947), I, 63–67; and II, 57, 134–35, 296, 368, 465, and 1015–22. Those who voted for the Ecuador proposal were: Bolivia, Brazil, Bulgaria, Colombia, Dominican Republic, Ecuador, Egypt, Ethiopia, Greece, Guatemala, Iran, Mexico, Panama, Peru, Saudi Arabia, and Venezuela. (See also the rather complicated criteria suggested by the international bureau in *ibid.,* pp. 122–33).

167. Docs., Brussels Postal Congress (1952), I, 181–82; and II, 370–71.

168. The overall position of the Swiss government as supervisory authority is explained below, pp. 191, 193, 203.

lishment of ceilings on ordinary expenses incurred by the congresses; the budgetary procedure carried out by the bureau and the Swiss government; and the accounting for expenditures in which the bureau, the Swiss government, the ELC, and the congress are involved.

For our purposes, the procedure begins with the postal congress which fixes, on the basis of the director general's report of the union's accounts for the preceding five years, the anticipated future needs of the union, and any changes in the functions or structure of the union made by the congress itself — the annual ceiling for net ordinary expenses during the period in which the new postal convention is in effect. The amount agreed upon is included in an article of the convention regulations for the guidance of the bureau and the supervisory authority. The ceiling set by the Congress of Ottawa in 1957 was 2,500,000 Swiss francs.[169] Congresses do not set the ceilings of the extraordinary expenses and thus leave the amount of this part of the expenses, and the items to be included in it under the definition contained in the convention — "expenses occasioned by the meeting of a Congress, Conference or special Committee and the expenses which may result from special tasks entrusted to the International Bureau" — to the discretion of the authorities who are in true control of the union's finances.

The ceiling on net ordinary expenses has been raised only eight times since the beginning of the UPU, and the four largest raises all occurred since World War II. The Berne Congress in 1874 set the ceiling for the first time at 75,000 francs. It was raised to 100,000 francs in 1878, to 125,000 in 1891, 300,000 in 1920, and 350,000 in 1929. The Paris Congress in 1947 raised the ceiling to 714,286, the Congress of Brussels in 1952 raised it to 1,357,143, and the Congress of Ottawa in 1957 to 2,500,000 Swiss francs. The ceiling for 1963 has been set at 3,500,000 francs by the executive and liaison committee.[170]

The next step is the submission and approval of the annual budget. The preparation of the budget is the duty of the director of the bureau. After preparation, the budget is submitted by the director, along with all required information, which must include an explanatory statement, to the political department of the executive branch of the Swiss federal government. It is this body which in effect approves the union's budget,

169. See Ottawa Postal Convention (1957), Regulations, Art. 112. In effect, the new ceiling always comes into being at the same time as the new final acts of the congress, unless other arrangements are made. The ceiling set at Ottawa did not come into existence until April 1, 1959.

170. See *Annotated Acts* (1957), 1ᵉʳ fascicule, p. 159, fn. 1, and *Annual Reports, 1949,* p. 30; *1954,* p. 30; *1959,* p. 39; and *1960,* p. 36. The circumstances surrounding the decision of the ELC will be dealt with below, p. 163. Until 1934, the ceilings were expressed in Swiss francs. In 1934, the Congress of Cairo changed the 1929 ceiling from Swiss francs to "gold francs." As a result of a slight fluctuation of the Swiss franc, the 350,000 gold franc ceiling was actually equivalent to about 500,000 Swiss francs by 1947. The figures given above for 1947, 1952, and 1957 are expressed in the Swiss franc equivalent of the gold franc ceiling.

although the right to do so is delegated to it by the Swiss federal executive, the Federal Council, which also reserves the right to make the final decision.[171]

Four different bodies are involved in the examination and control of accounts. First, each month the director sends a statement of accounts to the Federal Financial Control Office, a branch of the Department of Finance and Customs of the Swiss federal executive, for auditing. At the end of the calendar year, the Financial Control Office undertakes a final verification of the accounts of the union for the entire year, which is then submitted to the Political Department of the Swiss government for verification along with the director's financial report.[172] The director's approved financial report, along with a balance sheet attested to by the director of the Federal Financial Control Office, is then included in the director's annual report on the activities of the union.[173]

There are three further occasions on which at least a partial examination of the union's accounts can take place. Before being printed, the annual report, which includes the financial report for the year, is submitted by the director to the chairman of the executive and liaison committee, who gives his preliminary approval.[174] After this approval is obtained, the annual report is printed and submitted to the executive and liaison committee. It is the job of the ELC, according to the postal convention, "to approve the annual report on the Union's activities drawn up by the International Bureau and, where appropriate, to furnish observations on it." [175] The annual reports of the preceding five years, which still include the financial sections, are then examined by the next postal congress. Only after the postal congress has given its approval can the financial reports of the UPU be considered closed.

Although a thorough examination of the accounts of the union could take place on these occasions, in practice the previous work of the Swiss government and the international bureau in the matter makes it unnecessary. At the 1957 session of the ELC, for example, examination of the Annual Report for 1956 took a little less than an hour, and none of the discussions that took place was concerned with its financial aspects.[176] At the Congress of Ottawa in 1957, the financial committee took only five meetings to investigate the director's report on the union's finances for the five preceding years. There is no record of any controversy whatsoever in committee, and the committee's report was quickly approved

---

171. See Switzerland, Federal Council, *Règlement concernant l'organisation, le fonctionnement et le contrôle de l'activité du Bureau international de l'Union postale universelle,* of June 30, 1953 as amended, Art. 2, para. b; Art. 3, para. a; and Art. 6.

172. *Ibid.,* Art. 3, para. g; and Art. 7, para. 2.

173. See *Annual Report, 1962,* pp. 41–44.

174. *Ibid.,* p. 40.

175. Ottawa Postal Convention (1957), Art. 16, para. g, subsec. 3.

176. See, UPU, *Documents de la Commission exécutive et de liaison, Session d'avril 1957* (Berne, 1957), pp. 418–21.

in plenary session, to the accompaniment of "applause." [177] That the UPU has an excellent guardian of its finances in the international bureau, as well as in the Swiss government, is illustrated by the reserve fund of 120,403.67 francs that was accumulated for the union by the care the bureau takes over its centimes. In 1907 the UPU inaugurated the international reply coupon and directed the bureau to supply these coupons to member states at cost. While the cost to members was fixed at 1.50 Swiss centimes per coupon, it was found that the real cost was only 1.460782 centimes. The bureau carefully hoarded the remaining 0.039218 centimes per coupon over the years until it was able to present the UPU in 1957 with 120,403.67 Swiss francs for its reserve fund.[178]

NET ORDINARY EXPENSES, 1947–1961
(IN SWISS FRANCS)

Year	Official ceiling	Net expenses	Amount put into pension fund
1947	500,000.00	499,329.44	33,838.00
1948	671,627.94	671,627.94	36,535.96
1949	857,142.84	857,142.84	165,218.29
1950	857,143.00	855,701.67	50,473.19
1951	857,143.00	857,143.00	97,865.03
1952	857,143.00	798,288.00	80,221.20
1953	1,357,143.00	1,278,529.02	265,843.69
1954	1,857,143.00	1,647,961.69	394,878.27
1955	1,857,143.00	1,695,409.74	288,214.34
1956	1,857,143.00	1,640,529.52	226,355.83
1957	1,857,143.00	1,346,862.13	None
1958	1,857,143.00	1,450,713.12	None
1959	2,339,286.00	2,339,268.55	355,778.49
1960	2,500,000.00	2,499,282.15	362,900.73
1961	2,500,000.00	2,497,370.30	431,681.73
1962	2,500,000.00	2,484,698.46	None[179]

177. Docs., Ottawa Postal Congress (1957), II, 1143 and 1152–55. The greatest controversy that occurred was over a Greece-Yugoslavia proposal to give the ELC the power to draw up the union's annual budget. The proposal was finally withdrawn in committee, in view of the opposition, and a substitute proposal to direct the ELC to study the whole problem was defeated by a vote of 10 to 6.

178. See *ibid.*, p. 75.

179. See *Annual Reports, 1947*, p. 20; *1948*, p. 33; *1949*, p. 30; *1950*, p. 28; *1951*, pp. 28–29; *1952*, p. 32; *1953*, pp. 28–29; *1954*, pp. 31–32; *1955*, pp. 29–30; *1956*, pp. 39–40; *1957*, pp. 30–31; *1958*, p. 39; *1959*, p. 39; *1960*, p. 36; *1961*, p. 35; and *1962*, pp. 35 and 38. It should also be noted that the union's reserve fund may be used to keep the contributory units stable. In view of the small amount that it contains, however, this is not really significant. (See *Annual Report, 1961*, p. 39, and, UPU, *Documents de la Commission exécutive et de liaison, Séance constitutive [du 26 septembre 1957] et Session de mai 1958 de la Commission élue par le Congrès d'Ottawa* [Berne, 1958], p. 265.)

To conclude this section, it does not appear out of place to present a table showing the ceilings placed on the ordinary net expenditures and the actual net expenditures since 1947. One caution should be given, however. Since 1929 the UPU has been authorized to use any difference that remained between the real net ordinary expenditures and the ceiling to augment the union's pension fund.[180] The following table will, therefore, contain a column showing this item.

180. Docs., London Postal Congress (1929), II, 287.

Representative Organs

O F ALL THE INTERNATIONAL ORGANIZATIONS engaged in the essential task of solving communal problems by cooperative action, the structure of the Universal Postal Union is one of the simplest. In essence it consists of the congress — periodic meetings of plenipotentiaries, open to the representatives of all member countries and exercising supreme power — bodies of limited membership to exercise certain delegated powers in the interval between congresses, a technical study committee, and a permanent international secretariat. Very few demands have been made for a more complicated structure, none of which has received more than a minimum of support.

The purpose of this chapter and the next is to investigate the institutions to which the nations of the world owe so much in their attempt to create and maintain a modern, efficient, and rapid system of international postal communications. The present chapter will deal with the highest authority of the UPU, the congress, and the two permanent organs which have been created since World War II, the executive and liaison committee and the consultative committee for postal studies. The international bureau, the UPU's unique secretariat, will be the subject of the following chapter.

A. The Universal Postal Congress

"THE CONGRESS is the supreme authority of the Union." [1] As such it has the ultimate responsibility for the direction of the affairs of the union and the international postal system. Since there is no statutory division of powers between organs of the UPU, such as that between the General Assembly and the Security Council in the UN, the congress exercises

1. *Annotated Acts (1957)*, 1ᵉʳ fascicule, p. XVI.

all the powers of an international organization. As we will see later, congresses have recently created subordinate bodies and have given them certain functions to carry out in the intervals between the meetings of the supreme authority. These functions are limited, however, and decisions taken by these bodies within their terms of reference are valid only after they have been reviewed and approved by the succeeding congress. Further, as the creator of these organs, the congress holds ultimate responsibility for their continued existence.

The foundation of the supreme power of the congress lies in the provision of the universal postal convention which gives it the authority to revise all official acts of the union: the Universal Postal Convention, its Final Protocol, Regulations and Annexes; and the Agreements and their Final Protocols, Regulations and Annexes.[2] In addition to this basic function, which is primarily legislative in nature, congresses have given themselves certain other specific duties of an executive and administrative nature including: (1) appointing the country members of the executive and liaison committee; (2) fixing the upper limit on the ordinary expenses of the union and its major organs; and (3) examining the reports of the executive and liaison committee and the consultative committee for postal studies on their activities in the interval between congresses.[3] Congresses have also taken upon themselves the task of examining and approving the annual reports of the director of the international bureau on the work of the organization.[4] As stated in a congress document, the aims of a congress are to ". . . meet especially to perfect the Union's system, to introduce improvements judged necessary, and to discuss common affairs." [5]

Congresses meet "not later than five years after the date of the entry into force of the Acts of the preceding Congress." [6] The union has not always held to this interval, however. The Congress of Berne, 1874, set the interval between congresses at only three years.[7] The Paris Postal Congress of 1878 raised the interval to five years from the date of the preceding congress, where it remained until 1906 when the Rome Postal Congress set the interval at a maximum of five years from the date of coming into force of the *acts* of the preceding congress; there has been no change since that time.[8] As we have seen in Chapter Two, various other

2. The most recent statement of this power is found in Article 11, para. 1, of the Ottawa Postal Convention (1957) which reads: "Delegates of the Countries of the Union meet in Congress not later than five years after the date of the entry into force of the Acts of the preceding Congress in order to revise or complete those Acts as required."

3. See Ottawa Postal Convention (1957), Art. 16, para. 3; Art. 17, para. 7; Art. 20, para. 1; and Regulations, Arts. 103, para. 2, and 112, para. 1.

4. See the report of the work of the finance committee in Docs., Ottawa Postal Congress (1957), II, 1143 and 1152–57.

5. *Ibid.*, II, 35.

6. Ottawa Postal Convention (1957), Art. 11, para. 1.

7. Berne Postal Treaty (1874), Art. 18, para. 1.

8. Docs., Paris Postal Congress (1878), pp. 44–49, 250, 396, 507, and 635; and Docs., Rome Postal Congress (1906), II, 197.

situations, including the intervention of World Wars I and II, have led to the postponing of congresses beyond the statutory limits. Various proposals have been made since 1906 to extend the interval, but without exception they have received only insignificant support.[9]

"Each congress fixes the place of assembly for the next congress." [10] The usual procedure is for the delegate of the country which wants the congress — adequate facilities are always an important consideration — to broach the subject to the heads of delegations and receive an informal agreement before proceeding further. A sympathetic delegate then makes the formal proposal, usually quite late in the congress, which always is adopted unanimously with loud applause. On only four occasions has there been a contest of any kind.[11] It should also be noted that ten of the fourteen congresses have been held in Europe. At the time when Europe was actually the geographical center for the largest group of member countries, it was only normal that Europe should be the preferred meeting place for congresses. With improved methods of transportation and a wider geographical distribution of membership, it may become more difficult to justify the choice of Europe so often in the future. That member countries are becoming aware of this is demonstrated by the fact that four proposals were offered at Ottawa for the location of the fifteenth universal postal congress, only one of which was from Europe.[12]

1. Representation

All member countries have the right to be represented at each of the union's periodic congresses. This includes all regular members and the territories or postal administrations considered to be separate countries for the purposes of the postal convention. Each member may be represented by any number of delegates with plenipotentiary powers, and each delegation may have an indefinite number of advisers, but only one vote is allotted to a member. Proxy voting is permitted, but the maximum number of votes a delegation can cast in such cases is two.[13]

"Each country arranges for its representation at congresses by one

9. At the Paris Congress of 1947, for example, the Mexican delegation unsuccessfully attempted to change the interval from five to seven years. The major argument given was that the five-year interval was too short for some countries to gain adequate experience with previously adopted rules. (See Docs., Paris Postal Congress (1947), I, 42; and II, 424–25.)

10. Ottawa Postal Convention (1957), Art. 11, para. 3.

11. See, for instance, Docs., Brussels Postal Congress (1952), II, 1364 and 1405.

12. See Docs., Ottawa Postal Congress (1957), II, 1144–46 and 1148–51. Countries requesting the congress were Austria, Brazil, India, and Tunisia.

13. See Ottawa Postal Convention (1957), Art. 11. An official interpretation of the Congress of Stockholm in 1924 provides that a proxy vote may be cast only by regular members and not by territories or postal administrations considered to be separate countries only for the purposes of the postal convention. (See Docs., Stockholm Postal Congress (1924), II, 128, 206, and 217–18.)

or more plenipotentiary delegates furnished with the necessary powers by their government." [14] The "necessary powers," for the UPU, are government credentials designating individuals empowered to negotiate the revision of the acts of the UPU and to sign them in the name of their government.[15] "Government" in this respect has been defined by the UPU as the highest governmental authority of the delegate's country with the power to negotiate treaties, the executive authority.[16]

In order to eliminate the possibility that a member might not be invited because the host country does not have diplomatic relations with it, there is a provision in the postal convention to the effect that members may be invited also "through the intermediary of a third country." [17] The possibility that such an eventuality might occur was raised for the first time in the preparatory committee of the Congress of London in 1929 and resulted in an interpretation by that congress to the effect that diplomatic problems between member countries should not result in the refusal to invite or to permit the representation of any member country in any meeting of the union which it wished to attend. The decision was justified on the basis that the UPU was a "non-political" association, and consequently, politics should not be allowed to hamper its work.[18] The subject was not raised again until the 1952 Brussels Congress where, after a short discussion in which the possibility of having the international bureau issue invitations was discussed and rejected, the aforementioned provision was added to the postal convention.[19]

Although the congresses of the UPU are relatively small, there has been a steady increase in size over the years. The total number of delegates to the Berne Congress of 1874 was only 42. The delegates to the Rome Congress in 1906, however, numbered 125, and over 350 attended the Congress of Brussels in 1952. The increase has been due both to the increase in UPU members and to the increasing complexity of the matters under discussion. Larger delegations are needed in order to provide a variety of experts and to permit participation on all major committees. The size of the individual delegations, nevertheless, varies widely. In the Berne Congress of 1874, the largest delegation was that from Switzerland, the host to the congress, which numbered five. The next largest delegations were those of Belgium and Germany, with three. Five countries were represented by one delegate only.[20] At the Ottawa

14. Ottawa Postal Convention (1957), Art. 11, para. 2.

15. See Docs., Berne Postal Congress (1874), pp. 19–20.

16. Docs., London Postal Congress (1929), II, 134–35. It has also been agreed that it need not be mandatory that a delegate's credentials be signed by the chief of state of the country concerned. (Docs., Vienna Postal Congress, 1891, pp. 417–19.)

17. Ottawa Postal Convention (1957), Art. 11, para. 4.

18. Docs., London Postal Congress (1929), I, 1383; and II, 155. The Russian suggestion was undoubtedly prompted by the fact that the USSR had been refused an invitation to the 1927 Washington Radio Conference on the basis that the United States did not recognize the Soviet government. (See Codding, *op. cit.*, p. 116.)

19. Docs., Brussels Postal Congress (1952), I, 162; and II, 337–38.

20. Docs., Berne Postal Congress (1874), pp. 11–12.

Congress of 1957, in contrast, the largest representation was that of the United Kingdom, with 17, followed by Germany, with 12, and France, with 10. However, the host country, Canada, was served by only seven representatives and experts.[21]

Concerning make-up, the majority of the delegates to UPU congresses are experts in postal affairs. Since the early years of its existence the UPU has laid particular emphasis on the point that work can be done more efficiently and quickly by postal experts than by others. It is felt that professional diplomats, for instance, seldom know much about postal communications, and their presence would tend to intrude politics into primarily technical matters. There is a similar aversion to political appointees, such as ministers of postal services or, as in the United States, the Postmaster General. Consequently, delegations are usually headed up by an individual from the top professional level and assisted by other qualified experts from central headquarters. Nevertheless, at almost every congress a few member countries send as their representatives persons who are not postal experts but often a member of a diplomatic mission in the country where the congress is being held. It is usually the smaller countries which engage in this practice, especially those at a great distance from the congress or from Latin America. At the Ottawa Congress in 1957, the delegate of El Salvador offered a proposal to the effect that delegations should be made up *only* of "qualified functionaries of postal administrations." Although there was a great deal of sympathy for the purpose of the proposal, it was rejected on the basis that the congress should not attempt legally to restrict the right of countries to compose their delegations as they saw fit.[22]

Prior to World War II, it was an established principle that no one was to be admitted to union congresses except delegates from member countries and personnel from the secretariat of the international bureau. This prohibition applied to private and public international organizations as well as to casual observers. One of the more persistent demands during the interwar years came from the International Chamber of Commerce. The chamber requested but was refused permission to send an observer to the meetings of the preparatory committee of the London Congress (1928), to the congress itself in 1929, and to the Congress of Buenos Aires in 1939. Among the reasons given were: (1) the acceptance of observers from the chamber would in all likelihood give rise to requests from other interested organizations, such as the transport companies, which if accepted would hinder the work of the congress; (2) the users' representatives should not be given the right to consult directly with postal delegations who are limited by the instructions of their governments; and (3) the users should not be permitted to introduce proposals but rather should consult with postal administrations

21. Docs., Ottawa Postal Congress (1957), II, 44–53. In contrast, there were 600 delegates to the Atlantic City conferences of the ITU in 1947. The American delegation alone numbered 191. (See Codding, *op. cit.*, p. 223.)
22. Docs., Ottawa Postal Congress (1957), II, 339.

which, if impressed by their ideas, could present them as administration proposals.[23]

The Congress of Paris in 1947 changed the pattern, at least concerning other public international organizations. After a fairly long and arduous discussion in which the delegates from the three Scandinavian countries defended the thesis that no organization foreign to postal communication should be allowed in UPU meetings, the first plenary meeting of the Paris Postal Congress admitted an observer from the UN by a vote of 50 to 4, and an observer from the Provisional International Civil Aviation Organization (PICAO) by a vote of 46 to 4. Those arguing in favor of the admission of the two international organizations stressed the point that one of the major tasks of the Paris Congress was to determine the future relationships between the UN and the UPU. It was also noted that only five administrations had voiced disapproval when the possibility of inviting the UN to send observers had been suggested by the international bureau in a circular distributed to all members before the congress. Very little discussion centered around the request of the PICAO, and it can be assumed that its success was due to the action taken on the UN application.[24]

Since the decision of the Congress of Paris and the negotiation of the agreement between the UN and the UPU, public international organizations have been in regular attendance at UPU congresses. Observers from the UN and ICAO were joined by observers from UNESCO and WHO at both the Congress of Brussels in 1952 and the Congress of Ottawa in 1957.[25] An observer from the Postal Union of the Americas and Spain was admitted without much difficulty to the Brussels Congress, and observers from both this group and the Arab Postal Union were admitted without discussion to the Congress of Ottawa.[26] Despite the rather violent opposition of the Communist states, who argued that a purely "political" organization had no place in congresses of the UPU, the Congress of Brussels also admitted an observer from the Council of Europe.[27] The latter did not request permission to send an observer to the Congress of Ottawa.

One of the more difficult problems of representation for the UPU has been that of the private international organization, the Inter-

23. See Docs., London Postal Congress (1929), I, 1368–69, and II, 18; and Docs., Buenos Aires Postal Congress (1939), II, 19–20.
24. Docs., Paris Postal Congress (1947), II, 23–31.
25. Docs., Brussels Postal Congress (1952), II, 233–34; and Docs., Ottawa Postal Congress (1957), II, 17, 35, and 165.
26. Docs., Brussels Postal Congress (1952), II, 234, 236–37, and 244–47.
27. Ibid., pp. 234–36 and 277–79. It should be noted that the decision to admit the observer from the Council of Europe was made by 20 delegations voting in the affirmative, 11 against, and 48 abstaining. Voting in favor were: Algeria, Belgian Congo, Belgium, Brazil, Ceylon, Chile, China, Colombia, Egypt, France, French overseas territories, Ireland, Italy, Luxembourg, Peru, Philippines, Tunisia, Turkey, United States, and United States possessions. Voting against were: Albania, Byelorussia, Bulgaria, Czechoslovakia, Hungary, Poland, Rumania, South Africa, Switzerland, Ukraine, and USSR (see ibid., p. 236).

national Air Transport Association (IATA). Its predecessor, the International Air Traffic Commission, was refused permission to send an observer to the preparatory committee of the Congress of London in 1928 and to the congress itself in 1929, on grounds similar to those given in refusing the International Chamber of Commerce.[28] The request of the International Air Transport Association to send an observer to the Congress of Brussels in 1952 raised a storm of protest. The delegate from Canada expressed his most "energetic protest" against admitting a nongovernmental organization whose prime purpose was to obtain the highest possible airmail rates; the delegation from India felt that the presence of an observer from IATA would inhibit discussion; and the delegate from Lebanon argued that knowledge of the debates would place IATA in a position to let it take advantage of administrations in its fight for higher airmail rates. Nevertheless, when the request was put to a vote, the congress agreed to admit the IATA observer by a vote of 32 to 12, with 37 abstentions.[29] The head of the Canadian delegation was so incensed by the decision of the congress that he subsequently refused to accept the chairmanship of a subcommittee of the congress, one of the few times such an action has occurred in the history of the UPU.[30] IATA did not request permission to send an observer to the Congress of Ottawa. UPU congresses are still closed to the public.

2. Organization

The increased membership of the union and the steadily widening scope of the subject matter under its jurisdiction have resulted in an increase in the number of committees necessary to expedite the work of congresses. Nevertheless, the structure of congresses has been kept simple and uncomplicated, at least in comparison with many of the other specialized agencies of the United Nations. In essence, the UPU congress is composed of the plenary assembly — the congress in the strictest sense of the word — and its committee substructure. It is in the committee that the bulk of the substantive work of the congress is accomplished: winnowing out the important proposals from the trivial, exploring areas of agreement, and preparing acceptable drafts of changes in the final acts. Plenary assemblies, on the other hand, are usually devoted to the formalities which surround international meetings of any size and, of

28. Docs., London Postal Congress (1929), I, 1368–69; and II, 18.
29. Docs., Brussels Postal Congress (1952), II, 234 and 247–48. Those countries voting in favor were: Algeria, Australia, Belgian Congo, Belgium, British overseas territories, Brazil, Cambodia, Ceylon, Colombia, Dutch East Indies, Egypt, Ethiopia, France, French overseas territories, Great Britain, Iraq, Italy, Jordan, Laos, Luxembourg, Morocco, Mexico, Nicaragua, New Zealand, Netherlands, Philippines, Portugal, Saudi Arabia, Tunisia, Turkey, United States, and United States possessions. Those voting against were: Canada, Chile, Denmark, Iceland, India, Ireland, Lebanon, Norway, Paraguay, Sweden, Switzerland, and Yugoslavia (ibid., p. 248).
30. Ibid., p. 629.

course, give the stamp of approval to changes which the committees make in the final acts.

The overall organization of a congress is under the command of a bureau composed of a chairman of the congress, a vice chairman of the congress, and a secretariat. The chairman and the vice chairman act in the same capacity in plenary assemblies. Since the first congress in 1874, the post of chairman has always gone to a high official of the postal administration of the host country. At the Paris Congress in 1947, Mr. Joseph-Jean le Mouël, director general of French Posts, was chosen as chairman. At Brussels in 1952, the chairman was Mr. E. G. Pineux, the director general of the Belgian Post Office, and in Ottawa in 1957, it was Mr. W. J. Turnbull, deputy minister of Posts of Canada.[31] Prior to the Congress of Vienna (1891), no need was found for the post of vice chairman. As mentioned in Chapter Two, the Congress of Vienna created a vice chairmanship and the director of the international bureau was chosen for this position. The director of the bureau has held the post of vice chairman at all succeeding congresses.[32] The secretariat to the congress, ranging in number from two to seven persons, is usually provided by the international bureau, and the deputy director of the bureau acts as its chief.[33]

Since the Congress of Rome in 1906, it has also been the custom to appoint an even higher official of the host country to the post of honorary chairman of the congress, and quite often another to the post of honorary vice chairman. At Ottawa, for instance, Mr. J. G. Diefenbaker, prime minister of Canada, was named to the former and Mr. William Hamilton, postmaster general of Canada, to the latter.[34] It should be noted that all of these elections, both real and honorary, are a mere formality.

The Congress of Ottawa provides a good picture of the committee structure of a typical post-World War II congress. In all, the Congress of Ottawa created eight committees and two subcommittees. First was the General Committee. It was given jurisdiction over those parts of the postal convention and its regulations dealing with the structure and the organization of the union and other general questions not specifically concerned with the international mails. Among other decisions, the general committee decided to create a new organ of the union, the Consultative Committee on Postal Studies, and to direct the executive and liaison committee to inaugurate a study of the postal convention with a view toward its simplification and consolidation. The general committee also discussed the establishment of a single worldwide insignia for post boxes and the introduction of an international letter-writing week, and

31. Docs., Paris Postal Congress (1947), II, 17; Docs., Brussels Postal Congress (1952), II, 213; and Docs., Ottawa Postal Congress (1957), II, 162.

32. On three occasions more than one vice chairman was appointed: Rome in 1906, London in 1929, and Buenos Aires in 1939. In each case, however, the director of the bureau was among their number.

33. See, for instance, Docs., Ottawa Postal Congress (1957), II, 164.

34. Ibid., p. 162.

approved the report of the work done by the executive and liaison committee. The First Committee was given the task of examining all proposals concerning those parts of the postal convention and its regulations dealing with the letter post. The Second Committee had a similar mandate for the agreements concerning insured letters and boxes and the international parcel post. The Third Committee examined proposals for changes in all other agreements, e.g., postal money orders, postal traveler's checks, international postal checking account transfers, collect on delivery items, the international postal savings bank service, and subscriptions to newspapers and periodicals. The Fourth Committee, the drafting committee, was given the task of examining all proposals of a purely editorial nature and of drafting the final acts. In addition there were a Finance Committee and a Credentials Committee whose tasks are more or less self-explanatory.

Of special note at Ottawa were the Committee for a Program of Technical and Economic Studies and Committee 1 *bis*. The task of the former was to examine proposals for the establishment of a new consultative committee on postal studies and its terms of reference. As an ad hoc committee, its mandate ended with the presentation of its proposals to the general committee. Committee 1 *bis,* while technically a subcommittee, has a more permanent place in the UPU's congress structure. First created by the Congress of Paris in 1947, and re-created at the congresses of Brussels and Ottawa, Committee 1 *bis* is charged with examining all proposals concerning airmail. As airmail continued to increase in importance in the world's mail system, Committee 1 *bis* was raised to the position of a major congress committee. The one other subcommittee created at the Ottawa Congress was the Subcommittee on Forms, inaugurated by the Drafting Committee to deal with all administrative forms used in the international mail service.[35]

Committees have a chairman, one to three vice chairmen, and one to six rapporteurs, all chosen from the committee's membership, and a secretariat of one or two persons supplied by the international bureau. The number of vice chairmen and rapporteurs varies with the importance of the committee. At Brussels, for example, the general committee, the first three of the numbered committees, and Committee 1 *bis* all had three vice chairmen while the fourth committee and all the others had only one. The largest number of rapporteurs (six) was chosen by the general committee and the first committee. Rapporteurs for the other committees ranged from five for Committee 1 *bis* to one for the credentials committee and the finance committee.[36]

The UPU is not entirely democratic in the selection of countries

35. Concerning the creation of committees and subcommittees, see *ibid.,* pp. 36, 170, 174–75 and 177–78.

36. The information on the organization and staffing of committees at the Brussels Congress in this and following paragraphs, unless otherwise designated, is taken from Docs., Brussels Postal Congress (1952), II, 27, 30–33, 134, 182–92, 210, 213, 215, 216, 258, 306–10, 469–70, 578, 629–31, 774, 846, 892, 893, 1013, 1299, and 1301.

to provide the chairmen of committees. Since the Congress of Lisbon (1885), the first at which it was found necessary to have more than two committees, the chairmanship of the first committee has always gone to the United Kingdom. With one exception — the Congress of Brussels in 1952 — France has always held the chairmanship of the second committee. Further, from 1885 to 1939, the third committee had always been chaired by a delegate from Germany.[37]

In the membership of committees, the number varies according to the type of committee. Those dealing with the postal convention, its final protocol, its regulations, and its annexes have always been open to all delegations. At the Brussels Congress of 1952, for instance, all 92 countries represented at the congress were reported to have had delegates on the general committee, the first committee, and Committee 1 *bis*. Those dealing with the agreements and their regulations, on the other hand, have as full members only delegates who have ratified one or more of the agreements over which the committee has jurisdiction, or those who announce their intention to do so. Other interested delegations may send representatives but they do not have the right to vote. At Brussels, 84 countries were represented on the committee dealing with insured letters and boxes and the parcel post. Representation on the third committee, with jurisdiction over all other agreements, amounted to only 68. Drafting committees usually have a very restricted membership, with emphasis on countries with delegates who are proficient in French. The Paris Congress of 1947 limited membership on its drafting committee to nine, while the Brussels and Ottawa congresses limited membership to twelve.[38]

The voting procedure used by the UPU in its congresses is also deserving of special note. In the first place, the idea of required voting on any matter is traditionally abhorrent. It is almost traditional to have one or more speakers at congresses stress the importance of conciliation, cooperation, and unanimity, and the adverse effects that serious disagreements ending in votes might have on the smooth functioning of the international postal system.[39] Nevertheless, many problems arise at almost every congress which can be resolved only by a formal vote, and a fairly elaborate set of rules has been created to regulate the voting procedure.

Traditionally, there are two levels of decision: the committee and the plenary session. Voting at the committee level is similar to that of the plenary session, with one important exception. It has long been the practice in UPU congresses that a committee may not again discuss the same matter once a vote has been taken. Further discussion may take

37. See UPU, *Genèse des Actes de l'UPU*, No. R 091.52, pp. 3–18; and Docs., Ottawa Postal Congress (1957), II, 177.

38. The Brussels drafting committee was made up of representatives from Belgium, Canada, Denmark, Egypt, France, Haiti, Laos, Lebanon, Luxembourg, Poland, Switzerland, and Syria.

39. See, for instance, Docs., Paris Postal Conference (1880), p. 38; Docs., Cairo Postal Congress (1934), I, 2; and Docs., Ottawa Postal Congress (1957), II, 1177.

place only in plenary session; this includes either an affirmative or negative vote on any proposal. The plenary session, of course, has the privilege of changing any decision taken by a committee or any decision already taken in plenary session.[40]

Although the normal method of voting in UPU congresses is by a show of hands, provision is also made for a roll call vote. Either the chairman or a country delegation may request the latter. And, since the Congress of Paris in 1947, a secret ballot may be used at the request of any two delegations.[41] A secret ballot has often been used in UPU congresses, but prior to 1947 it was not made a formal part of the rules of procedure.[42] Secret ballots were used twice at the Congress of Berne in 1874, twice at the Congress of London in 1929, three times at the Congress of Paris in 1947, and frequently at the Congress of Brussels in 1952 and the Congress of Ottawa in 1957.[43]

Another change which resulted from the 1947 Paris Congress was the establishing of a specific quorum for voting in plenary sessions and committees. From the congress of 1874 to the congress of 1947, the rules of procedure provided only for a vote. No quorum being required, a simple majority of those present was sufficient for the making of all decisions. The 1947 Paris Congress, however, was confronted with two proposals to tighten the voting regulations. One, offered by the Swedish delegation, would have introduced, for all important decisions, a three-fourths majority coupled with a requirement of a quorum of at least three fourths of all the countries represented at the congress. Important decisions, in the Swedish definition, would include all decisions pertaining to such nonpostal matters in the postal convention as the provisions concerning the constitution of the union, its structure, and its relation to other international organizations. All other decisions could be made by a majority of those present and voting. The other proposal, by the delegate of the USSR, would have required "unanimous consent" to change many of the final acts of the union, including all of the articles covered in the Swedish proposal, the provisions of the convention dealing with the general rules of the international postal service, the final protocol to the convention, and six of the more important articles in the regulations. All other decisions would need a two-thirds majority. The Russian proposal did not, however, attempt to introduce any specific quorum. According to the Swedish delegate, stricter voting procedures were needed at Paris because of the seriousness of some of the decisions facing

40. An exception is made for committees that do not report to a plenary session of a congress, such as a preparatory committee, or one of the permanent organs of the union, such as the executive and liaison committee. (See Docs., London Postal Congress (1929), I, 1458; and Docs., Ottawa Postal Congress [1957], II, 1125–28.)

41. Docs., Paris Postal Congress (1947), II, 1054.

42. See Docs., London Postal Congress (1929), II, 22–23, and Docs., Buenos Aires Postal Congress (1939), II, 22.

43. See Docs., Berne Postal Congress (1874), pp. 66 and 82; Docs., London Postal Congress (1929), II, 254, 258, 261, 264, and 610–12; and Docs., Paris Postal Congress (1947), II, 42, 1052–55, 1058–59, and 1069–76.

the delegates, such as those relating to the agreement between the UN and the UPU, and the possibility of creating a new administrative council. The Soviet delegate simply argued that unanimous consent on all important items was a necessary procedure in any international cooperative undertaking.[44]

When the question was finally put to a vote, the Soviet proposal was rejected "by a great majority." [45] The Swedish proposal, on the other hand, after being amended to reduce the majority and the quorum needed from three quarters to two thirds, was accepted "by a great majority." [46]

The matter was not closed at that point, however. On two occasions delegations requested clarification on whether abstentions — a common practice in UPU congresses — were counted in the majorities agreed upon.[47] Finally, only six days before the end of the congress, the matter was raised again by the delegate of the United Kingdom, who stated that a great deal of confusion had been manifested at the congress over the proper majority needed to make valid decisions. To eliminate this confusion, he suggested that the congress change the voting provision by eliminating the two-thirds majority needed for a valid vote and by substituting a simple majority of those present. Despite the violent objection of the Soviet delegate and several others, the Paris Congress adopted the United Kingdom-sponsored change in a vote of 39 to 17. Twelve delegations abstained and eight were absent.[48]

The provisions of the rules of procedure of the Ottawa Postal Congress dealing with majorities and quorums, only slightly modified from that finally adopted at Paris, read as follows:

1] Issues which cannot be settled by common accord are decided by voting. Proposals dealing with questions concerning Part 1 of the Convention and with the relations of the Union with other international organs are not adopted unless: 1) at least two thirds of the members of the Union represented at the congress or on a committee and having the right to vote are present at the moment of the vote; 2) they receive more than half of the votes of the members of the Union represented at the Congress or on the committee.

2] In all other cases issues that cannot be settled by common accord are decided by the majority of the members present and voting, on the condition that at least half of the members represented and having the right to vote on the issue being put to the vote are present at the time of the voting. This condition does not, however, apply to the Fourth Committee [Drafting Committee]. The expression "members present and

44. See Docs., Paris Postal Congress (1947), II, 35–40.
45. *Ibid.,* p. 38.
46. *Ibid.*
47. *Ibid.,* pp. 39 and 61–67. The decision on both cases was in the negative. If two thirds of the delegations of the countries represented at the congress were present, a proposal could be carried if two thirds of those voting answered in the affirmative.
48. *Ibid.,* pp. 885–92.

voting" means those members voting "for" or "against." Abstentions are not taken into consideration. In a like manner, blank or invalid ballots cast in a secret vote are not taken into consideration. In the case of a tie, the Chairman casts the deciding vote.[49]

A substantial change has also occurred in recent years in the languages used by delegates in congresses. The official language of the UPU is French and has been so since the Congress of Berne in 1874. From 1874 to World War I, French was also the only working language permitted in union congresses. The question of the possible use of other languages in congresses was first raised at Madrid in 1920. A proposal to admit the use of Spanish was submitted by the Colombian delegation and a proposal to use English was submitted by the New Zealand delegate. In support of his proposal the New Zealand delegate pointed to the "inferior position" of those who spoke English, i.e., the difficulty of expression and of being "spontaneous." He also pointed out that two international organizations had adopted English as well as French for discussions, specifically, the League of Nations and the ILO at its Washington conference. The Colombian delegate pointed out that Spanish was a beautiful language, and that one third of the union's membership was Spanish-speaking.[50] At the suggestion of the chairman, who pointed out that the subject had been raised quite late in the congress, it was decided not to press the point but to ask the international bureau to look into the question for the next union congress.[51]

The Stockholm Congress in 1924 decided to continue to use French as the official language of the congress, as earlier congresses had done, but added a provision to its rules of procedure to the effect that, as an exceptional measure, the chairman of the congress could "authorize a delegation to make use of an interpreter designated by it to speak in its name and to present observations and proposals." [52] This formula was employed by all succeeding congresses up to and including the Congress of Paris in 1947, despite continued agitation for additional official working languages. At the Cairo Congress in 1934, for example, British India submitted a proposal to designate both English and French as official languages. Although the suggestion was supported by the United States, Australia, China, and Great Britain, the opposition, which included Canada, Chile, Germany, Iceland, Italy, Netherlands, Spain and Uruguay, was so strong that the proposal was subsequently withdrawn from consideration.[53] A British proposal of a similar nature was submitted, and later withdrawn without a vote, at the Congress of Buenos Aires in 1939.[54]

49. Docs., Ottawa Postal Congress (1957), II, 38.
50. Docs., Madrid Postal Congress (1920), II, 795–97. This section deals only with the spoken languages of congresses. For a discussion of the Union's official language see below, pp. 207–208.
51. Ibid., p. 797.
52. See Docs., Stockholm Postal Congress (1924), II, 28–31, 310, and 311.
53. Docs., Cairo Postal Congress (1934), II, 16–18.
54. Docs., Buenos Aires Postal Congress (1939), I, 60; and II, 21.

The 1947 Paris Congress was confronted with a series of requests for additional working languages. The Argentine delegation proposed that the delegates be allowed to use any language they wished and that the international bureau provide for interpretation into French and back. The Soviet delegation proposed that the congress adopt all five of the working languages used by the United Nations, the Lebanese delegate requested Arabic, and the Iranian delegate requested the right to use Iranian.[55] After it was pointed out that an enormous amount of time would be lost (simultaneous interpretation had not yet been introduced in 1947), and that the cost would be extremely heavy to bear, each of the proposals was voted down by large margins and the status quo was retained.[56]

By 1952 a system of simultaneous interpretation had been perfected and used in the meetings of many international organizations. Consequently, the main argument against the use of several working languages was no longer valid and the stage was set for the addition of other languages. Furthermore, two actions were taken preceding the Brussels Congress that were to have an important influence on the question: (1) there was a new provision in the draft rules of procedure, drawn up by the Belgian government in consultation with the international bureau, which provided for the simultaneous interpretation of debates into French, English, and Spanish; and (2) the Belgian government, with the help of the international bureau, had proceeded to install such a system in the building to be used by the congress.[57]

When the Brussels Congress reached its study of the rules of procedure, only the delegates from Denmark and the Netherlands made a spirited stand against additional working languages, and even they conceded defeat from the beginning. The gist of their arguments was that French had eminently proven its worth as the sole working language in the past and that a system of simultaneous interpretation would cost more than it was worth. The proponents, on the other hand, argued at length that the use of additional languages would make the work of the congress proceed at a much faster rate, that it would permit those whose mother tongues were not French to get their ideas across more readily and more clearly, and that the UPU should not fall behind the United Nations, the ITU, and other international organizations which accepted more than one working language in conferences.[58]

The only real point of disagreement occurred over the additional languages to be admitted. Almost immediately after the discussions opened, the delegate of the USSR made a formal request that Russian be added to the three languages already in the simultaneous interpreta-

55. Docs., Paris Postal Congress (1947), II, 33–34.
56. *Ibid.*, pp. 34–35.
57. Docs., Brussels Postal Congress (1952), II, 28 and 201. While the system was operating from the moment the congress was inaugurated, it was emphasized that it was a provisional measure only and should in no way prejudice the actions of the delegates.
58. *Ibid.*, pp. 261–71 and 275–77.

tion system. His proposal was supported by Albania, Byelorussia, Bulgaria, Czechoslovakia, Poland, Rumania, and Ukraine. The request for Russian was followed by requests for Arabic, Chinese, and Portuguese. So many languages were called for that at one point the Italian delegate asked that the discussions be closed in order to prevent the congress from disintegrating into a "tower of Babel." [59] After it was pointed out that the system in operation could not take more than four languages at a time, and it was agreed to reintroduce the old formula that permitted delegations to utilize interpreters to speak for them on the floor (this formula had been missing in the draft rules of procedure), the delegations requesting Arabic, Chinese, and Portuguese withdrew their proposals with a warning that their withdrawal was only temporary and that they retained the right to raise the point at future congresses. The Russian delegate, however, continued to insist on his proposal, and as a result Russian was included in the working languages of the congress.[60]

After a further discussion on the manner in which the expenses of the system should be apportioned, the following formula was adopted:

1]   French is the official language for the documents of the congress;

2]   An efficient system of interpretation into English, French, Russian, and Spanish is utilized for discussions in plenary assemblies and in all of the permanent committees with the exception of Committee 4 [the drafting committee];

3] *a)* The expenses of the installation and its upkeep are borne by the Union;

b) The expenses of the interpretation services are borne by the member countries which use English, Russian, or Spanish;

c) These expenses are divided into three equal parts. Each of the parts is apportioned between the countries belonging to each of these groups in proportion to their contributions to the general expenses of the Union.

4]   Exceptionally, the Chairman of the Congress or of a Committee may authorize a delegation to use an interpreter designated by it to present its observations or proposals in French, or in one of the other languages admitted.[61]

The fact that most of the specialized agencies of the UN, and the UN itself, recognize and utilize more languages in meetings than does the UPU will sustain constant pressure on the UPU congresses for the addition of more languages for more purposes. On the other hand, there is no question that the UPU has been able to carry on its work without too much difficulty with a minimum of languages. Whether this uniqueness

59. *Ibid.,* p. 266.

60. *Ibid.,* pp. 269 and 276. The official language for the congress remained French, however.

61. *Ibid.,* pp. 28 and 261–71. Of the 87 delegations which made their preference known, 36 opted for French, 22 for English, 20 for Spanish, and 9 for Russian. (See *ibid.,* pp. 276 and 301–303.)

will be allowed to continue, in view of what must be described as "language nationalism," is seriously in doubt.[62]

3. Submission of Proposals

One of the more difficult problems facing UPU congresses of recent years is that of the enormous increase in proposals from member countries. Prior to World War I, when the membership of the union was relatively small, the problem was insignificant. The Congress of Madrid in 1920, with its record of 2,248 proposals, however, marked a turning point. From that time on, the UPU has searched for a method that would ensure a thorough examination and discussion of all proposals submitted within a reasonable length of time.

The first suggestion on the matter was a proposal submitted during the 1924 Stockholm Congress by the delegate of Uruguay. He asked for a provision in the postal convention restricting discussion to proposals that had been submitted to the international bureau in time to be published six months in advance of the opening of a congress. The Uruguayan proposal was dropped on the basis that it was too drastic and perhaps unworkable. With an eye on the number of proposals that had been presented to the Madrid Congress, many of which had been introduced after the congress had begun its work, the delegates at Stockholm nevertheless acceptd a new provision of the rules of procedure eliminating from discussion all proposals of substance introduced after the ninth working day. The Congress of London (1929) lowered the interval for accepting new proposals to the fifth working day, where it remained until 1957.[63]

The Congress of Buenos Aires in 1939 in effect recognized the correctness of the principle of the 1924 Uruguayan proposal when, confronted with 1,108 proposals, it adopted unanimously a resolution calling upon administrations to deposit proposals as early as possible before congresses.[64] Although this resolution was obeyed to some extent at the Congress of Paris in 1947, the situation at the Brussels Congress in 1952 made evident the need for more drastic measures. The bureau sent out a circular to member administrations in March 1951, recalling the resolution of the Buenos Aires Congress and inviting them to try to have their proposals in Berne by August 31, 1951. Out of a total of 1,712 proposals submitted to the Brussels Congress which met on May 14, 1952, only 242 were in the hands of the bureau on the date suggested. By the end of December 1951, a little over four months before the opening of the Brussels Congress, the bureau had received a total of 988 proposals. All of the remainder were submitted in 1952, including 51 in January, 121 in February, 214 in March, 130 in April, and 208

62. See the additional information on languages below, pp. 207–208.
63. Docs., Stockholm Postal Congress (1924), II, 19–21, 121, and 310; and Docs., London Postal Congress (1929), II, 33–35.
64. Docs., Buenos Aires Postal Congress (1939), II, 517–18.

in May itself. The bureau was not able to get many of the proposals to the administrations until the Brussels Congress was already under way.[65]

The executive and liaison committee of the UPU took the problem under consideration at its 1955 session and came to the conclusion that since late proposals were either harmful or useless, legal methods should be introduced to eliminate or at least cut down their number. Such proposals were harmful, according to the ELC, because they complicated the work of the congress, its committees, and subcommittees, and placed a needless burden on administrations, the international bureau, and the secretariat of the congress. Late proposals were also useless because many were ignored by the delegates in the press of business. A certain delay was necessary in order to have the proposals printed, circulated (for some countries a month was necessary for surface mail transportation), and studied seriously. Furthermore, additional time was necessary for some administrations to translate the proposals from French into their own languages.[66]

The solution found by the committee, as modified in the Congress of Ottawa, was to add to the postal convention an article which subjected proposals to future congresses to the following rules:

A]   all proposals reaching the International Bureau at least six months before the date of the opening of a congress will be published in the list of proposals;

B]   substantive proposals reaching the Bureau in the interval between six and four months before the date fixed for the opening of a congress will be published only if supported by two other postal administrations;

C]   substantive proposals reaching the Bureau in the four months immediately preceding a congress will be published only if they are supported by eight other administrations;

D]   no proposal of a purely editorial nature would be accepted during the period of six months preceding the opening date of a congress.[67]

In addition, also at the suggestion of the ELC, the Ottawa Congress added a provision to its rules of procedure whereby no proposal of substance submitted after the formal opening of the congress would be considered. Amendments to proposals already submitted, on the other hand, would be considered in the congress only when they were handed to the secretariat by noon of the day before the pertinent proposal was scheduled to be discussed.[68]

Whether these provisions will have their desired effects on future congresses, or whether enough exceptions will be permitted to negate

65. UPU, *Documents de la Commission exécutive et de liaison, session de mai 1955* (Berne, 1955), pp. 170–71.

66. *Ibid.*, pp. 170–75.

67. *Ibid.*, pp. 175–79; Docs., Ottawa Postal Congress (1957), I, 282–83, and II, 375–76, 774, and 777–78; and Ottawa Postal Convention (1957), Detailed Regulations, Art. 101.

68. Docs., Ottawa Postal Congress (1957), II, 37.

their purpose, must await the passage of time. At least, the UPU has made an attempt to solve a serious problem.

4. Congress in Action

Although congresses differ in many ways, over the years a pattern has developed which each succeeding congress follows almost to the letter. Indeed, a stranger to the UPU with a knowledge of this pattern could find his way about any congress without too much difficulty. This section will be devoted to a description of the workings of a typical congress, not to enlighten our stranger who in any case would not be admitted, but to provide the student of international organization with an insight into a practice which tells much about the nature of the UPU.

Preparations for congresses must begin several years in advance of the date set for meeting. The host country needs time to arrange for housing of the congress, installation of facilities (including an interpretation system), hiring the necessary staff, and obtaining supplies. Preparations must be made for the housing of the delegates and the staff, and for their entertainment. Further, communication facilities must be prepared that will permit delegates to contact their embassies or their home governments. To aid it in these tasks, the host country fortunately has the services of the expert staff of the international bureau. For the Congress of Ottawa, for example, the international bureau made its first contact with the Canadian government in 1955 to prepare for the forthcoming meeting. In the summer of 1956, after consultation with the bureau, the Canadian government sent out the invitations to the Ottawa Congress with a convening date of August 14, 1957. This was followed by a circular from the bureau requesting administrations to inform it, at the earliest possible opportunity, of the size and composition of the delegations they proposed to send, and to submit their proposals for the modification of the union's final acts. In September 1956, the director of the bureau went to Ottawa to examine the status of preparations with representatives of the Canadian Ministry of Posts. In 1957, the bureau published the proposals that it had received and sent the necessary personnel to Ottawa to assist the Canadian authorities in running the congress.[69]

By August 14, 1957, most of the delegates had arrived in Ottawa, and the congress was ready to begin. The first official function of the Congress of Ottawa was a meeting in the Canadian senate chambers at 3:00 P.M., where the delegates heard welcoming speeches from the Prime Minister, the Canadian Minister of Posts, and the doyen of the congress, Sir Dudley Lumley, former vice director general of the British Postal Services.[70] At four o'clock the delegates retired to the chamber of the House of Commons, where the chair was taken by the doyen, who

69. See *Annual Reports, 1955,* p. 4; *1956,* p. 4; and *1957,* p. 20.
70. The first welcoming address at the 1952 Brussels Congress was given by King Baudouin, and at Paris in 1947 by French President Vincent Auriol.

proceeded to call the congress to order, read a congratulatory telegram
from President Eisenhower, and make an opening speech filled with
references to the history of the union, the tasks before the congress, and
a list of the important members of postal administrations and delegates
to previous congresses who had died in the interval since the preceding
congress. The doyen then announced the nominations for the bureau of
the congress, which had been made earlier on the basis of discussions between the Canadian government and the international bureau, and which
were accepted by acclamation. The newly elected chairman of the
congress then exchanged seats with the doyen, made an acceptance
speech which was followed by one from the vice chairman, proposed
and received the agreement of the delegates on the secretariat for the
congress, and then turned to the first real item of business.[71]

The first major item of business of any congress is the adoption of
the rules of procedure. According to Article 15 of the Ottawa Postal
Convention, "the provisions of the rules of procedure drawn up by the
previous Congress apply insofar as they are relevant to the debates."
Prior to World War II, there was no provision of this kind, and little
difficulty was experienced. The Congress of Paris in 1947, however, was
severely plagued by difficulties in the adoption of its rules of procedure,
much of which was due to the unsettled political climate. To eliminate
the possibility that the work of the congress would be hampered in the
future by a conflict in the adoption of rules of procedure, the Brussels
Congress added the above article to the convention.[72]

The rules of procedure for UPU congresses are usually quite brief.
That of the Congress of Ottawa, for instance, contains only fifteen
articles. Ten of these rules deal with procedures we have already
covered: aims of the congress; representation; observers; bureau of the
congress; committees; representation on committees; secretariat of committees; languages; proposals; and voting procedure. The other five deal
with the right of committees to create working groups; the nature and
means of approval of the minutes of meetings; the approval of final acts
in plenary assembly; discussions; and changes in the rules of procedure.
The rules on discussions in plenary assemblies and committees are as
follows: "1) It is recommended that delegates speak distinctly and without hurry. 2) Speeches are limited to 10 minutes except where authorization to speak longer is given by the chairman of the appropriate meeting." The one on changing the rules of procedure, also inserted because
of the difficulties that occurred at the Paris Congress, provides that all
subsequent changes must be supported by 10 other delegations and
receive a majority of two thirds of the delegations represented at the
congress.[73]

71. Docs., Ottawa Postal Congress (1957), II, 147–65.
72. See Paris Postal Congress (1947), II, 27–39, 61–67, 885–92, 992–95,
and 1054. See also Docs., Brussels Postal Congress (1952), I, 166–67; and
II, 341–43.
73. See Docs., Ottawa Postal Congress (1957), II, 35–39.

The adoption of the rules of procedure of the Ottawa Congress was completed during the second plenary assembly and was followed by the election of the chairmen, vice-chairmen, rapporteurs, and secretariats of committees. Two additional plenary assemblies were necessary at Ottawa, however, before the committees could begin their work. The third plenary assembly was devoted exclusively to the problem of representation of Communist China and the German Democratic Republic. The fourth took up the problem of the admission of observers to the congress and the report of the executive and liaison committee on its work since the Congress of Brussels.[74]

With one exception only, the next five weeks were devoted to committee work, the real work of the congress. The exception occurred on September 13 when the delegates reconvened in plenary assembly to discuss and adopt the reports of the ad hoc committee on a program of technical and economic studies and the credentials committee. Concerning the latter, although no delegation has the right to vote if credentials are not in order, it is customary in UPU congresses to permit all delegates to participate in both deliberations and votes until the report of the credentials committee has been approved in plenary assembly.[75]

The number of meetings that a committee holds and the length of its meetings vary from committee to committee. At Ottawa, the general committee held 15 meetings which lasted an average of about two and a half hours per meeting. The first committee held 18 meetings, committee 1 *bis* and the subcommittee on formulas, 10 each, the second committee, 8, and the third committee, 7. The "work horse" of the congress, the drafting committee, was forced to meet 28 times to complete its work. As a general rule committee meetings are held in the morning from about 10:00 A.M. to 12:30 P.M., or in the afternoons from 2:30 to 4:30 or 4:30 to 6:30.[76]

As the deadline for the closing of the congress approaches, there is a flurry of activity in plenary sessions, similar to that at any national parliament, in which the delegates rush to examine the reports of committees and to hammer out the details of the final acts. At Ottawa this occurred on Monday, Tuesday, and Wednesday, the 23d, 24th, and 25th of September. On those three days the 6th through 11th plenary assemblies were held, with delegates meeting both morning and evening to discuss and approve the bulk of the committee reports. About the only pause in these three hectic days of hard work occurred when the delegates turned from committee reports and elected the countries to be represented on the ELC for the next five years and when the date and place of the next congress were decided.[77] As a rule these decisions are

74. *Ibid.*, pp. 185–98.
75. *Ibid.*, pp. 35 and 320.
76. Information from *ibid.*, Vol. II. For an account of the "extracurricular" activities of the delegates to the Ottawa Congress see *Union Postale*, LXXXIII, No. 4 (April, 1958), 62A–63A.
77. Docs., Ottawa Postal Congress (1957), II, 1111–72.

not the subject of controversy, having been settled informally in the corridors well in advance. Now and then, however, hitches do occur that result in a spate of telegrams back and forth between delegates and administrations, as occurred at Ottawa when four countries made their bid for the next congress.

Although the congress is formally closed, there is another important official task that must be completed, namely, the signing of the final acts. This usually takes place several days after the closing of the congress, after a copy of the newly revised final acts has been assembled. In the case of the Ottawa Congress, the formal closing meeting was held on the morning of Friday, September 27, and the signing took place on October 3.[78] The word "task" is used advisedly for the ceremony of signing the final documents, since the number of signatures called for is large. At Ottawa there were five different documents concerning the postal convention alone that demanded a signature: the Universal Postal Convention; the Final Protocol to the Convention; the Regulations to the Convention; the Additional Provisions concerning the Airmail; and the Final Protocol to the Additional Provisions concerning the Airmail. The delegate whose country also participated in all of the ten agreements for various additional postal services was called on for 19 signatures more.[79]

Until the Congress of Vienna in 1891, the UPU followed normal diplomatic procedure whereby delegates signed a copy of each of the final acts for the archives of each of the countries represented. With the increase in membership, and the increase in the number of final acts, the signing procedure alone often took several days. Finally, at the suggestion of the international bureau, it was decided at the Congress of Vienna that only one copy of the final acts would be signed in the future, with that copy being kept in the archives of the host country. The other contracting countries would then receive a copy in which the signatures of the delegates were reproduced by mechanical means.[80]

The work of the international bureau does not end with the signing of the final acts, however. It must take copies of the final acts back to Switzerland, where they are printed and sent out to the member countries in numbers corresponding to their contributory share in the union's expenses. By the time this and other tasks that remain after a congress has been accomplished, it is almost time to begin preparation for the next one.[81]

78. Those delegates who had to leave Ottawa immediately were permitted to sign, without seeing the final documents, on the afternoon of the 26th (*ibid.*, p. 1147).

79. See Docs., Ottawa Postal Congress (1957), Vol. III.

80. See Docs., Vienna Postal Congress (1891), p. 718.

81. The documents of the Ottawa Congress, including the proposals submitted, the minutes of the meetings, and the final acts, amounted to 2,645 printed pages.

B. Extraordinary Congresses; Conferences

THE UNIVERSAL POSTAL CONVENTION provides for the calling of extraordinary congresses if a problem should arise between the regularly scheduled congresses that is of such immediate importance as to necessitate a meeting of representatives of member nations armed with plenipotentiary powers. On the other hand, if the problem is purely administrative in nature, one that representatives of administrations could handle and in which there is no need to sign a document of a diplomatic nature, an administrative conference can be called to resolve it.[82]

In either case it is necessary to obtain the agreement of two thirds of the membership of the union; "at least two thirds of the member countries" in the case of an extraordinary congress, and "at least two thirds of the Administrations" in the case of an administrative conference. In relation to other international organizations, the number needed for approval is large. The calling of a "special" administrative conference of the ITU, for example, requires only the consent of 20 members. Although the ITU does not provide for "extraordinary" plenipotentiary conferences (the ITU equivalent of the UPU extraordinary congress), the date of a scheduled plenipotentiary conference could be advanced in order to take care of any immediate or pressing problem, on the demand of 20 members or on request of the 25-member administrative council.[83] Even the United Nations provides for special sessions of the General Assembly if requested by the Security Council or a majority of the member nations.[84]

The universal postal convention provides a minimum of rules for the convening of such congresses. The place and date of meeting of extraordinary congresses are fixed by the countries taking the initiative in calling the congress, after agreement with the international bureau. The rules concerning representation and the right to vote, those dealing with the method of inviting member countries, and those regulating the submission of proposals, are the same as for regular congresses. The international bureau assists in the preparatory work and supervises the secretariat, and the director is given the right to participate without the right to vote. The convention provides further that extraordinary congresses shall adopt other rules of procedure, but until that is done, the rules of procedure of the preceding congress are applicable.[85]

With two exceptions, the rules applicable to administrative conferences are the same. First, invitations to conferences are sent out by the administration of the country in which the conference is to be held. Second, the time and date of meeting are fixed by the administrations

82. Ottawa Postal Convention (1957), Arts. 12 and 14.
83. ITU, *International Telecommunication Convention,* Geneva, 1959, Art. 7.
84. *Charter of the United Nations,* Art. 20.
85. See Ottawa Postal Convention (1957), Arts. 11, 13, and 15 and Regulations, Arts. 101 and 105.

of the countries taking the initiative in calling the conference, after consultation with the international bureau.[86]

In any event, only one extraordinary congress has been held, the Congress of Berne in 1900. This congress was called by the Swiss Federal Council to celebrate the 25th anniversary of the UPU, and the call was accepted by all member states. The agenda, according to the Swiss invitation, was made up of a formal opening session "with speeches" in which a committee was to be formed to discuss the problem of erecting a monument to the UPU, an excursion of two or three days in the Alps, and a closing session where the problem of erecting a monument was to be decided.[87] The Congress of Berne lasted four days, July 2 to July 5. The congress agreed to the erection of a monument to the UPU and allocated a credit of 200,000 Swiss francs to the Swiss Federal Council for that purpose.[88] By changing the date of meeting of the Congress of Stockholm (1924), the UPU was able to combine its 50th anniversary with a regularly scheduled congress.[89]

Only three meetings have been held under the auspices of the UPU which could qualify as "administrative conferences," the Conference of Berne (1876), the Conference of Paris (1880), and the Conference of The Hague (1927). Nevertheless, each one contained something in its make-up, or the manner in which it was convened, that sets it slightly apart from a strict interpretation of "administrative conferences" as defined in Article 14 of the Ottawa Postal Convention. The Conference of Berne, for instance, was held before the postal convention contained any reference to "conferences." Only regular congresses and a special meeting of interested parties to decide on sea transit rates upon the application for membership of an "overseas" country were provided for. It was under the second provision that the Conference of Berne was held. Further, the conference discussed only the admission of new members and postal rates between them and the other members of the union, and the participation was limited to the interested countries.[90]

By the Conference of Paris, in 1880, the postal convention had a provision for the calling of a "simple administrative conference" on the demand or on the approval of two thirds of the member "administrations." [91] This conference, however, was called by the international bureau under the specific authority of a decision of the 1878 Congress of Paris. It is not clear whether the international bureau made certain that two thirds of the membership were in agreement on the calling of the conference or whether it considered that the mandate given to it by the previous congress was sufficient to ignore the provisions in the postal

86. Ottawa Postal Convention (1957), Arts. 14 and 15, and Regulations, Art. 105.

87. *Mémoire* (Berne, 1949), p. 95.

88. *Ibid.,* pp. 95–96.

89. *Ibid.,* p. 135.

90. See above, pp. 35–36.

91. Paris Postal Convention (1878), Art. 19.

convention concerning simple administrative conferences.[92] In any case, this conference was taken out of the category of ordinary administrative conferences in that representatives of the participating countries were armed with plenipotentiary powers.[93]

The third conference under discussion, the Airmail Conference of The Hague, 1927, was also unique. The initiative for this conference came from the government of the USSR, acting on a suggestion made by the 1926 meeting of the air transport committee of the International Chamber of Commerce. After receiving the request from the USSR, the international bureau polled the postal administrations of members of the union as to the desirability of calling an airmail conference, and upon receiving 25 affirmative replies made arrangements with the Dutch government for the convening of such a conference.[94] Only after the delegates were assembled in The Hague was the question raised as to what type of conference was being held and what it was supposed to do.

In an introductory statement, the director of the international bureau pointed out that the conference had three alternative courses of action: (1) it could add to or modify the postal convention according to what the delegates felt were the needs of the airmail service; (2) it could proceed to create an airmail agreement, to be appended the convention; or (3) it could simply discuss the new airmail techniques and draw up a list of "suggestions" for the guidance of the next universal postal congress to be held in London in 1929. If the group adopted either alternative (1) or (2), according to the director, it would be necessary to determine whether two thirds of the members of the UPU were in agreement that it should be held before the discussions could begin, and the delegates would have to ask their governments for plenipotentiary powers. The rules of procedure of congresses would have to be applied.[95]

The Netherlands delegate proposed that the third alternative offered by the director be adopted and, in order to retain a cloak of legality, the meeting be considered as one held under the then Article 5 of the postal convention which approved the creation of restricted postal unions and special treaties of a nature that did not interest the union as a whole.[96] This was agreed to, and the delegates set to work creating a series of provisions which they considered would provide a better base for the international exchange of airmail. The final document of the conference was a "rapport," signed by the delegates and containing a recommendation that the newly drafted provisions be implemented by postal administrations on January 1, 1928, in order to provide a base of experience for

92. See the statement of Mr. Borel, director of the international bureau, in Docs., Paris Postal Conference (1880), pp. 37–40.

93. See *ibid.*, pp. 187–93.

94. See above, p. 58.

95. Docs., The Hague Airmail Conference (1927), pp. 103 and 117–20.

96. *Ibid.*, pp. 104 and 120.

the next postal congress.[97] Inasmuch as a restricted union was not created, however, it is still referred to as one of the union's three administrative conferences.[98]

The only other conferences held under the auspices of the UPU were the European Airmail Conferences of Brussels in 1930, The Hague and Paris in 1937, and Brussels in 1938. (There was also a preparatory committee meeting in Prague in 1931.) All of these conferences were held under the specific authorization of a provision of final protocol to the postal conventions, of London, 1929, Cairo, 1934, and Buenos Aires, 1939. Noting that it was in derogation to the postal convention, the articles in question provided for the calling of the special airmail conferences of interested parties at the request of *only* three administrations.[99]

While a similar provision was contained in the final protocols to the Paris convention of 1947 and the Brussels convention of 1952, no additional airmail conferences were held. The work carried out by these conferences was undertaken by the regular congresses and by the newly created executive and liaison committee. Noting that the provision had thus lost its significance, the Ottawa Postal Congress in 1957 agreed to its elimination.[100]

As a result of the action at Ottawa, the final acts of the UPU now provide for only three types of union meetings: regular congresses, extraordinary congresses, and administrative conferences.

c. The Executive and Liaison Committee

THE CREATION of the Executive and Liaison Committee by the Paris Congress of 1947 was the first important change in the structure of the UPU. Prior to 1947, the work of the UPU in the field of international postal communication had been carried out principally by its periodic congresses and the international bureau. Anything the congress or the bureau could not do was accomplished by calling a few ad hoc conferences and occasionally setting up preparatory committees.

1. Background

The incentive for the creation of an additional permanent body came from two sources. First, it had become apparent in the interwar years that congresses were having increased difficulty in giving adequate attention to all of the proposals for improvement of the international postal service submitted by the member administrations and in providing for

97. *Ibid.*, pp. 104 and 229–52.
98. See, for instance, *Annotated Acts* (*1957*), 1ᵉʳ fascicule, pp. 21 and 30.
99. See Docs., London Postal Congress (1929), I, 316–17; and II, 247–48 and 675.
100. See Docs., Ottawa Postal Congress (1957), II, 375.

an adequate study of, and exchange of views on, common technical problems. Neither the increase in the number of committees in congresses nor the expedient of creating preparatory committees was sufficient to provide a solution.

The first suggestion that the problem might be solved by a change in the union's structure came from the USSR at the Congress of London in 1929, when its delegate advocated the creation of a permanent international postal consultative committee similar to those then in use by the International Telecommunication Union. The duties of this organ would be to study operating techniques and procedures and make recommendations to members of the union and congresses. This was not being done in congresses, according to the USSR delegate, because of the press of time and detail. The London Congress did not spend much time on the USSR proposal, however. After a few delegates had expressed their opposition on the grounds that technical and administrative operating questions could be resolved on an administration-to-administration basis or through the good offices of the international bureau, the Russian proposal was voted down "by a strong majority." [101] The confidence of the majority in the traditional structure of the union did not, however, restrain them from creating a preparatory committee for the next scheduled congress.[102]

By 1947 the problem had become acute. In addition to a deluge of proposals and suggestions, there were the new problems of organizing a world airmail communication system and the intrusion, almost for the first time, of machines in post offices throughout the world. The appearance of airmail and mechanization added new dimensions to the work of the UPU. A great deal of study, more than could be accomplished within the confines of congresses, was indicated.

The second incentive for the creation of a new UPU organ came from the outside. By the time the first post-World War II congress had convened in Paris on May 8, 1947, the world had seen the creation of the United Nations and several other international agencies. Most of these organizations came equipped with bodies designed to perform certain functions in the interims between meetings of the plenary bodies. There was, therefore, a certain amount of pressure to conform. Even more important, however, was the "master plan" of close future cooperation between the United Nations and the various specialized agencies and among the specialized agencies themselves — those that had been created and those which were still in the planning stage. Inasmuch as the UPU was scheduled to become a specialized agency, there was need for an organ of a more continuous character than the congress to communicate with other agencies and with more authority to speak for union members than the bureau. There was even a call for close cooperation

101. Docs., London Postal Congress (1929), I, 13; and II, 105, 128–32, and 140–49. For a discussion of the creation of the ITU's consultative committee, see Codding, op. cit., pp. 35–36 and 121–22.

102. Ibid., pp. 255–59.

on the fixing of airmail rates from the International Air Transport Association.

The Paris Congress was confronted with three major proposals to create such an organ: one by France and Great Britain; one by Brazil, China, Egypt, and Portugal; and one by the USSR. Each of the delegations supporting one of these proposals advanced arguments based on the factors mentioned above.[103] After a majority of the delegations at Paris rallied to one or another of these proposals, the creation of a new permanent organ for the UPU was a foregone conclusion.

There was, however, a small vocal minority against any change in the structure of the union led by W. J. Turnbull, head of the Canadian delegation. In speaking for the status quo, Mr. Turnbull emphasized that the creation of such an organ would be neither desirable nor necessary. It was undesirable because its creation would tend to introduce "politics" into the union in the selection of countries to be its members. Further, according to the Canadian delegate, the creation of a body with restricted membership, as was advocated in all of the proposals, was undemocratic. No matter how it started out, it would tend to become more and more authoritarian and would tend to submit the previously democratic union to central control. Canada was against such a development in principle, and had made its opposition to such organs known when it had argued at San Francisco against the creation of the Security Council as a major organ of the United Nations. It was unnecessary, in his opinion, because the union had worked well for 72 years without any important change in its structure. Technical matters could be taken up on a bilateral basis between member administrations or on a larger scale through the intermediary of the international bureau. Liaison between the UPU and other international organizations could also be left to the bureau, or, if necessary, a special committee designated by a congress. The appeal for cooperation by IATA was the least of the UPU's worries, according to Mr. Turnbull. IATA was a nongovernmental agency "searching to create a monopoly" and desiring to use the UPU for these ends.[104]

Despite the eloquence of the appeal by the Canadian delegate, the Paris Congress was in favor of the new organ. The decision to create it, however, became bogged down in the first committee on a technicality and had to go to a plenary assembly for resolution. The committee first put the Russian proposal to a vote and it was rejected by 50 to 11, with 10 abstentions. Five delegations were absent during the voting. When the Brazil-China-Egypt-Portugal proposal came to a vote (the French-British proposal having been withdrawn in its favor), 43 delegations

103. Docs., Paris Postal Congress (1947), I, 46–51 and 57–59.

104. *Ibid.*, II, 390–92, 407–408, and 953–55. It is interesting to note that the problem of democracy versus centralized control was used by several smaller countries at the Congress of Buenos Aires in 1939 when a proposal for a preparatory committee for the next conference was turned down. (See Docs., Buenos Aires Postal Congress, 1939, II, 514–15.)

gave their support, 12 voted in the negative, and 16 abstained. Since the Paris Congress had by that time adopted a two-thirds quorum rule on important questions, the proposal failed.[105]

The authors of the multination proposal brought the matter up again in plenary meeting (they were prevented from bringing it up again in committee by the rules of procedure of the congress). The first victory of the proponents occurred when the delegate of the USSR agreed to withdraw his country's proposal and shift his support to the more favored one. Then, after another impassioned speech in opposition by the Canadian delegate, it was decided by a vote to enter into a discussion of the proposal. The vote was 52 for, 20 in opposition, and one abstention. Only three delegations were absent at this vote.[106]

The proposal to create a new organ for the UPU was then discussed and approved article by article. The changes that were made during the course of these deliberations will be treated as we proceed. It is interesting to note, however, that all this took up two complete plenary meetings and more than half of a third, time which might have been lessened considerably had the first committee had an opportunity to discuss it in depth.[107] During the plenary discussions it was also decided, this time without opposition, that the name of the new organ should be the Executive and Liaison Committee.[108]

2. Functions

The functions of the Executive and Liaison Committee, as established by the Paris Congress of 1947 and amended by succeeding congresses, place it in a unique category, in comparison to similar organs in other UN specialized agencies. The most outstanding characteristic, on paper at least, is its relative weakness. Despite the word "executive" in its title, it has little to do with the execution of the basic decisions of the congresses, it can do little to affect the work of the organization as a whole (it doesn't even have the power to call extraordinary congresses or meetings), and it has comparatively little control over the operation of the secretariat. It has a great deal less authority than the executive board of UNESCO, for example, and even less than the administrative

105. See Docs., Paris Postal Congress (1947), II, 417–18. Voting against the second proposal were: Argentina, Austria, Bolivia, Bulgaria, Canada, Denmark, Iran, Ireland, Paraguay, Uruguay, USSR, and Vatican City. Abstaining were: Afghanistan, Chile, Colombia, Curaçao and Surinam, Dutch Indies, Ecuador, Ethiopia, Finland, Iceland, Iraq, Italy, Netherlands, Norway, San Marino, Sweden, and Switzerland.

106. *Ibid.*, pp. 951–55. Those voting in the negative were: Afghanistan, Argentina, Belgian Congo, Belgium, Canada, Denmark, Dutch Indies, Ecuador, Finland, Iceland, Iran, Ireland, Luxembourg, Morocco, Norway, Paraguay, Sweden, Switzerland, Uruguay, and Vatican City. Austria abstained; Cuba, El Salvador, and Honduras were absent.

107. *Ibid.*, pp. 951–93 and 995–98.

108. *Ibid.*, p. 955.

council of its sister organization, the ITU.[109] However, as will become clear, it doesn't deserve the description given to it by the Lebanese delegate to the ITU's Atlantic City conference when he said that the UPU had created a body "whose only utility was to sit around during the period between two congresses." [110]

The basic decision to keep the executive and liaison committee a weak organ was made when the Paris Congress chose the Brazil-China-Egypt-Portugal proposal over Russia's and after the French and British proposal was withdrawn. Both the French-British and Russian proposals, for instance, would have given the committee power to convoke extraordinary congresses and conferences (on its own initiative under the French-British proposal but on the request of at least two thirds of the membership under the Russian proposal); to take direct control over the secretariat, and in general act as a true administrator of the union between congresses. The French-British proposal even went so far as to permit the committee to take any action it deemed necessary in the interval between congresses on problems that the postal convention did not anticipate.[111]

On the basis of the Brazil-China-Egypt-Portugal proposal, as modified in the discussions, the Paris Congress gave the executive and liaison committee the following six functions:

1] to maintain close contact with members of the union with a view to improving the international postal service;

2] to study technical and other questions and to communicate the results to postal administrations;

3] to make contact with the United Nations and other international organizations for the study of common problems and the preparation of reports to be approved by the members of the union, and to send a representative to take part in meetings of these international organizations;

4] to appoint the director of the international bureau and other higher officials on the proposal of the government of Switzerland;

5] to approve the appointment of some other bureau employees and to authorize hiring of supplementary personnel on the proposal of the director of the bureau;

6] to "establish" an annual report on the administration of the Bureau which it communicates to all members of the union.[112]

There was a clear tendency on the part of the Brussels and Ottawa congresses to increase the functions of the executive and liaison committee, although not to the extent that some countries would have liked.

109. See, for instance, *Constitution* of the United Nations Educational, Scientific and Cultural Organization, Art. v, and the International Telecommunication Convention (Geneva, 1959), Art. 9.

110. See Codding, *op. cit.*, p. 287.

111. Compare the provisions of the proposals in Docs., Paris Postal Congress (1947), I, 46–52 and 57–59.

112. Paris Postal Convention (1947), Art. 18.

At the Brussels Congress of 1952, for example, the United States delegation submitted a proposal that would have transformed the committee into a genuine executive body along the lines of the French-British proposal in 1947. The ELC would have been given the right to make fundamental decisions between the regular congresses in case of emergency, to convoke special conferences, to prepare the agenda of congresses, to control the work of the bureau and verify its annual account, and to "oversee the execution of the resolutions of congresses." [113] The Brussels Congress was not willing to go that far, however, but did agree that in the future the ELC would have the right to make proposals to congresses, or directly to member countries between congresses, on any question arising out of studies entrusted to it by a congress or out of the committee's statutory functions. The United States also attempted to give the ELC the power of commenting on all proposals submitted by member administrations to change the acts of the union between congresses and of having these comments appended to the proposals when sent out by the bureau. The congress agreed on the condition, however, that the country making the proposal request such comments.[114]

The Congress of Ottawa in 1957 took away from the ELC the right to study technical questions and gave it to the newly formed Consultative Committee for Postal Studies, but at the same time it gave the ELC the right to submit subjects for study to the newly created body for examination and report.[115]

While most of the delegates to the Brussels and Ottawa congresses were willing to approve a gradual expansion in the committee's functions, the Canadian delegations along with a few others attempted to turn back the clock. A Canadian proposal submitted to the Brussels Congress, for instance, would have changed the name of the ELC to "Consultative Committee" and confined its duties to advising the international bureau, studying questions raised by the United Nations or other international organizations, and submitting proposals in the intervals between congresses on the same basis as is permitted to member countries. The arguments presented by the Canadian delegation were, in general, a repetition of those presented at the Paris Congress when the ELC was created. They did, however, include a scathing attack on the amount of work that the ELC had accomplished and the amount of money it had cost. After a lengthy discussion in committee, in which the majority of the speakers praised the work accomplished by the ELC and stressed its importance to the UPU, the Canadian proposal was voted down in a secret ballot by 57 to 24 and was not raised again in plenary meeting.[116] A similar proposal introduced by the Canadian delegate at Ottawa — the only major difference was that the title of the ELC would be changed

113. Docs., Brussels Postal Congress (1952), I, 168–70.
114. Brussels Postal Convention (1952), Art. 6, para. e.
115. Ottawa Postal Convention (1957), Art. 16, para. 5.
116. See Docs., Brussels Postal Congress (1952), I, 170–72; and II, 343–59.

to Consultative and Liaison Committee — was withdrawn by its sponsor in committee after being subject to a few but unanimously disapproving statements.[117]

As modified by the Brussels and Ottawa congresses, the complete functions of the ELC are as follows:

A]   to maintain the closest contact with the administrations of the countries of the Union with a view to improving the international postal service;

B]   to study administrative, legislative and judicial problems of interest to the international postal service and to communicate the results of those studies to the postal administrations;

C]   to submit questions for study and opinion to the Consultative Committee for Postal Studies . . . ;

D]   to make useful contact with the United Nations, its councils and its commissions, and with the specialized agencies and other international organizations, for research and the preparation of reports to be submitted to the administrations of the countries of the Union for their approval; and to send as the occasion demands representatives of the Union to take part in meetings of these international organizations on its behalf;

E]   to formulate, as necessary, proposals to be submitted to member countries of the Union under the provisions of Articles 28 and 29 [proposals to amend the acts of the Union in the interval between congresses] or to congresses when the proposals concern studies entrusted by a congress to the committee or when they arise out of the committee's own activities as defined in this article;

F]   to examine, at the request of an administration of a country, any proposal which that administration forwards to the International Bureau under the provisions of Chapter v [proposals to amend the acts of the Union in the interval between congresses], to prepare observations on it and to charge the International Bureau with annexing these observations to the said proposal before submitting it for approval to the administrations of countries members of the Union;

G]   within the framework of the Convention and its Detailed Regulations:

1) to ensure the control of the activities of the International Bureau of which it appoints, when the need arises, and on the proposal of the Government of the Swiss Confederation, the Director and other higher officials;

2) to approve, on the proposal of the Director of the International Bureau, the appointment of officials of the 1st and 2nd salary grades after examining the professional qualifications of the candidates sponsored by the administrations of the Union, taking into account an equitable

117. See Docs., Ottawa Postal Congress (1957), I, 132–33; and II, 347–48.

geographical distribution with respect to continents and languages and all other relevant considerations, due regard being given to the Bureau's own internal promotion arrangements;

3) to approve the annual report of the Union's activities drawn up by the International Bureau and, where appropriate, to furnish observations on it.[118]

As a result of the postponement of the 15th congress, the powers of the ELC have been temporarily enlarged. After receiving word that India could not hold the congress in 1963, the president of the ELC asked the director of the bureau to consult UPU members as to whether the ELC should be permitted to make certain decisions that normally would be within the province of the congress which the ELC felt could not be postponed. Upon the approval of 82 administrations (10 replied in the negative and 25 abstained), the ELC proceeded to fix the maximum limit for the union's ordinary expenditure for the year 1963 at 3,500,000 Swiss francs (1,000,000 Swiss francs over the amount authorized by the Ottawa Congress) and approved a new staff insurance program, setting January 1, 1964 as the date for its coming into force.[119]

3. Composition

As presently constituted, the Executive and Liaison Committee is made up of representatives of 20 member countries, appointed by the congress on the basis of "an equitable geographical distribution." At least half of the membership must be renewed at each congress, and no country may serve more than two consecutive terms. The individuals who serve on the committee are chosen by the appointed countries.[120]

As simple as these provisions seem, they came about only after many hours of argument. The Paris Congress of 1947, for example, was confronted with three major proposals which demonstrated the widely differing views of governments on the proper composition of international bodies with limited membership. The original French-British proposal suggested a 14-member body made up of: (1) representatives of China, France, United Kingdom, United States, and USSR; (2) a representative from the country in which the seat of the union is located; (3) representatives of other countries which had provided chairmen of committees in the preceding congress; and (4) representatives of additional countries to fill out the membership to 14 and to meet the criterion of equitable geographical distribution. The four-nation proposal which became the basis for discussion provided for a body made up of the chairman of the congress and the chairmen and vice chairmen of the

118. Ottawa Postal Convention (1957), Art. 16.
119. See Dr. F. Koller, "The Annual Session of the Executive and Liaison Committee, 1963," *Union Postale*, LXXXIII, No. 9 (September, 1963), 127A.
120. Ottawa Postal Convention (1957), Art. 16, paras. 2–5, and Regulations, Art. 102.

first committee, committee 1 *bis,* the second committee, and the third committee.[121] The Russian proposal simply provided for a 15-member body made up of representatives from 15 member countries to be selected by each congress. While the other proposals permitted the committee to select its own officers, the Russian proposal gave the congress the task of electing a chairman and four vice chairmen.[122]

Although the four-nation proposal was adopted as a basis for discussion, and it was agreed that the new body should be made up of 18 members, there was complete disagreement on the manner in which the members were to be selected. Above all, a method had to be found which would permit a wider participation of countries on the new committee. The delegate of Indochina, for example, proposed that the entire membership of the committee be renewed each year in order that each member of the union have a chance to serve at least once between congresses. The Hungarian delegate quickly replied that a committee which changed its membership each year would be useless. A trip to a foreign country now and then by officials of a postal administration, in his opinion, would not be a sufficient reason for creating a useless body. He countered with a proposal that two thirds of the membership of the ELC be renewed every two years. Among the other proposals were one by the Canadian delegate that members serve the entire period between congresses, but that no country be reelected until all members who wished to serve on the committee had a chance; one by the delegate of Uruguay that one third of the membership be renewed every two years; and one by the delegate of Egypt to the effect that each congress should make its own decision.[123]

The dispute over composition died down after an alternative Canadian proposal was introduced and accepted, to the effect that at least half the membership of the new committee should be renewed at each congress and that no country could be chosen for more than two successive terms; but it flared again when the congress came to the problem of electing the countries to serve between the Paris Congress and the next congress.[124] The Egyptian delegation relit the fuse when it proceeded to nominate 18 countries, representing what it considered to be a good geographical distribution. The Egyptian nominations were attacked on the basis that the areas of the world that it had chosen were not representative, that small countries were being excluded, and that certain important powers were being excluded. South Africa complained that it should not be placed in the classification "rest of the world." [125]

The first step in bringing some order into the confusion occurred when the chairman of the congress asked for a vote on the portion of the original four-nation proposal whereby the members of the ELC were to be the chairmen of the congress and its committees — which somehow

121. Docs., Paris Postal Congress (1947), I, 47 and 51.
122. *Ibid.,* pp. 57–58.
123. *Ibid.,* II, 417–18 and 960–68.
124. *Ibid.,* p. 968.
125. *Ibid.,* pp. 998–1001.

had been forgotten. It was turned down by a vote of 29 to 19, with 14 abstentions.[126] Then, before the debates could really get under way again, the British delegate proposed that only the number of seats in each geographical area should be fixed and the countries that were to occupy the seats be determined by the countries in each of those areas. The British proposal (adopted by 28 to 14, with 16 abstentions and 18 absentees) gave nine seats to Europe, five to the Americas, and five to Asia, Africa, and Oceania.[127]

The delegates then adjourned to three separate rooms, depending upon the region they felt they belonged to, where they held elections to determine which countries should represent their region on the new executive and liaison committee. The countries chosen were: Argentina, Australia, Brazil, China, Colombia, Czechoslovakia, Egypt, France, Great Britain, India, Mexico, Netherlands, Portugal, Sweden, Switzerland, Turkey, United States, USSR, and Yugoslavia.[128]

The composition of the ELC was attacked at both the Congress of Brussels and the Congress of Ottawa. At Brussels, for instance, the United States and Egypt proposed that the rotation clause be eliminated. Egypt, in addition, proposed that the number of members be raised from 19 to 20. Brazil suggested that the number be raised to 21, and the USSR, Yugoslavia, and Turkey, among others, suggested that the status quo be maintained, but that a clause be inserted in the postal convention requiring that the membership reflect at all times the geographical distribution of the union's members.[129] By unanimous agreement the Brussels Congress agreed to include a geographical distribution clause in the convention and "by a very great majority" to increase the number of members from 19 to 20. On the other hand, the Brussels Congress voted 40 to 39 (with 3 abstentions) against the suppression of the clause providing for a renewal of half of the membership at each congress and 58 to 20 (with 5 abstentions,) against eliminating the clause which made members ineligible after being elected by two successive congresses.[130]

On the question of selection of members, the Brussels Congress was confronted with five different plans for dividing the world into regions, including one by the executive and liaison committee itself. The one chosen for debate (prepared by a small working group) divided the world into four major areas with the names of the countries to be included in each area in the following manner:

1. *Western Hemisphere:* Argentina, Bolivia, Brazil, Canada, Chile, Colombia, Costa Rica, Cuba, Dominican Republic, Dutch West Indies and Surinam, Ecuador, El Salvador, Guatemala, Haiti, Honduras, Mexico, Nicaragua, Panama, Paraguay, Peru, Uruguay, United States, United States possessions, and Venezuela (24).

126. *Ibid.,* p. 1001. Fourteen delegations were absent.
127. *Ibid.,* pp. 1007–1008. (See also, pp. 1001 to 1007.)
128. *Ibid.,* p. 1008.
129. Docs., Brussels Postal Congress (1952), I, 169, 173, and 404–10.
130. *Ibid.,* II, 409–10 and 445.

2. *Eastern Europe and Northern Asia:* Albania, Byelorussia, Bulgaria, Czechoslovakia, Hungary, Poland, Rumania, Ukraine, and USSR (9).

3. *Western Europe:* Austria, Belgium, Denmark, Finland, France, Great Britain, Greece, Iceland, Ireland, Italy, Luxembourg, Netherlands, Norway, Portugal, San Marino, Spain, Sweden, Switzerland, Vatican City, and Yugoslavia (20).

4. *Southeast Europe, Southern Asia, and Oceania:* Afghanistan, British overseas territories, Australia, Burma, Cambodia, Ceylon, China, India, Indonesia, Iran, Iraq, Israel, Japan, Jordan, Korea, Laos, Lebanon, New Zealand, Pakistan, Philippines, Portuguese territories in Eastern Africa, Asia and Oceania, Saudi Arabia, Syria, Thailand, Turkey, Viet Nam, and Yemen (27).

5. *Africa:* Algeria, Belgian Congo, Egypt, Ethiopia, French overseas territories, Liberia, Libya, Morocco, Morocco (Spanish Zone), Portuguese African territories, Spanish colonies, South Africa, and Tunisia (13).[131]

After a long discussion concerning the exact number of seats to be attributed to each region — Brazil and Egypt, for instance, wanted 6 seats for Region Three rather than the five suggested in the working document, and Russia wanted three seats rather than two for Region Two — a vote was held on the matter with the following results: Region 1, five; Region 2, two; Region 3, five; Region 4, six; and Region 5, two.[132]

The final problem before the Brussels Congress was the manner in which the seats were to be filled. In general, the debates centered around the question of whether to employ the method used by the Paris Congress — each region selecting its own representatives — or whether it might not be better to allow all the members of the union to participate in the election of representatives from each of the regions.[133] The interrelated problems of the total number of seats to be allotted, the countries to be in each region, and the number of seats to be given to each region, took so long to resolve that the question of the manner of election was not decided until the final day of the congress. On that day, the congress voted (40 to 37, with 12 abstentions) to permit all members of the congress to vote for the candidates in each region. Each delegation was permitted to cast a total of 20 votes, broken down according to the number of members that should come from each region.[134] It was also agreed that if more than half of the incumbents were reelected, the number in excess of one half who received the fewest votes would be dropped and replaced by new candidates in order to abide by the 50 per-

131. *Ibid.,* pp. 118–25.

132. *Ibid.,* pp. 424–45.

133. *Ibid.,* pp. 119, 139, 140, 424, 426–27, 431, 1380–81, 1383, 1386–87, and 1401–1403.

134. *Ibid.,* p. 1402. In general the delegates from Western and Eastern Europe voted for regional elections while the others voted for general elections. Also, many of the Middle East countries were abstainers.

cent turnover rule. As it turned out, however, only eight of the incumbents were reelected, so the issue of the 50 percent rule did not arise. Nevertheless, in one case both an incumbent (Mexico) and a new candidate (Chile) received the same number of votes. At the suggestion of the chairman of the congress it was agreed to give the seat to Chile.[135] The final result was as follows:

Members elected	No. of votes	Members elected	No. of votes
REGION 1: *United States**	74	Denmark	61
Venezuela	51	Italy	61
Brazil	48	REGION 4: Pakistan	79
Uruguay	44	Syria	61
Chile	42	*India*	60
REGION 2: Poland	68	*Australia*	59
USSR	67	Indonesia	53
REGION 3: Belgium	79	Japan	51
France	64	REGION 5: *Egypt*	81
Switzerland	63	South Africa	60

* Countries whose names are italicized are the incumbents who were reelected.

The Congress of Ottawa had the least difficulty of the three post-World War II congresses with this problem. Only one proposal was introduced to change the system. This proposal by Pakistan, to eliminate the ineligibility clause, was defeated 49 to 38 in committee and was not raised again in plenary meeting.[136] After a proposal by Yugoslavia to be moved from Region 3 to Region 2 was approved, and a proposal by the USSR to increase the number of countries to send representatives to the ELC for Region 2 from two to three was turned down, the Ottawa Congress decided to use the same system that had been employed by the Brussels Congress.[137]

The countries chosen by the Ottawa Congress to be represented on the ELC were:

REGION 1:	Argentina		*Italy*
	Canada		Norway
	Chile	REGION 4:	*Indonesia*
	Mexico		*Japan*
	Venezuela		Lebanon
REGION 2:	*Poland*		New Zealand
	Yugoslavia		*Pakistan*
REGION 3:	Germany		Turkey
	Belgium	REGION 5:	*South Africa*
	Great Britain		Libya[138]

135. *Ibid.*, pp. 1403–1405.
136. Docs., Ottawa Postal Congress (1957), I, 134; and II, 350.
137. See *ibid.*, II, 1111, 1112–14, and 1118–22. It should also be noted that the number of countries in several regions was changed as a result of the shift of Yugoslavia and the addition of new members.
138. *Ibid.*, pp. 1166 and 1167. The documents of the Ottawa Congress do not

The relative ease with which the Ottawa Congress resolved the problem of composition should not be taken as an indication that future congresses will continue to have an easy time of it. The very fact that the ELC is a limited membership body provides a built-in quality of conflict. It is inevitable that some countries will not be elected as often as they feel they should and that some regions will continue to feel under-represented. Additional new memberships, such as those from Africa of recent years, will create pressures. It can confidently be expected that future congresses will be faced with proposals to amend the composition of the ELC, either to increase the membership or rearrange the geographical apportionment.

4. Organization and Procedure

The manner in which the ELC organizes itself for its work is based on the rules of procedure which the committee adopts at each session and on certain provisions of the postal convention and its detailed regulations.

In the first place, the convention stipulates that each delegate of a country chosen by a congress to be represented on the ELC must be "a qualified functionary of a postal administration" and that while serving on the ELC must "exercise his function on behalf of and in the interest of the Union." [139] The Paris Postal Congress adopted a resolution to the effect that "a qualified functionary" was an individual who was a high official of a postal administration with at least ten years of service. This latter qualification was put to a test in 1950 when the Russian delegate was delayed and a consul from the Russian legation in Berne was sent to take his place until his arrival. By a vote of 12 to 1, it was agreed that the consul could serve until the proper delegate arrived, but without the right to vote.[140]

In general, the delegates to the ELC have indeed been qualified functionaries of their postal administrations. Of the 17 which were present at the session of April-May, 1956, for instance, six were the directors of their country's postal services, two were deputy directors, and four were "chiefs." The remaining four held titles of deputy postmaster general (South Africa), minister of communications (USSR), director of the Central Postal Administration (Poland), and Administrateur de classe exceptionnelle au Secrétariat d'Etat aux Postes, Télégraphes et Téléphones (France).[141]

The convention also provides that the individual members of the

---

contain the number of votes cast. Those countries whose names are in italics were members of the previous ELC.

139. Ottawa Postal Convention (1957), Art. 16, paras. 2 and 4.

140. See Docs., Paris Postal Congress (1947), II, 977 and UPU, *Documents de la Commission exécutive et de liaison, session de mai 1950* (Berne, 1950), pp. 140–41.

141. See UPU, *Documents de la Commission exécutive et de liaison, Session d'avril–mai 1956* (Berne, 1956), pp. 481–82.

ELC shall receive no pay from the union for their services, but the working expenses of the ELC are supported by the regular budget and each representative "has the right to reimbursement of the price of one first class ticket by air, sea, or land" to and from the meeting place.[142]

According to the detailed regulations, the first meeting of the newly elected body is convened by the chairman of the preceding congress and is devoted to electing its chairman and its four vice chairmen and adopting its rules of procedure.[143] In practice, the organizational meeting is held while the congress is still in session or immediately afterward, and the countries to provide the officers, rather than individuals themselves, are elected. Three organizational meetings have been held: Paris, July 5, 1947; Brussels, July 12, 1952; and Ottawa, September 26, 1957.[144] The Paris Congress, adopting a sort of geographical representation principle, selected France to provide the chairman and Brazil, China, Great Britain, and USSR to provide the vice chairmen. The Brussels Congress elected Belgium to provide the chairman, and Australia, Egypt, United States and USSR, the vice chairmen; and Ottawa elected the United Kingdom to provide the chairman, and Canada, Japan, South Africa, and Yugoslavia, the vice chairmen.[145]

Regular sessions of the ELC are held "in principle once a year" at the seat of the union, on convocation by its chairman. The international bureau is entrusted with the preparations for the meetings and with sending the documents of the meetings to the administrations represented on the ELC, other administrations requesting them, and regional postal unions. The bureau also acts as the secretariat for meetings and the director, as the secretary general with the right to enter into the discussions but without the right to vote.[146]

In 1953, at the suggestion of the United Nations, the ELC decided to hold its meetings whenever possible in the first two weeks of May. This would, according to the UN recommendation, eliminate the possibility of a conflict with meetings of the UN itself and other specialized

142. Ottawa Postal Convention (1957), Art. 16 and Detailed Regulations, Art. 102.

143. *Ibid.*

144. In view of the fact that the final acts of a congress do not come into effect until at least a year after its closing, various stratagems have been employed to permit the ELC to begin operation under the new organization before that time. The Paris Postal Congress used a resolution, the Brussels Congress, an "interpretation," and the Ottawa Postal Congress, a provision of the final protocol to its convention. (See Docs., Paris Postal Congress, 1947, II, 1041; Docs., Brussels Postal Congress, 1952, II, 444–45; and Ottawa Postal Convention, 1957, Final Protocol, Art. 17.)

145. See Docs., Paris Postal Congress (1947), II, 1109; UPU, *Documents de la Commission exécutive et de liaison, Séance constitutive (du 12 juillet 1952) de la Commission élue par le Congrès de Bruxelles et Session tenue à Berne du 4 au 15 mai 1953* (Berne, 1953), p. 3; UPU, *Documents de la Commission exécutive et de liaison, Séance constitutive (du 26 septembre 1957) et session de mai 1958 de la Commission élue par le Congrès d'Ottawa* (Berne, 1958), pp. 7–8.

146. Ottawa Postal Convention (1957), Detailed Regulations, Art. 102. See Annex I for a list of the meetings of the ELC.

agencies.[147] At its meeting in 1958, the ELC also decided that the committee itself should fix the "approximate date" of the annual sessions, but if circumstances so oblige it, the chairman of the ELC on consultation with the director of the bureau may change it. It also decided that a special session of the ELC may be held "exceptionally" either on the invitation of the chairman or, if it is requested, by two thirds of the members.[148] In practice the ELC usually sets a definitive date for the next meeting and adheres to it. Up to the present, there has never been a call for a special session.

Of particular interest is paragraph 4 of Art. 102 of the Detailed Regulations which gives the ELC an almost blanket right to invite observers to its meetings:

> The Committee may invite any representative of an international organ, or any other qualified person whom it desires to have associated with its work, to participate in its meetings without the right to vote. It can also invite, under the same conditions, representatives of one or more administrations of the Union interested in questions on the agenda of the Committee. The travel expenses of such representatives are the responsibility of their own administrations.

Under this power, the ELC has established two categories of observers, one consisting of those who will be invited as a matter of principle and one for all others. In the first category are:
1] representatives of the United Nations;
2] the chairman of the Administrative Council of the Consultative Committee on Postal Studies;
3] observers from regional postal organizations (allowed to speak in meetings only when authorized to do so by the chairman).[149]

In the May 1958 session, for instance, the United Nations was represented by the assistant to the deputy director of the European office of the United Nations, the International Civil Aviation Organization, by its assistant secretary general and a member of its staff in Paris, and the World Health Organization, by a chief of a section. The Arab Postal Union was permitted an observer in the person of the director of the permanent bureau of that organization. Mr. Greever Allan, director of the international postal service of the United States Post Office Department, was invited to be present in his capacity as chairman of the management council of the Consultative Committee on Postal Studies (CCPS) for discussions of two points on the agenda of the ELC of particular interest to the CCPS, as was Dr. V. Tuason, director of the Swiss Division of Posts, for the discussion of four points on the agenda

147. Docs., ELC, 1952/1953, pp. 69 and 162. By having its meetings in the spring, the council is also able to enjoy good Swiss weather and at the same time avoid the inconveniences of the annual summer influx of tourists.
148. Docs., ELC, 1957/1958, p. 240.
149. See ibid., pp. 238 and 239.

which were of particular interest to the Swiss postal administration.[150]

The freedom of the ELC to invite outsiders to participate in its work is not surprising in view of the nature of its work. It should also be noted that it permits the congresses to continue with a clear conscience to be sparing in issuing their invitations.

The ELC's rules of procedure provide that voting be carried out normally by a show of hands; however, on the demand of one member or at the suggestion of the chairman, a roll call vote may be held. Further, if it is requested by a member and supported by at least three others, a secret ballot may be required. A majority of votes will decide any issue, but in the case of a tie, the matter is considered rejected. Each member has one vote but in exceptional cases a member may also cast one proxy vote if the member authorizing another to cast his proxy vote has announced it in advance, in writing, to the chairman. A quorum of the ELC is at least 12 members.[151]

Usually, the reports of meetings of the ELC are singularly free of the use of voting to decide issues. This is due both to the nature of its work — few controversial issues come before it and it can seldom make decisions which are binding on the members of the union — and to the reflection in the ELC of the UPU's concern that wherever possible there should be a meeting of the minds. The only two votes that occurred in the 1958 session of the ELC, for instance, were over the election of new employees of the bureau. In one case the result was 18 to 0, and in the other 17 to 0, with one abstention.[152] There are exceptions, however, and the session of May 1950 is a case in point. In that session ten votes were taken in which there was some opposition. Seven revolved around the acceptance of the credentials of the representative of Communist China. In only three cases was there a division over a matter of substance; in one of the cases it was resolved by a vote of 12 to 3, with 2 abstentions; and in the other two cases there was only one representative in the opposition, and he voiced his displeasure by abstaining.[153]

The official language of the ELC is French, as it is for the UPU itself. English, Spanish, and Russian are admitted if requested, and a simultaneous interpretation system is provided. The expense of installation and upkeep of the system is met by the regular union budget, but the expenses of interpretation are charged to those countries whose delegates indicate that they desire to use one of the three nonofficial languages. Other languages are permitted, if requested at least six months in advance. In such cases, those requesting it must pay not only for the expense of interpretation but also for the necessary modifications to the system.[154] From 1947 to 1952 French was the language of deliberations. Non-French speakers were permitted to use an individual interpreter.

150. *Ibid.*, pp. 234, 257, 258, 277, and 344.
151. *Ibid.*, pp. 241–42.
152. *Ibid.*, pp. 269–70.
153. Docs., ELC, 1950, pp. 141, 145, 217, and 242.
154. Docs. ELC, 1957/58, p. 241.

From 1952 to 1957, English, Spanish, and Russian were used, and from 1957 to 1963 only English and Spanish were added to French. (The USSR was not a member of the ELC from 1957 to 1963 and no other country requested Russian.)

The ELC's rules of procedure also provide for the creation of "consultative sub-committees" with a membership restricted, in principle, to five. The meetings of subcommittees are scheduled by the chairman of the ELC and the chairmen of the subcommittees, after consultation with the director of the international bureau.[155] The heavy volume of work entrusted to the ELC has forced it to make extensive use of subcommittees. The 1958 meeting of the ELC, for instance, which was the first substantive meeting of that body after the Congress of Ottawa, created ten subcommittees. Three which had been active in the preceding five-year period were reconstituted: Airmail; Multilingual Vocabulary of Postal Terms; and Universal Decimal Classification. The following seven were created *de novo:* General Revision of the Convention; Rates; Transit Expenses; International Reply Stamps; Parcel Post; Money Orders; and Documents Published by the International Bureau.[156]

Most subcommittees hold one meeting a year immediately preceding the regular annual session of the UPU, and between sessions they carry out their work by correspondence. There are exceptions, however. Some, because of the nature or quantity of their work, are forced to meet more often. In the latter category is the subcommittee on the general revision of the convention, which met as a body twice a year in order to have its proposals available for the next congress.[157]

It should be noted also that the chairman of the ELC is given the power to treat urgent questions that may arise between sessions. If it is a matter of extreme importance, however, he must consult with the other members of the committee before making his decision and, if he judges it necessary, with all of the members of the union.[158]

5. The ELC at Work

In the few years of its existence — few in comparison to the age of the UPU itself — the Executive and Liaison Committee has proved its usefulness. One evidence of this can be found in the quantity of work it has undertaken. Its members, including representation on subcommittees, now devote a month or more during the year to union problems, which adds up to about five months of consultation between sessions of congresses. (Congresses themselves have never remained in session more than 61 days at a time.) That the ELC has a great deal of work to do is further evidenced by the decision of the Ottawa Congress to create a new organ of the UPU to take over the duties of the ELC in the scientific

155. *Ibid.,* p. 240.
156. *Ibid.,* p. 245.
157. *Ibid.,* pp. 288–89.
158. *Ibid.,* p. 240.

and technical fields alone. This decision, it should be noted, has not resulted in any permanent lessening in the length of the ELC sessions.

Concerning substance, the tasks of the ELC can be divided into three parts, the most important being that of serving as a preparatory organ for the periodic congresses. Essentially, the job of the ELC in this sphere is to undertake studies that congresses do not have the time for, or which cannot be done efficiently by correspondence through the intermediary of the international bureau. The ELC assumes these problems either under its terms of reference or through suggestions from congresses. The latter is perhaps the more important. The Congress of Ottawa, for instance, charged the ELC with the study of 29 different problems. Some were of a specific nature, such as "to examine all the documents published by the International Bureau as regards their form and content with regard to simplifying them as much as possible, to recommend to the next congress the suppression of those which have ceased to be of value and, eventually, to create new documents whose publications were expedient." [159] Others were of a more general nature, such as "to continue the examination of the general structure of the Universal Postal Convention" and, "within the framework of a study of the postal rate structure, also to examine the question of the problem of rates for newspapers." [160] Under its own terms of reference, for instance, the ELC studied the possibility of creating a new organization devoted to technical and scientific matters, and its report on the matter was used as the basis for the creation of the Consultative Committee on Postal Studies. In view of the activities of the ELC in these matters since 1946, it would not be wrong to say that the more important changes made in the postal conventions of Brussels and Ottawa stemmed directly from its investigations.

The second most important substantive area of concern of the ELC, at least with reference to the amount of time spent on it in meetings and its frequency on the agenda, is the review of the work of the UPU. At each annual session the ELC discusses and approves the annual report of the activities of the union which has been prepared by the international bureau and the report on the progress of the consultative committee for postal studies. Sometimes this scrutiny is perfunctory, but at other times it gives rise to a great deal of criticism. Most weighty, perhaps, are its activities with regard to the employees of the international bureau. This includes the routine approval of promotions to higher posts and a general discussion of the status of employees. At its May 1961 session, for example, the ELC discussed and approved a resolution to the Swiss government requesting that the salaries of the bureau personnel be raised to the level of those of its sister organization, the International Telecommunication Union.[161]

159. Docs., Ottawa Postal Congress (1957), II, 1157.
160. *Ibid.*, pp. 1156 and 1158.
161. UPU, ELC, *Compte rendu analytique, session de mai 1961* (Berne, 1961), p. 20. See also p. 211.

The third area of concern of the ELC, sometimes even more important than the second in view of the amount of time devoted to it, is the relation of the UPU to other international organizations. As a general rule, the ELC's major task is to investigate requests for collaboration of other international organizations with the UPU and, if approved, to execute them. Contacts that are arranged are carried out in various ways. The ELC has, for instance, created a special joint committee with the International Air Transport Association which holds sessions at various times throughout the year to work on common problems. Members of the ELC at times are sent as representatives to meetings of other international organizations, and they in turn send representatives to meetings of the ELC when matters of common concern are under consideration. Usually, however, contact with other international organizations is carried out by correspondence.[162]

In summary, while the work of the ELC cannot be considered earth-shaking, it is important to the efficiency and status of the Universal Postal Union as a major international organization.[163]

D. Consultative Committee for Postal Studies

THE CONSULTATIVE COMMITTEE FOR POSTAL STUDIES, created by the Congress of Ottawa in 1957, is the youngest organ of the UPU. Because of its nature and its emphasis on technical, operational and economic problems it, rather than the ELC, is the true descendant of the Russian proposal of 1929.

1. Creation

Real responsibility for the creation of the Consultative Committee for Postal Studies lies with the executive and liaison committee. The Congress of Paris, it will be recalled, considered creating a technical consultative committee, but action on the matter was sidetracked in favor of a body with a wider mandate, the ELC. Anything the new ELC could not do, it was pointed out, could be accomplished by consultation between administrations through the clearinghouse activities of the international bureau.[164] The delegates to the ELC, however, soon became aware that neither they nor the international bureau were equal to the tasks demanded of them. First, the number of problems needing study was more than they could possibly handle within a reasonable time, considering their duties in regard to the administration of the union and its relations with other international organizations. Second, many of the technical and operational problems with which they were confronted

162. *Ibid.,* pp. 7–8, and *Annual Report, 1960,* pp. 17–23.
163. Other examples of the work of the ELC can be found throughout this text.
164. Docs., Paris Postal Congress (1947), I, 57 and 61; and II, 419.

needed the kind of attention that they, as a restricted membership organ, could not give.

The feelings of the members of the ELC were first given voice in a Dutch proposal introduced at the ELC's session in May 1955. The Dutch administration was of the opinion that the ELC was not adequate to the task conferred upon it by the Paris Congress. What was needed, it was proposed, was a special committee of the UPU to deal primarily with technical problems, and one in which all members of the union could participate. "Several administrations," the Dutch delegation asserted, "have already created something in the field of postal mechanization, and it would be useful if a means could be found to bring together these creations, to exchange information on the subject, to try out the mechanical apparatus as perfected, and to arrive perhaps at a certain division of task and of research." [165] No opposition to the Dutch proposal was forthcoming, and, in fact, all the speakers praised it highly; but at the suggestion of the secretary general of the ELC (the director of the bureau) it was decided to postpone any action until the next session, at which time the secretary general would provide a report on the matter, in particular, its financial consequences. [166]

The secretary general's report, some 18 pages in length, was presented to the ELC at its meeting in April and May 1956. The report was exhaustive concerning the existing UPU organization. It treated technical study organs of other international organizations, including the consultative committees of the ITU, and the problems that would have to be overcome, both administrative and financial, if a new organ were to be created. In general, the report came to the conclusion that to attain the ends mentioned in the Dutch resolution, the best alternative would be to create an organ analogous to the electrotechnical committee of the International Organization for Standardization or the international consultative committees of the International Telecommunication Union. [167]

The report of the secretary general of the ELC provoked a spirited discussion between those who agreed that the UPU needed a new permanent organ for this purpose and those who felt that some other solution could be found. Among the suggestions by the latter group was one to the effect that technical problems could be handled adequately by a new subcommittee of the ELC. It was also suggested that the congress could create ad hoc interim committees which would achieve the same purpose. Several reasons were offered. Some were fearful that the authority inherent in a permanent organ might result in premature standardization of technical and mechanical apparatus and procedure. Others, Canada, for example, simply did not want to see a further complication of the organization of the UPU or were doubtful that the extra cost would justify the results that might be obtained. Debate at the 1956 session of the ELC was silenced when it was decided, by 13 to 5, that

165. Docs., ELC, 1955, pp. 78–79.
166. *Ibid.*, pp. 255–58.
167. Docs., ELC, 1956, pp. 195–212.

a new permanent organ was in order, and a subcommittee was created to prepare concrete proposals. The subcommittee was also ordered to undertake some technical studies on its own, both to help cut down on the ELC's backlog and to give it some background on the type of problems that the new organ would have to face.[168]

At its meeting in April 1957, the last before the Ottawa Postal Congress, the ELC heard the report of its subcommittee and, after rejecting a Belgian proposal to the effect that the Ottawa Congress should turn the matter over to an interim committee, agreed by a vote of 12 to 4 to recommend the creation of a new permanent organ.[169] The final results of the work of the ELC in this matter were presented to the Ottawa Congress in several forms. First, there was a recommendation from the ELC that a new organ of the union be created to deal with technical matters and that it be permanent and not temporary. Second, the ELC submitted a series of recommendations concerning the specifications of the new organization, based on its subcommittee's report and presented by the Netherlands delegation. Third, there was a resolution of the ELC containing a suggested list of questions to be studied by the new organ.[170]

The Congress of Ottawa created the new permanent technical committee, but only after additional discussion. First, the congress turned the consideration of the new organ over to the special committee on "a Program for Technical and Economic Studies" which had been created upon the recommendation of the international bureau, in agreement with the host country.[171] The first two sessions of this committee, open to participation by the entire membership of the congress, were devoted to a debate on the principle of establishing the new organ. It was approved unanimously. An agreed text was drawn up and submitted to the general committee. After seven more sessions, plus the additional labors of a special working group made up of delegates from Belgium, Egypt, France, Great Britain, India, Netherlands, Switzerland, United States, and USSR, the text was approved by the general committee and finally approved unanimously by the fifth plenary session of the congress, without any debate.[172]

Throughout the discussions on the proposed new technical study body it was evident that if such a body was to be created it would have to have an open membership. The subject matter under the competence of the new body was of universal interest because of its relevance to all internal postal systems and to the international postal system in general and, therefore, most nations would wish to participate. This concept was ratified by a special unanimous decision on August 23, 1957, in the com-

168. *Ibid.*, pp. 520–46 and 568–69.

169. UPU, ELC, *Documents de la Commission exécutive et de liaison, Session d'avril 1957* (Berne, 1957), pp. 321–93 and 449–70.

170. Docs., Ottawa Postal Congress (1957), I, 94–113, 116, 130, 134, 137–43, 186, 274, 281, 285–87, 290, and 293–94.

171. *Ibid.*, II, 18–19 and 174–75.

172. *Ibid.*, pp. 199–267. (See also the speeches of self-congratulation in *ibid.*, pp. 268–69.)

mittee on a program of technical and economic studies of the Ottawa Congress and approved in plenary meeting on September 13, 1957, also by a unanimous vote.[173]

Inasmuch as a committee of the entire membership of the union would be unworkable, it was necessary to create a small executive-coordinating body. It was the composition of this body, called the Management Council, which caused some conflict at Ottawa. A small group of delegates, led by the representative of Canada, argued that the management council should be composed of as small a group as possible, preferably four in the opinion of the Canadian delegate. A small group would be efficient and economical and could work closely with the international bureau. The group would not necessarily have to remain small, it was suggested, but could develop as experience and need dictated.[174]

The group desiring a small membership did not have enough support, however, and when the United States proposed, with the backing of eight other delegations, that the membership of the management committee be fixed at 20, the same size as the ELC, its cause was lost. The committee on a program of technical and economic studies approved the United States proposal by a vote of 38 to 20 after only two days of discussion.[175]

As for the study groups which would actually investigate various technical matters, there was no problem. From the beginning it was agreed that membership in these bodies would be open to any interested member of the union, and this was the decision taken by the Congress of Ottawa.[176]

2. *Structure and Authority*

The Consultative Committee on Postal Studies (CCPS), then, "is a permanent organ of the Union," made up of all the member countries of the union, and "charged with carrying out studies and issuing opinions on technical, operational and economic questions concerning the postal service." [177] It is composed of the committee sitting as a whole; the limited member management council; and a series of study groups in which any member may participate.

The only specific duties given to the committee by the convention are the election of the members of its management council, discussion and approval of the report of the council before it is submitted to a congress, and the adoption of the rules of procedure that govern the

173. *Ibid.*, pp. 214 and 267–68. The article as adopted (Paragraph 2 of Article 17 of the Ottawa Postal Convention of 1957) reads: "All the member Countries of the Union are, as of right, members of the Committee."

174. *Ibid.*, pp. 216–17.

175. *Ibid.*, p. 222.

176. See, for instance, *ibid.*, I, 144. Paragraph 5 of Article 17 of the Ottawa Postal Convention provides: "Countries which do not belong to the Management Council may, at their request, collaborate in the activities of the working groups."

177. Ottawa Postal Convention (1957), Art. 17, paras. 1 and 2.

work of the committee and its organs.[178] The rules of procedure of the committee provide, in addition, that it may "give opinions on technical, operational and economic questions concerning the postal service." [179]

The basic documents of the union fix no time for meetings of the committee. Article 104, para. 2, of the detailed regulations of the Ottawa Postal Convention simply provides that "the committee meets in plenary session at the request of the Chairman of the Management Council in agreement with the Chairman of the Executive and Liaison Committee and the Director of the International Bureau." The rules of procedure of the CCPS provide, however, that it shall meet in ordinary plenary session at the place and on the dates fixed for congresses. An extraordinary plenary session may be held at the request of the chairman of the management council after agreement with the chairman of the executive and liaison committee and the director of the international bureau.[180] The only plenary meeting to date was that held during the Congress of Ottawa for the purpose of electing the members of its management council and adopting its rules of procedure.[181] In view of the large membership of the commission, it is to be expected that it will hold only two meetings every five years. One will be an election meeting and another will be held in the early days of the next congress to discuss and approve the report of the management council before it is submitted to the congress.

The directing organ of the CCPS is its 20-member management council. This body meets once a year, at a place and date fixed by its chairman "in agreement with the Chairman of the Executive and Liaison Committee and the Director of the International Bureau," and is charged with "directing, fostering and co-ordinating" the work of the committee and its study groups. Specifically, its task is to establish study groups, to draw up a program of work to be undertaken during the following year, to publish study reports, to submit an annual report to the executive and liaison committee, and to draft a final report covering its work in the interval between congresses.[182]

The management council of the CCPS elects its own chairman and three vice chairmen. In addition to the duties mentioned above, the chairman represents the CCPS at meetings of the executive and liaison committee when questions of interest to his group are to be discussed. Other functions of the chairman are similar to those previously discussed for the chairman of a congress.[183]

The presence of 12 delegates constitutes a quorum, and the council may invite representatives of other international organizations, or any

178. *Ibid.,* Art. 17, paras. 3 and 7, and Regulations, Art. 104, para. 6.
179. From the Rules of Procedure of the CCPS as found in Docs., Ottawa Postal Congress (1957), II, 263–66.
180. *Ibid., p.* 263.
181. *Ibid.,* pp. 283–84.
182. See Ottawa Postal Convention (1957), Art. 17, and Regulations, Art. 104.
183. See CCPS, Rules of Procedure, *op. cit.,* p. 246.

other qualified person, to participate in its discussions. Other rules of procedure for meetings are similar to those laid down for congresses and for plenary meetings: the chairman votes in case of a tie; the official language is French, although other languages may be used in discussions with the aid of a simultaneous interpretation system; each member has one vote, although in exceptional circumstances a member may exercise one proxy vote in addition to his own; decisions are made by a majority; and, on the demand of one member supported by at least one other, the vote may be secret.[184]

Representatives of each country elected to the council, designated by their country's postal administration, must be qualified employees of the postal administration. Neither the delegates to the council, the committee as a whole, or the working groups receive payment from the union. Travel and accommodation expenses of those participating in the work of the committee, including the members of the council, are borne by the delegate's postal administration. The secretariats for the committee and its organs are provided by the international bureau. Its expenses and other "working expenses" of the committee, however, are met by the regular budget of the union.[185]

The management council is further divided into three sections: technical, operations, and economic.[186] Each section is headed by a vice chairman of the council who may, with the agreement of the chairman, call meetings of his section to coordinate the work of the working groups under his section's direction, to prepare reports, and to publish the results of the work on the questions under their competence. Members of the management council may participate in as many of the sections as they wish, and the sections may invite nonmembers to participate in their work at their own expense.[187]

The sections, in their turn, create working groups to investigate specific problems within their areas of competence. These groups, the real work horses of the CCPS, are made up of members of the appropriate sections, supplemented by representatives of any member country of the union interested in the problem under investigation. The vice chairman of the council designates a member of his section to head each working group and the latter is responsible to that vice chairman for the study of the particular problem assigned to the group, including the division of work, coordination, gathering of necessary information, and a final report.[188]

Wherever possible the working groups carry out their tasks by correspondence. Nevertheless, if it is judged necessary, the head of the working group may call a meeting upon approval of the appropriate vice

184. *Ibid.*, p. 266.
185. *Ibid.*, p. 263, and Ottawa Postal Convention (1957), Art. 17 and Regulations, Art. 105.
186. Ottawa Postal Convention (1957), Art. 17, paras. 4 and 6.
187. CCPS, Rules of Procedure, *op. cit.*, p. 265.
188. Ottawa Postal Convention (1957), Art. 17, para. 5, and CCPS, Rules of Procedure, *op. cit.*, p. 265.

chairman and the director of the international bureau. The CCPS has decided that whenever possible the working groups should base their studies on the practice and experience of postal administrations.[189]

To provide a better picture of the actual structure of the commission and its organs, as well as the work they are doing, the next section of the study will be devoted to the commission's work since the Congress of Ottawa which created it in 1957.

3. The CCPS at Work

The Consultative Committee on Postal Studies held its first ordinary plenary session on September 13, 1957, during the Ottawa Congress.[190] This first meeting, which took exactly 15 minutes, was devoted to two tasks: the adoption of the rules of procedure for itself and its organs, and the election of the 20 countries to provide the management council for the next inter-congress period. The rules, adopted without great discussion, were those which had been prepared for it by the committee on a program of technical and economic studies of the congress. Although neither the Ottawa convention nor the CCPS's rules of procedure contained any instructions as to the method of electing members of the management council, the CCPS was relieved of any difficulty in this respect when only 20 countries presented themselves as candidates. No formalities were observed, therefore, and the 20 candidates were elected by acclamation to provide the delegates, who were: Australia, Belgium, Bulgaria, China, Colombia, Czechoslovakia, Egypt, France, Germany, Great Britain, Italy, Japan, Netherlands, Paraguay, Rumania, Sweden, Switzerland, Tunisia, United States, and USSR.[191]

The management council of the CCPS then met during the Ottawa Congress on September 19 and 26, 1957, to elect its officers, to create its organization, and to fix the time and place of the next meeting. The United States was unanimously chosen to provide the chairman of the council and France, the Netherlands, and the USSR to provide the three vice chairmen. After consultation among the three countries involved, France was chosen to head the operations section, the Netherlands the technical section, and the USSR the economic section.[192]

The next important item of business was for the members of the management council to choose the sections with which they wished to be affiliated. Seventeen chose the operations section, 16 the economic section, and 12 the technical section. Nine countries chose to take part in all three sections, six to take part in two, and four — Bulgaria, China, Rumania, and Tunisia — to take part in only one, as follows:[193]

189. CCPS, Rules of Procedure, op. cit., p. 265.
190. The fifth plenary meeting of the congress, in fact, adjourned immediately after approving the creation of the committee in order that it might hold its first session.
191. Docs., Ottawa Postal Congress (1957), II, 283–284.
192. Ibid., II, 285–87.
193. Ibid., p. 290.

Country	Technical section	AFFILIATED WITH Operations section	Economic section
1. Australia	X		X
2. Belgium	X	X	X
3. Bulgaria			X
4. China		X	
5. Colombia	X	X	
6. Czechoslovakia		X	X
7. Egypt		X	X
8. France	X	X	X
9. Germany	X	X	X
10. Great Britain	X	X	X
11. Italy	X	X	X
12. Japan	X	X	
13. Netherlands	X	X	X
14. Paraguay		X	X
15. Rumania			X
16. Sweden		X	X
17. Switzerland	X	X	X
18. Tunisia		X	
19. United States	X	X	X
20. USSR	X	X	X
	12	17	16

Confronted with 45 questions proposed by the congress, covering almost every aspect of postal operations, the management council had as one of its major tasks the planning of its work schedule. First it was determined that 19 questions were primarily technical in nature, 16 operational, and 10 economic. For primarily financial considerations it was decided not to undertake all the studies at one time, but to divide the questions into two more or less equal parts and to begin the investigation of one half. The technical section chose seven topics on which to begin its work, the operations section chose eight, and the economic section chose five. Twenty working groups were then created, one for each question, and the members of the management council chose the working groups with which they wished to be affiliated. The size of the working groups established at Ottawa varied widely. One, the working group of the operations section to study "methods for defining the standard surfaces necessary for handling mail in postal establishments," was composed of only the delegates from Great Britain and the USSR. Another, the working group of the economic section dealing with the "cost price of separate postal operations," was chosen by 12 members of the management council.[194]

The management council of the CCPS has held five meetings since the organizational meeting of 1957: Brussels, May 19–29, 1958; The

194. *Ibid.,* pp. 291–95. This citation also includes a complete list of the questions submitted to the CCPS by the congress.

Hague, March 9–19, 1959; Eastbourne, June 27 to July 9, 1960; Tokyo, October 2–22, 1961; and Washington, D.C., October 28 to November 8, 1963. As a rule, only three or four days of each session are devoted to meetings of the council as a whole. On these days, the council discusses reports, makes organizational decisions, and in general plans the work of the sections and the working groups. About three days are devoted to meetings of the three sections, and the remainder to meetings of working groups.[195]

While the details of these meetings are not of great interest to us, note should be taken of some of the lessons learned in the first few years of activity of the CCPS. The most important is, without doubt, that the tasks confronting the CCPS were much greater than had been anticipated. First, there was the constant increase in the number of questions that administrations considered appropriate for study by the committee. Although it had started with only 45 questions in 1957, and 14 studies had been completed, at its meeting in 1961 the management council found that it still had before it a grand total of 41 questions. Second, many of the questions that had been submitted took much more time to investigate than had been planned. Some which it was hoped would be completed in a year or two were actually taking three years or more to study thoroughly. And third, some of the questions were of a permanent nature which would require continuing study as new developments took place.[196]

In view of this problem, the management council made some short-term recommendations. Among them was the recommendation that working groups contain a minimum number of experts in order to facilitate their work. However, few countries not members of the management council have expressed a desire to participate in working groups.[197] The management council has also made provision for coordination on questions found to touch on the work of more than one working group.[198]

Perhaps the most important decision of the management council was to form in 1961 a special working group made up of the chairman and vice chairmen of the CCPS along with the chairman of the executive and liaison committee to attempt to fix the probable line of development

195. See, for instance, Docs. CCPS, 1957/58, pp. 41–189.

196. See UPU, *Documents de la Commission consultative des études postales (CCEP), session d'Eastbourne 1960; Compte rendu analytique de la session d'Eastbourne 1960* (Berne, 1960), p. 10; and Emile Bühler, "The Annual Session of the Management Council of the Consultative Committee for Postal Studies, Tokyo 1961," *Union Postale*, LXXXVII, No. 1 (January, 1962), 9A–10A, and *Annual Report, 1961*, p. 24. The more important reports of the CCPS are summarized in the *Union Postale*. For some recent examples, see *Union Postale*, LXXXVII, No. 1 (January, 1962), 11A–14A; No. 2 (February, 1962), 20A–22A; No. 3 (March, 1962), 34A–35A; No. 4 (April, 1962), 53A–54A; No. 5 (May, 1962), 64A–65A; No. 6 (June, 1962), 80A–81A; and No. 9 (September, 1962), 128A–30A.

197. See Docs., CCPS 1957/58, *Compte rendu analytique de la session de Bruxelles 1958* (Berne, 1958), p. 9. In June, 1963, ten countries in addition to the members of the Management Council were participating in working groups.

198. Bühler, *op. cit.*, p. 7A.

MEMBERSHIP IN WORKING GROUPS OF THE CCPS MANAGEMENT COUNCIL AS OF JUNE, 1963

	A. Technical Section Working Groups											B. Operations Section Working Groups															C. Economic Section Working Groups								Number of Groups as	
	A1	A2	A3	A4	A5	A6	A7	A8	A9	A12	A19	B1	B2	B3	B4	B5	B6	B7	B8	B9	B10	B11	B13	B15	B16	B18	C1	C2	C3	C4	C5	C6	C9	C10	Reporting Country	Member Country
Members of the Management Council																																				
Australia	x	x	x		x	x	x		x	x				o	x		x			x		x	x	x	x		o	x	x		x	x		x	–	12
Belgium		x				x			x	x		x	x		x	x							o		x		x	x	x		x	x	x	x	3	20
Bulgaria							x			x		x												x			x	x							–	4
China																		x																	–	2
Colombia												x		x		x							x				x								–	4
Czechoslovakia		o	o			x		o	x		x	x	x	x	x	x	x	o	x	x		x	o		o	x	x	x		x		x	x		1	10
Egypt – U.A.R.	o	x	x	x	x	x		x	x	x		x	x	x	x	x	x	x	o	o		o	.	x	x	x	x	x	o	x		x	x		–	5
France	x	x	x		x	x	x	x		x	x	o		x	x	o	o	x	x	x	x	x	x	x	x	x	x	x		x	x	o	x	x	8	25
Germany (Fed. Rep.)	x	x		x	x										x	x	x	.		x		x	x	x	x		x	x			x		x		2	21
Great Britain							x			x				x	x	x	x	x		x	x	x		x	x		x	x		x		x	x		4	19
Italy		x			x	x		x			x																x	x	x	x	x	x	x	x	–	9
Japan			x	o			o							x	x		x	.	x	x	x	x	x	x				o		x	o				1	7
Netherlands	x	x	x	x	x	x	x	x	x	o	x	x	x	x	x	x	x	x	x	x	x	x	x	x	x		x	x	x	x	o	x	x	x	3	24
Paraguay																																			–	6
Rumania							x	x		x				x	x		x		x			x	x			o	x	x	x	x		x	x		1	6
Sweden	x	x		o	x			x	x		x			x	x		x	x	x	x	x		x	x			x			x		x	x	x	–	8
Switzerland					x	x	x					x	o	x				.	x			x	. x	x	x	o	x	x	x	x	o	x	x	x	2	22
Tunisia											x																x	x				x	x	o	–	10
U.S.S.R.	x	x			x	x			x	o	x	x		x	x		x		x				x	o			x	x	x		o		x		4	21
United States	x	x	x		x	x	x			x		x	x	x	x	x	x	.	x	x	x		. x	x	x	o	x	x		o	x	x	x	o	3	21
Other Members of the UPU																																				
Argentina																		x	x			x	x	x			x x								–	16
Austria	x											x			x		x		x					o				x						x	–	5
Denmark																			x				x				x	x	x		o				–	4
India					x														x				. x				x								–	5
Israel					x							x			x		x		x					x				x							–	3
Korea																		x	x					x			x x							x	–	3
Norway																			x															x	–	1
Poland												x							x			x							x						–	4
Turkey	x	x	x		x	x			x			x	x	x	x	x	x	x	x	x	x	x	x				x	x					x	x	–	2
Yugoslavia	x	x	x		x	x	x	x	x	x		x	x	x	x	x	x	x	x	x	x	x	x				x	x		x	x	x	x	x	–	22
TOTAL MEMBERS IN EACH WORKING GROUP	12	10	10	4	11	14	9	5	7	8	3	10	6	10	14	8	13	12	11	10	7	8	11	13	7	3	15	14	8	7	7	11	14	9	34	

Source: CCPS Aide - mémoire -- Session de 1963 du Conseil de gestion, June, 1963   x Member country   o Reporting country

of postal services during the next 15 to 20 years. The purpose is to provide the next postal congress with guide lines for its decisions on the future work of the CCPS.[199]

It should also be noted that the management council of the CCPS has made extensive use of a steering committee made up of the chairman and the vice chairmen in order to organize and coordinate its own work. When it was decided to postpone the 1962 meeting of the management council in order to relieve some of the burden on postal administrations (in view of the proximity of the next congress), the steering committee was ordered to meet at Berne from the 3d to the 6th of October 1962 and was given a mandate to settle all questions that might rise concerning the CCPS.[200]

Five years is too short a time to permit a definitive evaluation of the usefulness of the CCPS in the Universal Postal Union system. It will be necessary to give the CCPS time to find the organization and the methods best suited to its tasks. Above all, it will be important to await completion of a respectable number of studies and the application of those studies to the international postal service and to the various domestic postal services. Only then will the true potentialities of the CCPS become known.

199. *Ibid.*, p. 9A.
200. *Ibid.*, p. 24A. For further information on the work of the CCPS, see Emile Kern, "CCPS — Recent Events," *Union Postale*, LXXXVI, No. 8 (August, 1961), 104A–105A.

The International Bureau

U NTIL THE CREATION of the Executive and Liaison Committee in 1947, the international bureau was the only organ of the Universal Postal Union other than the periodic congresses.[1] Although the international bureau now shares the designation of permanent organ with congresses, the ELC, and the CCPS, and although some of its former duties are now shared with the ELC and to a certain extent with the CCPS, it remains the only real continuing organ of the UPU, and its duties are still vast. To have a true knowledge of the UPU, one must know its international bureau.

A. Background

THE DRAFT TREATY presented to the delegates at the Berne Postal Congress in 1874 did not provide for the creation of any organ other than the congress. It suggested only that "at least every three years a Congress of plenipotentiaries of the participants in the treaty will be held in order to improve the Union, to introduce necessary changes, and to discuss common affairs." [2]

The idea that the new international organization might need any-

1. "International bureau" is a term which has been in use longer than "secretariat" for the permanent personnel of an international organization. Some of the older organizations, such as the International Telecommunication Union, have changed the designation from bureau to secretariat. The UPU and some others have retained the original designation. In this latter category are the international bureau of the Permanent Court of Arbitration, the International Bureau of Weights and Measures, and the United International Bureaus for the Protection of Industrial, Literary and Artistic Works. The ILO has also retained the original, although "bureau" is officially translated as "office" in English.

2. Docs., Berne Postal Congress (1874), p. 7.

thing more in its structure was expressed for the first time at the second plenary meeting, during the discussion of a provision of the draft treaty concerning arbitration procedure. At one point, according to the records, Mr. Vinchent, a Belgian delegate, observed that the proposed arbitration procedure seemed a little too complicated for the settlement of minor disputes and suggested that for such disputes "he would see, with pleasure, the creation of an International Bureau comparable to that which existed for the telegraphs." [3] The organ of the "telegraphs" to which Mr. Vinchent was referring was the international bureau of the International Telegraph Union which had been established in 1865.

It was not until the fifth plenary session of the Berne Congress that Mr. Vinchent translated his observations into a concrete plan. At that session he offered a proposal, described by him as "an article similar to Article 63 of the International Telegraph Convention of Rome of 1872," which would create an international bureau, under the supervision of a country chosen by the congress, with the following duties: 1] to co-ordinate, publish, and distribute information of all types which might be of interest to the international postal service; 2] to give advice in legal disputes between member administrations; 3] to conduct inquiries for administrations on proposed changes to the convention and its regulations between congresses, and to notify the members of the results of these inquiries; 4] to assist members in clearing their international postal accounts; and 5], in general, to undertake studies and other work of interest to the postal union.[4] In general, the Vinchent proposal was quite close to one in the International Telegraph Convention, and reflected the duties of the Telegraph Union's bureau, with one major exception. The one function that the bureau of the Telegraph Union did not have was that of acting as an arbitrator on legal questions between members of the ITU.[5]

In presenting his proposal, Mr. Vinchent emphasized that the new bureau "would not be an *authority*, but simply a *help*" to the members of the new union. Administrations would owe nothing to it "except a very modest contribution to cover its expenses and the obligation to receive from it, and to send to it, certain documents." There was only one instance, according to the Belgian delegate, where the bureau would have any power even approximating the right to intervene in the affairs of administrations, that is in the arbitration of disputes; but in this instance the bureau could act only when requested to do so by an administration. "It is not, therefore, an authority," he concluded.[6]

3. *Ibid.*, pp. 32–33.
4. *Ibid.*, p. 55.
5. For a discussion of the origins of the ITU's bureau and its functions, see Codding, *op. cit.*, pp. 22–24 and 49–52.
6. Docs., Berne Postal Congress (1874), p. 55. This same reluctance to give the secretariat any real authority was evident at the creation of the ITU's bureau in 1868. According to the Belgian delegate on that occasion, the director of the ITU's bureau would have "no decision to make, no means to impose his ideas; the liberty of the administrations would remain complete." (See Codding, *op. cit.*, p. 49.)

By the end of the Berne Congress, the new bureau was given five additional tasks: (1) to serve as intermediary for "regular and general" notifications of information from administrations concerning international postal relations, and to receive all documents published by postal administrations concerning their internal postal service; (2) to distribute annually a general set of postal statistics; (3) to publish a journal in English, French, and German; (4) to aid the host country in preparing for congresses; and (5) to place itself generally at the disposition of member administrations for furnishing any special information that they might desire concerning the international postal service.[7]

In addition to a lack of authority, the bureau also was to have no real independence. Mr. Vinchent proposed, and his fellow delegates agreed, that the task of creating the new organ and of supervising its operations be given to one of the postal administrations signatory to the postal treaty. In addition to naming the individuals who would serve as employees of the bureau, the supervising administration would advance the bureau's necessary operating funds and draw up and distribute an annual financial report.[8]

One of the last acts of the Berne Congress, with reference to the bureau, was the selection of the postal administration which would be its supervising authority. Only two countries were nominated — Belgium and Switzerland — and a secret ballot was employed to choose between them. On the first round of voting each country received 10 votes and one ballot was invalid. On the second round, however, Switzerland received 12 votes to Belgium's nine, and a few days later the congress was notified that the Swiss government had agreed to undertake the task.[9]

Later the Swiss government named Mr. Eugène Borel, chief of its Department of Posts and chairman of the Berne Postal Congress, to be first director of the bureau. In 1874 Mr. Borel and two employees set up shop in rented offices in Berne, and the international bureau of the UPU was ready for business. Switzerland, it should be noted, had also been chosen to create the bureau of the International Telegraph Union, and Berne thus became the seat of both secretariats.

No great substantive changes were made in the functions or organization of the international bureau from its inception in 1874 to the first post-World War II congress in Paris in 1947. It remained primarily "an organ for liaison, information, and consultation." [10] However, the work of the bureau in all its aspects continued to increase with regularity.

Two threats, neither serious, were made to the autonomy of the international bureau before 1947. At the Congress of Lisbon (1885) the Portuguese delegate proposed that since the telegraph and postal services were united in most countries under the same administration, it would be useful to unite the international bureau of the UPU with

7. Berne Postal Treaty (1875), Detailed Regulations, Art. xxvii.
8. Docs., Berne Postal Congress (1874), p. 55.
9. *Ibid.*, pp. 82 and 99.
10. Wording added to the postal convention by the Stockholm Congress of 1924. See Docs., Stockholm Postal Congress (1924), ii, 850.

that of the International Telegraph Union. After a brief intervention by delegates from France and Belgium, who pointed out the difficulties of such a proposal and the advantages of separate organizations, the Portuguese delegate agreed to drop the proposal and let it stand in the minutes as simply a suggestion from his government.[11] In 1934 the Brazilian delegate proposed the possibility of uniting the same two bureaus to create an "International Bureau of the Union of the Posts and Telegraphs" or better, "Universal Bureau of the Union of the Posts and Telegraphs." The chairman of the preparatory commission in which the Brazilian proposal was made advised the Brazilian delegate that such a suggestion did not lie within the terms of reference of the commission, and the Brazilian delegate agreed to let it drop.[12]

As mentioned earlier, 1947 was the crucial year for the international bureau. The postwar reorganization of the world to eliminate threats to the peace and to provide for international cooperation in international welfare was well under way. The United Nations had come into operation and several specialized agencies had been created. All of these organizations had a much more complex administrative structure than the Universal Postal Union. It would have been expected, therefore, that there would be a great deal of pressure to "modernize" the UPU and to place it on a footing of equality with the other specialized agencies that had been created or were being planned. The remainder of this chapter will be devoted to the present-day organization of the international bureau and the changes that were made in its organization during and after the first post-World War II congress held in Paris in 1947.

B. The Status of the International Bureau

THE INTERNATIONAL BUREAU of the UPU has a unique status among the specialized agencies of the United Nations. While the secretariats of most specialized agencies are controlled by one or more organs of the agency in question, and to a certain extent by the government of the country in which their headquarters are located, the uniqueness of the international bureau's position stems from the manner in which this control is apportioned between the congress, the ELC, and the government where its headquarters are located. The ultimate authority of the international bureau is, of course, the congress. The second in command, however, is not the ELC but the Swiss government. It is the Swiss

11. Docs., Lisbon Congress (1885), I, 65; and II, 91 and 376.

12. Docs., Cairo Postal Congress (1934), I, 26, 28, and 1269. Two years previously, at Madrid, the International Telegraph Union and the International Radiotelegraph Union had agreed to merge to create the organization that is now known as the International Telecommunication Union. It is interesting to speculate whether, had the bureaus been merged as the Brazilian delegate had suggested, there would have been a serious effort to merge the UPU and the ITU. (For an account of the conference in which the Telegraph Union and the Radiotelegraph Union were merged, see Codding, op. cit., pp. 131–56.)

government which exercises the real day-to-day control over the bureau's administrative and financial operations. The ELC's powers are merely nominal and advisory.

The decision to give the international bureau the hybrid status that it now enjoys was made by the Congress of Paris in 1947, and the form it took resulted from a series of interrelated factors. In the first place, it was generally agreed that the Swiss government had done a good job on the supervision and control of the international bureau. There were no complaints whatsoever concerning the personnel or the manner in which they had carried out their functions. In general, nothing but praise was heaped on the Swiss for their running of the bureau in the decisive discussions at Paris in 1947.[13] Secondly, it was generally agreed that the Swiss government performed certain tasks in relation to the bureau for which it would be extremely difficult to find a substitute. For example, when additional personnel was needed the Swiss postal administration loaned its own staff to the bureau. Temporary personnel with competence in postal matters are, as pointed out by the Swiss delegation, sometimes difficult to find in a hurry. The Swiss government had also advanced operating funds to the bureau when the contributions of member governments were in arrears. In World War II, for instance, the Swiss government financed the bureau at a time when it was difficult for member nations to keep in contact with one another, much less make annual contributions to the expenses of the bureau. Finally, the Swiss government was in a position to aid the bureau in its material needs, such as postal and telegraphic services.[14] It might also be added, although it was not expressed openly, that there undoubtedly was recognition of the importance of having the organization's secretariat under the patronage of a "neutral" state.

The threat to the position of the Swiss government as the "high authority" of the international bureau, made in 1947, therefore, did not stem from any dissatisfaction with its work in the past. It arose rather out of the desire to create the ELC and the decision that had to be made concerning the scope of the powers of that new agency. If the new ELC were to be given the "normal" powers of an administrative organ, the functions left to the Swiss government would be minimal. On the other hand, if, as was actually the case, the ELC was to be given little or no power, the functions left to the Swiss government would remain numerous.[15]

Neither the Russian proposal for the new ELC, which was quickly defeated, nor the Brazil-China-Egypt-Portugal proposal, which was adopted as a basis of discussion, contained any reference to the future duties of the Swiss government — the former by design, the latter perhaps by inadvertence. The nations sponsoring the latter, at least, had

13. See, for instance, the statements in Docs., Paris Postal Congress (1947), II, 952, 954, 981, 985, and 987.
14. *Ibid.*, pp. 958, 981, 985, and 987.
15. Since the discussions were thus interrelated, reference should be made to the preceding material on the ELC. See above, pp. 159–63.

nothing to say against the work done by the Swiss government. The Chinese delegate, for example, emphasized only the argument that the proposed new ELC could take over some of the functions previously exercised by the old bureau.[16]

After a rather lengthy exposé by the Swiss delegate of the numerous duties that the Swiss government had undertaken for the UPU and the bureau in the past, the possibility of replacing the Swiss government by the new organ seemed to disappear, and the discussions shifted to the problem of just how much authority to transfer to the ELC. On the one side there were the delegations, the chief spokesman of whom was Canada, which desired that the ELC be given the minimum possible authority over the bureau. On the other side was a group, of which Bulgaria was a vocal member, which argued that the ELC be given a maximum amount of authority over the bureau. Specifically, one of the more thorny points turned out to be the amount of authority that the ELC should have over the employment of the bureau's personnel, a function previously in the exclusive province of the Swiss government.[17]

Finally, after an impassioned and confused debate — there were several at the Paris Congress — a number of decisions were reached by vote. Although some of the decisions contradicted each other, and this in itself was the subject of agitated debate, a compromise was finally reached. It did, in effect, give the ELC some authority to participate in the selection of the personnel of the bureau, but failed to make a genuine delimitation of the spheres of competence between the ELC and the Swiss government.[18] According to this compromise decision, which took the form of an addition to the postal convention, the ELC's functions in relation to the bureau were:

> e) within the framework of the Convention and its Detailed Regulations, to ensure the control of the activities of the International Bureau of which it appoints, when the need arises and on the proposal of the Government of the Swiss Confederation, the Director and other high personnel; to approve, on the proposal of the Director of the International Bureau, the appointment of other officials and to authorize the use of auxiliary personnel . . . ; and to establish an annual report on the administration of the Bureau which it communicates to members of the Union.[19]

On the other hand, the Paris Congress did not spell out the functions of the Swiss government. The only reference to the Swiss government, in fact, was contained in the short article of the convention dealing with the international bureau, the first paragraph of which read:

16. Docs., Paris Postal Congress (1947), I, 49–51 and 57–59; and II, 952–53.
17. See the discussions in *ibid.*, II, 950–98.
18. *Ibid.*, pp. 991–98.
19. Paris Postal Convention (1947), Art. 18, para. 11.

A central office, operating at Berne under the title of the International Bureau of the Universal Postal Union and placed under the general supervision of the Swiss Postal Administration, serves as an organization for liaison, information, and consultation for the countries of the Union.[20]

Since the exact delimitation of the authority over the bureau to be exercised by the ELC and the Swiss government (desired by the Paris Congress) cannot be gleaned from the official documents, the evaluation of the bureau itself is our best guide:

> The question of the delimitation of the prerogatives of the Swiss authorities and the ELC as regards the general supervision and control of the activity of the International Bureau was discussed in its general aspects by the Congress of Paris in 1947. It did not take any formal decision, but the Congress did tacitly accept a statement of the Chairman according to which . . . the competent Swiss supervisory authority would continue to exercise its supervision of the International Bureau in the areas and in the degree to which it had done so up to that time, whereas the ELC would control the International Bureau in those questions, undertakings and missions concerning the affairs which are under its exclusive competence, notably in matters relating to the relations of the UPU and the United Nations and other international organizations. It is also understood, in addition, that if this gives rise to borderline or doubtful cases, the ELC and the Swiss supervisory authority will consult to find out the line of demarcation.[21]

The congresses of Brussels and Ottawa did little in the way of changing the UPU's final acts to make this demarcation clear. The provision of the convention making the Swiss postal administration responsible for the general supervision of the bureau remains unchanged. Two changes have been made in the provisions regarding the authority of the ELC, however. The task of the ELC "to establish an annual report on the administration of the Bureau" has been changed to read "to approve the annual report on the Union's activities drawn up by the International Bureau and, where appropriate, to furnish observations upon it." [22] This was not a change in substance, however, but a drafting change to eliminate a contradiction between the Paris convention and its regulations and to reflect actual practice.[23] The Brussels Congress also modified the authority of the ELC over the bureau by replacing the phrase "to approve, on the proposal of the

20. *Ibid.*, Art. 26, para. 1.
21. *Annotated Acts, 1957*, 1er fascicule, p. 40, fn. 14. See also Docs., Paris Postal Congress (1947), II, 983–86.
22. Ottawa Postal Convention (1957), Art. 16, para. 5.
23. See Docs., Brussels Postal Congress (1952), I, 168.

Director of the International Bureau, the appointment of other officials and to authorize the use of auxiliary personnel," with "to approve, on the proposal of the Director of the International Bureau, the appointments of officials of the 1st and 2nd salary grades." The Brussels Congress also eliminated the need of approval by the ELC for the hiring of auxiliary personnel. Both changes, it should be noted, were proposed to the Congress of Brussels by the ELC itself.[24]

In practice, the ELC confines itself quite closely to "the affairs which are under its exclusive competence." It approves the annual report drawn up by the bureau, usually with a minimum of discussion, and approves the nominations of the director for the promotion of employees to the first and second class categories, also with a minimum of discussion. In 1960, for instance, it agreed to replace the director, Dr. Fritz Hess, on his retirement, with Dr. Edouard Weber. Although one member of the ELC abstained in the vote, no alternate candidate was proposed to run against the one selected by the Swiss administration.[25] It also requests the bureau to make studies when appropriate and supervises the sending of bureau personnel as UPU representatives to the meetings of the United Nations and other international organizations.[26]

On several occasions the ELC has taken under discussion affairs which might be interpreted as falling within the competence of the Swiss supervisory authority, such as pensions, salaries, cost of living supplements, or employees' emergency funds. The ELC has not, however, made any effort to force its recommendations on the bureau or the Swiss supervisory authority on its own initiative. When the subject matter is considered to be of major importance, the ELC has made it a practice to pass along its recommendations to the next congress for action. In some areas which do not need a constitutional enactment, the ELC has put its decisions or recommendations in the form of suggestions and submitted them to the Swiss supervisory authority.[27] As far as is known, this procedure has not given rise to any conflict between the ELC and the Swiss authorities. On the contrary, all evidence points to a good working relationship.

The remaining supervision of the international bureau rests with the Swiss authorities. As explained by the Swiss delegate at the Paris Congress, this supervision is carried out along two major lines. In the first place, the Swiss authorities assure conditions which will permit the bureau to carry out its duties under the most favorable circumstances. This includes the making of rules and regulations concerning the status of the headquarters, the legal capacity of the bureau, legal

24. *Ibid.*, I, 168; and III, 15.
25. See, ELC, *Compte rendu analytique de la session de mai 1960* (Berne, 1960), pp. 14 and 25.
26. See for instance, the *Compte rendu analytique* of the ELC's sessions from 1948 to 1961.
27. See, for instance, ELC, *Compte rendu analytique*, 1957, pp. 22–23; 1958, pp. 18–19; 1959, pp. 24, 26–27; 1960, pp. 22–23, 25; and 1961, p. 20.

and fiscal immunities, and the like. The Swiss government is responsible for the conditions of service and provisions for privileges and immunities for personnel. Included also are such activities as the nominating of individuals for higher posts, the lending of temporary personnel from the Swiss postal administration when necessary, and the providing of the bureau with certain services such as telephone and telegraph communications. The second function, perhaps the major one according to the Swiss delegate, is in the realm of finances. This area of supervision includes approval of the annual budget and the accounting for expenditures. It includes advancing funds for the bureau when the contributions of nations are in arrears or so late as to hamper the operations of the bureau, and the management of personnel insurance and emergency funds. Also, it was noted, the Swiss government contributes its services in the process of fixing postal rate equivalents as demanded by the postal convention. These activities, emphasized the Swiss delegate, were highly complex and purely gratuitous.[28]

In summary, the international bureau of the UPU is supervised by both the ELC and the Swiss government. The line of demarcation between the powers of the two bodies is not clear, but could be described as a division in which the ELC has certain restricted delegated functions, with all functions not thus delegated reserved to the Swiss government. It is too early to tell whether the vagueness of the convention and its regulations permit the ELC to increase its powers at the expense of the Swiss authorities if it should so desire.

Before turning to the actual functions of the international bureau, an explanation of the branch of the Swiss government which carries out the supervision of the international bureau is necessary. Article 19 of the universal postal convention designates the "Swiss Postal Administration" as the supervisory body. In point of fact, supervision of the bureau by the Swiss government is exercised by three divisions of the executive branch, namely, the Political Department (foreign affairs), the Department of Finance and Customs, and the Department of Posts and Railways. The Division of International Organizations of the Political Department handles diplomatic and personnel questions; the Department of Finances and Customs is in charge of budgetary and financial questions; and the postal administration of the Department of Posts and Railways is in charge of other matters, mostly of a practical nature, such as making temporary personnel available to the bureau when needed.[29]

Two attempts were made to change the wording of the postal convention so that it might more accurately reflect the true state of affairs, once at the Congress of Stockholm in 1924 and once at the Congress of Brussels in 1952, both of which failed. In 1924 Brazil proposed that "Swiss Postal Administration" be replaced by "Swiss

28. See Docs., Paris Postal Congress (1947), II, 980–81.
29. Docs., Brussels Postal Congress (1952), II, 364–65.

Federal Council," and in 1952 Brazil again proposed that it be replaced by "Government of the Swiss Confederation." [30] The reason for the two failures is simple; the proposed language did not fit in with the delegates' concept of the nature of the UPU. As stated by the Syrian delegate at Brussels (not too logically in view of the circumstances perhaps): "The UPU is an international organization founded on the principle of the equality of its members . . . It is preferable to leave the International Bureau under the control of the Swiss postal administration rather than under the government of a member country." [31] Or, as stated by the Swiss delegate: ". . . it is proper to avoid the interference of politics and the term 'government' is a political term while 'administration' is not. It is preferable, therefore, to maintain the status quo." [32]

c. Seat of the Bureau

THE SEAT of the International Bureau, and thus the seat of the union, is in Berne, Switzerland, and has remained there since 1874. Nothing was contained in the Berne Treaty of 1874 concerning the question of location. After it was chosen by the congress to do the organizing, the Swiss government decided on the Swiss capital city and there the bureau remained. After the period 1874 to 1927, during which time the bureau rented office space, it moved to a villa on Schwarztorstrasse, which was purchased for its use by the union. In 1948 the ELC was informed by the director that the villa would not be adequate to house the increased personnel needed to carry out duties designated for the bureau by the Congress of Paris in 1947. After a year of study the ELC agreed upon a new building, and in 1950 authorized the director to enter into contracts for its construction.[33] The new building, located at 46 Schosshaldenstrasse in Berne, was completed in 1953 and occupied by the UPU. At the Congress of Brussels in 1952, following the suggestion of the ELC, a new article was added to the universal postal convention which for the first time made Berne the official seat of the union. The provision in question reads: "The seat of the Union and its permanent organs is established at Berne." [34]

The legal status of the headquarters of the UPU on Swiss soil is regulated by The Provisional Agreement on Privileges and Immunities

30. See Docs., Stockholm Postal Congress (1924), II, 149 and 312; and Docs., Brussels Postal Congress (1952), I, 178, and II, 364–66.
31. Docs., Brussels Postal Congress, II, 364.
32. *Ibid.*, p. 366.
33. See UPU, *Le nouveau bâtiment de l'Union postale universelle inauguré à Berne le 9 mai 1953* (Berne, 1953), pp. 4–5.
34. Brussels Postal Convention (1952), Art. 2. (See also the debates concerning the possibility of having the headquarters of the ELC somewhere else in Docs., Paris Postal Congress, 1947, II, 955–59.)

of the United Nations Organization Concluded Between the Swiss Federal Council and the Secretary General of the United Nations Organization of April 19, 1946, which, the Swiss Federal Council declared on February 3, 1948, applied by analogy to the UPU.[35] In general, under this agreement, the premises of the UPU and its archives are inviolable. Its property and assets in Switzerland are immune from search, requisition, confiscation, and expropriation or any other form of executive, administrative, judiciary, or legislative interference. It may hold funds, including gold or currency of any kind, and it may transfer them freely. The possessions, revenues, and other goods of the UPU, including all objects imported or exported for official use, are exempt from all direct taxes, customs duties, and restrictions. The UPU is guaranteed freedom of official communication equal to that granted by the Swiss executive to any diplomatic mission; it is given the right to use codes and to send and receive communications by couriers or in bags in the same manner as diplomatic missions.[36]

Outside of Switzerland the legal status of the UPU is assured by the Convention on Privileges and Immunities of Specialized Agencies adopted by the General Assembly of the United Nations on November 21, 1947, and accepted by the members of the UPU in a consultation ordered by the ELC in 1959.[37] This document is similar to the previous one, but goes into much further detail. By the end of 1962, 32 countries had become parties to this treaty.[38] This is true except in the United States, where the union's legal status is assured unilaterally under that country's International Organizations Immunities Act.[39]

D. Functions of the Bureau

THE INTERNATIONAL BUREAU of the UPU has four primary duties. Two are, in general, comparable to those exercised by the secretariats of most international organizations: It acts as a clearinghouse for information concerning postal matters, and it provides the secretariat for meetings of representative and consultative bodies. The bureau also functions as a clearinghouse for international postal accounts and as conciliator and arbitrator in disputes over postal matters between administrations. The first three of these duties, along with some additional ones of lesser importance, will be treated at this point. The fourth, con-

35. See *Annual Report, 1948*, p. 1, and *Annotated Acts (1957)*, 1er fascicule, pp. 321–34.
36. *Ibid.*, pp. 322–23. Concerning privileges and immunities for personnel and representatives to meetings, see below, pp. 212–13.
37. See *Annual Report, 1949*, pp. 1–3, and Annotated Acts (1957), 1er fascicule, pp. 335–46.
38. See *Annual Reports, 1958*, pp. 3–4; *1959*, p. 3; *1960*, p. 3; *1961*, p. 9; and *1962*, p. 11.
39. See *Annual Report, 1957*, p. 3.

cerning the role of the bureau in conciliation and arbitration was dealt with in Chapter Three.[40]

In order to act as a clearinghouse for subjects of interest to postal authorities, the bureau must first receive information from the various administrations concerning their postal services. Article 109 of the regulations of the Ottawa Postal Convention, for instance, obligates members to submit to the bureau: *1]* a record of their application of the various optional clauses in the convention and its regulations; *2]* information concerning any reduction in mail charges below the limits set in the final acts of the UPU that have been agreed to in regional postal organizations or in bilateral agreements; *3]* information concerning the application of customs regulations to international mails, including prohibitions or restrictions on the entry and transit of various postal items and the type and number of customs declarations required for all items that are admitted; *4]* a list of routes and their distances followed by transit mails; *5]* a list of shipping lines operating from their ports and used for the conveyance of mails, including information concerning the distance and duration of the voyage between the port of embarkation and each of the successive ports of call, the frequency of the service and the countries to which the sea transit charges should be paid if the ships are used; *6]* "any necessary information concerning their organization and internal services"; and *7]* a statement of their internal postal charges.[41] As if that were not enough, the postal administrations are also required to "supply the International Bureau with two copies of the documents which they publish, whether relating to the internal or international service." [42] Additional information of a similar nature is demanded for each of the eight agreements to which an administration is a party.[43]

The information received by the bureau returns to the administrations in various guises. In the first place, the bureau publishes a monthly journal, the *Union Postale,* in seven languages, devoted to articles and information of various kinds concerning both the domestic and the international mails. From 1875 to 1920, the journal was published in English, French, and German. In 1920 Spanish was added and in 1947 it was decided to follow the UN pattern of official languages; Arabic, Chinese, and Russian were therefore added. In 1947 German was dropped, only to be restored in 1952.[44] The journal must contain a large portion of material on "the scientific and technical progress in the various countries, questions of mechanization and automa-

---

40. See above, pp. 115–17.
41. Ottawa Postal Convention (1957), Regulations, Art. 109, para. 1.
42. *Ibid.,* Art. 109, para. 3.
43. See, for instance, Agreement concerning Insured Letters and Boxes (1957), Regulations, Art. 101, and Agreement concerning Parcel Post (1957), Regulations, Art. 102.
44. Docs., Madrid Postal Congress (1920), II, 59, 150, 167, 326, and 912; Docs., Paris Postal Congress (1947), II, 373–76, 1061, and 1062; and Docs., Brussels Postal Congress (1952), II, 400.

tion," and essential economic problems of the postal service.[45] All articles must be at all times "strictly objective." [46]

In 1962, the *Union Postale* printed 34 articles, 26 of which were furnished by 14 postal administrations and the remainder were prepared by the international bureau. The total circulation of the *Union Postale* in 1962 was 3,805 copies.[47] Inasmuch as each article is published in seven different languages in each edition, in order to keep the size and costs down, the articles are not very long and do not go very deeply into any one subject.

The bureau also publishes some 15 lists, studies, and catalogues containing information of special interest to postal administrations, as well as a telegraph code of the international postal service and a multilingual dictionary of postal terms. Of special interest is the *Genèse des Actes de l'UPU,* a resumé of all the documents of all of the UPU congresses.[48] To keep much of this material up to date, and to keep administrations informed of current developments, the bureau publishes a small *Circulaire* as the need arises, and various supplements to its other publications. In 1960, the bureau issued 198 *Circulaires,* 81 bulletins, and 47 "printed letters." [49] Further, the bureau is charged by the convention with the printing and distribution at cost of postal identity cards and postal reply coupons for those countries which desire to use them. And, lastly, the bureau is required to draw up an annual report on the activities of the union.[50]

The best summary of the work of the bureau as a clearinghouse for information on postal matters is contained in Article 106 of the detailed regulations of the Ottawa Postal Convention where it states that the bureau "should at all times be prepared to furnish the Executive and Liaison Committee, the Consultative Committee for Postal Studies, and Administrations with any necessary information on questions relating to the service." In particular, "it is responsible for collecting, collating, publishing and distributing information of every kind relating to the international service . . . and, in general, for carrying out such studies and editorial work or documentation as the Convention, the Agreements, and their Detailed Regulations may assign to it or as may be referred to it in the interests of the Union."

A review of the work of the bureau in the information field would not be complete without a mention of the use of the bureau to conduct inquiries on questions of common interest. Ofttimes an administration has a question dealing with the operation of the international postal service or even of its internal service on which it needs additional help or advice. Upon receipt of such a request, the bureau proceeds to

45. Docs., Ottawa Postal Congress (1957), II, 64. (See also pp. 394–96.)
46. Docs., Buenos Aires Postal Congress (1939), II, 522.
47. *Annual Report, 1962,* p. 30.
48. Ottawa Postal Convention (1957), Regulations, Art. 110. (See also Docs., Paris Postal Congress 1947, II, 106.)
49. *Annual Report, 1960,* p. 23.
50. Ottawa Postal Convention (1957), Regulations, Arts. 108 and 111.

circularize the other members of the union for their opinions or information on the manner in which such a problem has been solved in their postal service. Copies of all replies received are sent to the administration which has initiated the inquiry as well as to all other member administrations of the union.[51]

Administrations make frequent use of this service. In the five-year period from 1955 to 1960, for instance, the bureau opened 60 inquiries on the request of member administrations. Of these requests, 28 dealt with problems of the international postal service and 32 dealt with internal postal service problems.[52] An example of an inquiry concerning the international service is the question posed by the French postal administration in 1956 as to whether other administrations permitted the transport of gas-operated cigarette lighters by mail, and if so, under what conditions. By the end of 1957, 40 postal administrations and 27 post offices had replied to the inquiry.[53] As for the internal postal services, an example is the question posed by the Argentine postal administration in 1958 as to whether other countries supplied dust masks to post office employees charged with the reception, opening, and tying of correspondence. By the close of 1959, 30 administrations had made their practices in national post offices known to the Argentine administration.[54]

The second major task of the bureau is to provide the secretariat for meetings of representative bodies and consultative committees including congresses, administrative conferences, special committees, and meetings of the ELC and the CCPS.[55] This includes the gathering and publishing of proposals. The bureau also classifies proposals as procedural or nonprocedural to aid the delegates in their work; mimeographs or prints other documents and the proceedings of the meetings; and, after completion of the meeting in question, publishes all proposals, proceedings, and final acts and distributes them to the members of the UPU.[56]

As has been mentioned previously, the bureau also provides expert assistance to countries which are chosen to host conferences or meetings. Several years in advance of the meeting, the bureau enters into communication with the host administration in order to go over all of the preparatory details. These contacts become increasingly frequent as the date for the meeting occurs, and are followed up by a

51. Authority for this service is given in the Regulations of the Ottawa Postal Convention (1957), Art. 106, para. 3. It should be noted that the bureau carried out this service many years before it was specifically mentioned in the documents of the union. (See Docs., Brussels Postal Congress 1952, II, 369.)
52. See *Annual Reports, 1955,* p. 17; *1956,* p. 22; *1957,* pp. 26–27; *1958,* p. 27; *1959,* pp. 28–29; *1960,* p. 28; and *1961,* p. 32.
53. *Annual Reports, 1956,* p. 22; and *1957,* p. 26.
54. *Annual Reports, 1958,* p. 27; and *1959,* p. 28.
55. See Ottawa Postal Convention (1957), Arts. 11, 12, 14, and 18; and Regulations, Arts. 102, para. 1, and 104, para. 8.
56. *Ibid.,* Arts. 101 and 105.

delegation from the bureau which takes up residence at the site of the conference. When the meeting finally convenes, the bureau provides the secretariat along with those individuals supplied by the host country. At the Congress of Ottawa in 1957, for instance, the vice director of the bureau was made chief of the secretariat, six of the higher-ranking bureau employees were named as secretaries, and five others, including three who were temporarily attached to the bureau for the congress, were named as assistant secretaries.[57] The vice director acted as secretary to the chairman of the congress in the plenary meetings, assisted by one or more members of the bureau with the designation of assistant secretary. The other secretaries, each with an assistant, acted in a like capacity for the various committees of the congress.[58] There is no doubt, therefore, that there is more than a grain of sincerity in the traditional statements which are made at the last session of congresses or committees when the members of the international bureau are warmly thanked for their help.[59]

Another service offered by the bureau to members of the union is a clearinghouse for international postal accounts. According to Article 106, para. 5, of the detailed regulations of the 1957 postal convention, the bureau "intervenes as a clearinghouse in the liquidation of accounts of every kind relating to the international postal service between those Administrations which claim such intervention." More specifically, Article 183 of the detailed regulations provides that "the general liquidation account of transit charges is prepared annually by the International Bureau; exceptionally, Administrations may agree to settle their accounts directly between themselves if they consider it expedient." Also, the international bureau acts as a clearinghouse for accounts resulting from the use of international postal reply coupons.

Despite discussion and recommendations, Article 106, para. 5, has remained a dead letter since 1916. This reference, or an equivalent thereof, has existed in the convention or its regulations since 1891. In 1892, its first year of operation, the bureau handled the equivalent of 10,973,785.00 Swiss francs in its general clearinghouse operations. Although this service never did appeal to many administrations, by 1914 there were 13 postal administrations taking advantage of it. In 1913, the year of the largest total operation, the bureau's clearinghouse reduced some 129,344,392.00 francs in debts to 67,719,104.00 francs. The abandonment of the free exchange of currencies and the gold standard, and the heightening of international tensions in Europe precipitated a wholesale desertion from the bureau's clearinghouse to a return to bilateral agreements. The last year in which the bureau operated its optional clearinghouse service was 1916, and in that

57. Docs., Ottawa Postal Congress (1957), II, 54 and 164. The director of the bureau had already been named vice chairman of the congress.

58. See *ibid.*, pp. 172, 178, 287, 300, and 405.

59. See, for instance, *ibid.*, p. 1175.

year the total accounts handled amounted to only 3,271,671.00 francs.[60]

At the Madrid Congress in 1920, the gold franc was chosen as the monetary unit for the payment of international postal accounts, and in 1921 an appeal was made to postal administrations to again make use of the bureau's clearinghouse activities. The number of administrations which expressed interest was not sufficient, however, to permit the bureau to renew the activity. Administrations preferred to continue taking care of their international accounts on a bilateral basis. A second appeal was made in the fall of 1940, after the economies of most countries had recovered from the difficulties of the 1930's, but the political situation again made it inappropriate. A third appeal was made in December 1959. No replies were forthcoming by the time the executive and liaison committee met in May 1960, and the ELC requested the bureau to make a further appeal for the use of its clearinghouse. At present there is no information as to whether the member countries are yet willing to take advantage of the facilities of the bureau.[61]

While the members of the union are hesitant to use the bureau as a clearinghouse where they have a clear option to do so, it has been used extensively in the two cases where it has been made more mandatory: for transit accounts and accounts created by the use of the international postal reply coupon. The Congress of Washington, D.C., in 1897 separated transit charges from the general clearinghouse activities mentioned in Article 105 when it suggested specifically that administrations should send their transit charge statements to the bureau for clearing operations.[62] The following congress (in Rome in 1906) tried to make the use of the bureau more obligatory by the addition of a new paragraph to the convention's detailed regulations to the following effect: "Except for contrary agreements between interested Administrations, the general liquidation account of transit charges . . . is established by the International Bureau." [63]

The postal administrations were quite serious in carrying out their self-imposed obligations before World War II. In 1935, for instance, 130 postal administrations participated in the transit account clearinghouse established by the international bureau. It has been estimated that without the clearinghouse operations of the bureau there would have been 945 separate payments between administrations, totaling some 16,744,829.00 gold francs, in 1935. As a result of the intervention of the bureau, the number of payments was reduced to 135 for a total of 9,033,445.00 gold francs.[64] Since World War II, despite stronger wording of the obligation to use the bureau as a clearinghouse for

60. *Annotated Acts (1957)*, 1ᵉʳ fascicule, p. 150, fn. 7.
61. See *ibid.* and *Annual Report, 1960*, p. 24.
62. Docs., Washington D.C. Postal Congress (1897), pp. 463–66, 502–602, 713, and 773.
63. Docs., Rome Postal Congress (1906), II, 52, 289, and 740.
64. *Annotated Acts (1957)*, 1ᵉʳ fascicule, p. 231, fn. 1.

transit accounts, there has been some reluctance on the part of postal administrations to do so. In 1947 there were 65 administrations using the bureau's clearinghouse for transit accounts, 16 above the previous year, and the number rose to 87 in 1958. In that year it is estimated that the bureau handled some 444 payments representing only 4,692,-605.00 gold francs. These 444 payments, however, were reduced to 86 for a total of 3,091,741.00 francs. The amount liquidated by other means in 1958 was 8,709,102.00 gold francs.[65] And this, despite the numerous occasions on which the international bureau has drawn the attention of administrations to the fact that "the liquidation of transit accounts by means of a general clearinghouse should be considered the rule which liquidation of accounts on a direct basis should be only the exception," and that the more administrations that participate in the clearinghouse, the more the liquidation of accounts is facilitated and simplified.[66]

Since 1906 the bureau has also acted as clearinghouse for accounts arising from the use of international postal reply coupons, which the bureau also prints and distributes.[67] In view of the fact that the use of international reply coupons is optional, and because the amounts of money that are involved are small, the bureau's task in this area is not very demanding.[68] In 1947, for instance, 65 administrations used the services of the bureau for a total amount of 411,586.40 gold francs. In 1961, 90 administrations took part, involving transactions totaling 525,169.00 gold francs.[69]

The following description of the manner in which the bureau acts as a clearinghouse is based primarily on transit accounts; however in its general form it is the same for the accounts resulting from the use of international reply coupons.[70] In the first place, administrations compile reports on transit charges according to the procedure set forth in the detailed regulations of the convention. After preliminary agreement between the administrations involved, each sends reports of amounts due to the international bureau. If there are differences between the amounts notified by the creditor and the debtor administration, "the international Bureau invites them to reach agreement." [71] If one ad-

65. *Ibid.*, p. 231, fn. 1. According to the 1962 Annual Report, p. 29, which gives fewer details, the number of participants had increased to 92 and a total amount of 8,335,800.00 gold francs was reduced to 4,322,452.00. The amount liquidated by other means in 1962, however, was 14,152,928.00. This is not much of a gain when one considers the increase in membership which has taken place in the UPU.

66. *Annual Report, 1960*, p. 24. (See also, *Annual Reports, 1947*, p. 7; *1949*, p. 9; *1951*, p. 9; *1961*, p. 29.

67. Docs., Rome Postal Congress (1906), II, 745.

68. Ottawa Postal Convention (1957), Regulations, Art. 188, and Final Protocol, Art. VII.

69. See *Annual Reports, 1947*, pp. 7–8, and *1962*, p. 29.

70. Compare Ottawa Postal Convention (1957), Regulations, Arts. 182–84 and 188.

71. *Ibid.*, Art. 183, para. 4.

ministration should submit a statement and the other administration involved fails to do so, the bureau must inform the second administration of the amount notified. "If, one month from the date of its letter, the International Bureau has received no comment, the amount on the statement already on hand is accepted as final." [72] At the end of the year the bureau prepares a general annual liquidation account of transit charges, including (1) the debit and credit of each administration; (2) the debit balance or the credit balance of each administration; (3) the sums to be paid by the debtor administrations; and (4) the sums to be received by the creditor administrations. The bureau then reduces the number of payments to be made by offsetting balances, and sends a final statement to the participating administrations. If payments are not made one year from the due date, the creditor administration may notify the bureau, "which invites the debtor Administration to pay within a period of not more than four months." [73] If the amounts due have not been paid on the expiration of this new four-month grace period, the international bureau includes them in the next general liquidation account to the credit of the creditor administration, and compound interest is charged.

The procedure seems simple enough and, in fact, the bureau maintains only one employee to take care of the clearinghouse activities for both transit accounts and reply coupon accounts, as well as the entire accounting work for the bureau. The individual in question must be a diplomat as well as an excellent accountant. With so many countries involved in the process, it is more than likely that some are involved in political disputes with others. It is also likely that some administrations, for one reason or another, do not pay their debts promptly. Consequently, the individual in charge must, if the accounts are to be cleared on a regular basis (as they in fact are), use the offsetting procedure in such a manner that debts are restricted wherever possible to friendly countries, that payments will be made in acceptable currencies, and that even the debts of habitual delinquents are paired off with countries of such stature as to offer the greatest likelihood of prompt payment.

E. Organization

THERE ARE TWO CHARACTERISTICS which set the International Bureau apart from the secretariats of most other specialized agencies: its small size and the control exercised over it by the Swiss government. As for size, on March 1, 1963, the total number of bureau employees was 59, including twelve under temporary contract.[74] This is the highest it has ever been. In the first 47 years of its existence, the bureau staff never

72. *Ibid.*, para. 5.
73. *Ibid.*, Art. 184, para. 1.
74. UPU, *Liste du Personnel du Bureau international, état au 1ᵉʳ mars 1963.*

numbered more than seven employees, including the director and vice director. In 1949 the number topped 20 for the first time in the union's history, and in 1955 there were only 34.[75]

Since the general delimitation of authority between the congresses, the ELC, and the Swiss government has been discussed previously in this chapter, at this juncture we will treat only the specific relations between the Swiss government and the bureau as it pertains to organization. The basis for this relationship is found primarily in an administrative decree of the Swiss Federal Council of June 30, 1953, as amended.[76]

This decree places the Swiss Federal Council and two of its subsidiary organs — the Political Department and the Federal Financial Control Office — in the actual organizational hierarchy of the international bureau.

The highest authority is the Swiss Federal Council, and it reserves for itself a few of the more important decisions such as:

1] presenting proposals to the executive and liaison committee for nominees for the posts of director of the bureau, vice director, and the next two highest categories of employees (counselors and superior counselors); fixing an equivalent for previous service in postal administrations for the calculation of their beginning salaries; and establishing the amount of their pensions on retirement;
2] approving the annual budget and advancing supplementary credits;
3] purchasing and selling important pieces of real estate in the name of the bureau;
4] hearing appeals against the decisions of the political department.[77]

The Federal Council's political department is responsible for the following affairs:

1] proposals to the Swiss Federal Council concerning points *1*], *2*], and *3*] above;
2] purchase or cession of parcels of land on the borders of the bureau's property as is necessary for changes in bordering public roads;
3] control of the employees' insurance funds;
4] fixing the general rules for official travel of the Bureau's employees, including the amount of per diem;
5] granting vacations in excess of one month;
6] fixing the compensation for employees acting as replacements for agents in a higher post and for overtime work;
7] verifying the financial aspects of the annual report;
8] hearing appeals of employees against decisions of the director.[78]

The Federal financial control office verifies the bureau's monthly accounts.[79]

---

75. Docs., Ottawa Postal Congress (1957), II, 47.
76. See *Règlement concernant l'organisation, le fonctionnement et le contrôle de l'activité du Bureau international de l'Union postale universelle.*
77. *Ibid.,* Art. 2.
78. *Ibid.,* Art. 3.
79. *Ibid.,* Art. 7, para. 1.

The most important individual in any international organization is the secretary general. The UPU is no exception to the rule, despite the facts that the title is director and that there is a relatively high degree of control over the activities of the bureau reserved to the Swiss government. Article 1, para. 2, of the *Arrêté* of 1953, provides that "the administration of the Bureau is entrusted to a Director." Paragraph 3 of the same article adds: "The advice of the Director will be taken into account by the controlling authority [the Swiss government] on all questions which . . . devolve on the latter." Further, Article 4 permits the director to initiate proposals concerning any of the subjects under the competence of the Swiss Federal Council and the political department of the Swiss Federal Council, as mentioned above.

The specific duties of the director are laid down in Article 5 and include the following:

> The management of the business of the Bureau devolves on the Director, who is its legal representative. He is competent to administer all the affairs of the Bureau which are not reserved for the Executive and Liaison Committee or the controlling authority . . . and, with this reservation, he represents the Bureau in relations with third parties and binds it by his signature.

Specifically, the administrative decree grants the director discretion over the following matters:

1] Appointment of all employees in classes 1 to 8 — with the reservation that the ELC must give its approval for appointments to classes 1 and 2 — and liquidation of the related problems dealing with: A] fixing an equivalent for previous employment in a postal administration; and B] fixing salaries and determining the amount of pensions and insurance to be received on retirement.

2] Organization of the work of the bureau.

3] Employment of temporary personnel and fixing of salaries within the framework of budgetary credits.

4] Authorization of short-term official travel and per diem expenses.

5] Granting permission for special leave which does not exceed one month.

6] Concluding contracts of all types dealing with activities of the bureau.

7] Payment of all expenses of the bureau, including maintenance and repair of property, within the framework of the budget approved by the Federal Council and other decisions taken by the supervisory authority.

All decisions taken in regard to *1*] and *3*] above must be brought to the attention of the supervisory authority.[80]

80. *Ibid.*, Art. 5.

In case of the absence or incapacitation of the director, his duties are undertaken by the vice director.[81]

In point of fact, the director of the bureau of the UPU exercises most of the normal authority of other secretaries-general of specialized agencies. The amount of supervision by the agencies of the Swiss government is minimal and routine; most of the work of the bureau is carried out by the director, and his suggestions to the supervisory authority are usually approved and acted upon with dispatch. After all, the director knows the problems of the bureau better than any other person in the Swiss government and he has an expert staff to help him prepare any requests that he might care to make.

There is another reason why the Swiss government is willing to defer to the wishes of the director; the director is a man of their own choosing. As stated above, it is the Swiss government that proposes to the ELC the name of candidates for the post of director. Further, the director has always been a Swiss national with prior service in a high capacity in the Swiss government itself. Of the nine bureau directors since its establishment in 1875, four have come to the directorship from the position of director general of the Swiss Post, Telegraph and Telephone Administration, and one from the post of director general of the Swiss Post Office. Three have been members of the Swiss Federal Council and one was a Swiss federal judge. The following is a list of the directors, the post from which they came, and their terms as head of the bureau:

1. Eugène Borel (1835–1892), member of the Swiss Federal Council from 1872–1875, director of the bureau from 1875–1892.
2. Edmond Höhn (1838–1899), director general of the Swiss Post Office from 1878–1892, director of the bureau from 1893–1899.
3. Eugène Ruffy (1854–1919), member of the Swiss Federal Council from 1893–1899, director of the bureau from 1899–1919.
4. Camille Decoppet (1862–1925), member of the Swiss Federal Council from 1912–1919, director of the bureau from 1920–1925.
5. Evariste Garbani-Nerini (1867–1944), Swiss federal judge from 1922–1925, director of the bureau from 1925–1937.
6. Reinhold Furrer (1875–1944), director general of the Swiss PTT from 1918–1935, director of the bureau from 1938–1944.
7. Aloïs Muri (1879–   ), director general of the Swiss PTT from 1943–1945, director of the bureau from 1945–1949.
8. Fritz Hess (1895–   ), director general of the Swiss PTT from 1945–1949, director of the bureau from 1950–1960.
9. The present director is Edouard Weber (1901–   ), who took

81. *Ibid.*

up his duties on January 1, 1961, and who had served as director general of the Swiss PTT from 1949 until that time.[82]

The average term of a director of the bureau has been eight years and the average age on taking up that post was about 55.

The bureau is organized along quasi-functional lines. The organizational plan of Dr. Weber, for instance, provides for an office of the director, an office of the vice director, an office of the assistant director, and six sections.

The functions of sections A through C were based more or less on the various parts of the final acts of the union as follows:

SECTION A — 1] Postal convention and detailed regulations (1st part: organic and general provisions).

2] Congresses, conferences and commissions (except for the CCPS).

3] Legal status of the Union.

4] General questions.

5] Arbitration.

SECTION B — 1] Postal convention and detailed regulations (2d part: letter post).

2] Agreements dealing with insured letters and boxes, parcel post, and subscriptions to newspapers and periodicals.

3] The postage stamp service.

4] The *Union Postale*.

5] Internal services of member postal administrations.

6] Loan and documentation services.

SECTION C — 1] Airmail.

2] Agreements dealing with negotiable instruments (money orders, transfers to and from postal checking accounts, cash on delivery items, collection of bills, and the international savings bank service).

The functions of sections D, E, and G, which took up the bulk of the remaining employees, were as follows:

SECTION D — 1] Secretariat of the CCPS.

2] UPU–International Organization for Standardization Contact Committee.

3] Seminars.

SECTION E — Common services: Personnel, finance, stores and buildings services (*Economat*), real estate, registry and archives, typing pool (*Chancellerie*), telephone switchboard, collation and expedition, concierge service and administrative and financial questions connected to technical assistance.

SECTION G — 1] Relations with the United Nations and other international organizations.

2] Technical assistance.

3] Expositions.

82. See various issues of *Union Postale,* from 1892 to 1961.

Sections D and G are under the supervision of the Assistant Director. Each section is headed by an employee of the rank of Counselor, and each section head is also an understudy for the head of another section so that in case of emergency he can take over his functions.[83]

One additional point which concerns the organization as well as the size of the Bureau will be treated before we proceed to a discussion of personnel management: the official language. Since 1874, the official language of the Bureau, as well as of the Union, has been French. Over the years, however, certain inroads have been made in the monopoly held for so long by the French language. As pointed out, the *Union Postale* has been multilingual since its start. Since the war, the bureau has also published a multilingual dictionary of postal terms. In addition, while French is legally the only language which the bureau has to accept in communications from postal administrations, for many years it has accepted communications in any language. Nevertheless, in the work of the bureau these inroads have all been minor. The bureau still replies to all communications in French, and with the two exceptions mentioned, all documents which carry the name of the UPU as publisher, including final acts of congresses, minutes of meetings, and technical papers, continue to appear only in French.

There has been a movement afoot for several years to change this state of affairs, however. One of the first attempts occurred at the Congress of Madrid in 1920 where an American proposal to place English and Spanish on an equal footing with French in the work of the bureau was defeated 22 to 3 in committee.[84] Since World War II, the attacks on the monopoly of French have taken two different phases. The first was to gain permission to use other languages in the debates of congresses and committees. As was shown in the previous chapter, it was successful.[85] The second phase was started in 1957, when three countries proposed additional changes. The Korean proposal, which was slightly different from the other two, requested simply that the official language be French, English, Spanish, and Chinese. The United States proposal, on the other hand, suggested that French be retained as the official language, but that the final acts of congresses and other documents for general distribution be published in English and Spanish also. The British proposal also envisaged that French be kept as the official language, but added that on the request of any six member countries the bureau should translate its documents into whatever language was requested.[86] After a long discussion in the general committee, concerned mostly with the increased expenses that additional languages would entail — including a statement by the director of the bureau that the addition of two official languages by the ITU had already resulted in a doubling of the expenses

83. See UPU, *Renseignements Généraux* (Berne, July 1, 1956), pp. 9–21, and *Organigramme du Bureau international de l'Union postale universelle* (Berne, 1963).
84. Docs., Madrid Postal Congress (1920), II, 326.
85. See above, pp. 144–46.
86. Docs., Ottawa Postal Congress (1957), I, 127–29.

of its secretariat — the committee decided to maintain the status quo by a very narrow margin.[87] After the Korean and American proposals had been withdrawn, a modified version of the British proposal was introduced in plenary session only to be beaten by a vote of 46 to 47, with 1 abstention and 2 absences.[88]

There is no doubt that succeeding congresses will be faced by similar proposals and there is also no doubt that a change in the status quo will have a profound effect on both the organization and size of the bureau. The great bulk of the work of translation is being undertaken by the regular employees who are encouraged to become efficient in at least three languages. This is sufficient for the present needs of the bureau. If additional languages should be admitted for any large portion of the union's documents, however, an extended and relatively expensive translation section would have to be created.

F. Personnel Administration

THE EFFICIENCY of the International Bureau, as with the secretariat of any international organization, depends upon its personnel. The concluding section of this chapter will be devoted to the policies which have been adopted by the UPU to obtain qualified personnel.

Perhaps one of the most striking aspects of the personnel administration of the UPU is the lack of official guide lines for employment practices in its basic documents. In recruiting, for instance, there are only two minor statutory directives. One is Article 16, para. 2, of the Ottawa Postal Convention, which provides that in approving the appointments of officials of the first and second salary grades, the ELC must examine "the professional qualifications of the candidates sponsored by the administrations of the union" and take into account "an equitable geographical distribution with respect to continents and languages and all other relevant considerations, due regard being had to the Bureau's own internal promotion arrangements." The second is the rule that "a candidate for a permanent post must, if required, submit to a medical examination before nomination." [89]

Similarly, it has not been found necessary to require any special oath or declaration on employment as is the rule in the United Nations and most of its specialized agencies. Further, regarding incompatibilities or conflict of interest, the only rule is that contained in Article 9 of the Swiss executive decree to the effect that "the agents of the Bureau may not exercise any other lucrative activity without the authorization of the supervisory authority [the Swiss government]. This authorization will not

87. *Ibid.*, II, 325–30 and 332–38. In point of fact the status quo actually lost by 43 to 47. Because of 3 invalid ballots, 1 abstention and 1 absentee, however, the 47 did not represent an absolute majority of those represented at the congress, as required by the rules of procedure.
88. *Ibid.*, pp. 1115–17 and 1122.
89. Swiss Federal Council, Regulations, *op. cit.*, Art. 13, para. 1.

be given if these additional occupations could prejudice the employee's service to the Bureau." [90]

In practice, the director of the bureau is free to evaluate the qualifications of candidates for employment, with an occasional assist by the ELC and the Swiss government. The background of most directors provides them with the necessary faculties for choosing employees who will fit the needs of the bureau. Further, since all recruitment is done in national postal administrations, the director has the advantage of previous screenings by the administrations involved. In view of the small number of agents employed by the bureau, administrations seem to take particular care to propose only candidates with solid postal backgrounds. At its 1958 session, for instance, the bureau hired four new employees. Mr. Fokke Albert Hofman, hired as vice director, came to the bureau from the position of superior director of the Netherlands Post Office. Dr. Rafel Barrientos Peréz of Bolivia, Dr. Zdeněk Caha of Czechoslovakia, and William Anthony Reid of Australia held, in their respective countries, the posts of chief of the international service of the Bolivian Post Office, member of the international division of the Czechoslovakian Ministry of Posts and Telecommunications, and research chief of the Division of Postal Services of the Post and Telecommunication Headquarters in Australia.[91]

The ELC and the director of the bureau must also take into account, when appointing employees of the first and second salary grades, "an equitable distribution with respect to continents and languages." Geographical distribution requirements for staffing of secretariats is common among the specialized agencies and has been since World War II. The UPU, however, did not introduce the geographical requirement until the Congress of Brussels in 1952. At Brussels the requirement was proposed by the delegate from Uruguay and adopted without a great deal of discussion.[92] Nevertheless, prior to that time, an attempt had always been made to include one or two employees of nationalities other than Swiss in the bureau. Mr. Eugène Borel, the first director, had in fact hired a Belgian and a Prussian as part of his first small secretariat. By 1945, eight non-Swiss had been employed by the bureau — three Germans, two Belgians, one Prussian, one Frenchman, and one Colombian (the only employee not from Western Europe). Since the decision of the Brussels Congress, there has been a genuine attempt to internationalize the bureau. Of the total of 27 non-Swiss employees who have been hired by the bureau on a permanent basis since 1875, 16 have been employed since 1953.[93]

As of March 1, 1963, 15 of the 47 of the Bureau's permanent employees were non-Swiss, including Mr. F. A. Hofman from the Netherlands, the vice director and Mr. A. M. Boënnec from France, the Deputy

90. *Ibid.,* Art. 9.
91. See ELC, *Compte rendu analytique, 1958,* pp. 18–19.
92. See Docs., Brussels Postal Congress (1952), I, 176; and II, 113, 116, and 410–16.
93. Information received from the bureau of the UPU.

Director. Other countries represented include Australia, Belgium, Bolivia, Czechoslovakia, Egypt, Germany, India, Japan, Luxembourg, Pakistan, Poland, Sweden and USSR.[94] The small number of employees, combined with the large number of member countries, eliminates any serious staffing problems resulting from the requirement of geographical representation. There are so many areas and languages of the world represented in the union that the director usually has a large number of nominations from which he can pick the best qualified candidate.

The 47 permanent employees of the bureau are grouped into two main categories: directorial and classified posts. The former includes the director, vice director, deputy director, counselors (6), and assist-ant counselors (2). The classified posts, which number 1 to 8, are: 1] first secretary (7); 2] second secretary (10); 3] third secretary (5); 4] assistant secretary (1); 5] clerk (2); 6] typist 1st class (4); 7] typist 2d class (and assistant concierge) (5); and 8] office boy, and technical assistant (2). For comparative purposes, Classes 1 to 4 could be considered as professional and 5 to 8 as nonprofessional. Classes 5 to 8 are recruited locally.

The salaries in Swiss francs for the various classes on January 1, 1962, were as follows:

A]	Director	51,600
B]	Vice Directors	40,000
C]	Superior Counselors	35,000
D]	Counselors	31,000
E]	Class 1	17,000 to 24,000
	Class 2	15,000 to 21,000
	Class 3	11,400 to 17,200
	Class 4	10,100 to 14,900
	Class 5	8,700 to 13,500
	Class 6	7,400 to 12,000
	Class 7	6,500 to 10,800
	Class 8	6,200 to 9,000[95]

As is evident, the salary level of UPU bureau employees was lower in 1962 than that of their colleagues in most other specialized agencies, which have adopted the UN salary scale. One important reason for this disparity appears to be the attitude of the Swiss government, as was evident also in its relation to the International Telecommunication Union. Before these two organizations became specialized agencies, most of the employees were Swiss nationals taken directly in most cases from the Swiss Post, Telegraph, and Telephone Administration. The Swiss government hesitated to raise the salaries of the two secre-tariats to the level of other specialized agencies because the resulting increase would, it was felt, be unfair to the regular employees of the

94. UPU List of Personnel, *op. cit.* For a complete listing, see Annex II.
95. Swiss Federal Council, Regulations, p. 10.

Swiss Post, Telegraph, and Telephone Administration, whose salaries were in general much lower. It was feared there would be discontent in the Swiss administration.[96] There have been regular salary raises since the UPU became a specialized agency, however, and at its session of May 1961, the executive and liaison committee adopted a resolution asking the Swiss government to introduce a new salary scale equivalent to that enjoyed by the employees of the International Telecommunication Union, a scale which, it should be noted, is the equivalent of that of other specialized agencies.[97] The Swiss government is now in the process of introducing the new pay scale.

With few exceptions, the other personnel policies of the Swiss government for bureau employees are similar to those of most specialized agencies. Newly appointed non-Swiss personnel have their own and their families' way paid to Berne, and are offered moving costs. Upon their retirement, the same policy prevails. Families of deceased employees are also paid the cost of return to their homes. Each agent has the right to an annual vacation of from three weeks to a month each year, and non-European personnel and their families receive payment for travel to their country of origin once every two years. Other than some of the specifics of the above rules, one of the minor exceptions to the general practices of most specialized agencies concerns the weekly working hours. Although the exact hours of work are fixed periodically by the director, the Swiss government sets a minimum of 33 hours a week. While normal working hours are usually close to the minimum, the staff of the bureau may be required to work up to 44 hours a week, if necessary, without additional compensation.[98]

As a general rule, a new employee will start in the first step in the grade of the post he is to occupy. In exceptional circumstances, the salary may be fixed at an advanced step in the grade, depending upon such things as "good service rendered in another situation," preparatory studies, or special knowledge. Each employee has the right to a salary increase each year, equal to one twelfth of the difference between the minimum and the maximum salary of his class. All employees are also entitled to an annual allowance for each child under 20 years of age not gainfully employed; an expatriation allowance; special bonuses equivalent to one month's salary upon achieving 25 years of service and 40 years of service; a group insurance plan; and retirement benefits. The retirement pension for permanent bureau employees is based upon length of service, varying from 15 percent of annual salary for those who are married, widows or widowers (a single person does not receive a pension until the completion of five years of service) up to a maximum of 60 percent for those who have served for 30 years or more. Previous employment with national postal administrations is taken into account when calculating years of service for pension pur-

96. See Codding, *op. cit.*, pp. 292–93.
97. See ELC, *Compte rendu analytique, 1961*, p. 20.
98. Swiss Federal Council, Regulations, Arts. 11, 12, and 13.

poses. However, except under special circumstances, the total pension paid by the bureau is reduced by the amount which the employee receives as pension or retirement payment from previous employers.[99]

An employee may be retired for physical or mental disability (in which case a medical certificate is required), at 60 years of age after at least 10 years of services (five of which must be with the bureau) and upon the employee's request, or at the age of 65 on a mandatory basis.

In cases where a post is eliminated, the employee may be released from service on the payment of an amount not to exceed the equivalent of three years' salary. The employee may, in addition, resign his post without compensation at any time upon three months' notice.[100]

The personnel regulations of the bureau also provide for disciplinary action: "The agent who violates his duties, either intentionally, or by negligence or imprudence, will be liable to a disciplinary penalty corresponding to the degree of the error." [101] The penalties include: A] a reprimand; B] a reduction or deprivation of ordinary salary increases; C] a reduction in salary; D] temporary suspension from duty with or without a reduction in salary; and E], dismissal. The director may give an employee a reprimand, but B], C], and D] are carried out only by the supervisory authority. An employee may be dismissed only by the authority which appointed him, with the reservation that the dismissal must be approved by the executive and liaison committee in cases where its approval was necessary for appointment. Disciplinary action may be carried out only after an official inquiry by the responsible authority, in which the accused is notified of the accusations against him and the acts upon which the disciplinary measure is based. The accused is guaranteed a delay of 20 days in which to vindicate himself. There are no appeals to disciplinary actions involving a reprimand or dismissal. All other disciplinary actions may be appealed to the Swiss Federal Council.[102]

Personnel of the bureau on official duties outside of Switzerland are accorded the privileges and immunities provided for in the Convention on Privileges and Immunities adopted by the General Assembly of the United Nations in 1947.[103] On Swiss territory, the bureau and the personnel of the UPU receive the benefits of the Provisional Agreement on Privileges and Immunities concluded on April 19, 1946, between the Swiss Federal Council and the secretary general of the United Nations.

The 1946 agreement gives the personnel of the bureau immunity of jurisdiction for "acts committed by them in their official capacity,

99. *Ibid.*, Arts. 16–27.
100. *Ibid.*, Art. 13, paras. 3 and 4; Art. 23, paras. 1 and 2.
101. *Ibid.*, Art. 10.
102. *Ibid.*
103. Except in the United States where they come under the provisions of the United States law entitled "International Organizations Immunities Act." (See *Annual Report, 1957*, p. 3.)

including speech and writings." They pay no taxes on their salaries. They and their families are exempt from all the immigration restrictions and formalities of registration for foreigners, and are given the right to import, without customs duty, their furniture and personal effects when they take up their functions in Switzerland. In addition, employees of the bureau and their families are given the "same facilities of repatriation as diplomatic agents" in periods of international crisis. All but Swiss employees are exempt from Swiss military service. The director and the Swiss Federal Council may, however, negotiate a "restricted list" of Swiss employees who, because of the importance of their functions, should be exempt from such service. In the case of mobilization of the Swiss Army, the director may appeal to the Federal Political Department for a delay in their recall, "or other appropriate measures." The director must communicate regularly to the Swiss Federal Council the names of the employees to which these provisions are applicable.[104]

In addition, the director and the vice director and their families and, if desired, the principal higher functionaries of the bureau are beneficiaries of all of the privileges and immunities accorded, "in conformity with international law," to diplomats.[105]

The agreement, however, points out that these privileges and immunities are granted to the bureau "uniquely" in the interests of the organization and not to the "personal advantage" of the recipients. Further, the director may lift the immunity of any employee in cases where, in his opinion, it may impede justice. The director is also required to collaborate with the responsible Swiss authorities in order to facilitate the good administration of justice, to assure the observation of police regulations, and to eliminate the possibility of any abuses of the privileges and immunities granted to his employees.[106]

104. Agreement on Privileges and Immunities, Secs. 14–15.
105. *Ibid.*, Sec. 16.
106. *Ibid.*, Secs. 17 and 18.

SIX

The UPU and
Other International Organizations

FOR A LONG TIME the UPU was a hermit among international organizations. It is only recently that it has experienced a drastic change
in this direction. Actually, during the early days of the UPU there were
few other international organizations, and these received no encouragement from the UPU. Even the creation of the League of Nations did
little to rescue the UPU from its self-imposed isolation. It was the
creation of the United Nations system which for the first time, although
perhaps a little reluctantly in the beginning, brought the UPU into
close contact with other international organizations. The UPU became
a specialized agency of the UN with all the cooperative relationship
which that implies, and even cooperated with some of the organizations
it had previously ignored. It is doubtful now whether the UPU could
revert to its previous isolation.

This chapter will treat this development toward cooperation. The
first section will deal with the League and pre-League days, and will be
followed by an analysis of the relations of the UPU with the UN.
The third section will be devoted to other international organizations,
especially the specialized agencies. The chapter will close with a section
dealing with the regional postal organizations which, although they
have been encouraged by the UPU over the years, have only recently
come into their own.

A. The League and Before

WITH ONE MINOR EXCEPTION, the documents of the UPU are silent as to
official contacts between the union and other international organizations in the period prior to World War I. The reason probably lies

in the fact that in the union's earlier days there was a dearth of international organs, especially ones of such a nature as to make official contact necessary or even desirable. Despite the lack of official cooperation between the UPU and other international organizations, it is undoubtedly true that there were unofficial contacts between the personnel of the few secretariats that did exist, although the documents of the UPU are silent on this also. The pioneering nature of the work of the primitive secretariats would have tended to bring their officials together to trade experiences, if nothing else. This was probably true in the case of the personnel of the bureaus of the UPU and the International Telegraph Union, both of which had their headquarters in Berne and many of whose employees had previously been employed by the same Swiss Ministry of Posts and Telegraphs. Although possible, it is less likely that there would have been as close a relationship between the bureau of the UPU with other secretariats, such as that of the International Bureau of Weights and Measures, which was also in Berne.

The one exception is a note in the documents of the Berne Congress of 1874 to the effect that a letter had been received from the chairman of the permanent committee of the International Statistical Congress requesting the elimination, or at least reduction, of postage for statistical documents. The only action taken by the congress was to "lay it on the table" for inspection by the delegates.[1]

After it appeared on the international scene, the League of Nations was never able to overcome the sense of independence that had been engendered in the UPU during its more than four decades of solitary existence. The attitude of the UPU toward Article 24 of the League Covenant is the most important case in point.[2] It was obviously the intention of the framers of the covenant that the bureau of the UPU would be one of the bureaus placed under the direction of the League, according to the provisions of Article 24. However, it did not come to pass.

One of the reasons why the UPU did not become subordinated to the League was, undoubtedly, the slowness with which the League

1. Docs., Berne Postal Congress (1874), p. 26. The UPU has always made it a practice to make any letter addressed to a congress, no matter what the source, available for inspection by the delegates.

2. This article of the Covenant reads as follows: "1] There shall be placed under the direction of the League all international bureaux already established by general treaties if the parties to such treaties consent. All such international bureaux and all commissions for the regulation of matters of international interest hereafter constituted shall be placed under the direction of the League. 2] In all matters of international interest which are regulated by general conventions but which are not placed under the control of international bureaux or commissions, the Secretariat of the League shall, subject to the consent of the Council and if desired by the parties, collect and distribute all relevant information and shall render any other assistance which may be necessary or desirable. 3] The Council may include as part of the expenses of the Secretariat the expenses of any bureau or commission which is placed under the direction of the League."

acted to implement Article 24. Although the League council approved
a report on June 27, 1921, concerning the "general principles to be
observed for placing the International Bureaus under the authority
of the League of Nations," it did nothing at that time to prepare the
rules that would permit the League to apply them.[3] In 1927, the
assembly of the League took the matter under further consideration
and adopted a report of its second committee to the effect that the time
had come to consider the general question of relations between the
League and other international organizations referred to in Article 24,
and requested the council to study the question and to report back
to it. The council obeyed, and submitted a report to the assembly at
its session in 1928. In its report the council came to the conclusion
that the "direction" that the council should exercise over international
organizations as specified in Article 24 should not include anything
that would harm their essential autonomy or make them of a similar
mold. The League's job, on the other hand, was one of coordination
in order to help achieve efficiency and to eliminate overlapping of
functions. Specifically, the organizations would have to: (1) make the
League a depository for all of their documents; (2) permit the secretary
general of the League or his delegate to be present at all meetings
as an observer; (3) give their observations on all questions within
their competence posed to them by League organs; and (4) submit
an annual report on their activity to the council for examination and
comment. Finally, the report recommended that the relationship between the League and international organizations coming under Article
24 should be established by means of a precise legal act, the nature of
which would be decided by the council.[4] The League council, however,
did nothing in the next few years to implement its report, and it soon
became preoccupied with other matters of a more serious nature.

Another reason for the failure of the implementation of Article 24
was the attitude of the Swiss government. It made no effort to encourage
the placing of the UPU's bureau under the authority of the League
council, which it could have done readily as the bureau's supervisory
authority. One of the best records of the Swiss government's official
attitude on the matter is contained in a "short question" to the Swiss
Federal Council posed in the Swiss parliament in 1925, and an equally
short answer. The question, posed by a National Council member
from Lausanne, concerned the impact of Article 24 on the bureaus
under the control of the Swiss government. The answer expressed the
Swiss executive's opinion that there was nothing that the Swiss government could do as long as some of the members of the UPU were not
members of the League. Further, nothing could be done until all of
the contracting parties requested a change and (noted the Federal
Council) the actual situation seemed to be completely satisfactory to

3. See SdN, Doc. A. 12. 1928. XII, p. 1.
4. *Ibid.*, p. 2.

all.[5] Never, it should be noted, did the Swiss government take any initiative to change the situation.[6]

The third reason stated by the Swiss Federal Council was the apparent lack of desire on the part of the contracting parties to the universal postal convention to see the UPU come under the authority of the League. A member country could have brought the subject up for action by either of two methods: through a congress and, between congresses, through the bureau. It suffices to note that the question was not brought up in any of the interwar congresses and no member requested the bureau to poll the other member countries in the interval between the congresses.

The only contacts that the UPU had with the League of Nations during the latter's existence were ad hoc and brief. At the Congress of Madrid in 1920, for instance, the UPU received a letter from the secretary general of the League requesting that it add a new article to the postal convention binding host governments of congresses to send copies of the revised UPU conventions to the League for registration as well as information concerning subsequent adherences and accessions. At the suggestion of the chairman of the congress, it was decided not to change the convention as requested, but simply to direct the bureau to supply this information.[7] At the Madrid Congress the UPU also studied its system of finances, this too at the suggestion of the League, but took no action.[8] The Congress of London in 1929 did, however, make a change in the UPU's final acts, at the suggestion of the League, that would help to discourage the traffic in opium and other drugs.[9] The UPU had other contacts with the League and some of its organs throughout the latter's existence, but none on the congress level.[10]

Returning to Article 24, some of the most valid reasons why it was not applied to the UPU bureau are given by Henri Boisson in a book published in 1932. According to Mr. Boisson, these reasons were: (1) the opposition of the irreducible enemies of the League; (2) the opposition of those who did not want to see any augmentation of the number of League organs, including those individuals in the League who feared a challenge to their own powers; (3) the opposition of those countries which were members of the UPU but not of the League; and (4) the opposition provoked by the fear that implementing the pro-

5. "Klein Anfrage im Nationalrat, vom 16. Juni 1925 und Antwort des Bundesrates, vom 5. Oktober 1925," *Amtliches stenographisches Bulletin der schweizerischen Bundesversammlung*, XXVI, No. 14, 89.

6. See also the similar statement of the Swiss delegate in 1923 regarding a project presented by the League's committee for communications and transit, as reported in Henri Boisson, *La Société des Nations et les Bureaux internationaux des Unions universelles postale et télégraphique* (Paris, 1932), p. 73.

7. Docs., Madrid Postal Congress (1920), II, 846–47.

8. *Ibid.*, II, 179–180 and 807–809.

9. Docs., London Postal Congress (1929), II, 202–203. (See also, however, pp. 199–200.)

10. See Annual Reports, 1920–1939.

visions of the covenant dealing with conflicts would harm the interested international organizations.[11] Whatever the reason, the UPU never came under the authority of the League and perhaps in a small way helped to contribute to the downfall of that organization.

B. The UPU and the United Nations

WHILE THE UPU was able to elude the League successfully, the United Nations was another matter. The world was ready after World War II to create a new international system which, it was hoped, would really be able to preserve the newfound peace. Unlike the framers of the League covenant, the framers of the UN charter considered economic and social matters to be essential components in the struggle against war. The UPU was considered an important part of the overall economic and social plan and consequently could not be permitted to escape. While the UPU did become a specialized agency of the UN, it did not prove to be as tractable as the UN might have wished.

The UN took the initiative when, at the suggestion of its economic and social council, it called a conference of postal experts at Lake Success to draw up a proposal for the establishment of relations with the UPU. The conference (which met from December 10 to 18, 1946) was attended by 39 representatives of governments which were members of both the UN and the UPU and two observers from the UPU's international bureau. While the conference came to the conclusion that it was advisable for the UPU and the UN to enter into an agreement, it did not accept the UN's proposals in their entirety — proposals which had been drawn up by the Economic and Social Council (ECOSOC) and which had been the basis for similar agreements with other specialized agencies. The result of the meetings was a compromise between the UN's proposals and a separate draft introduced by the British and French members which attempted to preserve much more independence for the UPU. The results were submitted to all UPU members by the international bureau.[12]

Despite the Lake Success meeting and its compromise, there was still a great divergence of opinion at the Paris Congress of 1947 as to the details of the proposed agreement between the UPU and the UN.[13]

11. See Boisson, op. cit., pp. 93–94. (See also Paul Guggenheim, Traité de Droit international public, Geneva, 1953, I, 243. Dr. Guggenheim places the blame primarily on the opposition of the United States and the states with supervisory powers over the bureaus to which Article 24 was supposed to apply. In the case of the UPU, this would be Switzerland.)

12. See Docs., Paris Postal Congress (1947), I, 21. (See also the pamphlet prepared by the postal administrations of Denmark and Sweden entitled L'Union postale universelle et l'Organisation des Nations Unies (Stockholm, 1947), pp. 3–15.)

13. The overall question of whether or not an agreement should be reached was answered early in the first committee when 68 delegates voted in the affirma-

In general there were delegations which wished to see a close future relationship between the UPU and the UN, at least as close as that provided in the Lake Success compromise draft, and those which wished to preserve a larger degree of independence for the UPU. Those who took the former position argued that a close relationship between the two organs would help the UN in its efforts to maintain peace, aid international cooperative efforts to solve the world's economic and social problems, and aid the UPU by putting it in close relationship with other international organizations—the specialized agencies as well as the UN — with common interests. It was argued further that most of the members of the UPU were obliged to opt for a closer relationship suggested by the UN since they were also members of that organization. Those who preferred a looser arrangement than that agreed to at Lake Success, on the other hand, based most of their arguments on the thesis that the UN was a political organization and the UPU was a technical organization, and any mixture of politics in the UPU would only be harmful. It could compromise its technical effectiveness, which was dependent upon independence, autonomy, and flexibility. Further, a close relationship might compromise its universality. Not all the members of the UPU, it was noted, were also members of the UN.[14]

The advocates of maximum independence won one of their most important victories when the first committee of the Paris Congress decided to consider a new draft agreement along with the one which came out of the Lake Success meeting. Submitted by 12 nations — Argentina, Belgium, Brazil, Canada, Cuba, Denmark, Egypt, Lebanon, Portugal, Sweden, Uruguay and Venezuela — it was an even paler reflection of the document originally submitted by ECOSOC. As it turned out, whenever disputes occurred over the relationship between the UPU and the UN, the members of the first committee could not resist the temptation to end the ensuing arguments by taking from the less radical document.[15]

The agreement finally accepted by the congress, and the UN, con-

---

tive. There were no dissenting votes and only three abstentions: Ireland, Sweden, and Vatican City. Guatemala, Saudi Arabia, Syria, and Uruguay were absent. (Docs., Paris Postal Congress 1947, II, 104–105.)

14. See arguments on both sides in Docs., Paris Postal Congress (1947), II, 92–96, 97–105, and 184–99. Additional arguments for close cooperation between the two organizations are to be found in Beelenkamp, 1949, *op. cit.*, pp. 2–15. This author argues that the UPU had become "immobile," and even backward over the years. The UN and ECOSOC, in his opinion, could stimulate the UPU into becoming dynamic once again. On the other side, note should also be taken of the arguments expressed in the pamphlet prepared by the Danish and Swedish postal administrations (*op. cit.*). In the first place, they cast aspersions on the whole Lake Success meeting, especially because the majority of the delegates were not in reality postal experts but members of embassy staffs. Perhaps the most important argument presented, and one that many of the delegates at Paris had in mind but refrained from voicing, was that a close relationship with the UN might in some way harm the UPU's tradition of equality of states, a tradition of special importance to the smaller countries.

15. *Ibid.*, pp. 201–33, 426–43, and 452–60.

tains many of the usual provisions in specialized agency agreements, such as those dealing with reciprocal representation in meetings, the reciprocal right to propose agenda items, the exchange of information and documentation, and the like.[16] On the other hand, there are important differences. The ECOSOC draft, for instance, contained an article concerning membership which permitted the General Assembly of the United Nations to recommend the rejection of a membership application to the UPU. The final agreement between the UPU and the UN contains no provision giving the UN any say in applications for UPU membership. Another example is the article dealing with personnel arrangements between the two organs. The World Health Organization–United Nations agreement on this subject, for example, consists of two major paragraphs and four sub-paragraphs. The content of this article is evidenced in the introductory words: "The United Nations and the World Health Organization recognize that the eventual development of a single unified international civil service is desirable. . . ." [17] The entire content of the companion article in the UPU–UN agreement, however, reads: "The United Nations and the Union agree to co-operate as necessary to ensure as much uniformity as possible in the conditions of employment of personnel and to avoid competition in the recruitment of personnel." [18] The same is true regarding budgetary cooperation. There is a detailed article in the WHO–UN agreement which provides for "close budgetary and financial relationships." [19] The corresponding article in the UPU–UN agreement is, in its entirety: "The annual budget of the Union shall be transmitted to the United Nations, and the General Assembly may make recommendations thereon to the Congresses of the Union." [20] Further, there is no mention in the UPU–UN agreement of possible recourse to the International Court of Justice for advisory opinions, and no obligation on the part of the UPU to offer that body information if requested.[21]

It is difficult to appraise the results of the UN–UPU agreement. On the one hand, there has been a steady exchange of documents between the two organizations and a periodic exchange of observers. In regard to the latter, the UN, as mentioned in Chapter Four, sent observers to the Brussels and Ottawa congresses and to all of the ELC meetings which have been held since the agreement came into effect.

16. See Ottawa Postal Convention (1957), Annex A, *Agreement Between the United Nations and the Universal Postal Union.*
17. WHO, *Basic Documents,* 11th Edition (Geneva, November, 1960), p. 46.
18. UPU–UN Agreement, *op. cit.,* Art. VII.
19. WHO, Basic Documents, *op. cit.,* pp. 48–49.
20. UPU–UN Agreement, *op. cit.,* Art. x.
21. In contrast, see ITU, *International Telecommunication Convention, Buenos Aires, 1952* (Geneva, 1953), Annex 6, *Agreement Between the United Nations and the International Telecommunication Union,* Art. VII. For a general discussion of the differences in the various agreements between the specialized agencies and the UN, see S. S. Goodspeed, *The Nature and Function of International Organization* (New York and Oxford, 1959), pp. 387–89. The complete agreement between the UPU and the UN is contained in Annex III.

The UPU has sometimes had an observer present at ECOSOC meetings when the UPU's annual report is under consideration (sometimes members of the bureau but more often a member of the U. S. Post Office, especially when meetings are held in New York). The UPU has also been represented at times at ECOSOC's administrative coordinating committee, the United Nations cinema council, and other UN and ECOSOC bodies dealing with such matters as public information, legal services, the transportation of dangerous merchandise, and narcotic drugs.[22]

The results of many of these exchanges of documents and observers are intangible. The UN bodies undoubtedly benefit from the advice of the representatives of the UPU in areas where they bring some expertise to the subjects under consideration, such as transportation of dangerous merchandise. The UPU, on the other hand, cannot help but benefit from the availability of services which it cannot afford, in the area of legal advice, or public information. Information on administrative matters gathered at the meetings of the UN bodies are likely to show up later in the bureau's administrative practices. Since most of the policy recommendations made by ECOSOC and other UN agencies dealing with postal matters and international organization in general are reported in UPU publications, the UN has an additional direct channel of communication to governments and in some cases to the branch of the government where action can be taken. The difficulty of documenting the effects of such cooperation is clear.

Evidence of tangible results of UN–UPU cooperation do exist, but are both rare and generally superficial. At the request of the UN, for instance, the UPU did participate in 1958 in the creation of a United Nations pavilion for the Brussels World's Fair and a United Nations exposition at the UN headquarters in New York and Geneva.[23] Another example is in the area of stamps. In 1959 ECOSOC decided to mark the tenth anniversary of the Declaration on Human Rights in several ways. A request by ECOSOC to governments to participate by issuing special commemorative stamps was forwarded by the international bureau to member administrations, and 27 agreed.[24] The High Commissioner for Refugees did the same in 1960 for the World Refugee Year, and with the help of the bureau was able to obtain the participation of 75 members of the UPU.[25] In addition, certain changes were made by the ELC and the international bureau in the format of the UPU's budgetary report at the request of the UN.[26]

Among evidences of a more substantive nature, one could include the convention on privileges and immunities for the specialized agencies

22. This and the following information about contacts between the UPU and the UN are taken from the UPU's Annual Reports from 1948 to 1961, unless otherwise indicated.

23. See *Annual Report, 1958,* pp. 19–20.

24. *Annual Report, 1959,* p. 17.

25. *Annual Report, 1960,* p. 18.

26. See Docs., ELC, 1952, p. 69.

mentioned above which the UN negotiated and the UPU accepted, and the supplementary agreement which gives the right to the UPU officials to use the United Nations laissez passer.[27] The contacts between the two organizations have resulted directly in two changes in the postal convention, although neither is really significant. In 1957, the Ottawa Postal Congress changed the designation "colonies" in two articles of the postal convention to "territories" at the request of the UN to make it more in keeping with the terminology adopted by the UN. At the same congress, at the request of the UN Commission on Narcotic Drugs, it was agreed to add narcotic drugs to the UPU's periodic list of objects forbidden in the mails.[28]

On the other hand, it is evident that the UPU is unwilling to make the contact between itself and the UN as close as the UN and its organs would wish. In 1948, for example, it was announced that the executive and liaison committee had decided that the UPU was not to respond to invitations from the UN to send observers to its meetings "except in those rare cases where the questions to be discussed affected the UPU directly or presented a positive interest to it." [29] In the five-year period for which the UPU gives figures (1954–1958), the UPU received 181 invitations from the UN and its organs but was represented at only 36 meetings. There are also numerous examples of a reluctance on the part of the UPU to follow through on recommendations and requests made to it as a result of the contacts that have been established, a few of which will suffice for illustration. In 1951 the ELC answered in the negative a query from the UN as to whether it could become a member of the UPU after the creation of a United Nations postal administration. The decision was upheld by the Brussels Congress in 1952.[30] The ELC elected by the Paris Congress turned down a request by the UN General Assembly that the UPU, as one of the specialized agencies, make public the names of countries whose contibutions were in arrears.[31] In 1958 the UPU declined to participate in an international public information conference and in 1959 it declined to participate in the UN publications program.[32]

Various reasons have been given for the refusals of the UPU to cooperate more fully with the United Nations, including its small operating budget, the strict technical nature of its activities, and the very detailed regulation of its activities by the universal postal con-

27. For the latter, see Ottawa Postal Convention (1957), Annex B, *Supplementary Agreement to the Agreement Between the United Nations and the Universal Postal Union*.

28. See Docs., Ottawa Postal Congress (1957), I, 49–50, 75, 126–27, and 289; and II, 318, 325, and 365.

29. *Annual Report, 1948*, p. 4.

30. See Docs., Brussels Postal Congress (1952), I, 50; and II, 372–79, 955, and 1348–51.

31. *Ibid.*, p. 51.

32. *Annual Reports, 1958*, p. 14; and *1959*, p. 15.

vention and its regulations.[33] While all of these reasons contain at least a grain of truth, it is apparent that the UPU's tradition of independence and autonomy, as well as its fear that anything political might harm its work in the postal field, have not yet been completely overcome. The real attitude of the UPU toward cooperation with the UN is excellently expressed by the leading sentence in the section of the 1958 Annual Report dealing with UN–UPU relations: "The United Nations Organ and the Universal Postal Union have continued to collaborate in a very effective manner in order to avoid all overlapping of their respective functions." [34]

1. Technical Assistance

The reluctance of the UPU to participate fully in the UN technical assistance program is an interesting case in point with reference to UPU–UN relations, and as such deserves closer attention.

Before considering this in detail, however, it is only fair to note — as the UPU does with regularity when the subject of technical assistance is raised — that the basic concept of technical assistance is far from foreign to the UPU; in fact it might even be said that the UPU was the originator of the idea. Since the Treaty of Berne of 1874, the UPU has provided its members with a procedure by which help can be obtained on any question — economic, administrative, financial and legal, as well as technical. This includes studies by the bureau staff and surveys of practices by postal administrations. Further, although it was not publicized in the past, there is a well-established practice among the members of the UPU of giving direct assistance to neighboring postal administrations on request, through the exchange of both information and experts.[35]

For all intents and purposes the UPU ignored the UN program during the latter's first few years of existence. Although the UPU was represented in various organs of the UN in which the subject was discussed, the UPU made no particular effort to offer its services, and it did not make application to participate in the expanded technical assistance program which was introduced in 1950.

In the three-year period 1952 to 1954, however, a series of incidents occurred which caused the UPU to recognize the existence of the UN program and to attempt to define a desirable relationship toward it. First, in 1952, the international bureau was approached by the United Nations Korean Reconstruction Agency (UNKRA) to aid it

33. See, for instance, *Annual Reports, 1957,* p. 15; *1958,* p. 13; and *1959,* p. 15.

34. *Annual Report, 1958,* p. 13.

35. See, for instance, Marcel Farine, "The Contribution of the Universal Postal Union to the Technical Assistance of the United Nations," *Union Postale,* LXXXV, No. 3 (March, 1960), 43A.

in finding an expert who could assist the director general of Korean
Posts in reorganizing and developing the postal service of his country.
In reply the bureau circularized the member administrations for candidates, and sent the responses to UNKRA. The following year the
bureau aided the staff recruitment service for technical assistance in
finding an expert in postal administration for Paraguay and provided
the Technical Assistance Administration with publications on the construction of post offices and their equipment for experts being sent by
the UN to Iran. In addition, in 1952 the public information center of
the UN published a brochure in which it was stated: "With the exception of the Universal Postal Union, all of the Specialized Agencies
are cooperating in the Expanded Technical Assistance Program and are,
consequently, represented on the Technical Assistance Board." [36]

The first reaction to the involvement of the UPU in the UN technical assistance program, and the comment that the UPU was shirking
its duty vis-à-vis the expanded program, was the drafting and submitting of a report on the subject by the director to the 1954 session
of the executive and liaison committee. The most important parts of
this report, for our purposes, were the reasons given by the director
for "the restrained extent" of the UPU's participation and his recommendations for the future. In the first place, according to the director,
the "technical side" of the postal services plays a relatively modest
role. Of the Swiss budget for technical installations in 1953, for instance, 99.2 percent was allocated to the telecommunication services
and only 0.8 percent to the postal service. The reason was, of course,
that the telecommunications services had to rely on their own installations for transmissions. The postal service, on the other hand, was
obliged to rely for transportation on services outside of the postal
administration such as railroads, airlines, and shipping companies. Second, as mentioned at the beginning of this section, postal administrations had their own system of technical assistance which had worked
well for a long time and would continue to provide help in the future.
Under it, if an administration wished to improve its existing services
or create a new one, all it had to do was request an expert from a
country with a more developed postal administration or send some
of its employees to the other administration for a study tour. Such
a system had always given entire satisfaction to all involved. This type
of direct aid was inexpensive and could be realized without the intervention of other governmental bodies. Further, the less fully developed
postal administrations could always make use of the UPU's docu-
mentational and informational services. Third, still according to the
director, technical assistance in the postal area should be given a low
priority by the UN. Food, clothing, shelter and culture were much
more important to newly developing nations, thus more of the avail-

36. See Farine, *op. cit.*, and UPU, *Documents de la Commission exécutive et de liaison: Session de mai 1954* (Berne, 1954), pp. 16–17.

able funds should be channeled through the Food and Agriculture Organization, the World Health Organization, and UNESCO, than through the UPU. When these countries had reached a higher level of development, they could then afford important additions to their technical postal equipment. A final reason given was that the UPU did not have the necessary funds.[37]

Concerning the future, according to the director, these reasons demanded that the UPU should not create a closer alliance with the UN's technical assistance program, but "in our view the International Bureau ought to continue to give its advice concerning the experts to be chosen by the Technical Assistance Administration and to continue to assist it in finding experts when it wishes. More particularly the International Bureau ought to keep up its contribution by giving the experts up-to-date information as regards the most extensive documentation at present in existence, which the Bureau could place at their disposal." [38]

The director's report was adopted by the ELC during its session of May 1954, but with the additional observation that the question of the possibility of overlapping activities between the UN and the UPU in this field should be examined more fully. This was accomplished in two meetings between the director of the bureau and the director general of the UN Technical Assistance Administration in 1954, and resulted in an agreement between the two which defined the tasks of the UPU in future collaboration with the regular UN Technical Assistance Program. In essence, this agreement made the UPU responsible for: (1) making observations on the requests sent in by governments for technical assistance and candidates recommended for experts' posts; (2) searching for experts, if necessary; (3) placing the lending service of the international bureau and the documents of the UPU at the disposal of the UN technical assistance program and the experts appointed; and (4) including the reports of experts on their activities in the documentation of the international bureau.[39]

This agreement remained the basis for all UPU participation in the UN technical assistance program for several years. By March 1960, it could be reported that the international bureau had made observations on 28 candidates for expert posts in ten different countries and had found four candidates itself for technical assistance missions. In addition the bureau had supplied the documentation which it considered useful to the experts and to the scholarship holders who had visited the seat of the union in Berne. Further, on several occasions the bureau had given its observations on the purpose of expert missions, including advice on the necessary technical installations. Finally, the bureau had added to its documentation the reports of the experts which had been forwarded by the UN's Technical Assistance Administration.[40] Subse-

37. See Docs., ELC, 1954, pp. 17–18.
38. See Farine, *op. cit.*, p. 41A.
39. *Ibid.*, p. 42A. From the translation of a summary of the UPU's duties.
40. *Ibid.*

quently the UPU also participated in the UN's OPEX program, which it could easily do under the terms of the agreement.

One of the interesting byproducts of the discussions between the UN and the UPU over the latter's participation in the UN's program was a heightened awareness and interest in the UPU's own technical assistance program. In 1957, for instance, the ELC decided that henceforth the director of the bureau should find out what the members of the UPU were doing in this field each year and publish his findings in the union's annual report. This was done and the results, it must be admitted, were astonishing. The report for 1961, for example, shows that: (1) ten nations received 300 employees from 18 other countries for additional study in postal techniques; (2) 157 employees from 16 countries went to 12 countries for a study tour or to obtain information; (3) four countries sent a total of 423 experts to 22 other countries to aid them in attacking postal problems; and (4) 15 countries sent information to 42 other countries on request.[41] As pointed out by the member from South Africa at the 1957 ELC meeting, the UPU's technical assistance program had been a very informal operation with, now and then, a more developed country sending groups of experts to investigate techniques of other countries. Any indiscretion in the matter might have the result of eliminating such contacts in the future.[42]

In 1959 the ELC went one step further and created a subcommittee to study how the UPU's technical assistance program could be intensified, especially in the promotion of the exchange of experts. As a result of the subcommittee's report, the director of the bureau was ordered in 1961 to make a full examination of the UN's technical assistance program, including an investigation of its advantages and disadvantages from the UPU's point of view and an opinion as to whether it could be adapted to the UPU's needs. The director was also asked to encourage more direct technical assistance between postal administrations by, among other means, inviting administrations to make their needs known, and attempting to obtain help for them from willing administrations.[43]

In view of the tenor of previous attitudes on the subject, it could have been safe to predict at this point that the UPU would continue to keep its distance from the UN's expanded technical assistance program. A new element was present, however, in Dr. Weber who had replaced Dr. Hess as the director of the bureau in January 1961. Dr. Weber decided to supplement the requested report with first-hand information from countries most concerned with assistance and proceeded to use his trip to and from the CCPS meeting in Tokyo as an opportunity to discuss the issue with government officials in seven countries of the Far East. In early 1962 he also traveled to Africa

41. See *Annual Report, 1961*, p. 13. The names of the countries are not given.
42. See Docs., ELC, 1957, pp. 425–26.
43. See Marcel Farine, "Technical Assistance in the Universal Postal Union," *Union Postale*, LXXXVI, No. 12 (December, 1961), 158A–59A.

where he consulted with officials of postal administrations and resident representatives of the UN in a number of new African states.[44] The results of his observations were evidently on the side of more UPU cooperation, for the president of the ELC, and the director of the bureau applied to ECOSOC on March 31, 1962, for permission for the UPU to participate in the UN's expanded technical assistance program.[45] The request was granted by ECOSOC on August 2, 1962, and final approval was given by the ELC at its regular meeting in Berne in September 1962.[46] The UPU was allotted some $93,000 in ETAP funds for 1963/4 and began participating on January 1, 1963. Thus, 13 years after the program had been initiated and long after most other specialized agencies had decided to cooperate, the UPU finally became a participant in the UN's expanded technical assistance program.

c. Other International Organizations

THE UPU HAS RELATIONS, some distant and some close, with a number of other international organizations. As would be expected, the closeness of the relations depends primarily upon the subject matter within the terms of reference of the organizations concerned. Those that are close and continuous are to be found where interests are complementary. Others take place on an occasional ad hoc basis when common problems arise and, as is often the case, when the UPU can help another agency. The idea that the UPU should have any relations with another international agency on any regular basis, it should be noted again, is strictly a post-World War II phenomenon.

The UPU has probably had more contacts with the International Civil Aviation Organization (ICAO) than with any other international agency. The key to this relationship is that ICAO has as its purpose the provision for smooth and safe functioning of civil aviation throughout the world, while the UPU determines rates for airmail, which makes up a large portion of the profits of the world's airlines. In order to aid the UPU in setting rates, the ICAO has provided periodic reports on the costs involved in the transportation of mail by air and on the general problem of profits and losses of airlines. ICAO, on the other hand, has received information from the UPU on the manner in which postal administrations portion out airmail to the various airlines. The two organizations have also collaborated on a study of the transportation

44. See "Technical Assistance within the Universal Postal Union — Some Reflections Consequent to my Journey in Africa," *Union Postale*, LXXXVII, No. 8 (August, 1962), 106A–109A.

45. See F. Koller, "The Annual Session of the Executive and Liaison Committee (1962)," *Union Postale*, LXXXVII, No. 12 (December, 1962), 165A. It should be noted that the entire report was not formally approved until the ELC acted on it at its meeting in September, 1962.

46. *Ibid.*, and LXXXVIII, No. 4 (April, 1963), p. 59A.

of dangerous merchandise. ICAO usually sends an observer to the meetings of the ELC and congresses, and the UPU occasionally sends an observer to the ICAO's general assembly.[47]

The second international organization which has important relations with the UPU is not a specialized agency of the United Nations, but the International Air Transport Association (IATA), a private organization made up of representatives of operating airlines. IATA, like ICAO, has a primary concern with airmail rates since a large portion of airline profits comes from this source. From 1947 to 1950, the contacts between the UPU and IATA were confined to an exchange of observers, but starting in 1950 when ICAO seemed to have turned over the problem of airmail rates to IATA, these contacts have increased tremendously. In 1951 a joint IATA/UPU conference was held in Cairo which resulted in the establishment of a joint committee which met at least once a year. The committee fell dormant in the mid-1950's, but was reconstituted in 1958 and has been working continuously since that time. It is now IATA, rather than ICAO, that works with the UPU for the setting of airmail rates. Any proposed changes are immediately communicated to IATA for its observations, which are taken very seriously in UPU circles. In addition, the two bodies have carried out studies on such related subjects as the basis for remuneration of air transport agencies by postal administrations, the setting up of an agreed list of airmail distances, and the manner and method of making payments to airlines for various postal services. Other studies include those on airline schedules, the transport of dangerous materials, and the return of empty airmail bags. If the ICAO continues to concede more and more authority in postal matters to IATA, it is quite possible that IATA might replace it as the UPU's most important sister organization.[48]

There are numerous other international organizations, both public and private, with which the UPU has had contacts since World War II. None, however, attains the consistency and complexity of the relationships with ICAO and IATA. UNESCO, for instance, has as one of its major tasks the encouragement of the free flow of information. Consequently, it has worked with various UPU organs on such problems as lower rates for printed matter and books, and in general has made suggestions which would encourage the free flow of information. Some of UNESCO's suggestions have found their way into the UPU's final documents. The World Health Organization (WHO) has collaborated with the UPU in order to obtain permission to send perishable biological materials through the mails; the International Atomic Energy Agency (IAEA) has done the same for certain types of radioactive materials; and the International Labor Organization (ILO) and the UPU have cooperated in the study of professional illnesses in the postal profession.

47. The material that follows, unless otherwise indicated, is taken from the UPU's *Annual Reports* for the years 1947 to 1962.
48. For other comments on the work of IATA, see above, p. 138.

Other public international organizations which have found a reason to enlist the help of the UPU on occasion for documents, special stamp issues and the like, include the International Telecommunication Union, the World Meteorological Organization, the Intergovernmental Maritime Consultative Organization, and the Council of Europe. Among nongovernmental international organizations, special mention should be made of the Iternational Organization for Standardization (ISO) with which the UPU has been collaborating recently (including the creation of a joint UPU–ISO contact committee) to study the standardizing of envelopes and postcards, a problem which is being posed by the mechanization and automation of letter handling in post offices. Other nongovernmental organizations with which the UPU has cooperated include the International Chamber of Shipping, the International Federation for Documentation, and the Union of International Associations.

While the number of other international organizations with which the UPU cooperates is not large, it has been growing and, unless the UPU should decide to return to its pre-World War II isolation, it should continue to grow.

D. Regional International Postal Unions

THE UPU is not the only intergovernmental agency with a primary interest in international postal matters. There are, at present, several other international postal organizations throughout the world with a like interest. While these bodies differ from the UPU in size and extent of organization and while most do not have an interest in all of the matters which the UPU claims as under its jurisdiction, the primary difference lies in membership. All are restricted to countries of more or less the same geographical region.

The pertinent article in the 1957 Postal Convention, similar in many ways to that found in all postal conventions since 1874, reads as follows:

ARTICLE 8

Restricted Unions. Special Agreements

1. Countries members of the Union, or their postal administrations if their legislation permits, may establish restricted unions and make special agreements concerning the international postal service provided always that they do not introduce provisions less favorable to the public than those laid down in the Acts [of the UPU] to which they are parties.

2. Restricted unions may send observers to congresses, conferences and meetings of the Union, to the Executive and

Liaison Committee as well as to the Consultative Committee
for Postal Studies.

One of the oldest of the restricted postal unions is the Postal
Union of the Americas and Spain. Founded originally as the South
American Postal Union at Montevideo in 1911, its name was changed
to the Pan-American Postal Union in 1921 and, after the admission of
Spain in 1923 and Canada in 1931, to the present designation. The mem-
bers of the Postal Union of the Americas and Spain include: Argentina,
Bolivia, Brazil, Canada, Chile, Colombia, Costa Rica, Cuba, Dominican
Republic, Ecuador, Guatemala, Haiti, Honduras, Mexico, Nicaragua,
Panama, Paraguay, Peru, El Salvador, Spain, United States, Uruguay,
and Venezuela.[49]
    Two other restricted unions with claims to longevity are the Nordic
Postal Union and the Balkan Postal Union. The former was founded
in 1946 between Denmark, Finland, Iceland, Norway, and Sweden.
However, this union was preceded by the Inter-Scandinavian Postal
Agreement of 1919 between Sweden, Norway, and Denmark, the origins
of which can be traced back to a postal agreement between the same
three countries dating from 1869.[50] The latter was founded in 1936
between Czechoslovakia, Greece, Rumania, Turkey, and Yugoslavia.
It fell into disuse in 1947, but was revitalized in 1955 by Greece,
Turkey, and Yugoslavia.[51]
    Of a more recent origin are the Arab Postal Union, founded in
1954, the Conference of European Postal and Telecommunications Administrations which came into being in 1959 at Montreux, Switzerland,
and the Asian-Oceanic Postal Union which was created by a conference
in Manila in January, 1961. The membership of the European grouping
includes Austria, Belgium, Denmark, Finland, France, Germany, Greece,
Iceland, Ireland, Italy, Luxembourg, Netherlands, Norway, Portugal,
Spain, Sweden, Switzerland, Turkey, and United Kingdom. Those in
the Arab union are Iraq, Jordan, Kuwait, Lebanon, Libya, Morocco,
Saudi Arabia, Sudan, Syria, Tunisia, and Yemen. And, the membership of the Asian-Oceanic postal union is made up of China, Korea,
Philippines, and Thailand.[52]
    There are several other restricted postal unions, the present status

49. See Otfried Brauns-Packenius, "The Nature of Restricted Postal Unions,"
Union Postale, LXXXVII, No. 4 (April, 1962), p. 55A. (See also, Roberto Arcinie-
gas, "The Postal Union of the Americas and Spain," *Union Postale,* LXXXVI, No. 11
(November, 1961), 150A–51A, in which the author argues that the foundations of
the Postal Union of the Americas and Spain were laid at the American Postal
Conference of Bogota in 1838 at which New Granada, Venezuela, and Ecuador
were represented.)
    50. See Thure Nylund, "The Northern Countries Postal Union," *Union
Postale,* LXXXII, No. 9 (September, 1957), 86A–89A.
    51. Brauns-Packenius, *op. cit.*
    52. *Ibid.,* pp. 55A–56A; *Union Postale,* LXXXIV, No. 11 (November, 1959),
145A; and Union of International Associations, *Yearbook of International Organizations, 1962–1963* (Brussels, 1962), p. 186.

of which is indeterminate because of recent political events. These include the Malayan Postal Union founded in 1949 between the Federated Malay States and the Crown Colony of Singapore (members of which were the postal administrations of Johore, Kedah, Kelantan, Malacca, Negri Sembilan, Pahang and the Province of Wellesley, Perak, Perlis, Selangor, Trengganu, Singapore, and Cocos and Christmas Islands) and the African Postal and Telecommunications Union founded in 1935 and including the postal administrations of Angola, Basutoland, Bechuanaland, Congo, East African High Commission, Cameroons, Central African Republic, Madagascar, Mozambique, Rhodesia and Nyasaland, South West Africa, Swaziland, and the Union of South Africa. Others of a doubtful status include the African and Malagasy Postal and Telecommunications Union (1961) and the African Postal Union (1961) consisting of Algeria, Egypt (UAR), Ghana, Guinea, Mali, and Morocco. Most of the other African regional groupings that have been proposed in the past few years, including the Organization of African Unity (created in Addis Ababa in 1963), have made reference to cooperation on postal matters. Until such time as the problems of African unity have been resolved, however, the status of the various African groupings must be considered as fluid.[53]

There is an enormous difference in the administrative structures of the various regional postal unions. That of the Postal Union of the Americas and Spain (PUAS) is, for example, the most complex. The Convention of Buenos Aires (1960) of the PUAS provides for seven different organs, the basic organ being the congress, which brings together delegates from its 23 members once every five years. There are also provisions for extraordinary congresses and conferences on the agreement of two thirds of the membership, the latter for the examination of technical and administrative questions. The Buenos Aires Convention also provides for a five-member technical consultative committee to keep in contact with various international organizations (including the UPU's ELC) and regional postal unions, to study technical and organizational problems, and to collect information of use to the member states. The PUAS also has a permanent secretariat, the International Bureau of the Union, located at Montevideo, and an international transshipment bureau located in Panama.[54] The Arab Postal Union is probably the closest to the PUAS. It has a congress which meets every three years, an extraordinary congress which can be called in the interval between congresses upon the agreement of a majority of the members, an executive committee of delegates from all member

53. See Brauns-Packenius, *op. cit.*; Dr. E. Weber, "The Universal Postal Union and Its Restricted Unions," *Union Postale*, LXXXVIII, No. 1 (January, 1963), 4A; A. Bakir, "A New Restricted Union, the African Postal Union (APU)," *Union Postale*, LXXXVIII, No. 2 (February, 1963), 23A–30A; and Yearbook of International Organizations, *op. cit.*, pp. 181–83.

54. See PUAS, *Congreso de Buenos Aires, Convenio y Acuerdos, 1960* (Montevideo, 1960), *Convenio Postal de las Américas y España*, Arts. 10–14 and 16–17.

countries which meets every year, and a permanent bureau which is located in Cairo. An interesting innovation in the Arab Postal Union is the High Arab Postal Institute, which provides a special course of training for employees of postal administrations.[55]

At the other extreme is the Conference of European Postal and Telecommunications Administrations. This is a very primitive type of international organization, in essence a series of administrative conferences. There is no permanent secretariat. At each conference, so far called once a year, one of the member administrations is chosen to organize the next conference and to carry out in the interim the secretarial duties necessary to ensure continuity. Between conferences studies are carried out either by correspondence or by formally constituted working groups and committees.[56] The Nordic Postal Union is similar with the exception that it publishes a Nordic Postal Review (*Nordisk Posttidskrift*) containing articles dealing with the postal service, under the editorship of a Swede aided by a local editor from each of the member states.[57]

While there is a wide variety of administrative structures in the various regional organizations, there is a great deal of common agreement as to the aims and purposes of these organs. On the one hand, all of the basic documents of the regional organizations state, either explicitly or implicitly, that their aim is to extend, facilitate, and improve the postal relations of the member countries. This general terminology can be broken down further into several concrete subdivisions. It includes the study of common problems, both technical and administrative. It is apparent that some of the problems facing a geographical region are different from those faced by the UPU as a whole; therefore, a concentrated effort on these problems in, for instance, the PUAS's technical consultative committee has an excellent chance of achieving substantive results. This is, however, one of the lesser areas of accomplishment of the restricted postal unions. The real area of accomplishment lies in the introduction of conditions more advantageous to the public than can be provided in the larger sphere of the UPU with countries which have much less in common. This is particularly true concerning rates. The final acts of almost all of the restricted unions provide for lower tariffs than those permissible under the provisions of the final acts of the UPU.[58] Further, several of the final acts, such as that for the Arab Union, provide for the elimination of transit charges.[59]

55. See *Convention of the Arab Postal Union, Concluded in Khartoum, Thursday, the 28th of Muharram 1378 [14th August 1958]* (Cairo, 1958; mimeographed), *Convention*, Arts. 8–10, 16, and 19–21.

56. See, "Conference of European Postal and Telecommunications Administrations," *Union Postale*, LXXXVII, No. 2 (February, 1962), 22A–23A.

57. See, *Arrangement concernant l'Union Postale des Pays du Nord* (Stockholm, March 24, 1960; mimeographed), Arts. 3 and 8.

58. See, for example, Art. 9 of the Nordic Postal Union Agreement, *op. cit.*

59. Article 26 of the Convention of the Arab Postal Union, *op. cit.*, reads as follows: "The land transit charges for conveyance of mails exchanged between the countries of the Union shall be cancelled. The sea and desert charges between

There is another important reason for the existence of the regional postal unions: to act as a pressure group for its members in the meetings of the Universal Postal Union. The postal union of the Americas and Spain make this explicit in its charter; the others do it by implication. The preamble of the convention of the PUAS, for example, states that one of the major aims of this regional group is to "establish a solidarity of action capable of effectively representing its common interests in the Congresses, Conferences, and other meetings of the Universal Postal Union. . . ." [60] This is also the reason for its "conferences prior to UPU conferences." The same intention is evident in the final acts of the Conference of European Postal and Telecommunications Administrations.[61] While the final documents of the other regional international organizations are silent on this point, there is evidence that pressure group activity in conferences and meetings of the UPU is not a forgotten element.[62]

In the earlier days of the UPU, the existence of regional postal unions did not create much of a stir. Their number was few and their activities were restricted. As a result of the recent increase in their number and in their activities, however, questions are being raised as to their proper function and their relationship to the UPU.[63] On the one hand it is evident that a regional grouping does tend to provide a more fertile ground for improving postal relations between its members, such as the lowering of rates and the elimination of transit fees, that cannot readily be accomplished on a worldwide basis. These unions can also be proving grounds for innovations which, if successful, can be introduced into the final acts of the UPU. On the other hand, it is also clear that there are dangers in the situation. There is the danger that the members of such unions will come to place so much reliance on their regional organs that they may tend to ignore their duties to the UPU or that they will make their regional unions actual competitors of

Syria and Iraq shall remain applicable." (See also, African Postal Union Agreement, *op. cit.*, Art. 14.) For further information concerning the accomplishments of the restricted postal unions in the rate and transit fields, see Brauns-Packenius, *op. cit.*, and the article of which it was a condensation entitled, "Das Wesen der engeren Postvereine und ihr Verhältnis zum Weltpostverein," which appeared in issue No. 3, 1961, of *Archiv für das Post- und Fernmeldewesen*, published by the Ministry of Posts and Telecommunications of the West German Federal Republic.

60. PUAS Convention, *op. cit.*, Preamble.

61. See Brauns-Packenius, *op. cit.*, p. 57A. This is also one of the central themes of an article written in 1950 by an official of the Dutch ministry of posts and telegraphs advocating the creation of a European Postal Union. See F. A. Hofman, "The Usefulness of a European Postal Union and its Tasks," *Union Postale*, LXXV, No. 1 (January, 1950), 2A–5A. (See also, Machold, "Difficulties and Advantages of a European Postal Union," *Union Postale*, LXXXI, No. 5, May, 1956, 38A–40A.)

62. See, for instance, Anouar Bakir, "The Arab Postal Union (AUP): History and Fundamental Principles," *Union Postale*, LXXXII, No. 4 (April, 1957), 38A–40A.

63. See, for instance, Dr. E. Weber, "The Universal Postal Union and its Restricted Unions," *op. cit.* LXXXVIII, No. 1 (January, 1963), 4A–6A.

the UPU. As stated by the director of the bureau, it is clear that such regional collaboration favors "centrifugal tendencies which, in the end, could have unfavorable repercussions on their relations with the Universal Postal Union.[64]

One method of ensuring against this tendency would be to provide for more representation at regional meetings by officials of the UPU. But, as was pointed out by the director, the bureau does not have the funds or the necessary personnel.[65] Perhaps the only real solution would be for a congress of the UPU, which would include all interested parties, to define the proper relationship between the UPU and its regional organs and to insert the definition in the UPU's basic documents. Certainly Article 8 of the postal convention, which states only that restricted unions shall not introduce provisions less favorable to the public than those in the UPU's basic acts, does not provide any real guidelines. In any case, the UPU cannot wait too long before beginning a serious search for answers to the problem.

64. *Ibid.*, p. 5A.
65. *Ibid.*, p. 6A.

SEVEN

Conclusions

D ESPITE THE FACT that there have been postal systems since earliest recorded history, and isolated bilateral postal agreements from the early part of the seventeenth century, all of the conditions necessary for the creation of an international organization to regulate the international mails were not prevalent until the middle of the nineteenth century. First, there had to be a number of independent states each with exclusive control over the postal communications within their respective borders. Consequently, it was necessary to await the rise of the nation-state, and the creation of state postal monopolies. There are a number of reasons why states created official postal services and excluded private mail carriers and the carriers under the control of other states, including the desire of monarchs to know what went on within their kingdoms, to add a new source of income to the royal treasuries, and to provide a more convenient and rapid method of sending official dispatches than other systems could provide. Whatever the reason, as soon as mail carrying became a state monopoly, the necessity arose for heads of state to enter into mutual agreements for an exchange of mails.

The second condition was met only after the public was in a position to use the mails. In essence it amounted to the existence of pressures for a larger, faster, and more convenient system for the exchange of international mails than that which could be provided by government systems based on bilateral agreements. The ability of the public to use the mails began only after the discovery of the printing press, combined with the general vulgarization of public education and the real development of international commerce. Even with these developments, however, only a small portion of the public was in a position to use the international mails because for a long time they remained too complicated and expensive. This is where men like Sir Rowland

Hill came into the picture. They led a demand for postal reforms which resulted in a lowering of postal rates and a simplification of procedures to the point where the public was able to take advantage of the mails. National postal reforms touched off a desire for a reform of the international mails; if the national mails could be made inexpensive and convenient, why could not the same thing be done for letters to foreign countries? Postal authorities were not ignorant of the faults in the international system. The difficulty of convincing the public that they should pay high rates and the problem of informing the public of the differences in weight limits and rates for sending a letter to another country along various alternative routes was only too apparent. Postal administrations were also aware of the expense involved in the existing international accounting system. They were ready, therefore, when U. S. Postmaster General Blair issued his suggestion for cooperative action in 1862.

If the delegates to the Paris conference in 1863 had had the foresight to draw up a binding treaty similar to that which was signed 11 years later, the UPU would have had the honor of being the oldest of the truly international intergovernmental agencies in existence today. The necessary foresight was lacking, however. Instead, the delegates to the Paris conference created what they considered to be a model bilateral treaty, to be used in place of existing ones, which would eliminate many of the obvious abuses that existed in international postal relations. There are two primary reasons why this was done. In the first place some countries were still experimenting with domestic postal reforms and wanted time to evaluate the results, especially regarding revenues, before they would be willing to obligate themselves. By creating only a model treaty, freedom of movement was retained. The second reason, and a very important one, was that there was no real precedent for such action. True, nations had previously entered into multilateral alliances for various purposes, and in some cases had created regional postal organizations such as the Austro-German Postal Union. Nevertheless, there was still no precedent for the creation of an international organization bringing together such geographically widely separated nations as those which were invited to send representatives to Paris.

By 1874 circumstances had changed. First, there was a recognized need for a more efficient international mail system. The model treaty of 1863 had been introduced into numerous postal relations, and the benefits were encouraging. The rates for letter mail between many countries had been lowered and standardized and administrative procedures had been simplified. The international mails were thus less expensive and more efficient from the public point of view, and the postal administrations were beneficiaries of lower costs. Since the coordination of postal efforts was still essentially a bilateral affair, however, discrepancies did occur between the 1863 model treaty and the postal treaties which were actually negotiated. The only way to eliminate these discrepancies was to bring all interested parties together to sign a binding multilateral agreement. Second, there was now a precedent. Delegates from 20 states had created the International Telegraph Union at a conference in Paris in 1865. While the problems that had confronted the telegraph experts were different in many respects, and the experts came mostly from Europe, there was no obvious reason why postal administrations could not also create an international organization. Additional stimulation undoubtedly came from the fact that in many of the countries which were represented at Paris in 1863 and 1865, both posts and telegraphs were controlled by the same government organ. It was an easy matter, therefore, for one group to influence the other. Third, there were people in official circles who possessed the necessary vision. One such man was Heinrich von Stephan. His success in convincing others of influence to take the next logical step gives ample justification for calling him the father of the Universal Postal Union.

The Berne postal conference of 1874, the starting point of the UPU, created an international organization with an important but limited objective. In the terminology of the UPU, this objective was to create a single postal territory for the dissemination of the international letter mail. In essence, this meant that the foreign mail of any given country should be able to move freely throughout the world. Intermediate states should, in all cases, provide fast and efficient transportation for foreign mails destined to another state. Terminal states should accept foreign mails without question or hesitation and deliver them to the addressees in a manner at least equal to that in which domestic mails were delivered. An important corollary was that of increasing the speed and efficiency of the international mails. This was to be achieved by setting standards for the handling of the international mails and by introducing to all administrations the new and improved methods discovered by the more advanced countries.

The basic organ of the new international organization was to be the periodic congress, made up of representatives from member countries, to revise and bring up to date the postal conventions and regulations which were to contain the rules and regulations of the postal service. A bureau, composed of a small secretariat, was created to act as a clearing house for information on postal problems and new techniques, to provide a core of experts to act as the secretariat for congresses, and to give unofficial interpretations of the final acts of congresses in the interval between congresses.

Although the achievements of the conference of Berne were modest, they provided an excellent foundation on which to build: in the 63-year period between the conference of Berne and the first post-World War II congress, the UPU went a long way toward achieving its goals. The main accomplishment of the UPU was in obtaining acceptance for the idea of a single postal territory for the international letter mail. Member nations found little difficulty in agreeing to rules that would give foreign mails at least the same consideration as domestic mails; once the foreign mails arrived at the frontier (or airport later), they were integrated into the domestic system, or transported to the next frontier by at least the same modes of transportation as were used for domestic mails. The second major accomplishment was the creation of a uniform set of rules for member postal administrations in the exchange of the international mails and for the handling of the resulting international postal accounts. Both the postal administrations and the public benefited from these innovations.

Although the primary concern of the delegates to the Berne conference of 1874 was with letter mail, throughout the years the UPU extended its work to other types of international services engaged in by postal administrations. Starting with insured letters and boxes in 1878, the UPU went on to include postal money orders and postal traveler's checks, the parcel post, the collection of bills, postal identity cards, subscriptions to newspapers and periodicals, and postal checking accounts. Cash-on-delivery items and the international savings bank services were not brought under the aegis of the UPU, as separate areas of concern, until 1947 and 1957, respectively. The UPU attempted to do for the non-letter services much the same as it had accomplished for the letter services: create a uniform set of rules for their exchange between administrations and for the handling of the international postal accounts that resulted.

There was one major failure on the part of the UPU during this period. It had been the dedicated intent of the framers of the postal treaty of 1874 to create, as a counterpart of the single postal territory, a single low postal rate for letters. Because of the different experiences which the delegates to the 1874 conference brought with them — some used the mails for revenue, some felt that it was primarily a public service — the single low letter rate was not immediately sought. As nations gained experience, however, they began to work toward this goal. By World War I, it had been achieved in essence. But the economic disruptions of World War I brought an end to this experiment. Instead of a single low rate, an ideal rate was introduced, with wide permissible variations. Attempts to return to the prewar uniform rates were frustrated by the depression of the 1930's and World War II. There has been little pressure to return to the battle.

A minor failure occurred concerning transit rates. Their abolition was hoped for by many postal administrations in the early days of the UPU. Gradually, however, it became obvious that some countries were natural transit areas for large amounts of mail, and that these countries would not give up compensation for the extra services that they performed. Consequently, the UPU concentrated its efforts in achieving uniformity of transit rates, and gave up the quest for their abolition.

The best indication that the task the UPU had set for itself was an important one, and that it was making good progress in achieving it, lies in its steady growth in membership. Only 21 countries sent representatives to the Berne conference of 1874. By the second congress (Paris, 1878) there were 37; by the third, 54; fourth, 59; fifth, 62; and at the sixth (Rome, 1906), the UPU had 71 countries on its membership rolls. Some countries joined even before they had completed their own domestic postal services. So great was the desire of nations to participate in the work of the UPU, that with the admission of China in 1914, the UPU's membership included almost all of the independent nations of the world. As has been noted, many nonindependent countries were also permitted to participate. To a certain extent, the rapidity with which the membership of the UPU increased was due to its extremely simple membership provisions. In essence, all a country had to do to be affiliated with the UPU was to make known its desire through diplomatic channels to the country in which the last congress was held. Although universality was for all intents and purposes achieved in 1914, the number of members continued to increase up to World War II. This was due primarily to the changes in political units which resulted from World War I and the appearance of newly independent countries whose postal communications had previously been represented by other member countries. In 1939, there were 88 members of the UPU.

The record of accomplishments of the UPU over these years was found in the Universal Postal Convention, the often-revised successor to the general postal treaty of 1874, and its regulations. These, the basic documents of the UPU, contained the rules and regulations to which all members had to agree. In general, the convention contained the provisions dealing with the organization of the union, the rules regulating the international postal service, the rules for the operation of the international letter service, and provisions dealing with other relations between postal administrations, such as the rules for settling international accounts. The regulations, although in the form of a separate document with its own formula for entry into force and duration, had the same force and effect as the convention proper. In principle this document contained, as its name implies, details of a primarily administrative nature for carrying out the provisions of the convention, which were of a more transitory nature. Perhaps, partially because the framers of the original postal treaty did not have the experience to know what was fundamental and what was transitory, and partially because no congress had had the time to eliminate the mistakes that had accumulated through the years, many transitory details found their way into the convention and many provisions of a permanent nature found their way into the regulations. To know all of their obligations, members had to be well acquainted with both.

One of the more important characteristics of these two documents was their large number of optional provisions. And then there was always a final protocol attached to the convention containing reservations to certain mandatory articles in the convention and regulations. Some of the reservations were for a limited number of countries and some covered all. This was a direct reflection of the UPU's caution throughout the years. The UPU seldom attempted to make the provisions of the convention and regulations obligatory in any case where there was a substantial amount of disagreement. Wherever possible, either by making articles optional or by permitting widespread use of the final protocol, the UPU encouraged but did not coerce.

The same attitude was evident in the UPU's handling of the rules and regulations of the non-letter services. Instead of incorporating them in the convention and regulations, even as separate chapters, the UPU placed them in separate documents attached to the postal convention and made the entire document optional. Only those countries which signed and ratified, or adhered to, these additional agreements and their regulations were bound by them, and there were always many which did not wish to do so.

An additional manifestation of the UPU's reliance on encouragement rather than coercion is found in its attitude toward the legal duty of ratifying the basic acts. Many nations failed to ratify the final acts of UPU congresses by their effective date, and some never ratified. From a strictly legal point of view, no nation incurs any obligations until it has completed the process of ratification. The UPU, however, was very lenient concerning ratification. All that was required was that delinquent members continue to make their modest financial contributions to the running of the union and undertake to introduce the modifications to the rules and regulations of the international mails on the date fixed for the final acts of congresses to come into effect. It was felt that the participation of as many nations as possible in achieving the goals of the UPU was more important than strict adherence to legal formality.

Another interesting feature of the pre-World War II UPU was the variety of methods provided for obtaining an interpretation of the final acts of congresses between meetings. These include obtaining the opinions of other member countries of the union through the good auspices of the international bureau and the opinion of the bureau itself. These two methods were, of course, not binding on the parties, but did tend to give an indication of the manner in which a problem would be settled if taken to court. If a legal dispute became a reality, the bureau's opinion could be sought. Again the decision was not binding, but the country which received the adverse opinion of the bureau could be certain that the decision of the legal body would in all likelihood not be too different. Finally, if a binding legal opinion was needed, recourse could be had to the arbitration article of the convention which provided for binding decisions by groups of administrations or by the international bureau acting alone. At first glance, this variety of methods for obtaining an interpretation of the basic documents would seem simply to mirror the desire of the UPU to avoid conflict. On the other hand, it should be noted that the nature of the international mails was also accountable. The UPU, unlike many other international organizations, dealt with physical objects. Physical objects, when lost or damaged, raised the problem of liability. Since these physical objects crossed frontiers in such large quantities, convenient methods for determining liability were necessary.

Before the Paris Congress of 1947, the organization of the UPU consisted of two organs: the periodic postal congress and the international bureau. The postal congress, meeting approximately every five years, was the supreme organ of the union with power to revise all of the basic documents of the UPU. All members were permitted to attend, and each delegation was given one vote. Decisions were made on the basis of a simple majority vote. The final documents of the previous congress were used as the basis for the work of the congress, and the congress lasted until all proposals for modifications were either accepted or rejected. Each congress decided on the date on which the revised final acts would come into effect and each chose the place where the following congress would be held. The only noticeable change in the postal congresses over the years was the increasing reliance on committees. While the Berne conference of 1874 could make do with one, by 1939 there were six regular committees and two subcommittees. More committees were necessary because of the steadily increasing load of work that the congresses had to undertake, resulting from the readiness with which member countries submitted proposals for the revision and modification of the basic documents, added to the steadily increasing membership, the innovations in the postal services, and the widening scope of competence of the UPU, especially in the non-letter mail field. Further, it should be noted, each congress entertained proposals for all of the basic documents, convention and regulations as well as the various agreements for non-letter services and their attached regulations. Despite the use of more committees, including now and then a preparatory committee, it became increasingly difficult for the congresses to carry out their responsibilities in a relatively moderate length of time.

The international bureau, the secretariat of the UPU, provided for continuity and carried out a complex array of tasks for the member administrations. It served as a clearinghouse for information on problems of the international postal service and on innovations in procedures and techniques. The bureau issued a series of publications, including the monthly *Union Postale,* and often contributed the results of studies taken under its own responsibility. It acted as a center for certain international accounts and as the intermediary for proposed changes to the basic documents of the UPU between congresses; made preparations for congresses; served as the secretariat for congresses; and gave interpretations of the basic documents upon the request of member administrations.

Of special interest were the small size of the bureau and its relationship with the Swiss government. At no time before World War II did the employees, including the director, number more than two dozen. There were no legal prerequisites for serving on the staff of the bureau. In fact, all of the directors were of Swiss nationality, the majority of whom came to the bureau from high positions in the Swiss postal service. The director's small staff was also made up primarily of Swiss nationals transferred from the Swiss postal service. While the duties of the bureau were set forth in the final acts of UPU congresses, the Swiss government provided all other rules and regulations. Further, the Swiss government handled the funds of the bureau, which were raised by a class unit method of contribution from member countries, as set forth in the regulations to the convention, and accounted for them to the members of the UPU.

Several forces have been at work since World War II to change the complexion of the UPU for the first time. First, there was the introduction of aircraft as a means for transportation of international mails. True, airmail had been introduced into various countries and regions of countries before World War II, and a series of conferences outside of the UPU had been called to discuss the manner in which it should be integrated into the world's postal service. However, it was the conversion of modern long-range aircraft, designed during the war, which provided for the first time a secure means of mail transport by air throughout the world, especially over the Atlantic and the Pacific. Since it was primarily only a new means of transportation, airmail did not radically change postal methods, but it did raise a number of problems. For instance, to take advantage of the speed of this new means of transportation, it was necessary to introduce new methods of handling mail that would permit swift passage from post offices to airport and, at the other end, from airport to post offices. Air transport was also expensive in view of the rapid speed and the small carrying capacity of aircraft in relation to older methods of transportation. A decision had to be made concerning compensation for air transport associations which would be adequate for the carriers and yet, at the same time, keep the cost down to the point where the public could use the service. Although the problem of compensation has taken up a tremendous amount of the time of the UPU and its organs, it has still not been solved to everyone's satisfaction. The second was the introduction of mechanization into post offices and the possibility of automation. In the past the basic work of post offices — reception and delivery of mail — depended primarily on manpower. Mechanization threatens to change this picture radically, and in doing so, affects the work of the UPU. New procedures and rules are necessary to pass on the advantages to the public. On the one hand, as was the case of airmail, it is necessary to introduce new methods to accommodate the resulting speed and efficiency. On the other hand, many nations would need help in order to obtain and operate the new machinery. The third was the creation of the United Nations system of international cooperation. The UN placed greater emphasis than did the League on economic and social matters as a possible means of eliminating the seeds of war. Included were communications in general, and the free flow of information in particular. The fourth and final force at work on the UPU is the cold war. This prolonged peacetime animosity between nations has had its effect on the work and the organization of the UPU. Not so much, perhaps, as it has had on other international cooperative enterprises which are more readily adaptable to national ends, but there has been a noticeable impact nevertheless.

The most obvious reflection of the new forces affecting the international mails and the UPU was the creation of the executive and liaison committee. It had long been evident that congresses were having difficulty in carrying out their tasks as thoroughly as they should. Preparatory conferences and open membership preparatory committees had proved to be overly time consuming and costly in relation to their effectiveness. The increasing mechanization of postal procedures, the threatened automation of post offices, and the introduction of aircraft as a normal means of the transportation of domestic and international mails demanded even more time than the existing organization could conveniently devote, not only from the point of view of creating appropriate new rules and regulations for the international mail service, but also from that of enabling all of the member postal administrations to take advantage of the innovations introduced by some. Preparatory work for congresses and studies in depth of some of the new issues and problems were both in order. In view of the tradition of the UPU that everything possible should be left in the hands of the congresses, aided by the international bureau, these might not have been considered sufficient reasons to create a new organ. The added stimulus came from the United Nations. The model for a specialized agency which the UN negotiators wished to see the UPU adopt had some sort of executive body in it which would meet more often than the plenipotentiary meetings in order to provide a closer supervision of the workings of the UPU secretariat and at the same time act as a liaison with the UN and the other specialized agencies. While the UN was able to convince the UPU of the need for the new organ, the UPU did not go quite as far as the UN would have wished.

The executive and liaison committee, as created by the Paris Congress of 1947, is primarily a research organ, secondarily a liaison organ, and only lastly an executive organ. Since its inception it has concentrated the major portion of its efforts on studies of problems of interest to member postal administrations, either as directed by the postal congresses or on its own initiative; most of these have resulted in suggestions for further action by postal congresses. A great deal of its time has also been spent on liaison with the UN and its bodies in the economic and social field and with other international organizations with similar or concurring fields of interest. Although the ELC has also engaged in studies dealing with secretariat affairs and has made suggestions to the Swiss government, its principal undertakings in this respect have been to review the bureau's annual report, to approve the Swiss government's choice for a director to replace Dr. Hess, and to approve the director's nominations for the first and second salary grades.

In form the ELC does not differ greatly from that of the administrative councils found in the hierarchy of many international organizations. It is made up of 20 representatives from member countries, elected with an eye to an equitable geographical distribution, meeting at least once a year at the union's headquarters. The bureau provides the secretariat for meetings and the ELC elects its own officers. As it has turned out, the warning of the Canadian delegate at the Paris Congress that the creation of the ELC would introduce a certain amount of "politics" in the UPU was correct. Because it is a restricted membership body, some countries must of necessity be excluded. Even before it became a going entity, membership on the ELC became a matter of national prestige. The novel method found by the postal congress for choosing members of the ELC, including rotation and limits on consecutive elections, has permitted the ELC to renew itself despite controversy.

The creation of the Consultative Committee on Postal Studies was the second major organizational change. The problems and prospects of the international mails, especially in the technical field, were so complex that the ELC was not able to give consideration to all of the tasks assigned to it. Another organ was needed to assume part of the burden. Consequently, the functions of the ELC were divided, leaving to it problems of an administrative, legislative, and legal nature, and giving to the new organ competence over problems of a technical and economic nature. The new organ, the CCPS, has plunged into its duties wholeheartedly. Although it is too early to give a definitive evaluation of the potentialities of the CCPS, it can safely be said that it has made an excellent start. Moreover, since it is primarily a technical study organ and does not have the power to make decisions seriously affecting member administrations, and since all member countries are welcome to work with its study groups, the problem of prestige that has caused "political" difficulties for the ELC has not arisen.

The break with tradition that has occurred since World War II is also apparent in the UPU's new position in relation to other international organizations. Prior to World War II, the UPU lived in splendid isolation. Cooperation with other international organizations was neither necessary nor desired, because there were so few other international organizations whose work was complementary. The UPU dealt with international postal matters and nothing else. The League's feeble attempts to bring the UPU under its wing were thwarted in its earlier days by a lack of decisiveness combined with the UPU's tradition of working alone. By the time the League was in a position to demand more, it was involved in other more serious problems. Close cooperation with the League was not desired because it was primarily a political organ. Politics, in the minds of those who worked in the UPU, could tend only to hinder the important work of the union by forcing congresses to devote some of their limited time to problems not related to the postal services. It might result in the substitution of diplomats for postal experts in UPU congresses, diplomats who could not understand the complexities of the postal services. Above all, it was feared that the League might interfere in the work of the UPU, which should be left to postal experts.

The United Nations was a different matter. National leaders were, almost without exception, wholeheartedly behind the United Nations concept. World War II had been so devastating that nations were willing to do anything possible to prevent World War III. While the League had been primarily an organ to stop conflicts of arms, the UN considered economic and social matters of primary importance. The UPU was needed in the United Nations system because communication was an important element in this concern. The UPU was also needed, because of its long history, to add to the prestige of the new United Nations.

Consequently, the UPU became a specialized agency of the UN. Despite the pressures on the UPU, however, the final agreement between the two organizations gave the UPU a greater degree of freedom than most of those negotiated with other international organizations. And, it must be admitted, if most of those postal experts who attended the Congress of Paris in 1947 had not been under pressure from their governments, the UPU's relations with the UN might have been even more tenuous than they became. In this respect, it is interesting to note that the first negotiating team, which was made up chiefly of non-postal experts, agreed to a much tighter liaison between the UN and the UPU than the one that was agreed to at Paris.

One would think that the successes of the United Nations, especially in the economic and social fields, would tend quickly to melt some of the UPU's aloofness. Although much progress has been made, it was slow in coming. This is especially evident with regard to technical assistance.

When considering the relations of the UPU with other international organizations, one should not overlook the regional postal organizations. The UPU has always concerned itself primarily with universal rules and regulations, the achieving of a minimum of workable practices. It is not surprising, therefore, that it would encourage the creation of organizations with smaller membership. These restricted unions can make changes, because of the common desires and backgrounds of their members, which would not be possible within the universal membership of the UPU. The success of these smaller unions in creating special conditions among their members has resulted in such a proliferation of their number since World War II that to know the rules and regulations of the international mails, one must look increasingly to their basic documents and treaties as well as those of the UPU.

There are certain other manifestations of the forces at work on the UPU since World War II, some of which reflect the prolonged state of international tension known as the cold war. One example is the necessity since 1947 of garnering a two-thirds vote for admission to membership in the union. In a similar vein is the establishment of a two-thirds quorum for valid votes in plenary sessions of postal congresses on matters dealing with the constitution and organization of the union, and at least half of the countries represented for valid votes on other parts of the postal convention and other official acts of the union. Previously, a simple majority only was necessary. Even more directly related to international politics is the refusal of the UPU to permit certain divided countries, such as the People's Republic of China, to be represented in the union's congresses and meetings. As a result, the UPU has retreated from the universality of membership that it achieved prior to World War I.

Interestingly enough, the international bureau and its functions have been the least affected. It is still small, at least in comparison with the secretariats of other specialized agencies of the United Nations, and it is still primarily controlled by the Swiss government. Its original character was preserved probably only by the decision of the Paris Congress to make the ELC primarily a study and liaison organ rather than an executive one. So far, the few powers given to the ELC have not been used to substitute its control for that of the Swiss government. The bureau has not escaped completely from change, however. The major evidence for this is the increasing number of employees.

There are certain problems that will continue to make meetings of the UPU lively in the future. Most deal with the UPU's constitution and organization, and one important one looms for the international mails. First, the UPU will continue to be a little less than "universal" for some years to come. This is a problem beyond the scope of the UPU, and one which it will not be able to solve on its own. As long as the cold war continues, it will be extremely difficult to restore the cooperation of some states with the UPU. But also, as long as the cold war continues there will be attempts by a minority to have them represented in UPU congresses and meetings, which will bring the UPU face to face with distasteful "political" considerations from time to time.

The organization of the executive and liaison committee will continue to create unpleasantness in the foreseeable future. Since it is a limited membership body, there will continue to be dissatisfaction concerning its composition and pressures to give it more power over the affairs of the union. These are not serious problems, however. Other international organizations have created limited membership organs with a great deal of executive power, and have learned to live with the situation and the inevitable controversy that it raises.

Tied to the problem of the powers of the ELC is the future of the Swiss government as the supervisory authority of the bureau. This unique feature of the UPU has worked successfully for a relatively long period of time. However, its uniqueness cannot help but bring attention to it, and some will compare the situation of the UPU with that of other international organizations. The question will then be raised as to why an important organ such as the international bureau should be under the control of one member government. There has been a reason, as we have seen, but this reason may lose its meaning as the memories of World War II recede and pressure mounts to make the UPU conform. After all, the ELC is in existence and power could easily be transferred to it from the Swiss government. The UPU is a conservative organization, and thus change comes with great difficulty. However, this is no guarantee that one day Switzerland will have no more power over the bureau than any other state.

Languages are also a problem of the future. Language nationalism has become more and more important in the post-World War II era and has succeeded in forcing several official languages on most international organizations. From one point of view, additional languages for documents are unnecessary. The UPU has gotten along well without them for a long time. The only real need for additional languages is in conferences and meetings, to enable those whose mother tongue is not French to make themselves understood, and that is being taken care of. The addition of other languages would be expensive. The bureau would have to be enlarged to take care of the extra languages, and costs would increase tremendously. On the other hand, now that the UPU is concentrating more on the field of technical assistance, including UPU technical assistance, the new nations would be able to get a great deal more from information in their own languages than in a foreign one. This new force of new members, combined with those of longer standing who have always wanted to have the use of their languages made official, might be enough to bring about a change in the near future.

On the functional side there is a problem that may loom larger in the years to come. It is evident that one of the major aims of the delegates who have come to UPU congresses since 1874 is that of achieving a certain amount of uniformity in the international postal system, the great complaint before the establishment of the UPU being the confusing and costly varieties in rates, weights of mail, and other national regulations in foreign mail. An absence of uniformity, it was rightly argued, was confusing to the user of the mails and postal administrations and caused costly procedures for postal administrations. The aim of creating "one postal territory" included the aim to create one set of rules which would be valid all over the world. An individual who wanted to post a letter in San Francisco would be faced with more or less the same regulations as an individual in Paris, and have the same services at his convenience. Further, the postal employee in a nation's capital as well as the postal employee in the smallest provincial post office would know the regulations; they would be simple and uniform. The ultimate aim would thus be to provide the user, as well as the postal administration, with one set of rules and regulations that would be valid for mail anywhere in the world.

Although uniformity has been achieved over the years in certain areas, in other areas it is receding further into the distance. Certain irregularities are not too serious, such as those relating to rates and weights. Even here, there are problems, however. In some countries the postal rates for dispatches of certain weights are so high that individuals send packages of mail to other countries, where the rates are lower, to be mailed from there. The UPU has been forced to add a provision to the final acts to discourage such practices. Further, especially with countries sharing borders, these differences in rates can cause discontent among the users. The more important consideration is that the user in any country cannot now know, unless he consults an up-to-date set of regulations in a large city, what sort of mail he can send to another country. This is due in a large extent to the numerous optional clauses in the convention and regulations and to the final protocols to conventions. It is due also to the optional nature of the agreements. Although this policy of the UPU makes for a happy choice of voluntary commitment or non-commitment at the member's pleasure, and has perhaps been a harmonious factor for many years, it also opens the way to dissatisfaction and disagreement. The time is not too far distant when the UPU will have to face again the overall problem of uniformity. For example, if a service such as parcel post is desirable, it might be well to make it obligatory on all of those who profess to believe in the principles of the UPU. Otherwise it should be eliminated, or restricted to purely bilateral agreement. The increase in the number of regional postal unions, each of which provides special services and lower rates for the individuals in their membership, cannot help but cause further deterioration in this uniformity.

So far, despite the changes that have occurred and the problems confronting it, there is nothing yet that poses a serious threat to the most outstanding characteristic of the UPU, its durability. The ability of the UPU to survive for such a long time, long at least in relation to other international organizations, rests on a number of interrelated factors that must be kept in mind constantly by anyone who wishes to make any major reforms in its organization or method of procedure. In the first place there is the UPU's primary concern, the international mails. Mail communication has, for almost a century, been a highly important element in the relations of nations. Nations cannot do without it, therefore they find it expedient to cooperate within the UPU in order to meet the changing needs of the times. Further, the long, successful experiment in cooperation has engendered a sort of nonpolitical tradition. This tradition has been fostered by the individuals who participate in the work of the UPU, both in their private capacities and as elements in the organs of the UPU. Engaging in international politics is not a tradition within the higher echelons of national postal administrations. Further, as long as postal officers keep politics out of their work in the UPU, they will not be replaced by the politicians or diplomats. As UPU decision makers, the postal authorities have done everything they could to avoid any incursion of the politician by setting technical qualifications for those who would attend UPU congresses and meetings. In addition, they have made a conscientious effort to avoid any major conflict between members. The tendency of the UPU to make any provision of the convention or regulations, on which there is any significant opposition, optional in nature is evidence of this concern. The same can be said of the constant use of final protocols and optional agreements on non-letter matters. Unanimous or near unanimous consent, especially concerning functional matters, is a key to the work of the UPU. By concentrating its efforts on the technical, on the important task of keeping the international mail up to the demands made of it, the UPU has been able to avoid international political conflicts that would have a tendency to weaken or perhaps destroy its work. This was probably one of the more important reasons why the UPU did not become a specialized agency, or its equivalent, of the League of Nations. While the UPU could not escape the plans laid for it by the UN, it did keep as much of its independence as possible, thus attempting to preserve its primarily technical nature and remove itself from political interference.

The second major reason for the durability of the UPU lies in its organization. The UPU has tended over the years to keep its organization as simple as possible. There were no real continuing organs upon which the UPU depended whose activities could have been curtailed or seriously hampered by the two major international conflicts of World War I and World War II. If the UPU had had an executive committee made up of representatives of member states, upon which the international bureau depended for direction, supervision, and finances, the impact of the two wars might have been serious enough to leave nothing which could be picked up after the wars to start it going again. Nevertheless, the same consequences might have taken place if the work of the UPU's one continuing organ, the international bureau, had been prevented from operating for a long period of time. Again, the continuity of the UPU might have been irreparably damaged. It is at this point that the third most important reason for the durability of the UPU enters: the nature of the country in which the UPU had its headquarters and the position of this country in relation to the international bureau. Since the UPU was on Swiss territory, it was not touched by the conflicts nor did it come under the control of one of the belligerents. And finally, the Swiss being in charge of the union's finances could continue to underwrite the bureau's activities until peace came and the member nations could resume their contributions. If any of these considerations had been drastically different, the continuity of the UPU might have been harmed enough to result in a call for its replacement with a different organization after World War II. Fortunately, however, this was not the case. In addition, from all evidence, the representatives of member countries who have participated in the post-World War II congresses have continued to respect those considerations which help to make the UPU unique among international organizations.

The problems and questions facing the UPU are not serious. The UPU has a factor working for it that most other international organizations lack — a real sense of tradition. The UPU has proved itself by virtue not only of its endurance of the trials of so many years — the span of which has encompassed both great conflict and great change — but also of its long record of accomplishment in its area of primary concern and its contributions to international cooperative efforts in general. Mistakes will undoubtedly be made in the future, as they have in the past. Since the work of the UPU will continue to be carried out by postal experts, however, these mistakes will not be irreparable as they might well be if the work of the UPU were to be entrusted to diplomats. Further, as postal experts, it is safe to predict that the delegates will never be so deeply engrossed in the world's continuing political problems as to ignore their essential work. This is an important advantage.

In summary, all indications are that the UPU will continue to pro-

vide a basis for international cooperation to solve the problems of the
international mails. The need for the Universal Postal Union is as great,
if not greater, than it was when the General Postal Union was created in
1874, and as long as men communicate by means of the written word,
this need will not disappear.

Meetings Under UPU Auspices

I. Congresses of the Union

1. Berne, 1874 (September 15–October 9)
2. Paris, 1878 (May 2–June 4)
3. Lisbon, 1885 (February 4–March 21)
4. Vienna, 1891 (May 20–July 4)
5. Washington, D.C., 1897 (May 5–June 15)
6. Rome, 1906 (April 7–May 26)
7. Madrid, 1920 (October 1–November 30)
8. Stockholm, 1924 (July 4–August 28)
9. London, 1929 (May 10–June 28)
10. Cairo, 1934 (February 1–March 20)
11. Buenos Aires, 1939 (April 1–May 23)
12. Paris, 1947 (May 7–July 5)
13. Brussels, 1952 (May 14–July 11)
14. Ottawa, 1957 (August 14–September 27)

II. Extraordinary Congresses

1. Berne, 1900 (July 2 to 5)

III. Administrative Conferences

1. Berne, 1876 (January 17–27)
2. Paris, 1880 (October 9–November 3)
3. The Hague (*Conférence sur la poste aérienne*), 1927 (September 1–10)

IV. Special Committees

1. *Commission d'études* (established by Lisbon Congress, 1885) — Brussels, 1890
2. *Commission d'études* (established by Madrid Congress, 1920): Zermatt, 1921; Nice, 1922; Florence, 1923
3. *Commission d'études* (established by Stockholm Congress, 1924) — Cortina d'Ampezzo, 1925;
   Commission préparatoire (for London Congress) — Paris, 1928
4. *Commission technique du transit* [CTT] (established by Buenos Aires Congress, 1939; reestablished by Paris Congress, 1947): Interlaken, 1949; Pontresina, 1951

V. Airmail Conferences and Meetings

1. Restricted Conference, Brussels, 1930
2. Airmail Conference Preparatory Committee, Prague, 1931
3. European Airmail Conference, The Hague, 1937
4. European Airmail Conference, Paris, 1937
5. European Airmail Conference, Brussels, 1938

VI. Executive and Liaison Committee

A. *Organizational Meetings*

1. Paris, July 5, 1947
2. Brussels, July 12, 1952
3. Ottawa, September 26, 1957

B. *Sessions*

1. Berne, April 6–15, 1948
2. Berne, October 11–23, 1948
3. Berne, May 16–25, 1949
4. Montreux, May 15–26, 1950
5. St-Gall, May 21–June 1, 1951
6. Berne, January 21–28, 1952
7. Berne, May 4–15, 1953
8. Lucerne, May 3–14, 1954
9. Lugano, May 2–13, 1955
10. Berne, April 30–May 11, 1956
11. Lausanne-Ouchy, April 1–12, 1957
12. Berne, May 5–16, 1958
13. Berne, May 14–23, 1959
14. Berne, May 16–21, 1960
15. Berne, May 15–20, 1961
16. Berne, September 21–29, 1962
17. Berne, June 1–8, 1963

VII. Consultative Committee for Postal Studies

A. *Plenary Assemblies*

  1. Ottawa, September 13, 1957

B. *Management Council Meetings*

  1. Ottawa, September 19 and 26, 1957
  2. Brussels, May 19–29, 1958
  3. The Hague, March 9–19, 1959
  4. Eastbourne, June 27–July 9, 1960
  5. Tokyo, October 2–22, 1961

List of Personnel of the Bureau of the UPU

As of March 1, 1963

I. *Permanent Agents*

Directorial			Year of Birth	Date of First Nomination to Bureau
Director	1.	E. Weber	1901	Jan. 1, 1961
Vice-Director	2.	F. A. Hofman (Netherlands)*	1896	Jan. 1, 1959
Deputy Director	3.	A. M. Boënnec (France)	1897	June 1, 1956
Counselors	4.	A. Vuilleumier	1908	Apr. 1, 1937
	5.	M. Rahi (Egypt-UAR)	1912	July 1, 1950
	6.	R. Barrientos Pérez (Bolivia)	1909	Sept. 16, 1958
	7.	Z. Caha (Czechoslovakia)	1913	Jan. 1, 1958
	8.	M. Akbar (Pakistan)	1915	Oct. 1, 1962
	9.	S. N. Das Gupta (India)	1911	Oct. 1, 1962
Asst. Counselors	10.	W. Schlaefli	1912	July 1, 1938
	11.	N. Siplet (Belgium)	1903	Sept. 1, 1953
Classified				
1. First Secretaries	12.	P. Piguet	1902	Jan. 1, 1944
	13.	M. Froidevaux	1902	Jan. 1, 1953
	14.	S. Bäckström (Sweden)	1921	Jan. 1, 1961
	15.	M. Herwich		

* Where no country designation is given, the employee is of Swiss nationality.

	(Poland)	1907	July 1, 1959
16.	R. Büschi	1910	Jan. 1, 1948
17.	L. Koster		
	(Luxembourg)	1916	July 1, 1953
18.	F. Koller (Germany, Fed. Rep.)	1926	Jan. 1, 1963

2. Second Secretaries

19.	W. A. Reid (Australia)	1924	July 1, 1958
20.	S. Tanaka (Japan)	1908	July 1, 1959
21.	E. Bühler	1914	Jan. 1, 1954
22.	E. Léchaire	1914	Jan. 1, 1948
23.	A. Berney	1920	Jan. 1, 1953
24.	L. Chaubert	1927	Apr. 1, 1959
25.	A. Petrentchuk (USSR)	1922	Jan. 1, 1962
26.	M. Senft	1918	Jan. 1, 1953
27.	J. Guenot	1920	Jan. 1, 1953
28.	M. Farine	1924	July 1, 1950

3. Third Secretaries

29.	M. Fitzé	1920	Jan. 1, 1954
30.	J. Brasey	1921	Jan. 1, 1955
31.	A. Kunz	1922	Jan. 1, 1955
32.	R. Voeffray	1924	Jan. 1, 1959
33.	C. Paris	1926	Jan. 1, 1959

4. Asst. Secretaries

34.	A.-M. Giroud	1920	Jan. 1, 1953

5. Clerks

35.	O. Chappuis	1904	July 1, 1945
36.	A. Schönmann	1922	Feb. 1, 1947

6. Typists, First Class

37.	M. Gex	1914	Jan. 1, 1950
38.	E. Vonlanthen	1921	Jan. 1, 1953
39.	F. Cuérel	1929	Oct. 1, 1958
40.	J. Deladoey	1931	Mar. 1, 1959

7. Typists, Second Class (Asst. Concierge)

41.	O. Fleischmann	1926	Jan. 1, 1960
42.	O. Hermann	1920	Jan. 1, 1955
43.	O. Spicher	1931	Jan. 1, 1961
44.	D. Balmer	1917	Jan. 1, 1962
45.	S. Robert	1928	Jan. 1, 1962

8. Office Boy (Technical Assistant)

46.	H.-L. Gentizon	1938	Jan. 1, 1962
47.	J. Combe	1942	Jan. 1, 1962

II. *Temporary Agents*

48.	A. Guèye (Senegal)	1938	Aug. 1, 1962
49.	B. Larabi (Tunisia)	1934	Aug. 28, 1962
50.	M. Mazou (Congo, Brazzaville)	1936	Aug. 28, 1962
51.	G. Beney	1934	Oct. 1, 1962
52.	A. Léger (Canada)	1926	Jan. 14, 1963
53.	F. Cicéron (France)	1929	Mar. 1, 1963
54.	V. Scarpatetti	1941	Jan. 22, 1962
55.	C. Garrido (France)	1934	Aug. 1, 1962
56.	L. Doux (France)	1939	Aug. 1, 1962
57.	J. Roy	1913	Jan. 1, 1963
58.	J.-P. Pilloud	1940	Dec. 1, 1962
59.	H. Renner	1893	Jan. 12, 1959

ANNEX III

A

Agreement Between the United Nations and the Universal Postal Union

PREAMBLE

In consideration of the obligations placed upon the United Nations by Article 57 of the Charter of the United Nations, the United Nations and the Universal Postal Union agree as follows:

ARTICLE I

The United Nations recognizes the Universal Postal Union (hereinafter called "the Union") as the specialized agency responsible for taking such action as may be appropriate under its basic instrument for the accomplishment of the purposes set forth therein.

ARTICLE II

Reciprocal Representation

1] Representatives of the United Nations shall be invited to attend all the Union's Congresses, administrative Conferences and Commissions, and to participate, without vote, in the deliberations of these meetings.

2] Representatives of the Union shall be invited to attend meetings of the Economic and Social Council of the United Nations (hereinafter called "the Council") of its Commissions and Committees and to participate, without vote, in the deliberations thereof with respect to items on the agenda in which the Union may be concerned.

3] Representatives of the Union shall be invited to attend the meetings of the General Assembly during which questions within the competence of the Union are under discussion for purposes of consultation, and to participate, without vote, in the deliberations of the main Committees of the General Assembly with respect to items concerning the Union.

4] Written statements presented by the Union shall be distributed by the Secretariat of the United Nations to the members of the General Assembly, the Council and its Commissions, and the Trusteeship Council as appropriate. Similarly, written statements presented by the United Nations shall be distributed by the Union to its members.

ARTICLE III

Proposal of Agenda Items

Subject to such preliminary consultation as may be necessary, the Union shall include on the Agenda of its Congresses, administrative Conferences or Commissions, or, as the case may be, shall submit to its members in accordance with the provisions of the Universal Postal Convention, items proposed to it by the United Nations. Similarly, the Council, its Commissions and Committees and the Trusteeship Council shall include on their agenda items proposed by the Union.

ARTICLE IV

Recommendations of the United Nations

1]   The Union agrees to arrange for the submission as soon as possible, for appropriate action, to its Congresses or its administrative Conferences or Commissions, or to its members, in conformity with the provisions of the Universal Postal Convention, of all formal recommendations which the United Nations may make to it. Such recommendations will be addressed to the Union and not directly to its members.

2]   The Union agrees to enter into consultation with the United Nations upon request with respect to such recommendations, and in due course to report to the United Nations on the action taken by the Union or by its members to give effect to such recommendations, or on the other results of their consideration.

3]   The Union will co-operate in whatever further measures may be necessary to make co-ordination of the activities of specialized agencies and those of the United Nations fully effective. In particular, it will co-operate with any body which the Council may establish for the purpose of facilitating such co-ordination and will furnish such information as may be required for the carrying out of this purpose.

ARTICLE V

Exchange of Information and Documents

1]   Subject to such arrangements as may be necessary for the safeguarding of confidential material, the fullest and promptest exchange of information and documents shall be made between the United Nations and the Union.

2]   Without prejudice to the generality of the provisions of the preceding paragraph:

    a) the Union shall submit to the United Nations an annual report on its activities;

b) the Union shall comply to the fullest extent practicable with any request which the United Nations may make for the furnishing of special reports, studies or information, subject to the conditions set forth in Article XI;

c) the Union shall furnish written advice on questions within its competence as may be requested by the Trusteeship Council;

d) the Secretary-General of the United Nations shall, upon request, consult with the Director of the International Bureau of the Union regarding the provision to the Union of such information as may be of special interest to it.

ARTICLE VI

Assistance to the United Nations

1] The Union agrees to co-operate with and to give assistance to the United Nations, its principal and subsidiary organs, so far as is consistent with the provisions of the Universal Postal Convention.

2] As regards the Members of the United Nations, the Union agrees that in accordance with Article 103 of the Charter no provision in the Universal Postal Convention or related Agreements shall be construed as preventing or limiting any State in complying with its obligations to the United Nations.

ARTICLE VII

Personnel Arrangements

The United Nations and the Union agree to co-operate as necessary to ensure as much uniformity as possible in the conditions of employment of personnel and to avoid competition in the recruitment of personnel.

ARTICLE VIII

Statistical Services

1] The United Nations and the Union agree to co-operate with a view to securing the greatest possible usefulness and utilization of statistical information and data.

2] The Union recognizes the United Nations as the central agency for the collection, analysis, publication, standardization and improvement of statistics serving the general purposes of international organizations.

3] The United Nations recognizes the Union as the appropriate agency for the collection, analysis, publication, standardization and improvement of statistics within its special sphere, without prejudice to the right of the United Nations to concern itself with such statistics so far as it may be essential for its own purposes or for the improvement of statistics throughout the world.

ARTICLE IX

Administrative and Technical Services

1]   The United Nations and the Union recognize the desirability, in the interests of the most efficient use of personnel and resources, of avoiding the establishment of competitive or overlapping services.

2]   Arrangements shall be made between the United Nations and the Union in regard to the registration and deposit of official documents.

ARTICLE X

Budgetary Arrangements

The annual budget of the Union shall be transmitted to the United Nations, and the General Assembly may make recommendations thereon to the Congress of the Union.

ARTICLE XI

Financing of Special Services

In the event of the Union being faced with the necessity of incurring substantial extra expense as a result of any request which the United Nations may make for special reports, studies or information in accordance with Article v or with any other provisions of this Agreement, consultation shall take place with a view to determining the most equitable manner in which such expense shall be borne.

ARTICLE XII

Inter-Agency Agreements

The Union will inform the Council of the nature and scope of any agreement between the Union and any other specialized agency or other intergovernmental organization, and further agrees to inform the Council of the preparation of any such agreements.

ARTICLE XIII

Liaison

1]   The United Nations and the Union agree to the foregoing provisions in the belief that they will contribute to the maintenance of effective liaison between the two organizations. They affirm their intention of taking in agreement whatever measures may be necessary to this end.

2]   The liaison arrangements provided for in this Agreement shall apply, as far as appropriate, to the relations between the Union and the United Nations, including its branch and regional offices.

ARTICLE XIV

Implementation of the Agreement

The Secretary-General of the United Nations and the President of the Executive and Liaison Commission of the Union may enter into such supplementary arrangements for the implementation of this Agreement as may be found desirable in the light of the operating experience of the two organizations.

ARTICLE XV

Entry into Force

This Agreement is annexed to the Universal Postal Convention concluded in Paris in 1947. It will come into force after approval by the General Assembly of the United Nations, and, at the earliest, at the same time as this Convention.

ARTICLE XVI

Revision

On six months' notice given on either part, this Agreement shall be subject to revision by agreement between the United Nations and the Union.

Paris, the 4th day of July, 1947.

(signed) *J.-J. Le Mouël*

Chairman of the xiith Congress of the Universal Postal Union.

(signed) *Jan Papanek*

Acting Chairman of the Committee of the Economic and Social Council on Negotiations with Specialized Agencies.

B

Supplementary Agreement to the Agreement Between the United Nations and the Universal Postal Union

❰ WHEREAS the Secretary-General of the United Nations has been requested by resolution 136(VI) of the Economic and Social Council, adopted on the 25th of February 1948, to conclude with any specialised agency which may so desire, a supplementary Agreement to extend to the officials of that agency the provisions of Article VII of the Convention on the Privileges and Immunities of the United Nations and to submit such supplementary Agreement to the General Assembly for approval; and
❰ WHEREAS the *Universal Postal Union* is desirous of entering into such supplementary Agreement to the Agreement between the *United Nations* and the *Universal Postal Union* entered into under Article 63 of the

Charter:

IT IS HEREBY AGREED AS FOLLOWS:
ARTICLE I

The following provisions shall be added as an additional Article to the Agreement between the *United Nations* and the *Universal Postal Union*:
"The officials of the Universal Postal Union shall have the right to use the laissez-passer of the United Nations in accordance with special arrangements to be negotiated under Article XIV."

ARTICLE II

This Agreement shall come into force on its approval by the General Assembly of the *United Nations* and the *Universal Postal Union*

For the Universal Postal Union: *For the United Nations:*

Done at Paris, the 13th of July 1949.

(Signed) *J.-J. Le Mouël*

Chairman of the Executive and Liaison Commission of the Universal Postal Union.

Done at Lake Success, New York, the 27th of July 1949.

(Signed) *Byron Price*

Acting Secretary-General.

Members of the Universal Postal Union

As of December 1961

Country Member	Date of entry into union as country member	Contribution class
1. Albania, Popular Republic of	March 1, 1922	6
2. Afghanistan	April 1, 1928	6
3. Algeria	Oct. 1, 1907	3
4. Argentina	April 1, 1878	1
5. Australia, Commonwealth of	Oct. 1, 1907	1
6. Austria	July 1, 1875	5
7. Belgium	July 1, 1875	3
8. Bolivia	April 1, 1886	6
9. Brazil, United States of	July 1, 1877	1
10. Bulgaria, Popular Republic of	July 1, 1879	5
11. Burma	Oct. 4, 1949	6
12. Burundi	April 6, 1963	7
13. Byelorussia, Soviet Socialist Republic of	May 13, 1947	5
14. Cambodia	Dec. 21, 1951	7
15. Cameroun	July 26, 1960	7
16. Canada	July 1, 1878	1
17. Central African Republic	June 28, 1961	7
18. Ceylon	July 13, 1949	5
19. Chile	April 1, 1881	5
20. China	March 1, 1914	1
21. Colombia, Republic of	July 1, 1881	5
22. Congo (Brazzaville), Republic of the	July 5, 1961	7
23. Congo (Leopoldville), Republic of the	Jan. 1, 1886ᵃ	6
24. Costa Rica, Republic of	Jan. 1, 1883	6
25. Cuba, Republic of	Oct. 4, 1902	6
26. Cyprus, Republic of	Nov. 23, 1961	7
27. Czechoslovakia, Socialist Republic of	May 18, 1920	3
28. Dahomey, Republic of	April 27, 1961	7
29. Denmark	July 1, 1875	4
30. Dominican Republic	Oct. 1, 1880	6
31. Ecuador	July 1, 1880	6
32. El Salvador, Republic of	April 1, 1879	6

Country Member	Date of entry into union as country member	Contribution class
33. Ethiopia	Nov. 1, 1908[b]	6
34. Finland	Feb. 12, 1918	4
35. France	Jan. 1, 1876	1
36. French Overseas Territories	July 1, 1876	3
37. Gabon Republic	July 17, 1961	7
38. Germany	July 1, 1875	1
39. Ghana	Oct. 10, 1957	6
40. Greece	July 1, 1875	5
41. Guatemala	Aug. 1, 1881	6
42. Guinea, Republic of	May 6, 1959	6
43. Haiti, Republic of	July 1, 1881	6
44. Honduras, Republic of	April 1, 1879	6
45. Hungary, Popular Republic of	July 1, 1875	4
46. Iceland, Republic of	Nov. 15, 1919	7
47. India	July 1, 1876	1
48. Indonesia, Republic of	Jan. 1, 1922	3
49. Iran	Sept. 1, 1877	5
50. Iraq	April 22, 1929	7
51. Ireland	Sept. 6, 1923	4
52. Israel	Dec. 24, 1949	7
53. Italy	July 1, 1875	1
54. Ivory Coast, Republic of	May 23, 1961	7
55. Jamaica	Aug. 29, 1963	7
56. Japan	June 1, 1877	1
57. Jordan, Hashemite Kingdom of	May 16, 1947[c]	7
58. Korea, Republic of	Jan. 1, 1900[d]	4
59. Kuwait	Feb. 16, 1960	7
60. Laos	May 20, 1952	7
61. Lebanon	May 15, 1946	7
62. Liberia, Republic of	April 1, 1879	7
63. Libya	June 4, 1952	7
64. Liechtenstein	April 13, 1962	7
65. Luxembourg	July 1, 1875	6
66. Malagache Republic	Nov. 2, 1961	6
67. Malay Federation	Jan. 17, 1958	6
68. Mali, Republic of	April 21, 1961	7
69. Mexico	April 1, 1879	3
70. Monaco, Principality of	Oct. 12, 1955	7
71. Mongolia, Popular Republic of	Aug. 24, 1963[e]	
72. Morocco	Oct. 1, 1920[f]	4
73. Nepal	Oct. 11, 1956	6
74. Netherlands	July 1, 1875	3
75. Dutch Antilles and Surinam	Jan. 1, 1922	6
76. New Zealand	Oct. 1, 1907	1
77. Nicaragua	May 1, 1882	6
78. Niger, Republic of	June 12, 1961	7
79. Nigeria, Federation of	July 10, 1961	5
80. Norway	July 1, 1875	4
81. Pakistan	Nov. 10, 1947	1
82. Panama, Republic of	June 11, 1904	6

Country Member	Date of entry into union as country member	Contribution class
83. Paraguay	July 1, 1881	6
84. Peru	April 1, 1879	5
85. Philippines, Republic of the	Jan. 1, 1922	7
86. Poland, Popular Republic of	May 1, 1919	3
87. Portugal	July 1, 1875	4
88. Portuguese provinces of East Africa, Asia, and Oceania	Jan. 1, 1922	4
89. Portuguese provinces of West Africa	Jan. 1, 1922	4
90. Rumania, Popular Republic of	July 1, 1875	3
91. Rwanda	April 6, 1963	7
92. San Marino, Republic of	July 1, 1915	7
93. Saudi Arabia, Kingdom of	Jan. 1, 1927	7
94. Senegal, Republic of	June 14, 1961	6
95. Sierra Leone	Jan. 29, 1962	7
96. Somaliland, Republic of	April 1, 1959^g	7
97. South Africa, Republic of	June 1, 1910	1
98. Spain	July 1, 1875	1
99. Spanish territories of Africa	May 1, 1877	7
100. Sudan, Republic of	July 27, 1956	7
101. Sweden	July 1, 1875	3
102. Switzerland	July 1, 1875	3
103. Syria, Arab Republic of	May 15, 1946	7
104. Tanganyika	March 29, 1963	7
105. Tchad, Republic of	June 23, 1961	7
106. Thailand	July 1, 1885	6
107. Togo	March 21, 1962	7
108. Trinidad and Tobago	June 15, 1963	7
109. Tunisia	July 1, 1888^h	5
110. Turkey	July 1, 1875	3
111. Ukraine, Soviet Socialist Republic of	May 13, 1947	3
112. Union of Soviet Socialist Republics	July 1, 1875^i	1
113. United Arab Republic	July 1, 1875	3
114. United Kingdom of Great Britain and Northern Ireland	July 1, 1875	1
115. British Overseas Territories	July 1, 1940	3
116. United States of America	July 1, 1875	1
117. United States Territories	October 1, 1907	3
118. Upper Volta	March 29, 1963	7
119. Uruguay, Republic of	July 1, 1880	6
120. Vatican City State	June 1, 1929	7
121. Venezuela, Republic of	Jan. 1, 1880	6
122. Viet Nam	Oct. 20, 1951	6
123. Yemen	Jan. 1, 1930	7
124. Yugoslavia, Federal Popular Republic of	Dec. 24, 1921	3

(*a*) From January 1, 1886 to 1908 as an independent state and from 1908 to July 1, 1960, as Belgian Congo.
(*b*) Under Italian occupation from 1936 to 1941.
(*c*) From May 16, 1947, to June 7, 1951, under Transjordan.

(d) From January 1, 1900, to January 1, 1922, membership as the Empire of Korea, and from January 1, 1922, to December 17, 1949, as Chosen.

(e) Contribution class not yet determined.

(f) From October 1, 1920, to October 15, 1956, two memberships; Morocco (excluding the Spanish Zone) and Morocco (Spanish Zone).

(g) Membership for Somaliland (under Italian administration) from April 1, 1959, to July 1, 1960.

(h) From July 1, 1888 to October 1, 1907, membership as Regency of Tunis and from October 1, 1907, to November 1, 1956, as Tunisia (under French administration).

(i) As Russia before June 24, 1924.

BIBLIOGRAPHY

1. UPU Publications

A. OFFICIAL RECORDS — CONGRESSES

Documents du Congrès postal international réuni à Berne du 15 Septembre au 9 Octobre 1874 (Berne, 1875).

Documents du Congrès postal universel de Paris, 1878 (Berne, 1879).

Documents du Congrès postal universel de Lisbonne, 1885, Vols. I and II (Berne, 1886).

Documents du Congrès postal universel de Vienne, 1891 (Berne, 1892).

Documents du Congrès postal universel de Washington, 1897 (Berne, 1898).

Documents du Congrès postal de Rome, 1906, Vols. I and II (Berne, 1906).

Documents du Congrès postal de Madrid, 1920, Vols. I and II (Berne, 1920 and 1921).

Documents du Congrès postal de Stockholm, 1924, Vols. I and II (Berne, 1924).

Documents du Congrès postal de Londres, 1929, Vols. I, II, and III (Berne, 1929).

Documents du Congrès postal du Caire, 1934, Vols. I and II (Berne, 1933 and 1934).

Documents du Congrès de Buenos Aires, 1939, Vols. I, II, and III (Berne, 1939).

Documents du Congrès de Paris, 1947, Vols. I, II, and III (Berne, 1948).

Documents du Congrès de Bruxelles, 1952, Vols. I, II, and III (Berne, 1952 and 1953).

Documents du Congrès d'Ottawa, 1957, Vols. I, II, and III (Berne, 1958).

B. OFFICIAL RECORDS — CONFERENCES AND EXTRAORDINARY CONGRESSES

Actes de la Conférence postale de Berne, Janvier 1876 (Berne, 1876).

Documents de la Conférence postale de Paris, 1880 (Berne, 1880).

Documents de la Conférence tenue à Bruxelles pour élaboration d'un projet d'Arrangement concernant le service international des abonnements aux journaux et aux publications périodiques, 1890 (Berne, 1890).

Documents du Congrès postal de Berne 1900 (25ᵉ anniversaire de la fondation de l'Union postale universelle) (Berne, 1900).

Documents de la Conférence sur la poste aérienne de La Haye, Septembre 1927 (Berne, 1927).

Conférence aéropostale européenne: Documents de la Conférence, 1ʳᵉ partie [Documents préparatoires] (Berne, 1933).

Conférence aéropostale européenne: Cartes-annexes à la 1ʳᵉ partie des Documents (Berne, 1933).

Conférence aéropostale européenne: Documents, 2ᵉ partie [Conférences de La Haye, de Paris 1937 et de Bruxelles 1938] (Berne, 1938).

Conférence aéropostale européenne: Cartes annexées aux Documents de la Conférence (2ᵉ ed. Berne, 1931).

C. OFFICIAL RECORDS — EXECUTIVE AND LIAISON COMMITTEE

Documents de la Commission provisoire exécutive et de liaison: Première séance tenue à Paris le 5 juillet 1947 et Première session de travail à Berne du 6 au 15 avril 1948 (Berne, 1948).

Documents de la Commission exécutive et de liaison: Session d'octobre 1948 (Berne, 1949).

Documents de la Commission exécutive et de liaison: Session de mai 1949 (Berne, 1949).

Documents de la Commission exécutive et de liaison: Session de mai 1950 (Berne, 1950).

Documents de la Commission exécutive et de liaison: Session de mai-juin 1951 (Berne, 1951).

Documents de la Commission exécutive et de liaison: Session de janvier 1952 (Berne, 1952).

Documents de la Commission exécutive et de liaison: Séance constitutive [du 12 juillet 1952] de la Commission élue par le Congrès de Bruxelles et Session tenue à Berne du 4 au 15 mai 1953 (Berne, 1953).

Documents de la Commission exécutive et de liaison: Session de mai 1954 (Berne, 1954).

Documents de la Commission exécutive et de liaison: Session de mai 1955 (Berne, 1955).

Documents de la Commission exécutive et de liaison: Session d'avril-mai 1956 (Berne, 1956).

Documents de la Commission exécutive et de liaison: Session d'avril 1957 (Berne, 1957).

Documents de la Commission exécutive et de liaison: Séance constitutive [du 26 septembre 1957] et Session de mai 1958 de la Commission élue par le Congrès d'Ottawa (Berne, 1958).

Documents de la Commission exécutive et de liaison: Session de mai 1959 (Berne, 1959).

Documents de la Commission exécutive et de liaison: Session de mai 1960 (Berne, 1960).

Documents de la Commission exécutive et de liaison: Session de mai 1961 (Berne, 1961).

Documents de la Commission exécutive et de liaison: Session de septembre
1962 (Berne, 1962).

Documents de la Commission exécutive et de liaison: Session de juin 1963
(Berne, 1963).

Documents de la Commission exécutive et de liaison [élargie]: Session de mai
1959: et de la Sous-Commission de la revision générale de la Convention:
Réunions de novembre 1958 et de mai 1959 [Révision générale de la Con-
vention] (Berne, 1959).

Documents de la Commission exécutive et de liaison: Session de mai 1960:
et de la Sous-Commission des frais de transit: Réunions de mai 1958, mai
et octobre 1959 et mai 1960 [Frais de transit] (Berne, 1960).

Documents de la Commission exécutive et de liaison [élargie]: Session de mai
1960; et de la Sous-Commission de la révision générale de la Convention:
Réunions de septembre 1959 et de mars 1960 [Révision générale de la
Convention] (Berne, 1960).

D. OFFICIAL RECORDS — CONSULTATIVE COMMITTEE
FOR POSTAL STUDIES

Documents de la Commission consultative des études postales (CCEP) et de
son Conseil de gestion: Sessions d'Ottawa 1957 et de Bruxelles 1958
(Berne, 1958).

Documents de la Commission consultative des études postales (CCEP) et de
son Conseil de gestion: Session de La Haye 1959 (Berne, 1959).

Documents de la Commission consultative des études postales (CCEP) et de
son Conseil de gestion: Session d'Eastbourne 1960 (Berne, 1960).

Documents de la Commission consultative des études postales (CCEP) et de
son Conseil de gestion: Session de Tokyo 1961 (Berne, 1961).

Documents de la Commission consultative des études postales (CCEP):
Session du Comité directeur, de Berne 1962 (Berne, 1962).

Documents de la Commission consultative des études postales (CCEP) et de
son Conseil de gestion: Session de Washington 1963 (Berne, 1964).

E. OFFICIAL RECORDS — OTHER

Comité de contact IATA/UPU. Réunion de Cheltenham (Grande-Bretagne),
1951: Compte rendu des réunions de Cheltenham (Grande-Bretagne),
18 au 21 september 1951 (Berne, 1951).

Comité de contact IATA/UPU. Réunion de Cheltenham (Grande-Bretagne)
1951: Ordre du jour des réunions de septembre 1951 à Cheltenham
(Grande-Bretagne) et documentation (Berne, 1951).

Comité de contact IATA/UPU. Réunion de Cheltenham (Grande-Bretagne)
1951: Réunion préparatoire tenue à Cheltenham (Grande-Bretagne) par
les délégués postaux, 13–14–15 et 17 septembre 1951 (Berne, 1951).

Comité de contact IATA/UPU. Compte rendu des travaux de la session du
Caire, 31 janvier et 1er février 1955 (Berne, 1955).

Comité de contact IATA/UPU. Compte rendu de la session de Rome, 13–16
février 1956 (Berne, 1956).

Compte rendu des délibérations de la Conférence mixte IATA/UPU du Caire 1951 (Berne, 1951).

Commission technique du transit. Premier rapport de la Commission technique du transit: Session du 1ᵉʳ au 16 juin 1949 à Interlaken (Berne, 1949).

Commission technique du transit. Rapport du groupe d'études de la Commission technique du transit sur les travaux de sa session d'Axenstein du 25 au 29 septembre 1950 (Berne, 1951).

Commission technique du transit. Second rapport [rapport definitif] de la Commission technique du transit: Session du 6 au 15 juin 1951 à Pontresina (Berne, 1951).

F. SERIAL PUBLICATIONS

Annual Reports (See *Rapport sur les activités de l'Union.*)

Bulletins. (Published as the need arises to modify and bring up to date certain serial publications.

Carte mondiale des communications postales de surface et annexe à ladite carte. (Occasional.)

Cartes des lignes aéropostales. (Occasional until 1953.)

Circulaires. (Published as the need arises.) Contain information of general or particular interest to postal administrations.

Dictionnaire des bureaux de poste. (Occasional.)

Formulaire de l'UPU. (Occasional.)

Liste des adresses des Administrations postales. (Occasional.)

Liste des Chefs et des fonctionnaires supérieurs des Administrations postales. (Occasional.)

Liste des distances aéropostales. (Occasional.)

Liste des distances kilométriques afférentes aux parcours territoriaux des dépêches en transit. (Occasional.)

Liste des lignes de paquebots [loose leaf]. (Occasional.)

Liste des objets interdits. (Occasional.)

Liste des Pays éloignés et assimilés. (Occasional.)

Liste des publications du Bureau international. (Occasional.)

Liste des surtaxes aériennes [loose leaf]. (Occasional.)

Liste du Personnel du Bureau international. (Occasional.)

Liste générale des services aéropostaux [loose leaf]. (Occasional.)

Mises à jour. (Published as the need arises to modify and bring up to date the bureau's loose-leaf publications and the *Genèse des Actes de l'UPU.*)

Nomenclature des pays, territoires, etc., du monde avec leur situation géographique. (Occasional.)

Rapport de Gestion. (See *Rapport sur les activités de l'union.*)

Rapport sur les activités de l'Union. (Published annually since 1875; before 1953 entitled *Rapport de Gestion.*)

Recueil de renseignements sur l'organisation et les services internes des Administrations. (Occasional.)

Recueil des taxes postales des services internes des Administrations. (Occasional.)

Recueils officiels des renseignements d'intérêt général concernant l'exécution de la Convention et des Arrangements. (Occasional.)

    a. *Recueil officiel des renseignements d'intérêt général concernant l'exécution de la Convention et de son Règlement.*

    b. *Recueil de renseignements concernant l'exécution de l'Arrangement des lettres et des boîtes avec valeur déclarée.*

    c. *Recueil de renseignements concernant l'exécution de l'Arrangement des Colis postaux.*

    d. *Recueil des Articles d'argent; Mandats de poste et Bons postaux de voyage; Virements et Valeurs domiciliées dans les bureaux de chèques postaux; Remboursements et Recouvrements.*

    e. *Recueil de renseignements concernant l'exécution de l'Arrangement des abonnements aux journaux et écrits périodiques.*

Statistique complète des services postaux. (Published every three years.)

Statistique des expéditions dans le service postal international. (Published every three years.)

Statistique réduite des services postaux. (Published every year in which the *Statistique complète des services postaux* and *Statistique des expéditions dans le service postal international* do not appear.)

Suppléments. (Published as the need arises to modify and bring up to date certain bound publications.)

Taxes et droits du service international. Cahier No. 1; Équivalents en monnaies nationales des taxes et droits exprimés en francs — ou dans la Convention et les Arrangements. (Occasional.)

Taxes et droits du service international. Cahier No. 2: Taxes réduites appliquées dans les Unions restreintes ou en vertu d'Arrangements spéciaux. (Occasional.)

Union Postale. (Published monthly, from 1875 to 1921, in French, English, and German; from 1922 to 1948, in French, German, English, and Spanish; from 1949 to 1953, in French, English, Arabic, Chinese, Spanish, and Russian; since 1953, in French, German, English, Arabic, Chinese, Spanish, and Russian.)

G. OTHERS

Les Actes de l'Union postale universelle revisés à Buenos Aires 1939 et annotés par les soins du Bureau international.

    a. *1er fascicule. Convention postale universelle* (Berne, 1940).

    b. *2e fascicule. Arrangements concernant: (1) Les lettres et les boîtes avec valeur déclarée; (2) Les colis postaux* (Berne, 1940).

    c. *3e fascicule. Arrangements concernant: (3) Les mandats de poste; (4) Les virements postaux; (5) Les recouvrements; (6) Les abonnements aux journaux et écrits périodiques* (Berne, 1940).

Les Actes de l'Union postale universelle revisés à Paris, 1947 et annotés par les soins du Bureau international.

    a. *1er fascicule. Convention postale universelle* (Berne, 1949).

    b. *2e fascicule. Arrangements concernant: (1) Les lettres et les boîtes avec valeur déclarée; (2) Les colis postaux* (Berne, 1949).

c. *3ᵉ fascicule. Arrangements concernant: (3) Les mandats de poste; (4) Les virements postaux; (5) Les envois contre remboursements; (6) Les recouvrements; (7) Les abonnements aux journaux et écrits périodiques* (Berne, 1949).

Les Actes de l'Union postale universelle revisés à Bruxelles 1952 et annotés par les soins du Bureau international.

a. *1ᵉʳ fascicule. Convention postale universelle* (Berne, 1954).

b. *2ᵉ fascicule. Arrangements concernant: (1) Les lettres et les boîtes avec valeur déclarée; (2) Les colis postaux* (Berne, 1954).

c. *3ᵉ fascicule. Arrangements concernant: (3) Les mandats de poste et les bons postaux de voyage; (4) Les virements postaux et le Supplément visant le règlement par virement postal des valeurs domiciliées dans les bureaux de chèques postaux; (5) Les envois contre remboursement; (6) Les recouvrements; (7) Les abonnements aux journaux et écrits périodiques* (Berne, 1954).

Les Actes de l'Union postale universelle revisés à Ottawa 1957 et annotés par les soins du Bureau international.

a. *1ᵉʳ fascicule. Convention postale universelle* (Berne, 1959).

b. *2ᵉ fascicule. Arrangements concernant: (1) Les lettres et les boîtes avec valeur déclarée; (2) Les colis postaux* (Berne, 1959).

c. *3ᵉ fascicule. Arrangements concernant: (3) Les mandats de poste et les bons postaux de voyage; (4) Les virements postaux; (5) Les envois contre remboursement; (6) Les recouvrements; (7) Le service international de l'épargne; (8) Les abonnements aux journaux et écrits périodiques* (Berne, 1959).

Catalogue général des informations de toute nature concernant le service postal et des documents disponibles pour le service de prêt [loose leaf] (Berne, 1953).

Code télégraphique de l'UPU (Berne, 1959).

Collection d'Études Postales publiées sous les auspices de l'UPU:

No. 1. *Ambulants automobiles sur route* (Berne, 1950).

No. 2. *Utilisation des véhicules à moteur pour le transport des correspondances à l'intérieur des grandes villes* (Berne, 1950).

No. 3. *Procédés modernes pour le lavage, le nettoyage et la réparation des sacs postaux* (Berne, 1950).

No. 4. *Transports postaux et tri dans les wagons-poste* (Berne, 1950).

No. 5. *Procédés méchaniques et autres, ansi que mesures prises pour l'amélioration des conditions d'hygiène des locaux postaux et du matériel postal* (Berne, 1951).

No. 6. *Utilisation de l'avion pour les transports strictement postaux* (Berne, 1951)

No. 7. *L'éclairage artificiel des locaux postaux* (Berne, 1951).

No. 8. *Mobilier et matériel pour le tri des correspondances et des colis — Machines à ficeler* (Berne, 1951).

No. 9. *Mobilier et appareils du service des guichets* (Berne, 1951).

No. 10. *Conception, construction, et équipment des véhicules ferroviaires postaux* (Berne, 1951).

No. 11. *Plan général de construction et d'aménagement d'un bureau de poste type dans une localité de moyenne grandeur* (Berne, 1952).

No. 12. *L'hélicoptère au service de la poste* (Berne, 1952).

No. 13. *Méthodes de formation et d'enseignement professionnels du personnel postal* (Berne, 1952).

No. 14. *Le traitement méchanique du courrier dans les grands bureaux de tri* (Berne, 1952).

No. 15. *Utilisation de l'automobile pour les transports postaux dans les relations à moyennes et à courtes distances [à l'exclusion des transports urbains]* (Berne, 1952).

No. 16. *Comptabilité mécanique d'un centre de chèques postaux français* (Berne, 1952).

No. 17. *Origine, structure, méchanisme, et développement des bureaux de chèques postaux belges et suisses* (Berne, 1955).

No. 18. *Les services d'épargne de l'Administration des postes de Grande-Bretagne* (Berne, 1955).

No. 19. *Les moyens utilisés pour le transbordement du courrier postal. Exploitation et technique* (Berne, 1955).

No. 20. *La distribution postale urbaine* (Berne, 1956).

No. 21. *Les méthodes de statistique postale* (Berne, 1956).

No. 22. *Les distributeurs automatiques de timbres-poste de l'Administration des PTT suisses* (Berne, 1956).

No. 23. *La poste pneumatique à New York et à Paris. Les tubes pneumatiques des PTT suisses* (Berne, 1956).

No. 24. *L'utilisation des containers et des palettes pour les transports postaux* (Berne, 1956).

No. 25. *Organisation des services sociaux en Belgique, au Brésil, en Italie, et en Uruguay* (Berne, 1957).

No. 26. *Le calcul des prix de rivient dans les Administrations postales* (Berne, 1957).

No. 27. *L'organisation du service postal rural* (Berne, 1957).

No. 28. *Systèmes utilisés pour l'instruction du personnel et le perfectionnement professionnel des cadres supérieurs, des ingénieurs et des techniciens des éstablissements postaux* (Berne, 1960).

No. 29. *Classification décimale postale à l'usage des Administrations postales — basée sur la classification décimale universelle* (Berne, 1961)

No. 30. *Méthodes de détermination de l'efficacité économique de la mécanisation et de l'automatisation des bureaux de poste* (Berne, 1961)

No. 31. *Machines à enliasser — Principes retenus. Information sur les réalisations et les expériences en cours* (Berne, 1961).

No. 32. *Mécanisation du tri des colis, des paquets, etc.* (Berne, 1961).

No. 33. *Organisation générale des bureaux de poste (autres que les centres de tri). Division en Sections. Liaision entre Sections* (Berne, 1961)

No. 34. *Machines de guichet* (Berne, 1961).

No. 35. *Organisation du Service des guichets des bureaux de poste. Répartition des attributions. Entraide* (Berne, 1961).

No. 36. *Redressage automatique en vue de l'oblitération des objets de correspondance* (Berne, 1961).

No. 37. *Méchanisation et automatisation du tri des lettres. Principes retenus. Informations sur les réalisations et les expériences en cours* (Berne, 1961).

No. 38. *Méthodes de définition des normes de surface nécessaires à la manipulation du courrier dans les établissements postaux* (Berne, 1961).

No. 39. *Normalisation des formats d'enveloppes de lettres, des couleurs, etc., et du libellé des adresses des correspondances. Dimensions et valeurs des timbres-poste, couleurs et encres employées à les obtenir* (Berne, 1962).

No. 40. *Organisation des centres de tri non mécanisés* (Berne, 1962).

No. 41. *Elaboration et fondement économique des tarifs afférents aux différentes catégories d'envois de la poste aux lettres* (Berne, 1962).

No. 42. *Possibilité de créer un sac universel pour l'échange des correspondances — Méthodes de manipulation et de contrôle des sacs* (Berne, 1962)

No. 43. *Système d'indices pour l'évaluation générale et l'analyse du travail des bureaux de poste* (Berne, 1962).

No. 44. *Organisation du travail dans les services postaux.* (Berne, 1962).

No. 45. *Distributeurs automatiques de timbres-poste, de cartes postales, de carnets ou enveloppes de timbres-poste, etc. Equipement des petits bureaux antomatiques (dits bureaux muets à libre service, etc.)* (Berne, 1962).

No. 46. *Organisation du travail (Etude des méthodes d'exploitation rationnelle)* (Berne, 1962).

No. 47. *Tendances principales du développement et du progrès technique des services postaux au cours dès 15 à 20 prochaines années* (Berne, 1963)

No. 48. *Etudes prévisionnelles de la rentabilité des prototypes et des ensembles mécanisés* (Berne, 1963).

Fêtes commémoratives du 75ᵉ anniversaire de l'Union postale universelle (Berne, 1949).

Fêtes du Jubilé de l'Union postale universelle célébrées à Stockholm à l'occasion du VIIᵉ Congrès postal universel — 16 août 1924 (Berne, 1924).

Genèse des Actes de l'UPU [loose leaf]. Two vols. (Berne, 1956–).

Le nouveau bâtiment de l'Union postale universelle inauguré à Berne le 9 mai 1953 (Berne, 1955).

Organigramme du Bureau international de l'Union postale universelle (Berne, 1963).

Rapport sur l'ensemble de l'activité de la Commission exécutive et de liaison 1947–1952 (Berne, 1952).

Rapport sur l'ensemble de l'activité de la Commission exécutive et de liaison 1952–1957 (Berne, 1957).

Renseignements généraux (Berne, 1956).

Résumé alphabétique et méthodique des Documents des Congrès et Conférences de l'Union postale universelle 1874–1931, Vol. I (Berne, 1932) and Vol. II (Berne, 1933).

L'Union postale universelle, sa fondation et son développement. Mémoire publié par le Bureau international à l'occasion du 50ᵉ anniversaire de l'Union 1874-1924 (Berne, 1924). *Supplément* (Berne, 1929).

L'Union postale universelle, sa fondation et son développement, 1874-1949 [*Mémoire*] (Berne, 1949).

L'Union postale universelle, sa création et son développement (French ed., Berne, 1958; German ed., Berne, 1959; English ed., Berne, 1959; Spanish ed., Berne, 1955; Italian ed., Berne, 1955; Russian ed., Berne, 1954).

Vocabulaire polyglotte du service postal international: 1st ed., 8 vols., Berne, 1954 and 1955; 2nd ed., 7 vols., Berne, 1957, 1958, and 1959; and, 3rd ed., 4 vols. completed, Berne, 1961, 1962 and 1963.

II. Other Official Publications

African and Malagasy Postal and Telecommunications Union. *Convention conclue par l'Union Africaine et Malagache des Postes et Télécommunications* (Tananarive, 1961).

Arab Postal Union. *Convention of the Arab Postal Union, Concluded in Khartoum, Thursday, the 28th of Muharram 1378* [*14th August 1958*] (Mimeograph; Cairo, 1958).

Denmark and Sweden, Postal Administrations. *L'Union postale universelle et l'Organisation des Nations Unies* (Stockholm; 1947).

East African Post and Telecommunication Administration. *Annual Report, 1961* (Nairobi, 1962).

Egypt, Ministry of Communication. *Les postes en Egypte* (Cairo, 1934).

El Salvador, Directorate General of Posts. *Legislación Postal Internacional* (San Salvador, 1961).

Europäischer Postkongress, Wien, 1942. Berichte und Vereinbarungen (Vienna, 1942).

Finland, Administration of Posts and Telegraphs. *Posti-ja Lennätinlaitos* (1937).

France. *Commission international des postes, Paris, 1863* (Paris, 1863).

France, Ministère des postes et télécommunications. *Centenaire de la réunion de la première Commission internationale des Postes – Paris mai 1863* (Paris, 1963).

France, Ministère des travaux publiques, sous-secretariat d'État des Postes et des Télégraphes. *Conférence internationale pour l'amélioration des Communications postales et ferroviaires, télégraphiques et téléphoniques et radiotélégraphiques* [*7-13 juillet 1920*] (Paris, 1920).

Great Britain, Foreign Office. *Universal Postal Union: Agreement for the Exchange of Insured Letters and Boxes.* Cd. 3558 (London, 1907).

———. *Ibid., 30th November, 1920.* Cmd. 1538 (London, 1921).

———. *Ibid., Agreement Concerning Insured Letters and Boxes, London, June 28, 1929.* Cmd. 3685 (London, 1930).

———. *Ibid.* [*with Final Protocol*] *Paris, July 5, 1947.* Cmd. 7794 (London, 1949).

———. *Ibid., Brussels, July 11, 1952.* Cmd. 8998 (London, 1953).

———. *Ibid., Agreements Concerning Insured Letters and Boxes; Postal*

Parcels [*together with final protocols, detailed regulations and annexes*], *Ottawa, 3d October, 1957.* Comd. 586 (London, 1958).

——, Postmaster-General. *The Post Office: An Historical Summary* (London, 1911).

——, Post Office. *Réunion de la Conférence européenne des Administrations des Postes et des Télécommunications — Torquay* [*12–22 septembre 1961*] (London, 1961).

International Air Transport Association. *IATA — The First Three Decades* (Montreal, 1949).

——. *Ten Years of Global Air Transport, 1945–1955.* Bulletin No. 21 (Montreal, 1955).

International Civil Aviation Organization, *Air Mail Study.* Doc. 5348 — AT/654 (Montreal, 1948).

——. *Air Mail Study.* 1962 ed., Doc. 8240 — AT/716 (Montreal, 1962).

International Chamber of Commerce. *International Postal Service.* Brochure No. 147 (Paris, 1951).

International Telecommunication Union. *International Telecommunication Convention, Buenos Aires, 1952* (Geneva, 1953).

Netherlands, General Directorate of the PTT. *60 jaar hoofdbestuur PTT 1893–1953* (1954).

Nordic Postal Union. *Arrangement concernant l'Union Postale des Pays du Nord* [Mimeograph] (Stockholm, March 24, 1960).

Philippines, Postal Administration. *Asian Oceanic Postal Convention signed at Manila, January 23, 1961* (Manila, 1961).

——, *Manila Postal Conference, 1961* (Manila, 1961).

Postal Union of the Americas and Spain. *Congreso de Buenos Aires, Convenio y Acuerdos, 1960* (Montevideo, 1960).

Switzerland, Federal Council. *Règlement concernant l'organisation, le fonctionnement, et le contrôle de l'activité du Bureau international de l'Union postale universelle* (June 30, 1953, as amended).

Switzerland, Nationalrat. "Klein Anfrage im Nationalrat, vom 16. Juni 1925 und Antwort des Bundesrates, vom 5. Oktober 1925," *Amtliches stenographisches Bulletin der schweizerischen Bundesversammlung,* Vol. XXVI, No. 14.

Union of International Associations. *Yearbook of International Organizations, 1962–1963* (Brussels, 1962).

Union of South Africa. *The African Postal Union Agreement as Amended at Cape Town, November, 1948* (Pretoria, 1948).

United Nations Educational, Scientific, and Cultural Organization. *L'Odyssée du timbre-poste. L'Union Postale Universelle présentée aux maîtres et à leurs élèves* (Paris, 1953).

U. S. Congress. *Universal Postal Convention. Signed Vienna, July 4, 1891, approved May 24, 1892* [Stat. L v. 28, pp. 1078–1182] (Washington, D.C., 1895).

U. S. Department of State. *Universal Postal Union. Convention Revising the Universal Postal Convention of May 23, 1939, Signed at Paris, July 5, 1947* [Treaties and Other International Acts, Series 1850] (Washington, D.C., 1949).

————. *Ibid. June 5, 1947, Signed at Brussels, July 11, 1952* [Treaties and Other International Acts, Series 2800] (Washington, D.C., 1953).

————. *Ibid. July 11, 1952, Signed at Ottawa, October 3, 1957* [Treaties and Other International Acts, Series 4202] (Washington, D.C., 1959).

U. S. Post Office Department. *Annual Report of the Postmaster General, 1894* (Washington, D.C., 1894).

————. *Ibid., 1895* (Washington, D.C., 1895).

————. *Cost Ascertainment Report, 1954* (Washington, D.C., 1955).

————. *Convention of Washington, June 15, 1897* (Washington, D.C., 1898).

————. Foreign Mail Service, "Convention [concluded June 15, 1897, revised March 26, 1906]. Done at Rome, March 26, 1906," pp. 49–84 in *Report, 1906* (Washington, 1906).

————. *Report of the Committee to Rearrange the Universal Postal Convention-Anticipation of the Stockholm Congress, to Meet June 4, 1924* (Washington, D.C., 1923).

————. *Universal Postal Union, Convention of Buenos Aires, May 23, 1939* (Washington, D.C., 1940).

————. *Ibid. Cairo, March 20, 1934* (Washington, D.C., 1934).

————. *Ibid. London, June 28, 1929, with Regulations for its Execution* (Washington, D.C., 1930).

————. *Ibid. Madrid, November 30, 1920, with Detailed Regulations for its Execution* (Washington, D.C., 1921).

————. *Ibid., Stockholm, August 28, 1924, with Detailed Regulations for its Execution* (Washington, D.C., 1925).

————. *Ibid., Universal Postal Convention Concluded Between Germany, United States [and other Powers]. Signed Rome, May 26, 1906, Approved October 16, 1906* (Washington, D.C., 1906).

World Health Organization. *Basic Documents,* 11th ed. (Geneva, November, 1960).

III. Books

Alexandrowicz, Charles Henry. "The Universal Postal Union," *World Economic Agencies* (New York, 1962), pp. 1–34.

Beelenkamp, C. J. *La Cooperation entre l'Organisation des Nations Unies et l'Union postale universelle* (Overeen, 1949).

————. *Les lois postales universelles* (The Hague, 1910).

————. *Réformes postales internationales* (Bloemendaal, 1947).

Belloc, Alexis. *Les Postes françaises* (Paris, 1886).

Blayac, Raoul. *Origine, évolution, et organisation de l'Union postale universelle.* Thesis. (Montpellier, 1932).

Boisson, Henri. *La Société des nations et les Bureaux internationaux des Unions universelles postale et télégraphique* (Paris, 1932).

Budelot, Suzanne. *Messageries universitaires et messageries royales* (Paris, 1934).

Bühler, Hans. *Der Weltpostverein; eine völkerrechtsgeschichtliche und wirtschaftspolitische Untersuchung* (Berlin, 1930).

Buser, J. *Zur Entwicklung des Weltpostvereins und des Weltpostrechts* (Zurich, 1935).

Chambe, René. *Histoire de l'aviation* (Paris, 1949).

Clark, Keith. *International Communications* (New York, 1931).

Codding, George A., Jr. *The International Telecommunication Union* (Leiden, 1952).

Constantinoff, Jean. *Le droit aérien français et étranger — droit interne et droit international* (Paris, 1932).

Cushing, Marshall H. *The Story of our Post-Office* (Boston, 1893).

Diena, Enzo. *L'Unione Postale Universale*. Thesis, University of Rome (Rome, 1950).

Fazelly, Mohammed K. *L'Union postale universelle*. Thesis, University of Paris (Paris, 1959).

Furrer, Reinhold. *Le problème des frais de transit des correspondances du service postal international* (Berne, 1946).

Gallois, Eugène. *La Poste et les Moyens de communication des peuples à travers les Siècles* (Paris, 1894).

Gewande, Herbert W. *Geschichte der Luftpost* (Leipzig, 1934).

Gneme, Giuseppe. *Della "Unione internazionale delle telecomunicazioni" e della "Unione postale universale"* (Rome, 1941).

Goodspeed, Stephen S. *The Nature and Function of International Organization* (New York and Oxford, 1959).

Guggenheim, Paul. *Traité de droit international public,* Vol. I (Geneva, 1953).

Haass, Friedrich. *Weltpostverein und Einheitsporta [Welt-Pennyporto]* (Berlin, 1913).

Harlow, Alvin F. *Old Post Bags* (New York, 1928).

Hemmeon, Joseph C. *The History of the British Post-Office* (Cambridge, 1912).

Hill, G. B. and Sir Rowland. *The Life of Sir Rowland Hill and the History of Penny Postage* (London, 1880).

Hill, Sir Rowland. *The State and Prospects of Penny Postage* (London, 1844).

———. *Post Office Reform: Its Importance and Practicability* (3d ed., London, 1837).

Jung, J. *Der Weltpostverein und sein Einfluss auf den Weltverkehr und die Weltwirtschaft* (Strasburg, 1903).

Kammerer, Ludwig. *Johann von Herrfeldt und die Idee des Weltpostvereins* (Hamburg and Berlin, 1963).

Kiderlen, A. *Die Funktion des Weltpostvertrags im zwischenstaatlichen Postverkehr*. Thesis (Geislingen, 1946).

Krains, Hubert. *L'Union postale universelle* (Berne, 1908).

Lacroix, Georges. *Exposé du système général de l'Union postale universelle*. Thesis (Toulouse, 1910).

Lapham, Ruth B. *Dr. Franklin, Postmaster General* (New York, 1928).

Lewins, William. *Her Majesty's Mails* (London, 1864).

Mance, Brig. Gen. Sir Osborne. *International Road Transport, Postal, Electricity and Miscellaneous Questions* (London, 1947).

Meeker, Royal. *History of Shipping Subsidies* (New York, 1905).

Moynier, Gustave. *Les Bureaux internationaux des unions universelles* (Geneva, 1872).

Poinsard, Léon. *Études de droit international conventionnel* (Paris, 1894).

Rich, Wesley E. *The History of the United States Post-Office to the Year 1929* (Cambridge, 1924).

Roberts, William. *History of Letter-Writing from the Earliest Period to the Fifth Century* (London, 1843).

Robinson, Howard. *The British Post Office: A History* (Princeton, N.J., 1948).

Roper, Daniel C. *The United States Post-Office* (New York, 1917).

de Rothschild, Arthur. *Histoire de la poste aux lettres depuis ses origines les plus anciennes jusqu'à nos jours* (Paris, 1873).

————. *Histoire de la poste aux lettres et du timbre-poste dupuis leurs origines jusqu'à nos jours* (Paris, 1876).

Sasse, Horst. *Der Weltpostverein* (Berlin, 1959).

Schroeter, Karl. *Der Weltpostverein* (Berne, 1900).

Smith, Alfred D. *The Development of Rates of Postage* (London, 1917).

Stephan, Heinrich von. *Weltpost und Luftschiffahrt* (Berlin, 1874).

————. *Geschichte der Preussischen Post von ihrem Ursprunge bis auf die Gegenwart* (Berlin, 1859).

Summerfield, Arthur E. and Charles Hurd, *U. S. Mail* (New York, 1960).

Vaillé, Eugène. *Histoire générale des postes françaises.* 3 vols. (Paris, 1947 and 1950).

Weithase, Hugo. *Geschichte des Weltpostvereins* (Strasburg, 1895).

Zilliacus, Laurin. *From Pillar to Post* (London, 1956).

————. *Mail for the World* (New York, 1954).

IV. Articles

Akzin, Benjamin. "Membership in the Universal Postal Union," *American Journal of International Law*, XXVII, No. 4 (October, 1933), 651–74.

Anglade, H. "Trafic postal et cycle économique," *Études et Documents*, Institut National de la Statistique et des Études Économiques, Série TH–1 (Paris, 1946).

Arciniegas, Roberto. "The Postal Union of the Americas and Spain," *Union Postale*, LXXXVI, No. 11 (November, 1961), 150A–151A.

Bäckström, Sven. "The Consultative Committee of Postal Studies in 1962," *Union Postale*, LXXXVIII, No. 1 (January, 1963), 14A–16A.

Bakir, Anouar. "A New Restricted Union — The African Postal Union (APU)," *Union Postale*, LXXXVIII, No. 2 (February, 1963), 23A–26A.

————. "The Arab Postal Union (AUP): History and Fundamental Principles," *ibid.*, LXXXII, No. 4 (April, 1957), 38A–40A.

Barrientos Perez, Rafael. "The VIIIth Congress of the Postal Union of the Americas and Spain," *Union Postale*, LXXXVI, No. 4 (April, 1961), 48A–50A.

Beck, Guillaume. "Postal Monopoly of the Tour-and-Taxis Family in the Papal States (1522–23)," *Union Postale*, LXXXV, No. 5 (May, 1960), 76A–80A.

Blazek, Bronislaw. "The Problem of the International Rates," *Union Postale*, XXII, No. 4 (April, 1947), 111–117.

Borgmann. "History of the Postcard and its Importance in International Relations," *Union Postale*, I, No. 10 (July, 1876), 149–158.

Brauns-Packenius, Otfried. "The Nature of Restricted Postal Unions," *Union Postale*, LXXXVII, No. 4 (April, 1962), 55A–58A.

――――. "Das wesen der engeren Postvereine und ihr Verhältnis zum Weltpostverein," *Archiv fur das Post- und Fernmeldewesen*, XIII, No. 3, 1961, pp. 153–173.

Bühler, Emile. "The Annual Session of the Management Council of the Consultative Committee for Postal Studies, Tokyo, 1961," *Union Postale*, LXXXVII, No. 1 (January, 1962), 2A–10A.

"The Central American Press and the Universal Postal Union," *Union Postale*, V, No. 10 (October, 1880), 202–205.

Chaubert, L. "The Organs of the UPU at Work. The Annual Session of the Executive and Liaison Committee (1961)," *Union Postale*, LXXXVI, No. 8 (August, 1961), 106A–112A.

China, Postal Administration. "Historical Survey of the Postal Services in China," *Union Postale*, L, No. 5 (May, 1925), 67–70 and No. 6 (June, 1925), 83–86.

"Conference of European Postal and Telecommunications Administrations," *Union Postale*, LXXXVII, No. 2 (February, 1962), 22A–23A.

"Le Congrès Postal Universel de Bruxelles," *Union Postale*, LXXVII, No. 12 (1952), 140A–164A.

"Contribution to the History of Postage Stamps," *Union Postale*, V, No. 7 (July, 1880), 145–149.

"The Couriers of Montezuma," *Union Postale*, V, No. 8 (August, 1880), 166–167.

"The Cursus Publicus of the Romans," *Union Postale*, IV, No. 9 (September, 1879), 175–182.

Das Gupta, S. N. "The Expanded Programme of Technical Assistance and the Post Office," *Union Postale*, LXXXVIII, No. 5 (May, 1963), 66A–69A.

De Paola, Hugo R. "The Golden Jubilee of the International Bureau of the PUAS and the Participation of the American Countries in Working Out Postal Legislation," *Union Postale*, LXXXVII, No. 10 (October, 1962), 143A–145A.

Desenne. "The Chinese Posts," *Union Postale*, IV, No. 10 (October, 1879), 204–209.

――――. "The Names Given to the Post, and their Origin," *ibid.*, VI, No. 8 (August, 1881), 165–175.

――――. "Origin of the Postal Monopoly," *ibid.*, IV, No. 7 (July, 1879), 131–145.

Eckhardt, Carl C. "Heinrich von Stephan, Founder of the Universal Postal Union," *University of Colorado Studies*, Ser. C, I, No. 2 (May, 1941), 131–143.

Emmenegger, Franz. "Technical Assistance for Countries Needing to Develop their Postal Services," *Union Postale*, LXXXVIII, No. 5 (May, 1963), 73A–74A.

"European Congress of Vienna," *Union Postale,* LXVII, No. 10/11 (October/November, 1942), 291–299.

"Extract from the Report of the International Bureau of the Universal Postal Union for the Year 1941," *Union Postale,* LXVII, No. 4 (April, 1942), 84–101.

"Extract from the Report of the International Bureau of the Universal Postal Union for the Year 1943," *Union Postale,* LXIX, No. 3/4 (March/April, 1944), 43–61.

Farine, Marcel. "The Contribution of the Universal Postal Union to the Technical Assistance of the United Nations," *Union Postale,* LXXXV, No. 3 (March, 1960), 39A–44A.

———. "Technical Assistance in the Universal Postal Union," *ibid.,* LXXXVI, No. 12 (December, 1961), 157A–161A.

"The First 100 Years of the Bavarian Royal State Posts," *Union Postale,* XXXVI, No. 10 (October, 1911), 155.

"First South American Continental Postal Congress at Montevideo," *Bulletin of the Pan American Union,* XXXVI (April, 1911), 689–98.

Furrer, Reinhold. "Repeal and Ratification as Understood in the Universal Postal Convention," *Union Postale,* LXIV, No. 12 (December, 1939), 554–558.

A German Postal Officer. "Past and Present," *Union Postale,* XV, No. 6 (June, 1890), 85–91; No. 7 (July, 1890), 101–107; No. 8 (August, 1890), 117–121; and No. 9 (September, 1890), 133–137.

Glover, Irving L. "The Third Pan American Postal Congress," *Bulletin of the Pan American Union,* LXVI, No. 3 (March, 1932), 169–71.

"The Hellenic Post," *Union Postale,* IV, No. 3 (March, 1879), 49–59.

Henrioud, Marc. "The Franco-Swiss Postal Relations from the 13th Century to the Year 1815," *Union Postale,* LVIII, No. 6 (June, 1933), 196–211; No. 7 (July, 1933), 255–266; and No. 8 (August, 1933), 288–302.

———. "A Proposal for the Reform of the International Postal Service," *ibid.,* LV, No. 10 (October, 1930), 357–367.

Hess, Fritz. "Human Rights and the Universal Postal Union," *United Nations Bulletin,* XI, No. 10 (December 1, 1951), 448.

———. "Peace Through Universality," *ibid.,* p. 431.

———. "The Postal Union's Wide Field of Operations," *United Nations Review,* II, No. 2 (August, 1955), 43–44.

———. "Universal Postal Union in 1950," *United Nations Bulletin,* X, No. 1 (January 1, 1951), 36–37.

Hill, N. L. "World and Its Mail," *South Atlantic Quarterly,* XXX, (July, 1931), 309–17.

"History of the German Post," *Union Postale,* III, No. 8 (August, 1878), 160–161.

"History of the Posts in Spain," *Union Postale,* VII, No. 4 (April, 1882), 65–83.

Hofman, F. A. "The Usefulness of a European Postal Union and Its Tasks," *Union Postale,* LXXV, No. 1 (January, 1950), 2A–5A.

Hudson, Manley O. "American-Norwegian Postal Arbitration," *American Journal of International Law,* XX, No. 3 (July, 1926), 534–536.

Hürlimann, Werner. "The Cursus Publicus," *Union Postale*, LXXXVI, No. 1 (January, 1961), 8A–13A.

"An International Postal Treaty of the Year 1660," *Union Postale*, XX, No. 9 (September, 1895), 146–56.

Kelly, Helen G. "International Mails During Wartime," *Union Postale*, LXX, No. 8 (August, 1945), 113–123.

Kern, Emile. "CCPS–Recent Events," *Union Postale*, LXXXVI, No. 8 (August, 1961), 104A–105A.

Koller, Fritz. "The Annual Session of the Executive and Liaison Committee (1962)," *Union Postale*, LXXXVII, No. 12 (December, 1962), 164A–167A.

———. "The Annual Session of the Executive and Liaison Committee, 1963," *ibid.*, LXXXVIII, No. 9 (September, 1963), 126A–129A.

Laffay, "Union postale universelle (UPU) et Union internationale des télécommunications (UIT)," *Journal des Télécommunications*, Vol. 18, No. 3 (March, 1951), pp. 86–104.

Le Mouël, J. J. "The Universal Postal Union," *Union Postale*, LXXV, No. 11 (November, 1950), 168–170; No. 12 (December, 1950), 182–183; and LXXVI, No. 1 (January, 1951), 2A–4A.

Linares, Fleytas A. "Breve resena sobre las actividades desplegadas por la Union Postal Universal," *Diplomacia*, XLII, (November, 1949), 33–34.

Loeper. "Contribution to the History of the University Messenger Service," *Union Postale*, IX, No. 8 (August, 1884), 165–177; No. 9 (September, 1884), 189–197; and No. 10 (October, 1884), 210–222.

———. "History of the Letter and of Letter-writing," *ibid.*, IV, No. 7 (July, 1879), 145–152.

———. "The Most Ancient Town Post Arrangements," *ibid.*, VI, No. 12 (December, 1881), 249–260; and VII, No. 1 (January, 1882), 1–13.

———. "The Most Ancient Work Published in France on the Posts," *ibid.*, IV, No. 10 (October, 1879), pp. 195–204.

———. "The Oldest German Historical and Legal Work on Postal Arrangements," *ibid.*, VI, No. 9 (September, 1881), 189–201.

———. "The Post in Universal Literature," *ibid.*, IX, No. 1 (January, 1884), 22–31; No. 2 (February, 1884), 33–44; No. 3 (March, 1884), 57–66; No. 4 (April, 1884), 89–98; No. 5 (May, 1884), 110–119; and No. 7 (July, 1884), 150–161.

———. "A Wurtemberg Post and Butcher Regulation of the Year 1622," *ibid.*, IV, No. 8 (August, 1879), 166–173; and No. 9 (September, 1879), 183–191.

Machold. "Difficulties and Advantages of a European Postal Union," *Union Postale*, LXXXI, No. 5 (May, 1958), 38A–40A.

"Meeting, 1920, Madrid," *Bulletin of the Pan American Union*, LII (February, 1921), 146–148.

"Montgomery Blair–Postmaster General," *Union Postale*, LXXXVIII, No. 8 (August, 1963), 119A–120A.

Mouquet, [Mrs.] D. "Centenary of the First Meeting of the International Committee of Posts, Paris–May 1963," *Union Postale*, LXXXVIII, No. 8 (August, 1963, 112A–114A.

Muri, Alois. "UPU Services Progressively Extended," *United Nations Bulletin,* VIII, No. 1 (January 1, 1950), 34–36.

Naumann, Joseph K. F. "Letters in the Course of the Ages," *Union Postale,* LXX, No. 1 (January, 1945), 8–20.

"News from the International Bureau," *Union Postale,* LXXXVIII, No. 6 (June, 1963), 89A–90A.

Nylund, Thure. "The Northern Countries Postal Union," *Union Postale,* LXXXII, No. 9 (September, 1957), 86A–89A.

"Organization of the Administration of the Imperial German Posts," *Union Postale,* V, No. 1 (January, 1880), 1–4.

"Organization of the Postal Administration of Portugal," *Union Postale,* V, No. 10 (October, 1880), 189–198.

"Organization of the Postal Administration of Sweden," *Union Postale,* V, No. 6 (June 1880), 107–120.

"The Organization of the Postal Administration of the United States of America," *Union Postale,* V, No. 4 (April, 1880), 69–82.

"The Origin and Development of the Letter," *Union Postale,* II, No. 5 (May, 1877), 98–102.

Olivera. "Origin and Progress of the Posts in the Ancient Spanish Colonies of South and Central America," *Union Postale,* III, No. 9 (September, 1878), 188–190.

"Pan American Postal Congress at Buenos Aires," *Bulletin of the Pan American Union,* LIII (August, 1921), 149–151.

"Permanent Committee of the European Postal Union," *Union Postale,* LXIX, No. 2 (February, 1944), 24–26.

"The Postal Congress at Washington," *Harper's Weekly,* XLI, No. 2101 (March 27, 1897), 326.

"Postal and Commercial Roads in Switzerland," *Union Postale,* I, No. 8 (May, 1876), 115–124.

"The Postal Conference of Paris in the Year 1880," *Union Postale,* V, No. 12 (December, 1880), 246–260, and VI, No. 1 (January, 1881), 12–32.

"Postal Union Changes," *Bulletin of the Pan American Union,* LXXII, No. 1 (January, 1938), 45–46.

Quesada, Arturo. "Fifth Congress of the Postal Union of the Americas and Spain," *Bulletin of the Pan American Union,* LXXXI, No. 3 (March, 1947), 142–143.

Rahi, M. "The Universal Postal Union, Its Tasks and Its Working as a Specialized Agency," *Union Postale,* LXXXVIII, No. 1 (January, 1963), 7A–14A.

"Responsibility for Cases Beyond Control," *Union Postale,* XLI, No. 6 (June, 1916), 83–85.

Risch. "The Tasks and Aims of a European Postal Union," *Union Postale,* LXVII, No. 9 (September, 1942), 246–252.

Rübsam, Joseph. "Francis von Taxis, the Founder of the Modern Post, and Johann Baptista von Taxis, his Nephew," *Union Postale,* XVII, No. 8 (August, 1892), 125–131; No. 9 (September, 1892), 141–149; and No. 10 (October, 1892), 157–162.

————. "History of the Oldest Postal Arrangements in Tirol and Adjacent Countries," *ibid.,* XVI, No. 12 (December, 1891), 197–206.

Ruger, C. "The Development of the Postal Service in China," *Union Postale,* LXV, No. 10 (October, 1940), 288–302.

Runk. "Establishment of a Public Postal Service in China," *Union Postale,* IV, No. 4 (April, 1879), 77–87.

Salz, Claude. "Choice and Calculation of Equivalents for Charges and Fees," *Union Postale,* LXXXVIII, No. 7 (July, 1963), 101A–104A.

Sargent, S. D. "International Aspects of Postal Services [Organization and Activities of the Universal Postal Union]," *Journal of the Institute of Transport,* XXVI (January, 1956), 271–284.

Scheuffler. "The Ratifications in the Universal Postal Union," *Union Postale,* LXVII, No. 10/11 (October/November, 1942), 260–290.

"Seventy-five Years of Service," *United Nations Bulletin,* VI, No. 11 (June 1, 1949), 603–604.

Sly, John Fairfield. "The Genesis of the Universal Postal Union," *International Conciliation,* No. 233 (October, 1927), pp. 395–443.

Sokolow, N. J. "Historical Facts Respecting the Origin and Growth of the Russian Post," *Union Postale,* XXI, No. 11 (November, 1896), 173–179; and No. 12 (December, 1896), 187–199.

Spencer, John H. "The Franking Privilege for Postal Communications with Prisoners of War," *American Journal of International Law,* XXXV, No. 2 (April, 1941), 365–371.

Swedish Post Office. "The Swedish Posts Before 1636," *Union Postale,* XXXIII, No. 8 (August, 1908), 113–118; No. 9 (September, 1908), 129–134; and No. 10 (October, 1908), 151–157.

Thieme. "The Posts of the Califs," *Union Postale,* IV, No. 12 (December, 1879), 231–246.

Tuason, Vincente. "Free Postage for Prisoners of War and Victims of War," *Union Postale,* XXX, No. 9 (September, 1945), 134–154.

"Twelfth Congress of the Universal Postal Union," *U. S. Department of State Bulletin,* XVII, No. 429 (September 21, 1947), 585–588.

"Universal Postal Union Agreement Drafted; Relationship with United Nations Recommended," *United Nations Bulletin,* I, No. 22 (December 31, 1946), 43–44.

"Universal Postal Union's One World," *United Nations Review,* IV, No. 2 (August, 1957), 40–42.

"UPU to be Related to United Nations," *United Nations Bulletin,* III, No. 3 (July 15, 1947), 108–109; and No. 4 (August 12, 1947), 231.

Vaillé, Eugène. "The Postal Feudal and Hereditary Rights of the Family of Taxis, as Discussed in 1757 by a French Diplomat," *Union Postale,* LXXIII, No. 3 (March, 1948), 70–92; No. 4 (April, 1948), 126–136; and No. 5 (May, 1948), 166–176.

Weber, Edouard. "Freedom of Transit, a Fundamental Basis of the Universal Postal Union," *Union Postale,* LXXXVII, No. 4 (April, 1962), 48A–52A.

———. "The Post as an Economic Undertaking," *ibid.,* LXXXVIII, No. 9 (September, 1963), pp. 125A–127A.

————. "Technical Assistance Within the Universal Postal Union," *ibid.*, LXXXVII, No. 8 (August, 1962), pp. 105A–109A.

————. "The Universal Postal Union and Its Restricted Unions," *ibid.*, LXXXVIII, No. 1 (January, 1963), 4A–6A.

————. "The UPU To-day and Tomorrow," *ibid.*, No. 8 (August, 1963), pp. 115A–119A.

Williamson, F. H. "The International Postal Service and the Universal Postal Union," *Journal of the Royal Institute of International Affairs*, IX (January, 1930), 68–78.

INDEX

INDEX